THE STATE OF THE LIBRARY ART

Publications of

THE GRADUATE SCHOOL OF LIBRARY SERVICE
Rutgers - The State University

THE STATE OF THE LIBRARY ART, edited by Ralph R. Shaw
Volume I, Parts 1 and 2 (in one volume) $8.00
Cataloging & Classification, by Maurice F.
Tauber; Subject Heading, by Carlyle J. Frarey
Volume I, Parts 3 and 4 (in one volume) March, 1961 $8.00
Classification, by Maurice F. Tauber and
Edith Wise; Gifts & Exchanges, by Donald E. Thompson
Volume II, Parts 1 and 2 (in one volume) $5.00
Training Laymen in Use of the Library,
by George S. Bonn; Bibliographical Services,
by Margaret S. Bryant
Volume II, Part 3 January, 1961 $8.00
Charging Systems, by Leila H. Kirkwood
Volume III, Parts 1-3 (in one volume) $5.50
Library Buildings, by Ralph E. Ellsworth;
Shelving, by Louis Kaplan; Storage Warehouses,
by Jerrold Orne
Volume IV, Parts 1-5 (in one volume) March, 1961 $8.00
Notched Cards, by Felix Reichman; Feature
(Peekaboo) Cards, by Lawrence S. Thompson;
Punched Cards, by Ralph U. Blasingame, Jr.;
Electronic Searching, by Gerald Jahoda;
Coding in Yes-No Form, by Doralyn Hickey
Volume V, Part 1 $5.00
Production and Use of Micro-Forms, by
Reginald R. Hawkins
Volume V, Part 2 $5.00
Reading Devices for Micro-Images, by
Jean Stewart and others
Volume V, Part 3 $8.00
Full-Size Photocopying, by William R. Hawken

Metcalf, Keyes D. ed.
Studies in Library Administrative Problems. $5.00

Distributed by
The Rutgers University Press
New Brunswick, New Jersey

the state of the library art

edited by Ralph R. Shaw

volume 2, part 3

Charging Systems

by

Leila H. Kirkwood

Graduate School of Library Service
Rutgers - The State University
New Brunswick, N.J.   1961

L. C. Card No. 60-16771

This volume is one of a series of studies
in librarianship published by the Graduate
School of Library Service * Rutgers - The
State University and distributed by the
Rutgers University Press

Preface

Pierce Butler planted the seed of this work some thirty years ago when he attempted to persuade me to follow my translation of Georg Schneider's "Theory and History of Bibliography" with an English rendering of Milkau's "Handbuch der Bibliothekswissenschaft." As we discussed this in his cubbyhole at the University of Chicago it became increasingly apparent that for all the excellence and usefulness of the Milkau, a version in English would require such wide revision and additions as to constitute a completely new work, and the project was, I thought, abandoned. Over the years, however, it remained a subject of, perhaps sometimes sub-conscious, dreaming, thinking, and occasionally some work.

When the Council on Library Resources was organized its need for information on the state of the library art resulted in almost spontaneous germination of Pierce Butler's long dormant seed. This resulted in a grant to the Graduate School of Library Service at Rutgers for preparation, under the direction of the undersigned, of a review of the status of our current knowledge of librarianship. From the inception of this project it was recognized that the initial grant could cover only somewhat less than half of the vast field, and there are many areas of librarianship still to be covered.

An advisory committee helped in the design of the program and in determining priorities for treatment of the various aspects of the field.

The advisory committee included: Dr. Julian H. Bigelow, Institute for Advanced Study at Princeton, New Jersey, Mr. Verner W. Clapp, President of the Council on Library Resources, Mr. Donald Coney, Librarian of the University of California, Mr. J. W. Kuipers, Apparatus research and development in Itek Corporation, Dr. Robert D. Leigh, Dean of the School of Library Service at Columbia University, Dr. Lowell A. Martin, Dean of the Graduate School of Library Service at Rutgers, Professor A. J. Riker of the College of Agriculture at the University of Wisconsin, Dr. Melville J.

Ruggles, Vice-President of the Council on Library Resources, Mr. A. N. Sears, Vice-President of Remington Rand, and Dr. Eugene H. Wilson, Vice-President of the University of Colorado.

Since the volumes now completed and being prepared for publication cover perhaps forty percent of the entire range of librarianship and bibliography, the plan of publication is in the familiar "Handbuch" form so as to permit the addition of volumes as financial resources and dedicated writers become available.

In preparing these for publication it appeared best to permit some variations in style from one volume to another rather than to devote a large percentage of our resources to achieving a standard style for all.

The general pattern followed in these studies consists of a survey of the published and unpublished literature of each facet of the field. In this survey, as a first step, each compiler attempts to summarize what the literature says with a minimum of redundancy but without editorial comment. Each statement is accompanied by a footnote so that investigation in depth can be conducted when necessary, but for most purposes, if we have adequately performed our primary task, it should be unnecessary to search the literature for information on the topics covered. A second step, provided in most cases, is examination of the evidence provided to support each allegation or statement in the literature and an indication of whether that particular bit of "the art" is empirical or the extent and reliability of the objective data provided to support it.

This pattern of presentation is modified in a number of the parts of the series since, except for the sake of external uniformity, it would serve little purpose to repeat substantially every statement in this second part followed by the words, "no objective evidence."

It was initially planned to present each summary in the historical perspective of the development of its field but this method of treatment was found unsuitable for some of the subjects. In some cases, such as the study of "Reading Devices for Micro-Images," both historical and topical treatments are presented; in others the treatment is historical only, and in still others primary emphasis is given to topical treatment. Here as in the review of evidence, suitability for each topic is given priority over external uniformity of the set.

While a few of these reports were prepared by staff assistants, as indicated by the list of titles and research staff, we were fortunate in enlisting participants of outstanding authority and reputation in most of the subject areas treated. In most cases the resultant first draft was read by one or more additional specialists in the field and in this work we had the assistance of such well known authorities as: Hubbard W. Ballou, Ralph H. Carruthers, Ralph Esterquest, Robert A. Fairthorne, John Fall, Charles F. Gosnell, Lutz Helbig, Laurence Kipp, Alfred H. Lane, Chester Lewis, Calvin N. Mooers, Robert H. Muller, Maurice F. Tauber, Lawrence S. Thompson, and others.

This is the concerted work of many hands, and many more than those listed above have helped in almost countless ways. Such value as may reside in this series is the result of professional contributions of high order by many people. Final responsibility for the plan of work, selection and supervision of research staff, revision of manuscripts as well as editing them and production of the volumes rested solely on the undersigned and he accepts full responsibility for the imperfections to be found in this series. It is hoped that this review of the library art will, on balance, be found to make a useful contribution and that it may some time be carried forward to cover the whole field of librarianship.

Ralph R. Shaw

Table of Contents

Introduction

In 1893, Mary W. Plummer defined charging systems as follows (583):

> The charging or loan system is that part of a library's administration by which chiefly its communications with borrowers is carried on. The word loan applies to it because the books are lent, and the word charging because every library, no matter how small, with any pretence at all at having a method, has some way of keeping account of these loans.
>
> The characteristic of a loan system best appreciated by the public is the speed with which it can receive and deliver books ....
>
> Another requisite is simplicity. The more complicated the system the greater the chance for error.
>
> The third thing to keep in mind is that the less the borrower's part in the operation the better he likes the system ....
>
> On the other hand a library, even a free library is a business institution, and must keep a record of its transactions ....
>
> The library, if it keeps pace with the rest of the world must know what it is doing ....
>
> The charging system should, to a great extent, answer the question whether or not the library is really of use to the community, and in order to do this it must put the library in possession of certain statistics.

The work of the loan department is often varied, according to Louis R. Wilson and Maurice F. Tauber who said that it "may include such activities as lending library materials to individuals and libraries, maintaining loan records, shelving and caring for the cataloged stack collection, issuing borrowers' cards, replacing books as required, and interpreting loan policy (584)."

According to H. G. Bousfield, "A good circulation system should save the borrower's time, reduce costs, speed up charging and discharging, and allow circulation librarians

maximum opportunity for professional work. These are
sound and practical objectives (585)." In emphasizing one of
his points he drew attention to the fact that the "type of circulation system employed often determines the level of work
circulation librarians perform; this alone justifies careful selection of the system best suited to a particular library. The
separation of professional and clerical work, if not a major
reason for introducing simplified circulation methods, is an
important objective (586)."

In 1941, E. V. Baldwin and W. E. Marcus conducted a
study on library costs and budgets. They felt that the "operations involved in the lending of books for home use, covered
by the caption 'circulation' have, as a general rule, been sufficiently standardized in libraries to admit a more accurate
comparison (587)." It seemed that (588):

> The process of the actual charging of the book to the bor-
> rower is an extremely simple, almost mechanical task,
> taking at the longest, as the borrower may easily see for
> himself, only a few seconds of time. It consists merely
> of the stamping of the date the charge is made (or the
> date on which the book falls due) on the book card, and by
> placing the same date either on a slip pasted in the book
> or by inserting a card bearing that date in a special pock-
> et provided in each book.
>   The introduction of machines for the automatic transfer
> of the borrower's number and date for the charge to these
> cards has further simplified this routine and, at the same
> time, has eliminated the possibility of errors through a
> transposition of figures.

However, they believed that the library which recorded
a longer time taken for book circulation did so "not by taking
a proportionately longer time for each unit of distribution,
but rather that its emphasis upon circulation is the result of
a skimping of the amount of time devoted in other ways to the
service to its patrons (588)." They also saw that a library
may concentrate much of its informational service and assistance to readers at the charging desk where it becomes a part
of the circulation routine.

In 1949, W. O'D. Pierce studied work measurement in
public libraries but noted that the "data obtained on charging
and discharging time is not very reliable due to lack of definition. However, some analysis has been possible in relation to the groups and the charging systems used (589)."

Still, it was not always a matter of simple acts of book charging not being defined; a tendency toward real complexity existed with many circulation systems. G. F. Shepherd dealt with this tendency in his discussion of recent trends (590):

> For many years most libraries have been penny-wise and pound foolish, particularly in circulation procedures. The methods and procedures used have too often been complicated, devious, and difficult.... The most books to the most readers at the least cost is a policy to which less lip service and more practical attention is given today.
>
> The circulation function is being performed in all libraries with greater emphasis on simplified procedures for the borrower....
>
> In both public and college libraries, multitudes of records have diminished toward a minimum. The beauties and conveniences of air tight controls can no longer be justified on the use or cost basis. The irreducible minimum record in the public library is one enabling to recall or reclaim books that are kept beyond reasonable time limits. Standing files for instant location of books not on the shelf are not considered as essential as they used to be, nor are files of charges standing by name of borrower.
>
> Loan periods are being lengthened generally. This minimizes the importance of a date-due file and lessens the work load of writing overdue notices....
>
> Further simplification, especially in the college and university library, has come with the elimination of the borrower's card....
>
> Even though the borrower's card is still essential in the lending procedures of most public libraries, efforts are being made to shorten the time required to issue these cards in the first place, and furthermore, the internal library routines concerned with registration are being simplified....
>
> The actual mechanics of the loan transaction has undergone a mild revolution in recent years. Every effort is made to deal with the reader quickly. Various streamlining devices are being incorporated into the charging routines. Photographic, mechanical, and marginal punched card charging systems have become widely used. The various mechanical systems which use primarily a transaction number for each withdrawal are most adaptable in the public library where it is not critically necessary to have a file by call number for books out of the library....

Upon reading the rules and regulations of public and
academic libraries a few decades ago, it was quite common to see specific limitations on the number of books a
reader might have out on loan at a given time. Except in
areas where there may be acute shortages, little thought
is now given to limitations.

In order to fully appreciate present day trends, the
background and history of charging systems must be understood. Ralph R. Shaw dealt with this briefly. He divided
the history of public library charging systems into four periods (591):

The first of these was the era of exploration and con-
flict....
The second period during which Newark charging won
virtually complete victory, might be termed the "borrowers' card period." Its distinguishing philosophical concept
was that of control of borrowers rather than of service to
them, and this philosophy was epitomized in the laborious
stamping and restamping of the borrowers' cards to make
sure that Johnny withdrew no more than four books and
that Johnny's mama borrowed at least one book of non-
fiction for every book of fiction.
The third era was symbolized by a new spirit of service, and it brought with it widespread elimination of controls over the amounts or kinds of materials borrowed.
This era might be termed the "identification card period,"
and its highest achievement was Ralph Ulveling's time-
and labor-saving, self-charging system....
The fourth era, in which we still lie arrested, may be
termed the era of gadgets. This period brought forward
no new systems but rather confined itself to the replacement of hand labor by machine labor; thus, one machine
copies the Newark charging system with minor modifications, while another is a slower and more expensive method for carrying out the Detroit system.

But this was written in 1941, and at that time he felt a lack
in what had been done. He wrote, "It is important to note
that these mechanical variations on our old charging themes
appear to make no basic contribution to the theory of charging or to the philosophy of librarianship, while the schemes
developed by librarians really did have fundamental theoretical variations from older accepted philosophies or theories.
Charging machines might have freed us from the drudgery of
numerical registration and from all the extra work thus caused

in registration and in handling overdue notices (591)."

W. S. Yenawine labeled "the processes and services which result in bringing users and library materials into productive relationship" as the circulation function of libraries (592). He pointed out that during the past one hundred years this concept has changed radically. "In all sincerity and through a sense of obligation in a scientific age, librarians have used machines to replace critical manpower, speed up processes, and reduce unit costs.... The circulation function ... is now symbolized by the charging machine, and the reader services, formerly an integral part of the circulation function, are gone (593)."

Continuing this same thought, S. E. Gwynn mentioned the following (594):

> The general circulation or charging counter, which in most libraries remains a major point of public contact, in many cases has been stripped of all functions save those associated with the delivery and charging of books. Here the reader finds that "circulation work" has come to signify, in the strict contemporary definition of the term, those library operations that take place after the patron knows the specific title he wants and either requests it at the delivery desk or procures it himself from the shelves and brings it to the desk for charging.

Edward Dudley summarized these thoughts when he gave us the following reasons for the recent interest and work in this field (595):

> First, the emphasis on the provision of personal service for the reader from qualified and experienced staff which is surely one of the really progressive trends in British postwar librarianship.... Second, the converse problem presented by the necessity for professional staff to carry out routine counter duties in many smaller libraries and, at busy periods, in larger ones. Third, the realization that the prospect of long hours of counter duty is a potent factor in the failure to recruit and retain junior staff. Fourth, that present issue systems involve great cost in staff labor-time, even if much of the work is done by junior librarians. Fifth, that the greater book issues of public libraries have as their concomitant greater inconvenience for the reader.
> An issue method as part of the working mechanism of

a busy library is not susceptible to controlled investigation and experiment in the same manner as, for example, the processes of overdues and book reservations. This fact, added to librarians' rather natural reluctance to undertake an exploratory work which might prejudice the running of their libraries, is one reason for delay....

....A further reason preventing widespread advance... is that many librarians make either unnecessary or impossible demands of an issue method and refuse to consider change until these are embodied in some practical scheme.

Surely it becomes clear that an issue method succeeds or fails by the measure of efficiency it achieves in the carrying out of its basic task - the recording of the issue and return of the books.

Chapter I

Early Systems of Charging

The charging systems which were in vogue during the latter part of the nineteenth century expressed a variance of viewpoint and differing library policy. H. J. Carr noted this when he made his Report on Charging Systems in 1889. He stated that, "A notable distinction is usually apparent in charging systems of libraries, dependent upon whether the book or the taker is given precedence in the records." He found that some libraries keep simple accounts (either by ledger or slips) in which the leading factor is the book number; others emphasized the name or number of the taker when filing the entry. He noted that a few libraries keep a double or triple entry system in which the book and the taker are of equal importance (1).

In 1899, J. D. Brown remarked that during this early period, in fact for the past thirty-six years, various types of indicators were in use in English libraries as aids in locating books and keeping records of loans (2).

Although ledger charging was used almost exclusively until the early days of the Civil War, its shortcomings were noted by many. Modifications and adaptations developed. Helen T. Geer remarked that an "important one was the dummy system, developed to eliminate the necessity for writing the title each time a book was borrowed and to avoid paging through lists of names and titles to find a specific book (3)."

Jennie M. Flexner traced the remaining events of this era in her Circulation Work in Public Libraries:

Both the temporary slip and the permanent card are merely substitutes for dummies, kept together at a central desk instead of scattered through the shelves, thus concentrating records in a flexible arrangement. As the body of readers increased in size and complexity, a method had to be devised to identify the individual. Since cards had proved to be effective for the book record, a two-card system de-

17

veloped; (1) a card for the book, and (2) a card for the reader, which he kept. The first readers' cards were identification cards. The incorporation of the book charges on the reader's card followed as increasing use required more complete records.

The attitude of a librarian toward circulation records is revealed in the tight controls and perfection of service desired in his day. Jacob Schwartz outlined the qualities which he thought necessary for the "perfect system" (5):

1st. In regard to the Books it should show: (a) Where every book is that is absent from its shelf. (b) How often every book has been issued. (c) The character of the reading of each day's issue.

2nd. In regard to the Readers, it should show: (a) The number of books taken out, with the dates of their issue and return. (b) There should be a receipt for every book returned. (c) The reader should have in his possession the means of knowing when his book is due.

3rd. In regard to Time, it should show: (a) The number of volumes issued each day. (b) The number of volumes issued each day. (b) The books overdue, so that they can be sent for without delay.

Melvil Dewey found necessary one more bit of information. He suggested, in regard to the "perfect system" of Schwartz, it should tell "not only the date of issue and return of each reader's books, but what those books were (6)."

One librarian, C. K. Bolton, believed that it was only necessary to know "Is a given book out? ... If out, who has it? ... When is it to be sent for as overdue? ... How many books were issued on a given day?" In referring to the question of "Has a given person a book charged to him?" he remarked, "I am not convinced that a fair reply would not be: 'You ought to know for what you are responsible.'" This last bit of information must be given up or "we must have a double-entry charging system. A librarian should ask himself then: Does a double-entry system charge books with the least delay and labor? If so, are tabulating statistics, considered solely on their merits, worth the time spent on them? If it does not, should a single-entry system prevail, at the sacrifice of statistics...? (7)"

The Ledger System

The ledger system was used early in the history of libraries, according to J. D. Brown, who described its use in the early Monastic Libraries (8):

Books lent were entered in a Brevis Librorum, or register, which appears to have corresponded with some of the varieties of modern ledgers or day books. At the annual distribution, which was also a stock-taking, these register-entries would no doubt be marked off and fresh entries made of the new borrowers and the books issued. It is a curious commentary upon some recent claims to the invention of the so-called "Two-book" System, to find that in the Carthusian Monasteries the issue of two books at a time was permitted.

This same writer revealed the thoughts of The Rev. Mr. Kirkwood, who was intent on establishing libraries in the "Highlands" in 1700 (8):

The following regulations as to borrowing, throw additional light upon the methods considered wise in the past....
7. "That he who borrows any book, consign a fourth part more than the real value of it; thereby to prevent the turning the Libraries into Book-sellers' shops."
8. "Besides, the borrower of any treatise ought to enter his name into a book of the Library to be provided for that purpose, together with the time in which he is to restore it, upon pain of forfeiting the money consigned. This seems likewise needful to prevent the embezelling of books."
18. "That they who are intrusted with the charge of books, give good security to leave them in as good case as they were in when they were first intrusted with them."
26. "No book shall be lent unless the person who comes for it bring with him conveniences to carry it without damage [sic]."
27. "No person at one time shall have more than two books."
28. "If any do neglect to return any book by the time limited, the Librarian shall take care to send him notice, the charge of which message he shall pay, besides the forfeiture."

In describing these early ledgers, Brown had this to say (9):

The very earliest type of Ledger used in connection with Lending Libraries was a kind of receipt book, in which were entered particulars of the book borrowed, and this register was signed by the person who took away the book. We ... believe it was simply an ordinary blank volume, in which the entries succeeded each other without columns or other classified features.... As books multiplied and Libraries increased a gradual extension would occur all round, and the necessity would arise for some ready method of distinguishing books returned from those still on loan. Thus would the column method of ruling come into existence, with its many varieties and uses. One form was designed to show by the presence or absence of a signature whether books were out or in....

With the advent of Subscription and Public Libraries fresh requirements arose, and the forms of charging ledgers entirely changed as regards the information recorded, although remaining the same in registering a day's work in consecutive order, instead of the issues of a certain book or to a certain reader.... Ledgers of a later pattern have been designed to get over the waste of time and liability to mistakes caused by the multiplication of details....

Melvil Dewey sought to acquaint us with the ledger daybook system used in his day (10):

A simple blank book has the date at the top of a page, a left-hand column for the reader's numbers, then columns for the book numbers. These lines are filled as the books are issued, and they can be charged very rapidly, as only two numbers - of reader and of book - have to be charged. It is much faster than a ledger system, where the page must be found for each entry. A column at the right is filled with the date of return. Unless this day-book is posted to a reader's or book-account ledger, nothing can be found except by knowing the date. In this respect it is no worse than the common slip system, arranged entirely by dates....

...Though little used, it is the most natural system of charging, for nearly all mercantile business is done on this day-book principle.... An incidental advantage of the plan is the ease with which different classes of books can be issued for different numbers of days, e.g., books of one, two and three weeks. The one-week books can be charged on the regular page for the day; the two-week books, on the page to be used two weeks from today for the regular one week books. Thus all the books on any page will be due the same day, and the sending of delinquent notices, etc., will be reduced to the greatest possible simplicity. This plan would require loose sheets which would be best any way for this kind of an account .... At the sacrifice of both book and reader accounts this gives an admirable system. These advantages can be secured by posting, but ... I fear this would be too cumbersome.

This "day-book" system was used in Litchfield, Connecticut Circulating Library in 1870 where a unique book auction took place each month. A. E. Bostwick mentioned this to those attending the American Library Institute(11).

The members having assembled, the president, or his representative, standing before them, proceeded to read the authors and titles of the books, with their serial numbers, from a catalogue, held in his hand.... No bid of less than two cents was entertained, and there was no superior limit. Books, as taken, were charged by the librarian in a blank book, using their serial numbers, and the name of the successful bidder.

The system used at Russell Library was designed simply to furnish an easy, rapid, and convenient way of accounting for books. This was stressed by W. K. Stetson in an article which contained the following description (12):

I use a book ruled vertically into columns and horizontally, the columns designed to receive, 1st, serial number of the day's issue (1, 2, 3, 4, etc.) which serial number is placed on the borrower's card, for convenience in checking off return of book; 2nd, number of borrower's card; 3rd, the book number (one column for each class of books). For example:

Feb. 9

No.	Card	Phil	Theol	Sociol	Philol
1	825	150.2			
2	1,892		220.4		
3	763			330.6	
4	3,789				409.8

G. W. Arnold suggested the use of four columns in the day-book system. He recorded, "It takes but about five minutes a day to run over the delivery of over 200 volumes to find the class circulation (13)."

In order to distinguish the type of material circulated

for statistical reports a Vermont librarian suggested the following table (14):

accession no. alone	=	adult fiction;
accession no. + class no.	=	adult nonfiction;
a ession no. + j	=	juvenile fiction;
accession no. + j & class no.	=	juv. nonfiction.

There were many merits in the day-book system, but,
according to H. J. Carr, it was superceded by other ledger
systems. He said, "Using the day-book method, and subsequently posting its successive charges to individual ledger accounts, it was an easy transition for someone to adopt the
idea of making the charge on the ledger direct to the personal account in the outset, and so dispense with the day-book
(15)."

This account with the reader was in book form, with an
alphabetical index to find each reader's page. Dewey mentioned this and gave a detailed description of the account with
the borrower (16):

By giving each reader a page and assigning him its number much is gained, as the use of the index is avoided,
except where a reader forgets his number and comes without his card, which of course bears it.... The book
should be ruled in five columns, for class or shelf, book
and volume numbers, date drawn and date returned....
The ledger is opened to the reader's page.... The number of class or shelf, book, and volume, if the work is in
volumes, with the day of the month drawn, is filled in, and
the charge is complete.... When the book is returned, opening to the page, the clerk enters the day of the month in
the returned column, assigns the fine, if any, and the
transaction is completed and is recorded in a clean compact line.

This record can also be kept on ledger cards, continued
Dewey (16):

The same rulings as in the book, on a card 10 x 15 cm.,
give 52 entries to the 4 columns of 13 lines each. This
is filed exactly like the book. It cannot be handled quite
as quickly, but saves time in being its own index, for the
cards are arranged alphabetically.... The cards are
placed and handled like a card catalogue, but must be removed in making entries.... After many experiments at

Amherst College we preferred this system of charging,
and have been using it for three years. It has special advantages for a college library, where it is desired to preserve a record of the reading of each of the students.

It may take the form of a Laced Ledger Sheets Reader Account, he added (17):

This plan is simply the shelf catalog binder, with sheets
ruled as in the book ledger.... It combines the merits of
the book with those of the ledger-card and box above described. While never getting out of order, it involves much
more labor in adding, removing, or changing sheets....
When removed they are filed away alphabetically the same
as cards. They are of course less convenient to handle
when removed from the binder.

Dewey had something to say about the methods involved
in keeping accounts with books (18):

The number and title of the book are written at the head,
instead of the number and name of the borrower. In place
of the book number we write the number of the reader
who takes the book. The name could be used, but would
be an intolerable labor. The loaned and returned columns
would be the same, and filled the same, as in the reader
accounts....
The book and laced-sheet form of ledger are almost
never used for this account with books, since so many
pages are required for even a small library. If to be preserved, it is kept on ledger cards; otherwise on temporary
slips.

The type of library and its purpose dictated its policy
in choosing a form of record, thought Brown (19):

In many of the proprietary and commercial subscription
libraries the plan of keeping an account with every sub-
scriber of books on loan was common, and is, to a certain extent still used, though the most usual practice is to
keep such records on cards....
In public lending libraries it is generally recognized
that accounts kept with the book issued, instead of with
the borrower who has it are much more helpful and exact
than other forms. Although now almost invariably kept on
cards, this form of ledger was formerly kept in book form
.... Each book was given a folio.

A system which combines the use of day-book and reader and book accounts was brought to light by H. J. Carr
(20):

> [An] ingenious scheme submitted by Mr. John Coffin Jones
> Brown (while one of the Trustees of the Public Library), was
> entitled "a system of record devised and proposed for the
> use of the Public Library, July, 1861 (Printed for the use
> of the Trustees) Boston, 1866...."
> Each borrower was to sign in a register against a con-
> secutive number, constituting the "Borrower's Number."
> A card catalog was to furnish an alphabetical index to same,
> and a re-registration was intended once in ten years. Each
> person so registered was to be given an "Application Card,"
> having thereon the borrower's number and name, and plac-
> es for numbers of books to be applied for. Usual old-
> style public library cards served as the model for that
> purpose.
> Secondly, there was to be prepared a "Delivery Card"
> for each person, made up from his signature in the reg-
> ister, and containing borrower's number, name, and res-
> idence, and to be placed in its numerical order in a re-
> ceptacle for that purpose. Such card to be 5 1/2 x 8 in-
> ches, ruled on both sides with space for record of 120
> loans or deliveries. Each entry consisting of day, week,
> loan number, shelf number, and volume of book. When
> full to be replaced by new cards; and, in fact, constitut-
> ing perpetual ledgers.
> A "Daily Record" was to be made on sheets (22 inches
> long by 20 inches broad with space for 1,000 loans)
> against a series of numbers commencing with unity each
> day; adding a designating number for each day, in order
> to distinguish one day's entries from another. Additional
> sheets for excess over 1,000 loans in a day. Against
> each daily loan number to be blanks for borrower's num-
> ber, shelf number, and volume, class number, and date
> of return. The sheets to be bound in a volume each year,
> thus making a day-book containing a compact, complete,
> and concise account of all the transactions of the loan de-
> partment for the year. The form might also be adapted
> to add the titles of the books, and take signatures in re-
> ceipt, if so wished.
> Inside the cover of each volume was to be placed a pa-
> per for the entry of borrower's number and loan number,
> and thus connecting each volume lent with its borrower;
> also making known its relative use, and a certain credit
> to the right person on its return. The delivery cards were

to be placed in drawers or compartments for each day of
delivery, and in order of loan numbers; each card thus
representing a book out of the library and finally indicating delinquents.

This plan of Mr. Brown's was probably deemed a little too complete, and so that of Prof. Jewett's in 1866,
was adopted instead (in connection with a re-registration),
and in lieu of ledgers, for recording loans.

Yet modifications of Mr. Brown's scheme are readily
recognized in the methods of several leading libraries today, and result in much satisfaction, so far as concerns
thoroughness and exactitude. But they entail some extra
labor, and in some respects do not admit of the fullest
speed.

The Subscription Library of the Royal Medical and Chir-
urgical Society made use of a large Folio Ledger where each
reader had a separate page of account to himself. B. R.
Wheatley wrote that the folio number from the reader's page
is given on a daily slip record and an alphabetical index is
kept to all titles which are listed in the ledger. "When works
are returned they are easily struck off in both books from
either direction, index or ledger (21)."

The Newburgh, New York Library used a charging system of a "novel sort" (22):

One ledger with borrowers in the common form is supplemented by another, where the number of the book is given
at the left, and the number of the page of the person who
has it out follows. By reference to any number it is seen
whether the book is in, or if out, who has it. It is the
slip system put into ledger form.

The ledger system proved useful to the Sunday School
Library, according to Shute, who described the plan he devised (23):

It is arranged for 500 persons and 1,000 books, and costs
$1.50. There is no need of dividing the library case in-
to cells or apartments [as in another Sunday School Library system].

The larger figures in the perpendicular columns represent the tens and hundreds in the library numbers of the
books; the other perpendicular columns represent the unit.
For instance, No. 125 would be represented by 5 in small
type, on the line of 120 in full-faced type.

One full column, from the calendar to the bottom of
the page, is assigned to each scholar. At the top of the
column, over the calendar, is the scholar's number. If
desired, write the names of the scholars directly under
the calendars on Sundays; each page will hold ten names,
generally sufficient for a whole class. Allow a double
page for larger classes. When a book is drawn out, check
with a small stroke the first, second, third, fourth or fifth
Sunday of the month, represented by 1, 2, 3, 4, 5, on the
line of the month; and also with a similar stroke the number in smaller type representing the book drawn out. When
a book is returned, draw a cross stroke over the date on
which it was taken out, and also over the number of the
book; then all is ready to charge again. A very little
practice will show how rapidly the entries can be made.
By marking the calendar in pencil, it can be used another
year after erasing.

In case the librarian prefers to make the record by the
scholar's number only, without writing the name under the
calendars, it will be desirable to use the two pages preceding the record for a numerical list of the scholars'
names. Reference can then be made at any time to this
list in order to ascertain what scholar is represented by
any special number.

Whenever it is necessary to ascertain who has a book
that is wanted the librarian need only run his eye along
the horizontal line containing the desired number until the
column is found in which the number is charged. The
scholar's name or number will be found at the top.

"The ledger," wrote Carr, "practically held its own in
the libraries of the United States, til the early days of our
Civil War of 1861. As late as 1856, Dr. N. B. Shurtleff
(well known in the history of the Boston P.L.), ... recommended changes to be made in a loan-book, having five accounts on a page; ten on two pages or the folio; then the
ninth account on folio 365 would be 3659, etc. (24)."

Even in 1940 we read of its use in small libraries.
C. H. Hull recommended the use of a large-sized exercise
book for book charging (25).

Permanent Card System

It is difficult, even impossible, to say when or where
cards were first used for library records, according to J. D.

Brown, who remarked, "...as they have been used for commercial purposes for years before the Public Library System was thought about, it follows that many minds must have
discovered the utility and convenience of movable entries
(26)."

These movable entries were managed in the fashion of
baggage checks in one library, observed Mr. Peck, in con-
versing with his friends (27):

> Mr. Peck. - A pastor adopted this system to save work-
> ing on Sunday. There was a board for borrowers, filled
> with pins on which were hung numbered checks corres-
> ponding to the number of borrowers; and another board
> for the books with pins and checks corresponding to the
> books. When a book was taken the book-check was hung
> on the borrower's pin and the borrower's check on the
> book-pin.
>
> Mr. Dewey. - We found the same system in use at the
> college library at Kingston, Can.
>
> Mr. Davidson. - The system is crude and liable to errors.
>
> Mr. Dewey. - From it has developed the card and pocket
> system.

The permanent card system was recommended by W. I.
Fletcher, who further stated (28):

> To this advantage of a self-registry of overdue books is
> to be added that of the comparative ease with which it can
> be learned at once who has any book which is out. This
> method of charging books, or some modification of it, is
> in use in nearly all progressive libraries, and is to be
> recommended in its simplest form for the smallest ones.
> It has the general features of the American baggage-check-
> ing system, and is as superior to the ledger-account meth-
> od as that system is to the happy-go-lucky way of dealing
> with "luggage" on European railways.

One of the earliest methods of card charging which we
know of in any detail is described by H. J. Carr, who knew
of its organization by C. C. Jewett. It was never used by
him in its complete form (29).

In 1861, Prof. C. C. Jewett, Superintendent of the Boston

P.L. put forth in a pamphlet of twenty pages a "plan for circulation and use of the books in the Upper Hall of the [Boston] Public Library." This plan proposed to permit all holders of Lower Hall cards to have a further or special card for use in the Upper Hall. This special card was to be left at the library (in pawn, as it were), for each book drawn thereby. In addition, a receipt was to be taken on a blank form having a coupon or stub, which coupon was to be surrendered to the borrower upon return of the book, canceling by its detachment the borrower's receipt. The date of lending the book was further to be stamped or written on a ticket (or abstract of the regulations), attached to the book cover, so that the borrower could thus see when it was due, and also that such ticket might give a progressive record of the use of that particular book.

The receipts were to be placed in a drawer or pigeonholes, arranged alphabetically in order of names of borrowers, each day's issues by themselves. The borrower's cards (which were devised for both identification and for giving lists of call numbers) being retained at the library in lieu of the books drawn, in addition to the receipts were to be placed in other drawers in alphabetical order....

The foregoing all sounds very much like an account of some "combined charging systems," which have been elaborated long since then, and urged as new devices. But so far as now known, the idea was original with Prof. Jewett.

In 1879, J. Schwartz described a "combined charging system" which makes use of the borrower's card and the book slip. He goes into greater detail in describing the filing procedure and discharge (30):

The card is deposited in the charging box in the order of its class and accession number, in its proper division, and as the same process occurs as each successive book is issued, the box will contain, at the end of each day, all the loans in a classified form, so that the necessary statistics can be at once obtained and recorded; the cards are then removed to the return-box....

As the return boxes contain a card for every book out, and as the books themselves have a record of the date when issued, together with the number of the reader's card, it is only necessary that the attendant refer to the slip and accessions number of the book returned to find the corresponding card.... As no card can be found except by means of the book charged on it, the mere fact of having the card before him is proof of the return of the previous book。

As the cards of each week are kept separate, and as every book returned requires a card to be withdrawn from its respective week, the number of finable books can be easily ascertained。 [When a week's charges have become delinquent these cards] ... are to be distributed into six heaps, according to the respective days of the week ... and all the delinquents of that week will be in regular order, so that the necessary notices can be sent each day to those a week overdue。

He felt that this method had certain advantages (31):

1st。 The reader is not obliged to carry around and take care of his card, as it is always kept in the library。

2nd。 Orders can be given either verbally or in writing - in the latter case the list is returned to the reader, and can be again used。

3rd。 The only writing necessary is the entry of the class and accessions number on the borrower's card, and the pencilling of the borrower's number and date of issue on the book-slip。

4th。 Most of the information, and in fact all that is necessary, is given in a form for permanent preservation.

5th。 The permanent and annual expense of the system for a library of say 10,000 readers need not exceed fifty or sixty dollars。

6th。 Any desirable number of clerks can be engaged at the same time in charging books, so that the greatest possible speed can be secured whenever necessary。 Returns can be managed in a similar manner。

Another librarian who felt that the record should be a classified arrangement by date was Cadwallader.   He introduced a card for the book which stayed with it while it was not in use (32):

The specimen check inclosed is ruled with three columns - the one at the left hand (the card being on its side) is for the number of the borrower's card, the middle is for the date when loaned, and the right-hand column was intended for the date when returned。 [now left blank] ...。

Printed blanks, three by three
and one half inches, with upper
corners trimmed for convenience
in handling, are provided - one
for each book.... As long as the
book remains on the shelf, the
check is left in it. In loaning a
book the date is stamped on the
check the same as on the borrower's card, and the number of the
card is written opposite the date
in pencil. The checks of books
loaned each day are placed in an
apartment by themselves in the
record box.

Those not returned at the end of the twenty-one days are
placed with other delinquent checks, and "notices" are
sent to the borrowers. Another apartment contains the
checks of books lost, also of books which are at the bindery, or elsewhere other than regularly loaned - the proper sign indicating the whereabouts. In returning a book,
the check is taken from the box and placed in the book
next to the front cover.

The record of books charged became quite elaborate in
the hands of Mr. George Parr, according to Cutter, who
wrote (33): "At the London Institute a subscription library
is used, a most ingenious and original system invented by
the sub-librarian, Mr. George Parr. It is a card system
by which the reader's time and book accounts are kept without stamping or writing, by means of arrangement, color,
and a series of projections on the cards (33)."

Brown speaks of Parr as the "inventor of the best card-
ledger we have ever seen (34)."

The main feature of this system, which was described at
Manchester in 1879, is a fixed alphabetical series of borrowers' names on cards, behind which other cards descriptive of books issued are placed. The system is worked
as follows: Every book has a pocket inside the board
somewhat similar to that used at Bradford and Chelsea,
in which is a card bearing the title and number of the
book. When the book is issued the card is simply withdrawn and placed, with a coloured card to show the date,
behind the borrower's card in the Register. When it is
returned the title card is simply withdrawn from behind

the borrower's card, replaced in the book, and the transaction is complete.... Mr. Parr has introduced many
refinements and devices whereby almost any question that
can be raised as regards who has a book, when it was
issued, and what book a given person has, can be answered without much labor.... As regards its application to a popular public library, the absence of a permanent record would in most cases be deemed objectionable, but there seems no reason why, with certain modifications, it could not be adapted to the smaller libraries,
where neither pocket system nor indicator are in use.

A description of the materials he used and the advantages, as Parr saw them, are given below (35):

Borrower's cards.... I have used white and green cards
alternately for each alphabetical character: the names beginning with A are on white cards, with B on green cards,
with C on white cards, etc.
      Book cards.... Ten colours are used for these cards,
the colours indicating sets of numbers; for instance, books
numbering 1 to 999 are white cards, nos. 1000 to 1999
are red cards, etc, etc., so that in 10,000 volumes there
would be ten colours of 1000 each; the process being repeated in every additional 10,000 volumes. These colours
are for the purpose of enabling the librarian to see the
book-cards as they stand in the tray, so that without taking them out he may be able to identify the volumes they
represent - to this extent at least, that he will know to
what particular thousand they belong. Having thus assisted him so far, I go further, and by means of projections
from the upper side of the cards, and inclining some to
the right and some to the left, I subdivide the thousands
into hundreds, each projection representing a hundred, and
the particular hundred being known by the position of the
projection. The projection on the left being the first hundred in each thousand, the projection on the right the tenth
hundred in each thousand, the other hundreds occupying in-
termediate positions. Thus a white card with projection
No. 1 will show that the volume to which it belongs is one
of the set numbered 1 to 100, projection No. 5 indicates
501 to 600, projection No. 10 indicates 901 - 1,000, and
so with the rest. By means of these colours and projections the librarian can find with remarkable ease who is in
possession of any particular book....
      Date-cards.... Where three weeks are allowed for
reading, it would be desirable to have date-cards running

over a space of two months, a different color being used
for each month; those cards used in January being available again in March, those used in February being available again in April. The projections on these cards have
five positions; the number on the projection marking the
day of the week, and the position of projection the week
of the month.

Short-time cards denote that their borrower has received a book which, being much in request, is to be returned within a shortened period. They stand side by side
with the date-cards in the tray, and can be seen without
turning a single card, so that no searching is required.
The advantages accruing from the use of these cards will
be obvious to every librarian. Thereby special lists of
books in request, with their borrowers, are rendered unnecessary, whilst delinquencies are instantly checked.

.... the following results are gained: -

No writing is required in the issue or return of books.

With 10,000 volumes in circulation, one can trace the
borrower of any particular volume in two minutes; taking
the average, only fifty cards would have to be glanced at
to find the one required.

A borrower desiring to know what works he has out
(a matter of common occurance where more than one is
allowed), the librarian can at once read the titles off to
the inquirer by turning to his account.

Should a borrower dispute the possession of a book
charged against him, it must be on the shelf if returned,
for had any other member presented the book at the
issue-desk, the book-card would, of course, be missing,
and the error thus detected could at once be rectified.

No error can be made in the date when a book is taken
out, as only the cards for that particular day would be in
use.

No searching of accounts is required for books overdue,
this being shown by the projections on date-cards.

Short-time books are shown with date when issued, without turning a card.

When the books require binding, the cards act as a
binder's check.

.... One thing it does not give: The number of times
any particular work may go out; this, as far as I see at
present, could only be obtained by a mark on the book-
card at each time of issue.

In the Albany YMCA Library a self-service system was
practiced using book cards and pockets and members' cards

kept at the desk. "All book-cards of books off the shelves
are kept in the order of call numbers. The members' cards
are arranged by date of charge and alphabetically under each
date (36)."

The use of book cards was mentioned by Melvil Dewey
in 1878. He called them ledger cards (37).

> A variation on the ledger card plan is to keep the cards
> of the books out in a separate box, ... A larger check
> box is used, and the cards arranged by dates or subjects
> .... The ledger cards of books in are kept in another
> box, or in the book itself on the shelf. The latter plan
> seems to me by far the best, as each book on the shelves
> has inside its cover a complete history of its reading
> since the current card was put in. This system is really
> a combination of the ledger card and slip system....
> The slips are the most convenient in examining the li-
> brary without closing.... It is of course only one of the
> many uses to which we put the ability to know almost in-
> stantly the whereabouts of any book.

The basic idea of keeping book cards at the desk while
books are on the shelf was dealt with by M. W. Plummer,
who recommended "when a book is in, its card is kept in a
tray, or box with partitions, with those of other books not in
use, in order of the call-numbers." She also recommended
keeping the borrower's card on file at the library. "This
system answers all possible questions.... It prevents the annoyance of lost cards, as the borrower has nothing to do with
his card. It prevents also all tampering with the dates on
the cards. By keeping the book-cards at the desk the librarian can tell if a book is in without going to the shelves (38)."

A detailed example of one such system was given by
Estabrook, who recommended that the borrower keep his ticket (39).

> The borrower, having selected a book, simply presents
> his card to the desk attendant, who enters on it, with pen
> and ink, the number of the book taken, and stamps the
> date, to guard against errors or alterations. This card
> is retained by the borrower, and presented whenever he
> returns or borrows a book. The book-card is taken from
> its box, the number of the borrower's card entered upon
> it, and placed under its proper date in the borrower's
> card-box, also kept on the table. When the book is re-

turned, the charge on the borrower's card is cancelled
with a conductor's punch, and the book card taken from
the dated box and placed in its numerical order in the
box containing the cards of all books on the shelves....

Each half of the borrower's box is composed of 7 tiers
of 10 apartments each. Tin partitions, running lengthwise of the table, divide the 14 tiers into 140 apartments.
Each tier of ten apartments has at the top the date of the
day when it was filled.... Thus, the date on the borrower's card tells in what tier, and the last figure of the
number in what apartment of the tier to look for the book
card.

Brown suggested a similar file of cards for all books
in the library in numerical order, "distributed in hundreds
and tens, shown by projections, to facilitate finding." He
does not include in his plan a separate file for books checked
out (40):

When a book is asked for all that the assistant has to do
is to write its number in the borrower's card, the number of the borrower's card and the date on the book label,
and then to issue the book, having left the borrower's
card in the Register. The period of issue could be indicated by differently coloured cards to meet the overdue
question, and a simple day-sheet ruled for class letters
and numbers of books issued would serve for statistical
purposes. The register of book numbers could be used
as an indicator by the staff in many cases, and such a
plan would be as easily worked, as economical, and as
accurate as most of the charging systems in use.

Incorporating the use of a classified book file and a
borrowers' file, C. A. Cutter introduced his double record
system used at the Athenaeum Library (41).

The plan is this. A pocket of stout linen paper, 10 cm.
high by 9 cm. wide, pasted inside the back cover of each
book, holds two cards, each 5 cm. wide, one of manila,
15 cm. long, and the other white, 12 1/2 cm. long. The
manila is ruled from side to side into 18 spaces, 36 on
both sides; the white into 15 which later are again divided by a lengthwise line into 30 spaces, or 60 on both
sides. Across one end of each is written the class and
author number of the book, and the author's name and a
prominent word or two of the title. When taking out
books the borrower takes the cards from the pocket, signs

his name on the first vacant line of the manila card, and
hands book and cards to the clerk. The clerk by a glance
sees that the numbers on book and card are the same, de-
livers the book to the reader, stamps the date on the
white card, and drops it into that reader's place in the
alfabetical [sic] box of borrowers, and the manila card
into another box. At her leisure, she, or another clerk
if it is a busy day, arranges the manilas in the order of
their class-numbers and distributes them in a case in
which all the manila cards of books out are arranged in
that order.

We have then two series of cards, manila in class order, white in the order of readers. The white cards show
how many books each borrower has out, what they are,
and when they were taken. The manila cards enable us
to find at once whether a given book is out and who has
it, and also what books are out in a given class. Counting them just before they are distributed in the case gives
the circulation for the day classified.

When a borrower returns his book, the clerk picks out
the white card from its place in the box, stamps on it the
date of return, compares that with the date of issue to
see if any fine is due for overtime, collects the fine, if
there is one, puts the card in the pocket and the book on
a wire-guarded shelf. From this shelf it can be taken
only by the clerk, who picks out the manila card from the
class case and puts it in the pocket, after which the book
is ready to be placed upon its shelf.... It will be seen
that the clerk does not have to do any writing, that the
borrower writes only his name, and does not have to carry a library card about with him.

W. E. Foster's modification of the system used by
Cutter showed two variations: "The runner, when taking a
book from the shelf to bring it to the delivery-desk, writes
the applicant's registration number on both slips. The delivery clerk carefully compares these numbers." Later when
slips are filed the book file "is arranged in the order of the
book numbers, and in a separate numerical order for each
one of the 14 days (42)."

A colored borrower's card aided in noting overdues in
this system by A. P. Massey, which he claimed to be somewhat modified from those of Mr. Schwartz and Mr. Cutter
(43):

Our tickets date from four points in the year, and we use

a different color for each quarter, as well as one for life
members, and one for extra entries of any sort. I was
not able to find six colors in ordinary stock that were
light enough to show pencil marks readily in all lights. I
therefore had some cards printed with colored ink on white
board, with a border about an eighth of an inch wide, of
the same color on the top and bottom of the card. This
shows in the rack as though colored all the way, while it
gives a white surface to write on. It adds nothing to the
cost.

We have the following assortment now in use: White
card, buff card, white with red border, do. light blue
border, do. black border, also white, with the word
"complimentary" in place of the border, and a bright yellow card unprinted for extra books, etc.

Klas A. Linderfelt discussed a system for which he
gave credit "for the ground work" to W. E. Foster, later
hearing that it really originated with Cutter modified in several particulars (44).

When the member withdraws a book, the number of this
book is entered on the slip corresponding to his card, but
no date stamped opposite. When the book is returned,
however, the date of such return is stamped on the member-slip, opposite the book number. The presence on the
member-slip of a number without a date opposite therefore
shows there is a book out on this card; the contrary, that
it is not at present in use.

.... the system is extremely simple in its workings;
that the actual writing done each time is exactly the same
as is necessary with Mr. Poole's charging system [used
formerly], and that the infinitesimal quantity of extra time
required for getting the member-slip, and stamping the
date once more, is amply compensated for by the greater
security, and the comparative immunity from mistakes,
which it affords.

In order to cut down the time involved in discharging of
books, A. R. Hasse introduced this plan of dividing the issue
file (45):

The two cases hold the book cards for the loans of the odd
and even days respectively, and during the greater part of
the day each case is in charge of an individual attendant,
the receiving force being reduced to one during the first
two hours of the day and during the latter part of the ev-

ening. Two short rails have been erected on the outside
of the counter, dividing the delivery-desk into stations
for the delivery of books loaned on odd and even days respectively, each station being indicated by a sign a little
over the level of the eyes.

The time saved by the present method is very percept-
ible both to the borrower and to the library staff. In
charging, the only thing it is necessary to write now is
the borrower's number on the book-card, instead of as
formerly, the book-number, borrower's number, and the
charging clerks number, the stamp being used twice as
formerly, both on the borrower's card and on the book-
card or charging slip. The book-cards ... at night are
counted and segregated by the clerk on duty in the reference room.

H. C. Bolton suggested the following to aid in showing
the borrower when his book is due (46):

Now, being myself averse to uselessly burdening the memory, I have been in the habit of writing on a slip of stout
paper the date on which the book should be returned. This
I then use as a book-mark. Believing this simple exped-
ient might be approved by librarians, I send you a specimen of my "improved book-mark." Stout paper slips
measuring 15 x 5 cm., with the name of library, and
simple instructions printed thereon, as shown in the margin, can be very cheaply made in quantity. A blank space
for the date and one for the rate of fine can be filled by
the clerk giving out books.

To this the editor of Library Notes appended a few remarks
(46):

Libraries using a pocket will of course use a book-mark
of the same size as the book card, and insert it in the
pocket when the book card is removed in charging. At
Columbia we long practiced putting a blank slip in this
pocket with date of return stampt [sic] on. Where no
pocket is used, the size outlined in Prof. Bolton's letter,
the old standard book-mark size, is best.

..... Except that the book mark is not necessary in order to draw books, and that its loss causes no inconvenience, this slip answers the same purpose as the reader's card, which most public libraries require to be presented in drawing books. To economize the book-mark
may hav [sic] a heading, "This book must be returned on

or before the last date stampt [sic] below, or a fine of
5 c₀ per day will be collected." Then the rest of the
card is ruled in squares, and the dater, set two weeks
or a month ahead, struck in the first vacant square. One
book-mark made of better card may thus be used a score
of times.

Another problem occurred to C. K. Bolton. Libraries
were finding it difficult to limit the number of books circulated to an individual and yet allow him more than one at a
time. Bolton suggested the following (47):

To meet this need the public library at Brookline devised
a card on which two books may be taken at one time, or
on different days, as the reader wishes. He may keep a
history a month (by renewal), and read 20 novels during
the same period; or he may take two books other than fiction.... The card is divided in the middle; the left has
"Fiction" at the top, the right "Other works." The date
of delivery of a book is stamped on the proper side of the
card, and also on the book itself.
   G. M. Jones mentioned other plans (48):
   .... The simplest plan is to issue an extra card, not
good for fiction, bearing the same number as the regular
card with the addition of some simple mark, such as X
or S. The special card should also be of a different col-
or.
   The reader should keep track of his cards, and there
should be no more difficulty through their getting mixed
than there is now with several cards in one family.
   With the "two-book" system, as with the single book,
the only safe method is to keep two accounts, book and
borrower. This involves looking up two charges when the
book is returned, and therefore seems not feasible when
there is a large circulation....
   .... I have learned of 18 libraries which are using the
"two-book" system. Four use two cards and 14 use one
card. Of the latter, six use a card with two divisions,
"fiction" and "other works," and eight make all charges
in the same column. Four write the number of the book
in the return column. The two Philadelphia libraries
simply mark "C" against the non-fiction date.

While many small libraries adopted what Dewey called
the "ledger-card system" he felt "it would not be too much
to say that 'account with the book' means to most library
people the temporary slip system.... It is not necessary to

date the slip on the return of the book, its removal from the
check-box being sufficient evidence of the return (49):

Temporary Slip System

The early use of temporary slips for the record of
loans was traced historically by H. J. Carr in his Report
on Charging Systems. He said (24):

> ... the fact that the transactions to be recorded were
> loans and not sales, led ... [the English libraries] to
> also incline toward taking receipts for the books loaned.
> At first the receipting or signing of the borrower's name
> was done on the margin of the entry in the day-book or
> ledger, opposite the name or number of the book charged
> .... Later on (and obviously derived from making on a
> blank or sheet of paper a schedule or list of works want-
> ed) the idea of having such a "call-list," as we would now
> term it, signed and retained as a receipt or voucher,
> seems to have become much in favor, and, in fact, to
> have been the forerunner of most recent methods of using
> such slips and tickets in library service in the many ways
> with which we are familiar.

Using this method, F. Vinton remarked, the "labor
may be thrown mainly upon the borrower, who finds blanks
within his reach. These are somewhat oblong having separate lines for 'author's name,' 'Title of the book,' 'Borrower's name,' 'Date.' When a borrower presents his book and
the receipt he would give for it, a careful comparison of the
two requires but an instant (50)."

Carr reported on the charging details involved in Jewett's
system of 1866 (51).

> Its chief features were the use of a slip of paper for each
> loan, as being simple and adaptable to charging exigen-
> cies, and readily assorted in various ways.
> The slip was to show: First, date of loan; second,
> some brief indications of the title of the book lent; third,
> shelf and order number of the book; and fourth, name and
> residence of the borrower.... He preferred also a print-
> ed form for the slips, and use of a serial or consecutive
> numbering of same, through each day. Date of issue was
> to be stamped on each slip; also on cover of book, inside,
> and on the borrower's card. Date of return was in like

manner to be stamped all around, but in different colored
ink.

Cutter's slip system became a double record method.
He used a typewriter to record the loans (52):

A long strip of paper 5 cm. wide passes over the roller
of the typewriter. It is divided down the middle by a
perforated line at intervals of 5 cm. by horizontal perforated lines. When a book is brought to be charged, the
clerk prints on the first line of the left half the book no.;
on the right the borrower's no.; on the second line under
the borrower's no. the book no.; and under the book no.
the borrower's no.; on the third line the day of the year,
thus:

372.34	5249
5249	372.34
247	247

The strip then is moved on around
the cylinder, so as to be ready
for the next charge. When convenient the strip is pulled apart along
the perforated lines, and the left
hand 5 x 2 1/2 cm. slips arranged
in check boxes in the order of the
book nos., while the right hand
slips are arranged in the order of
the borrowers' nos.

The librarian at Harvard, J. Winsor, arranged the
charge slips by book-number after posting the information to
the individuals' accounts in a ledger (53).

One arrangement produces a borrower's record, according to M. Dewey, who stated (54):

In practice I believe no library arranges these cheap slips
by themselves, but by means of larger slips of stiff card.
The stiff slips are arranged as in the other system, as if
to be written on. Then, instead of making the charge on
the stiff card, where it will be preserved, no writing is
done, but the slip on which the reader calls for the book
is simply dropped in against his card and the book is
charged. When returned, the slip is taken out and thrown
away, or preserved for statistics. This system saves
writing and is quickly managed, but it sacrifices all the
advantages of a record of each reader's books.... In this
plan the stiff card contains full name, address, date of
joining, time to which paid, etc., etc.

Carr suggested a date arrangement: "Each day's bundle of slips was to be placed in separate pigeon-holes (in order of book numbers), progressing forward till the thirteenth day, and thus showing overdue or finable books (51)."

It would be possible to supplement the borrowers' file by a book location file, according to Vinton, who suggested copying the slips by a "papyrograph" (50).

In commenting on this, Mary Plummer said, "Whenever there is copying done there is an extra liability to mistakes, and the writer suggests instead the use of the registering machine used by many dry-goods and notions houses to make duplicate checks for goods bought. Both entries would be in the same writing, made simultaneously, and if one was correct the other would have to be (55)."

In discharging the book, Vinton recommended, "When the book is returned, a colored pencil stroke by the librarian, across the face of the receipt, frees the late holder from the obligation he contracted and yet the receipt may be held by the librarian. These, being preserved in alphabetical order, form the literary history of the borrower, of his class, and of the institution (50)."

Carr believed that the slips should be "sorted, so as to bring together all slips for the same book, and thus show its use and frequency of subjects read upon and the like (51)."

The slips can be used for the above mentioned purposes, Cutter remarked, or be returned to the borrower as a receipt (56). Others felt that the slip should be destroyed (57).

The details of the Peplow system were related in 1939. It differs markedly from the usual temporary slip system in several particulars (58).

Mr. W. A. Peplow... has now introduced this system which obviates the chief faults of the card charging and other systems. It allows for a hundred per cent service from each assistant, it permits of unlimited extension of service and allows for the discharge of over 300 volumes per hour by each assistant with the minimum of fatigue. Also it ensures that only one book be borrowed per reader's ticket.
Staff. While engaged on the work of charging or dis-

charging books, each assistant is seated at a desk in the
counters, for it is unnecessary under this system to refer
to files or issue trays, though during very slack periods
discharges may be made direct from the files without making a record on the recording pad. Obviously when the
service is in full operation the counters present an order-
ly appearance, and the staff suffer much less fatigue.

..... At the outset all book cards are discarded and each
borrower's ticket is provided with a number.

Each book is provided with a pocket and a date label.
Unlike the card charging system the borrower's ticket remains in the pocket in the book while it is in the reader's
possession.....

Each reader will be provided with a stiff manilla ticket.

The spaces ruled on the borrower's ticket are used for
stamping the date of return of each book borrowed and as
both sides are ruled the ticket is available for 50 issues.
Issue and Discharge of Books.

..... A pad of foolscap paper (13" x 4 1/2") is provided
for each assistant issuing books. On this he enters the
book number and the borrower's ticket number. He then
stamps the date of return on the date label in the book and
on the borrower's ticket and inserts the ticket in the pocket. The issue pad is thumb-indexed by classes for Non-
Fiction and by 1,000's for Fiction so that the numbers are
recorded in approximate order. At the end of the day the
pads used by the charging assistants are assembled and
placed in a file bearing the date. The files holding each
day's issues are kept in a series of pigeon holes at the
entrance side of the counter.

It is found necessary to have just 31 such files, one
for each day of the month, for after a month the few outstanding entries can be copied on to a single sheet and
filed in a special file for overdue books.

Assistants at the entrance counter have pads similar
to those just described, the only difference is that the
thumb index is by date for the current two weeks, with
separate sheets for overdue books.

On the return of a book the assistant enters on the
appropriate page the book number and the reader's ticket
number. He then cancels the last date on the reader's
ticket with a special rubber stamp. This cancelling of
the date on the reader's ticket is intended as the borrower's receipt for the return of the book. Should, however,
a reader produce a ticket with the last date uncancelled,
it is clear that he still has a book charged to him on that
ticket and this can be easily proven by referring to the

issue files.

It is possible to have a number of assistants, each
with a pad and pencil, discharging books independently of
one another and without having to refer to the issue files.
New Borrowers and other enquiries are dealt with at a
special enquiry desk. Thus a steady and expeditious service is maintained.

The records of books returned are carefully filed and
cancelled from the issue files at slack periods, at the end
of the day, or by an assistant especially detailed for the
work. The essential feature of the system is that borrowers are not kept waiting while this work is done, nor
are the books held up.

The process of cancelling returned books in the issue
files is quite simple and with a little practice can be done
very quickly. Each sheet in the pads at the entrance
counter bears the date the books are issued (or returned,
whichever is preferred) and contains about thirty entries.
The assistant when cancelling returned books takes the
issue file bearing the corresponding date and proceeds to
cross out each book returned, and as the sheets in the
file are in classified order and arranged by number, as
already explained, the entries can be easily traced.

The system suggested by M. E. Buhre in 1896 had been
used also in the Chicago Public Library (59).

The slips are of manilla paper, size less than half that of
a card, made into blocks of 100 slips each, glued together
at the side. In issuing a book we write on the slip the
card number, accession number of the book and class number (first figure only), stamping both slip and card with
the date. The card is placed in the pocket of the book
and the slips thrown loosely into a box until the next day.
They are then counted by classes, and a record made of
the number in each class issued for that day. After this
they are arranged numerically by the upper (card) number,
and placed in the tray with the date designated as in the
... [card] system.

When the book is returned, the date upon the card
shows us in which division of the tray we must look for
the slip, the number of the card gives us the number of
the slip, which, when found, is taken out, and the accession number upon it compared with that of the book. If
they agree the slip is destroyed and the card stamped with
the date of return.

We think this latter method is less expensive than the

former [card method], and that by it books can be exchanged more rapidly; the slips also occupy less space
in the tray than cards. But we cannot keep a record of
the number of times a volume has been issued, as is the
case when the book card is used.

In discussing this disadvantage of the temporary slip,
among others, J. Meisoner said (60):

Charging and discharging take but a moment. The only
criticism that has been made is to the effect that it takes
time to transfer the charges to the readers' cards and to
check return books. That hour could not be better spent,
for it enables the circulation librarian to know just what
books have been drawn or returned. Such a familiarity
with the records and readers is a positive necessity.

Poole, in writing of the system adopted at the Chicago
Public Library, reminded librarians that a charging system
must be adjusted to meet local needs (61).

Without modifications, so rigid a method would not be
practicable in a Western library. Applicants are not required to fill printed blanks, and are not limited to any
specific method of applying for books. They may do it
verbally, or they may give a list of shelf marks of such
books as they desire; and often they need and receive
assistance from the attendants in selecting their books....
All the writing for the registry is done by the attendant,
which saves the applicant this trouble and secures a more
legible record.... The limit of business that can be done
at a circulating library is determined by its capacity of
receiving books, and not of delivering them.

Winsor recommended the slip system because the "moment the book is delivered the borrower departs; there is no
longer delay in signing and waiting the turn to sign (53)."

Dewey believed the "plan is simple, cheap, rapid, and
in careful hands reasonably accurate (62)."

Dummy System

This system of book charging may have had its start
among the legal fraternity. H. J. Carr writes of a practice
which has "sometimes been followed in loaning books to

brother lawyers which has in it the elements of simplicity
and yet of fair effectiveness (24)."

> If the borrower sends by messenger (as not at all unusual)
> a written request for some particular book, it takes but
> a moment to put the note or card in the place on the shelf
> from which the book was taken. If borrowed in person,
> then, as a business measure, a memorandum of like im-
> port, on a card or scrap of paper, is made to answer in
> the same way, the memorandum not only keeping the space
> open, as it were, for the return of the book, but also
> standing ready to tell any other inquirer the why and where-
> fore of its absence.

This idea was carried out in some reference libraries.
W.S.C. Rae revealed (63):

> In libraries where access is not allowed to the shelves
> all books are applied for on specially printed forms....
> [In the Michell Library, Glasgow] when a book is issued
> the form is placed on the shelf in the space made by the
> withdrawal of the book, and is not removed until the book
> is replaced.

Melvil Dewey, much earlier, suggested a system which
involved leaving a borrower's card in place of the book on
the shelf (64).

> I devised a year ago a new charging system, which seems
> to me admirably adapted to very small, and perhaps to
> larger libraries. Issue to each reader a card with his
> name and number, and a statement that the library will
> loan on this card one book. If two or three books are
> allowed to each reader, or it is desired to grant special
> privileges, issue as many cards as desired, numbered
> with a subscript number, or lettered a, b, c, etc. This
> card should be ruled for book numbers and dates of draw-
> ing and return, the same as if to be used in a ledger box
> .... This card is treated like a baggage-check or pawn
> ticket. When presented at the desk, with a book number
> written in the proper column, the book is taken from the
> shelf, the card left in its place, the date of the loan being
> first marked or stamped, and the charge is complete.
> Any one consulting the shelves for the book finds this
> card, which has the name and date. When the book is re-
> turned, it takes the place of the card, which is returned
> to the borrower, the date of return being first entered to

show that the book really came back.... The plan is very simple and rapid in a small library, where all the books are near the delivery desk. No ledgers, check-boxes, or other machinery are needed....

This little system gives us both a book account, by which we know the whereabouts of every book off the shelf, and a reader account, for on the card is the complete list of the reading of each person.

In 1881, one Sunday School library used the dummy system in another manner, according to L. T. Chamberlain, who described the method by which the librarian is "enabled to know the number of times each book has been drawn, as also the books drawn by each person during the year (65)."

First: The scholar's library-card, filled out with the number of the class and of the scholar, as also the scholar's name, is that which I suppose to be in general use. Second: The shelf space of the library is divided by thin partitions, so that each book has its own niche or cell. These cells are numbered in order, from one upward, on their respective lintels, and the books, as they are placed in their cells are numbered accordingly. Third: From a nail or tack driven in each lintel depends a tag, of light cardboard, of which a fac-simile is here given. An eyelet admits of its ready hanging or removal. The tag bears the number of the class and scholar; for example: 4 for the class number, and 1 for the scholar's number. A scholar draws a book, and the number of it is entered on the tag which covers the cell of that book, in the space designated for that Sunday. When the book is returned, its number on the tag is crossed; and as the tag has spaces for all the Sundays of the year, it constitutes a perpetual yearly record. To keep the record of the number of times each book is drawn, a simple tally-score is kept in pencil on the edge of the

0		
4 1		
Jan	May	Sept
Feb	June	Oct
Mar	July	Nov
Apr	Aug	Dec

cell to which the book belongs.

G. T. Little carried the idea a bit further with the use
of blocks of wood which served as the borrowers' records
(66):

> This system consists in merely replacing each book loaned
> by a wooden dummy bearing the name of the borrower.
> These dummies are pieces of board one inch in thickness,
> four in width, and six in length.... Each has the name
> and registration number of a borrower painted or other-
> wise plainly marked on the edge or narrow surface which
> corresponds to the back of a book.
> The two wider surfaces, or sides, are covered with
> sheets of note-paper, lined perpendicularly as well as hor-
> izontally, so as to give spaces in successive rows for
> book numbers and dates, and attached so as to be removed
> when filled.
> To charge a book the number or location mark is put
> on the dummy of the borrower, and this is plaaced in the
> vacant space left by the book. When the latter is returned
> the dummy is removed, the date marked on the space ad-
> joining the book number, and the account is balanced.
> Foremost among its excellences I place accuracy....
> Under favorable conditions as to the arrangement of
> volumes this method of charging is a rapid one....
> From my own experience I feel authorized in saying
> that a circulation of a hundred volumes a day can be at-
> tended to in two-thirds of the time demanded by the ledger
> account....
> Fully as important as either of the advantages just
> mentioned is the ease with which the selection of a book
> can be made. If a borrower is desirous of obtaining a
> particular volume he mentions its location-mark, and, in
> case it is not in, can be informed at once who has it and
> when it will be due.

The fact that dummies not in use were kept in alphabetical order was mentioned by Carl Vitz, who further stated:
"For libraries with few books and few borrowers and no access to shelves this method is as satisfactory as any (67)."

Indicator Charging System

When libraries were first established in England under
the provisions of the various Acts of Parliament, according

to J. D. Brown, two things happened which heralded the appearance of Indicators (68):

> ... a building, suitable or otherwise, was provided; and, the readers in a town increased in number to an enormous and unprecedented extent. Straitened means generally led to the provision of a cramped and inconvenient building, in which the space set apart for books was often ridiculously inadequate, with the result that lofty shelves were the rule, which secured economy of storage at the expense of rapidity of service.... Delays in service occurred continually and the poor librarian was often abashed or offended at the freely expressed scepticism with which the public received his reports of books being out. From these factors was evolved the idea of the indicator, which by and by took practical shape as a machine for saving the legs of the librarian and his assistants from frequent and fruitless climbs to high shelves, and enabling readers to satisfy themselves that books were actually in use. The original indicators were intended only for showing, by means of numbers, the novels which were out or in, but since then a considerable number of libraries have applied them to all classes.

In 1899, there were at least twenty different varieties; however Brown further stated: "It is not quite accurate to assume, as has been done by various writers, that the indicator system is used 'almost universally' in English Public Libraries, or is even to be found in a 'majority' of them (2)."

By way of defining this system, Brown revealed (69):

> A library indicator, as its name implies, is a device for indicating or registering information about books in such a way that it can be seen either by the staff alone, or by the public and staff both. The information usually conveyed to the public is some kind of indication of the presence or absence of books, and the methods of accomplishing this almost invariably take the form of displaying numbers qualified in such a way as to indicate books in and out. Thus, small spaces on a screen may be numbered to represent books, and their presence in the library indicated by the space being blank, or their absence from the library shown by the space being occupied by a card or block. Or, colours may be used to indicate books in and out, or a change in the position of a block representing a book. No doubt the idea of the mechanical indicator

was early evolved from the needs of the first Public Libraries.

W. Pollitt gave a useful specification when relating the
indicator to book charging (70).

> In a number of cases indicators do nothing of the actual
> charging, and are only worked in conjunction with it. A
> pure indicator system merely shows whether a book is
> "in" or "out," but a charging system must record the ac-
> tual current borrower of any book....
> An indicator is not necessarily a system of book-char-
> ging although it may be, as illustrated by the Cotgreave
> and Duplex.

The earliest English indicator seemed to be the Dyall
Indicator of 1863, recorded Brown, who said that the "charge
was made in a ledger, and the contrivance was used as an
indicator pure and simple (71)."

Brown then introduced us to the various indicator systems. Some of them exhibited the borrower's card, as the
basic loan record, in the indicator to reveal the location of
books (72).

> There can be hardly any doubt that Mr. Dent's indicator
> is the first to combine indicating with charging, and that
> it suggested several succeeding devices.... the provision
> of a series of numbered shelves in columns, with spaces
> between to take the borrowers' cards when the books
> were out. The back of the borrower's card was to be
> ruled to allow of numbers and dates being pencilled there-
> on, and, of course, the presence of a borrower's card
> under a number indicated a book "out".
> [The Elliot Indicator, 1870] differs from Mr. Dent's
> idea in having the numbers alongside the ticket shelves
> or spaces, instead of over them, and in having a special-
> ly thick borrower's ticket with coloured ends to show
> books out and overdue.... The borrower scans the indi-
> cator till he finds the space opposite the number he wants
> vacant. This indicates that the book he wants is in, and
> he then hands his ticket to the assistant, stating the num-
> ber of the book he requires. The assistant enters the
> book number and date of issue in the borrower's card,
> and inserts it in the indicator in the space against the
> number. The book is then fetched, and before issue it is
> registered on a specially ruled day-sheet, by means of a

stroke, to record the day's circulation for statistical purposes. When the book is returned its number directs to
the space on the indicator occupied by the borrower's card
which is withdrawn and returned to the owner, when all
liability for fines is cleared. Overdues are detected by
means of differently coloured ends to the borrowers' cards,
or the periodical examination of the indicator.

With the Kennedy Indicator, 1875, wrote Brown, "four
different coloured ends on the cards are for the purpose of
indicating overdues, a new colour being used in every period
of a few days (73)."

Mr. Yates reported more fully on the charging procedure in his description of the Leed's Indicator (74).

When a person has consulted the Indicator and fixed upon
a certain book, he asks at the issue-counter for the number - for instance, E 4269. The assistant gives him the
book, upon the receipt of his card, upon which the following entry is then made: 1   12 May   E 4269 and it is also entered upon the librarian's sheet as above. When the
book is returned, the date is placed in the column for
that purpose, and the card given to the borrower.

With the Wright-Stanlake Indicator, 1879, the book request form was dated. Brown said further, "the slips thus
certified are taken by an attendant, and affixed by a gummed
end to a strip of wood with a red edge [signifying that the
book is borrowed], and the slip thus mounted is placed in the
indicator rack opposite to the title of the book issued. The
borrower's receipt, in his own handwriting, is thus retained
in the Indicator until the book is returned, when the wood
strip is withdrawn, the tin shelf left empty, the application
form cancelled, and the book replaced upon its shelf (75)."

Another group of indicators stress the book record and
are formed by allowing a block of wood, slip, or tag to represent each book. Brown quotes from a descriptive circular
these words about the Cotgreave Indicator (76):

It consists of a wooden or iron frame, fitted with minute
zinc shelves, generally one hundred in a column. Upon
each of these shelves is placed a small metal-bound ledger containing a number of leaves, ruled and headed for
the number of borrower's ticket, and date of issue; also
date of return or other items as may be required, num-

bered or lettered at each end, and arranged numerically
in the frames. One part of it is also lettered for entries
of date of purchase, title of book, etc.... A borrower
having chosen a book from the catalogue, consults the indicator, and finding the required number to be on blue,
denoting in, asks for the book corresponding; at the same
time tendering his library ticket. The assistant withdraws the Indicator ledger, makes the necessary entries,
inserts borrower's ticket, and reverses the ledger which
then shows the red colour, signifying out. He then hands
out the book asked for. The borrower's ticket will remain in this number until he changes his book, when his
ticket will, of course, be transferred to the next number
required, and the returned number will be reversed again,
showing by the blue colour that the book it represents is
again in, and is immediately available to any other reader
requiring it. The entries need not be made...until a
more convenient time.

Brown further states: "It is also, in my opinion, superior
to other varieties in its provision of a fixed place for numbers and the relative records of issue. Mistakes are less
likely to occur than with Indicators already described, which
only provide vacant pigeon-holes for receiving the record of
issue. On the other hand, unless worked with a check card
system, it is apt to encourage the tendency of assistants to
place borrowers' cards in the wrong numbers, and when this
occurs, it is often impossible to trace the error, when no
separate card or ledger account is kept (76)."

W.S.O. Rae informed us that the ticket used with the
Cotgreave Indicator has "four colours, two at each of the
narrow ends, which by reason of their position in the ledger,
say red on the left and green on the right, make the finding
of overdues a comparatively simple matter (77)."

The Chivers Indicator turns the slip into a book record
(78).

Each number has under it a longitudinal slot in which is
placed a card. This bears the Book number and class
and represents the volume whose number it has.
When this card is in the slot it has the effect of under-
lining unmistakably the number of the book represented,
and thus shows it IN to the readers....
Mr. Chivers justly claims for his Indicator that it ex-
cels all others in the following important aspects: -

It does more work, is simpler and more quickly worked, occupies less space, costs less and is a more handsome piece of furniture.

To aid in locating overdue books, the Bonner Indicator exhibited a new feature, according to Brown (79):

The frame of the Indicator invented by Mr. Bonner of Ealing, is made to hold little five-sided blocks, on each side of which the number appears on a differently coloured ground, say black, red, blue, green and brown, and it is by the changing of these colours that books are indicated "Out," "In," or "Overdue.".... If Blue represents books In, any of the other colours showing at the front will be Out. Thus suppose you take Brown to indicate the first week's issue, Green the second, Blue the third, and Red the fourth, a complete series of changes is effected, and when Red is the current colour the Browns and Greens will be overdue. Black, of course, always indicates to the assistant that books are in. The merit of this Indicator consists in what its inventor calls its "self-contained" character, that is, no extra appliance of process is necessary to denote the period of issue at the moment of service beyond the simple turning of the blocks.

A. W. Robertson described the features of his Duplex Indicator in these words (80):

First of all then, the indicator is so constructed that each compartment of it accommodates a block of wood, 4 by 2 1/2 by 3/8 inches, one for each book in the library issuable to the public. This block is covered with paper ruled so as to be capable of recording fifty issues. On one end there is affixed a printed title, indicating plainly and intelligibly the author and subject matter of the book, and the shelf number at one corner. The other end is blank except that it also shows the shelf number, but at the opposite corner. The idea with regard to each block is that it shall be as the alter ego of some one book belonging to the library, and for this reason, in addition to its title, it bears on the flat top surface its shelf number in full, its class letter, and its accessions number, this last by a reference to the library stock book giving the whole history of the book since it was incorporated in the library.
    ... To each [borrower], on joining the library, is given a library ticket. This ticket bears on its surface all

the information with regard to the borrower usually required - his name, address, ticket number, date of ex-
piry of ticket, etc.... Twelve... [borrowers' ticket] registers, one for each day, contain the register of tickets
received in exchange for books issued during a fortnight
....
    It dispenses with day sheets, or any other kind of
sheets, and yet embodies in its system of working all
their accuracy and security at the cost of much less time
and trouble.

    In another paper was given the charging procedure (81):

When a volume which is "in" is asked for by a Borrower,
say, "Life and Letters of Herbert Spencer," No. 15, 1592
(Biography), the assistant abstracts the block from the
Indicator (this also verifying whether the book is out or
in), obtains the volume from the shelf, stamps it with
date of issue, and enters its number on the Borrower's
ticket. Both block and Borrower's Ticket are placed together in a counter tray, and the counter transaction is
completed. In due time, as opportunity in the course of
the day occurs, the Borrower's Ticket is entered in one
of the numbered compartments of the dated Ticket Register; on the book block are noted the date of issue, and the
number of the compartment in the Ticket Register in which
the Borrower's Ticket is to be found. The block is then
re-inserted in the Indicator, with the blank end toward
Borrowers showing the book "out."
    The converse operation - when a Borrower returns a
book - is as follows: The assistant, book in hand, abstracts from the Indicator the corresponding block, thence
is guided to the dated case in the Ticket Register, and to
the particular numbered compartment, whence the Borrower's Ticket, is abstracted, and handed over - and the
counter operation is completed. Subsequently, the book is
examined and returned to the shelf; the block is re-inserted in the Indicator, title-end to Borrowers, showing that
the book is now "in."

    In recommending his indicator, Robertson made the fol-
lowing claims (82):

(1) At the moment of issuing a book only one entry or
record, namely, the borrower's ticket number, has to be
made, all the other details of the transaction being de-
ferred till the library is closed, or till such time as may

be found more convenient.... In handing out borrower's tickets in exchange for books returned, no entry or cancelling of an entry is required.

(2) Of every book belonging to the library, whether in or out, it is possible, at a glance, to tell the name and address of the last borrower, also when it was last issued. In a similar way, the history of the past issues of any book can be traced indefinitely; and conversely, the history of each borrower's reading. The advantage of the double process will be appreciated by all practical librarians.

(3) Of every book, in or out, it is possible at a glance to tell the class to which it belongs, and also its accession number, by reference from which to the stock book the history of the book as part of the library property can be ascertained.

(4) The moment a book is issued or returned the fact of its issue or return is notified to the public.

(5) In the all important matter of indicating to the librarian or his assistants how long a book has been in a borrower's keeping, the "Duplex indicator" system is practically unerring. As soon as the period (usually a fortnight) allowed for reading a book expires, the borrower's ticket on which it is issued passes into a special compartment, indicating a fine of one penny. If not claimed by the borrower during the subsequent week, it again, at the end of that week, passes into another compartment, where its presence indicates a fine of twopence. In either case the librarian or his assistant is, on the return of the book, at once directed to the right compartment for the borrower's ticket, and by the same direction knows without any process of calculation what fine to exact. Books still further overdue are treated in a somewhat similar fashion; and it is at all times possible for the librarian to ascertain at a glance how many books are overdue, to whom they have been issued, and for how long they have been out of the library.

.... the system has ... the advantage of showing to the public, in a clear, bold type, the author's name and the title of every book in the library at any moment. As soon as a book is issued its title disappears, and conversely, as soon as it comes back to the library its title reappears.

In Ontario, at Carleton Place, a wooden plug represented each book in the indicator. This idea is carried further at the Cobalt Library where it became more than an indicator.

This discovery was revealed in the Ontario Library Review
in these words (83):

> Cobalt library was similarly equipped for book charging,
> though here the telephone exchange switchboard has evi-
> dently served as a pattern.... The holes were all num-
> bered to correspond with the numbers of book titles in
> the catalogue pamphlet which was sold to members at 25
> cents. When a book was lent the record was kept by in-
> serting a peg in the opening bearing the proper number.
> To the peg was attached a borrower's card, on which the
> last entry was the registered number of the last borrow-
> er. A red card attached to this indicated overdue.

M. W. Plummer recorded information about the tag
system of catalog and indicator combined which she saw at
the Sacramento Public Library (84):

> All along one side of the room, strung on a rod, are tags,
> each bearing the name of an author and title of his book.
> These are arranged in classes, according to the subject.
> Around the edges of these tags are printed the figures 1,
> 2, 1, 2, in double rows so that between 50 and 60 figures
> occur on a tag. When a book first goes out, the first fig-
> ure 1 is punched; when it comes in, the first figure 2. A
> second issue causes the punching of the second figure 1,
> and so on.

In order to answer the demands of librarians and attempt a solution to various problems, adaptations were made.
E. W. Neesham presented this solution to the haphazard arrangement of book numbers (85):

> [The Cotgreave Indicator] can, with a little labour, be
> turned into an author-indicator and furthermore, an indi-
> cator that has certain advantages over the "Graham" [indi-
> cator of 1905], as for instance, obviating the need for
> separate charging and indicator numbers [which was part
> of the Graham system] and doing away with the double op-
> eration, necessary when the indicator worked in conjunct-
> ion with a card-charging system....
> It will be seen that this system could easily be adapted
> to any library, the only expense being the new numbers,
> etc., and once instituted, the scattering of almost every
> author's works on the shelves and on the indicator would
> entirely cease.

The Librarians' Workshop in 1899 became concerned with the restricted counter space (86).

> Counter space is particularly liable to become restricted owing to the growth of the indicator and one of the shifts adopted has been the application of one number to several copies of the same book and to works in more than one volume. Such an arrangement necessitates provision being made for keeping a record of the issues of such books apart from the indicator.

J. D. Brown, being concerned with this problem forwarded these suggestions (87):

> The fundamental principle of all the indicators in general use is that they show all the numbers of books in the library and as a consequence, it becomes necessary to provide for two regular, though disproportionate growths [expansion of stock and collateral growth]. My idea of such limitation is that the dimensions of the indicator should be governed by issues, and not by stock....
>   ... I suggest the use of movable columns of book numbers to be displayed in single trays which are independent of all the others. These trays are perfectly free within their inner surfaces, so that suitable blocks can be moved about at pleasure throughout the entire length. The height of such trays must be decided by local conditions but in a tray 3 feet high, about one hundred number blocks, such as I have prepared, can be stored. The trays forming the indicator can be grouped by classes or thousands....
>   The borrowers' cards supply the movable blocks on which the book numbers are displayed. Each card is simply a little block book, with a few blank leaves at the beginning, in which will lie a card or slip bearing the number of the book it represents. These slips are made of card, with linen centres, and are turned over at each end to form little flaps on which the book numbers can be boldly printed. A little pocket is provided in each book, and in this the book number remains when the work is in the library.... The method of working is as follows:-
> A borrower having ascertained from the indicator that the book he wants is in, writes its number in his card and hands it to the assistant. The assistant fetches the book, removes the book card and places it in the borrower's card, and then in its numerical or class order in the indicator column. He may next stamp the book with the date of issue, enter it in a day sheet, and then hand it

to the borrower. When the book is returned, the conjoin-
ed book and borrower cards are withdrawn from the indicating column and restored to book and borrower respectively....
    The advantages of the system seem to lie in its ad-
justability, comparatively small size, and cheapness.

    C. T. Davis proposed to move the indicator off the
counter entirely, that is, if someone possessed sufficient ingenuity (88).

[The new Indicator] may consist of two or more parts perfectly distinct from one another, yet so intimately connected that any record made in the one part shall be in-
stantaneously made in the other. You all know the electric organ, where the keyboard is yards and yards away
from the pipes which produce the rich melody to charm
our ears. Well it may be possible to produce an Indicator, worked by electricity, or some other subtle force,
of which the part to be consulted by the public is against
a wall, and the other part altered by the staff would be
put in any convenient place not necessarily on the counter.

He touches on the crux of the problem a bit more seriously
in this way (89):

It does at the first blush seem strange that a work not
costly should be put in the Reference Library; yet the
Lending Library is generally cramped by the space which
can be devoted to Indicators, and we thus curtail the usefulness of those works which, going out so rarely, would
only take up space in the Indicator, by placing them in
the Reference Library....
    Divide the books into Reference Library and Lending
Library, but the Lending Library sub-divide into two divisions....first, those books issued through the Indicator,
and second, the rest, and often the greatest part of the
books in the library, for which no Indicator is provided.

    Some people, Miss James for one, objected to the me-
chanization involved (90):

I have very little to say on this subject, except that I regard indicators of any kind as barriers between librarian
and reader, and as such I am a strenuous opponent to
them, for the more we tend to mechanical and automatic
appliances in libraries the less chance there is of librar-

ianship being regarded as a dignified profession, such as
I understand members of the community desire to make it.

A. K. Gill's remarks revealed the more practical problem of the expense involved. He compared card charging
with indicator charging in a "closed" library (91).

The points to be noted in favor of the indicator, then, are
that it saves a certain amount of time and labour, and indicates to the public whether required books are in or out.
In order to do this in a library of 10,000 volumes, an initial expenditure of about £62 must be incurred.
    Card-charging.
    .... While more systematic and economical than the
indicator, however, it necessitates occasional delays, and
affords no information to borrowers as to whether required books are in or out. For a library of 10,000 volumes, this system costs about £12....
    Card-charging, with Indicator for Fiction.
    .... It is claimed by the advocates of this issue meth-
od that the good points of the other two systems are retained, while their bad points are eradicated.... As it is
only required for the 2,000 volumes of fiction in a library
of 10,000 volumes, the indicator, instead of £60, costs a-
bout £13; which, together with £12 for the card-charging
requisites, gives a total of £25 for the system complete.

Cotgreave worded his answer in this manner (92):

The cost of upkeep of the Cotgreave Indicator is practically nil, and I think it will be obvious to any open-minded
reader that a larger staff is required in a closed card-
charging library, where the assistants have to ascertain
which books are "in" either from the shelves or from a
time-wasting collection of cards.

At the same time W. J. Harris wrote in favor of open
access libraries where borrowers could choose their own
books and had no need for an indicator. He gave a detailed
picture of the expenses involved (93).

The cost of an Indicator is approximately £6 per 1000
numbers. In considering this question, however, the cost
of the Indicator is, unfortunately, not the only item in the
bill of costs. It takes 5-ft., of counter to carry effectively 4,000 Indicator numbers, and the cost of a good
counter is about £2 per foot run. In addition to this, some

little decoration in the form of a frame for the Indicator
is usually considered necessary; in fact in many libraries
I could mention, gorgeous frames have been erected, eq-
ualling in cost quite 50 per cent of the Indicator itself.

It appeared as though open access and card charging
were gaining in importance and the indicator was "on the way
out." This was uniquely expressed by W. K. Oswald, who
wrote of a supposed visit to the library of a nearby town
(94).

I ... noticed a room on the right with a tall curious looking arrangement standing on a long counter. Half a doz-
en or more spectacled people were peering anxiously at
this thing, and I came to the conclusion that it was part
of the museum.... the model of an Eastern tomb, with
the coffins arranged on tiny ledges....
My attention was instantly fixed on a very kindly-look-
ing and benevolent old gentleman with long white hair, at-
tired in a long dark green coat and wearing a tall hat....
After a little watching I felt my heart go out to my old
friend, for I thought that he had a kind of St. Vitus's
dance, for no sooner had he looked on a dirty torn book
than he went to this puzzle, and adjusting his spectacles
to the uncertain light appeared to read or try to decipher
a narrow piece of the exhibit running in one line from the
top to the bottom. He repeated the same methods or tac-
tics half a dozen or more times, scrutinizing the frame-
work closely and each time running his finger down different parts of the frame, and then coming suddenly to a
dead stop whenever his index finger touched a certain spot
....
...if I were a member of that library, or of any other
library, I would always wish to find my way among the
shelves and choose for myself the books which I wanted.
I had not time to go to the newsroom owing to this
Patience Exerciser, or Obstructor ... though the machinery may 'be loaded with some kind of ingenuity it must add
to the confusion of those who want a certain book - and
who naturally have no interest in its number.

In the book, Public Library Administration, W.S.O. Rae
made this statement: "It was felt that while ledgers and indicators were accurate enough in the recording of issues,
movability and adjustment were missing, and in order to obtain these necessary features the card system was introduced
and is gradually gaining favour throughout the country (95)."

Chapter 2

Two Trends in Card Charging

"To meet the requirements of a closed or indicator library, a card charging system was devised, about 1873, by Mr. Virgo, late librarian of the Bradford Public Libraries," wrote F. C. Cole in 1907 (96).

J. D. Brown recorded the details of this new type of book charging sixteen years earlier in an article on charging systems. Virgo's plan made use of the card in book pocket idea later advocated by George Parr [see reference to Parr's system as described by Brown, reference no. 34].

At Bradford this method was supplemented by another, perhaps more unique idea. Brown continued: "To each reader is issued on joining a cloth-covered card and a pocket made of linen, having on one side the Borrower's Number, Name, Address, etc. and on the other side a calendar. The pockets are kept in numerical order at the Library, and the readers retain their cards (97)." Brown then mentioned a system on somewhat similar lines which was used at Liverpool and Chelsea (98).

In an article written by J. H. Quinn in 1893 he said that he had modified a system used first by Virgo and later simplified by Mr. Cowell of the Liverpool Free Libraries (99).

This idea of the borrower's pocket became an integral part of the system devised and promoted by N. E. Browne in 1895 which was called the Browne System (100).

It had an impressive start in American libraries but, according to Flexner, was short-lived. "Except for very small libraries without much prospect of growth, this system would prove inadequate (101)."

English libraries saw the values in the borrower's pocket system and used it extensively, L. M. Harrod remarked,

60

saying, "the largest systems in England use this system,...
and some of these libraries issue two thousand books in a
day from one department alone (102)."

Another type of charging became important around the
turn of the century. F. P. Hill traced its early beginnings
back to Bassett Cadwallader, of Evansville, Indiana [see reference to Cadwallader's system, no. 32]. F. P. Hill wrote,
"The credit for the foundation of this system must be given
to the Evansville (Ind.) Library, where was devised a plan
of a slip for every book ... and a borrower's card.....
Modifications of this scheme were made by Jacob Schwartz
of the General Society of Mechanics and Tradesmen's Library,
New York City, J. F. Sargent, Paterson (N.J.) Library, and
the writer (103)."

In 1897, J. Schwartz refuted this connection with the
Evansville system, claiming to be the originator of the system he used (104).

This method of book and borrower control by which each
book contained a pocket, a date due slip, and a card while
the book was in the library and each borrower owned a borrower's card was put into use at the Newark Library by
J. C. Dana, who worked out its difficulties and explained the
details of its workings in 1896 (105).

F. M. Crunden, in writing of the system which he a-
dopted, said, "It has come to be known as the Newark system, though it was in use before Newark had a public library
(106)."

In 1917, experimentation began on an attempt to do a-
way with the borrower's card, maintaining instead a visual
file of borrowers kept at the charging desk. Notice of this
appeared in the Wisconsin Library Bulletin. "Two librarians
formerly connected with the Wisconsin Library Commission
have, after joint consideration, each adopted in her own library a new method of charging books without using readers'
cards. Miss Zana K. Miller, then librarian of the Public
Library at Menomonee, Michigan, and Miss Jeanette M. Drake,
librarian of the Public Library at Sioux City, after going over
the matter together, put this method in operation in their respective libraries (107)."

A later issue of Wisconsin Library Bulletin contained
an article which draws attention to a system in use at the

Detroit Public Library, which "has secured all the advantages
of dispensing with the borrower's card without these disadvantages, by the use of a small identification card (108)."

R. A. Ulveling, in 1930, described his system as "the
simplified Newark rearranged and further shortened; shortened
by the elimination of several operations, and rearranged so
that as many steps as possible will be completed prior to the
charging proper. This leaves a minimum of work during the
time of greatest pressure and permits a quick flow of patrons
past the charging desk (109)."

However A. E. Bostwick complained about the failings
of the two-card systems with which many readers lose or
mislay their cards. He wrote: "The frequency of error due
to improper or illegible charging, very apt to occur in the
pressure of a rush, has caused librarians to look for relief
in some device for automatic charging, and in 1927 a 'charging machine' was put on the market, which has met with
considerable favor (110)."

The background of this Dickman Charging Machine was
revealed by G. I. Lehman (111).

> The late Mr. Edwin White Gaillard of the New York Pub-
> lic Library recognized the value of a mechanical device
> for public and university libraries fully thirty-five years
> ago. He attempted to solve this problem at that time,
> but unfortunately, after constructing such a machine at
> a cost of approximately $3,500, it was found to be entire-
> ly unsuitable.
> Nothing further was done for a period of years, until
> Dr. George F. Bowerman, librarian of the Public Library
> of Washington, D. C. requested the United States Bureau
> of Efficiency to help solve the problem.

In 1928, Grace Finney prepared a paper for the ALA
Convention which introduced librarians to the Dickman Charging System (112).

Three years later, Sara Patterson wrote an article
which appeared in the Library Journal which told of the electric charging machine which Gaylord Bros. had devised (113).

In this same year an article appeared in the Library
Journal which was reprinted from the Library Assistant. This
dealt with book charging in England and contained the follow-

ing note (114):

> To the lumbering and effete mind of a European, it seems
> obvious that this lengthy process can be curtailed by the
> adoption of the ticket-pocket and the use of a rubber date
> stamp. They think differently in U.S.A., and have evolv-
> ed machines complete with electric motors, stencil plates
> and switches which are guaranteed to charge books at a
> rate which can be exceeded by an English junior of three
> weeks' standing, armed with a rubber stamp. And yet
> people say that Laputa was exaggerated in its satire.

Harrod speculated that a "combined Gaylord-Demco, or
Dickman-Demco system, will probably eventuate, thus approx-
imating as nearly as possible to the Browne system which has
been used in England for many years. Such a system will
then be almost as speedy as the Browne, but will have the
advantage of permitting more than one book to be issued on
one ticket (115)."

Also looking for a future solution for unsolved problems,
C. H. Brown and H. G. Bousfield in 1933 wrote (116):

> The methods used in charging books have remained the
> same for a long period of years, while records used in
> the business world have been revolutionized. It is pos-
> sible and even probable that during the next decade the
> method here described will have become antiquated and
> will be replaced, possibly by a system employing a vis-
> ible index or automatic charging device more satisfactory
> than any now in use.

Browne System

The borrower's pocket system as devised by Virgo was
operated as follows (117):

> When "Mr. John Smith, No. 1807," wishes a book, he
> hands in a list of numbers and his card to the assistant,
> who procures the first book he finds in, say, "East Lynne,"
> B21, Class E. He next selects from the numerical series
> of pockets the one numbered, "1807, John Smith." The
> title card is then removed from the book and placed in the
> reader's numbered pocket, and the date is written in the
> date column of the book pocket. This completes the pro-
> cess at the time of service. At night the day's issues

are classified and arranged in the order of the book numbers, after the statistics are made up and noted in the
sheet ruled for the purpose, and are then placed in a
box bearing the date of issue. When a book is returned
the assistant turns up its date of issue, proceeds to the
box of that date, and removes the title card which he replaces in the book. The borrower's pocket is then restored to its place among its fellows. The advantages of
this plan are greater rapidity of service as compared
with the Ledger systems, and a mechanical weeding out
of over-dues somewhat similar to what is obtained by the
"Duplex" Indicator system. Its disadvantages are the absence of permanent record, and the dangers which must
exist of title-cards getting into the wrong pockets, and so
placing the whole system at the mercy of accident.
    .... A system on somewhat similar lines is worked
at Liverpool and Chelsea, the difference being that in
these Libraries a record is made of the issues of books,
and books read by borrowers.

Quinn's modifications included the use of colored cards
to denote different classes. The labels of the books might
correspond in color with the cards so that the green card
will not be put into a book with a red label. He kept two
files of borrowers' cards - one for those with books checked
out and the other for those who had not. He also suggested
keeping a borrower's number book in which a note was made,
opposite a borrower's number, of the date upon which a book
was not taken and the entry cancelled when borrowing was
resumed. He remarked, "I have yet to learn that any further or more permanent record is being kept by any library,
where the methods are not cumbersome and red-tapey and
the staff larger than necessary (118)."

The system promoted by N. E. Browne revealed many
of these qualities (100).

It requires a book card, a book pocket, and a reader's
pocket. The use of the book card and book pocket is the
same as at Newark and Salem. The reader's pocket,
then, becomes the point of variation. Instead of the usual
card, each reader has a pocket of special design which
bears the reader's registration number, his name and
address.

As adapted in one English library, the Exeter Public
Library, the borrower's tickets were made of three grades

for adults (119):

>A general ticket with which any book in the lending library
>except music, may be borrowed; 2) A non-fiction ticket
>which is available for books other than fiction, magazines
>and music, and a music ticket with which only music can
>be obtained.
>   In order to distinguish the various tickets different col-
>ors are used, e.g., blue for general, red for juvenile,
>green for music and brown for non-fiction. These tickets
>are in the form of small cloth covered pockets into which
>the charge card is slipped.

The charging operation was very simple, remarked
Browne (100).

>The reader presents his pocket with a call slip. This slip
>need not bear his number or name, because the pocket
>will show these items, and the chances of separation are
>slight. Persons who use libraries where each call slip
>must be signed with name and address will appreciate this
>saving. The attendant after finding a book takes its book
>card from the pocket at the back and places the card in
>the reader's pocket and stamps the date upon the book
>preferably upon the book pocket. The book is then given
>to the reader.

At the Exeter library the book cards were kept at the
library desk. Tapley-Soper wrote, "On a counter between
the assistant and the borrower are arranged, in numerical
order, contained in trays, the charge cards.... From the
inside cover of the book the assistant notes the progressive
number and selects from the trays the corresponding card
(120)."

Browne explained that after charging the books the
book cards are kept until the end of the day when they are
filed (each still in its borrower's pocket) in book number order in a tray bearing the date. She added, "This arrangement of the book cards shows what persons have the books,
as well as the time when they were taken and when due. If
a record of the circulation of each book is desired, the attendant can at any time during the day write on the book
cards the readers' numbers and stamp the date. The advantage is that the reader is not detained while a record, which
is of no apparent value to him, is made (100)."

A suggestion was made by B. McDonald that "little notes - such as 'last book returned in bad condition' or - 'five cents fine owing on R273, returned five days overdue,' may be put in the borrower's pocket; thus surprising him with your wonderful memory (121)."

Cutter kept the charges in book number order but provided a date record by "putting into each pocket a slip of red cardboard, bearing the date when the book is due (122)."

As the number (not the month) projects above the charging card it is easy to pick out the cards of any date wanted.

The study pockets, whose books are not obliged to be returned at the end of a fortnight, but may be sent for at any time if someone has asked for them, have a white slip, not projecting, stamped with the date after which the book can be sent for....

The new method in a trial of three weeks has given entire satisfaction. The only draw back is that more cards have to be alphabeted in the overdues. In the old plan many of the books charged in the 12-days file were returned before their time was up and these pockets never went into the general file. Now everything must be distributed. But this work can be done at leisure, whereas the searching was usually at hurried moments.

In 1895, N. E. Browne suggested the following plan for discharging a book (100).

When the reader returns the book, he must get his pocket in order to begin the process over again. The book, therefore, must be discharged immediately upon presentation. The date on the book pocket shows in which tray the card is. The special form of the reader's pocket makes it a simple matter to find the card since the cards cannot stick together. The card, when found, is placed in the book-pocket and the reader's pocket is returned to him.

The reader comes to the library generally in tolerably good humor, and is more willing to see his book discharged, thus releasing him from all obligations, than to wait while an attendant stamps the date three times and writes a long number, as in many systems.

In 1908, Browne advocated another plan of discharge if the earlier method took too much time (123).

When the reader returns a book and wishes a new one,
all that is necessary is to stamp the date on the slip in
the new book before handing it to the reader, removing
its book card and laying it in the book returned.

At any leisure time this book may be discharged by a
simple process which the reader need not witness.... The
process requires the taking of each book in turn. The
date on the book slip shows where the book card is to be
found. When found, return it to the book pocket, and in
the reader's pocket just emptied place the book card of
the new book, which had been laid in the book returned
when the reader was present. When the book card in the
reader's pocket has been filed under the proper date the
charging of the new book is complete.

Another suggestion was mentioned in an article appearing in the Librarian and Book World in 1935 (124).

It was suggested that a "check system would enable readers to pass at once into the library, and whilst they are
in the library looking for their books, their tickets can
be found, fines calculated or damage to books assessed..
..

"The proposal is to have a number of duplicate numbered checks and pockets on the 'In' Counter....

"As the reader returns a book he is given a numbered
check and passes at once into the library. A pocket with
the same number as the check is placed in the book, which
is then passed to centre desk for discharging, the reader's
ticket is found, and if 'all clear' the ticket is placed in the
numbered pocket and passed to the end of the 'Out' Counter,
where it is placed in numerical order to await the reader.

"If a fine has been incurred the receipt can be placed
with the ticket in the pocket for collection.

"It would seem preferable for an assistant to deal with
the reader at the 'Out' Counter, to receive his check and
hand over ticket before he passes on to have the book
charged which he wishes to borrow....

"The merit of the system is that by dividing the work
of the charging desk into three sections it enables readers
to be passed into the library rapidly and gives more time
for attention to books returned."

Various suggestions were made for ways to deal with
the lines of people which formed at the discharge counter,
according to an article entitled "Six Day Wickets." The best
of these suggestions was outlined more fully than others (125).

The counter (or tables elsewhere) should be divided into
Monday, Tuesday, Wednesday, etc., and the book trays
for those issues for the two weeks kept in front of each
division.... A borrower returning a book would pass
down the counter to the section required, as shown by the
date. If he had several books of various dates he would
pass from one section to the other progressively, obtaining his ticket for each book at the different counter sections or tables.... Overdues, queries, and errors would
be dealt with after "Saturday" where time could be devoted
to correcting the error without "blocking up the gangway."

As the cards in the trays are arranged according to
date, overdues are revealed automatically. Browne saw that
with her system the "work involved in sending out fine notices
is also lessened. Since the reader's pocket bears the name
and address, the attendant has only to copy (100)."

W. E. Doubleday dealt with the matter of renewals in
the following manner (126):

Methods of adjusting the charges in the issue trays when
books are not brought back for renewal vary.... If the
"charges" are left in their first position the renewal date
may be stamped upon the book-card or a slip denoting renewal may be inserted, or a narrow card slip bearing the
letter "R" may take its place; but if the "charges" are removed to a later tray it will be necessary to place a guide
in the positions so vacated.

Two points were supremely in mind when Browne devised the system: "1) less bother to the reader by eliminating
the carrying of a card; 2) less work to the desk attendant by
eliminating writing and stamping (127)."

As to the first point, E. P. Clarke had this to add
(128):

In a small library the necessity for speed is not so great
as to counterbalance the risk of the card being lost or forgotten - that daily annoyance to the librarian, so effectually
prevented by the card being always on file at the library.
But in a large library, the holding of the card by the reader would, no doubt, be a great saving both of time at book
issue and of space in the charging tray.
But even with the added consultation of one file, the
Browne system is one of great speed.

B. W. Pennock mentioned several other advantages
(129):

> There are several systems by which books can be dis-
> charged as rapidly as by this one, but I know of none by
> which they can be charged so rapidly and so accurately
> ₒₒₒₒ A person who is fairly quick and accustomed to the
> system will deliver books about as rapidly as readers will
> take them from the desk.
> While books cannot be discharged quite as rapidly as
> they can be charged, it is seldom that the discharging-
> desk is crowded in our library, though in the busiest days
> we deliver more than 1000 volumes.

In this same vein, Tapley-Soper remarked that "provided an assistant is relieved from [minor interruptions]...
it is probable that an issue of at least 100 per hour could be
easily recorded (119)."

As to the matter of overdues, Pennock pointed out:
"since overdue notices are not sent without looking upon the
shelf, the mistake of sending an overdue notice when the book
has been returned is almost impossible (130)."

But she mentioned also the difficulties of the system
(131):

> In busy times it is easy for the person discharging to take
> from the case the wrong book card and put it into the pock-
> et of the book to be discharged. This is a source of trou-
> ble in several ways; the book is liable to be put on the
> shelf with the wrong card, and when the book belonging to
> that card comes in the card cannot be found. Then the
> card of the book which went on the shelf with the wrong
> card still stands in the charging case, and the envelope
> of the person who returned it is of course there too; and
> when a book is found for him there is no envelope with
> which to charge it. Or it may be that the mistake is not
> noticed at the charging-desk and the book is charged in the
> envelope, which was wrongly discharged - that is, the book
> is charged to the wrong person....when there was added
> to these mistakes the ones occasionally made of taking up
> the wrong envelope when the right one was at hand, we
> found ourselves in considerable difficulty.
> That these difficulties were not inherent in the system
> I was confident, and after studying the case for a few days I
> adopted a suggestion of Mr. Cutter's that it was better to call

the reader's name from the envelope rather than from his
card, which, with a rearrangement of desk attendants, almost entirely removed the difficulty.

L. M. Harrod gave the following information about the
space needed for the issue file (102):

The pocket-ticket charge takes about three times as much
space as the single book-card charge, but as far as I
know, this has not become a really serious problem in
any English library. When books are discharged at the
rate of three or four hundred an hour, it is desirable to
have the issue spaced out or the staff may get in each
other's way.

A revolving charging case was introduced by C. W.
Smith to take care of expanding files. "Whether there be only
one clerk for both charging and issuing of books, or whether
two clerks have the case stand between them within easy
reach, the contrivance will soon prove itself a great convenience (132)."

M. E. Hyde compared Browne charging with the Newark system. "The time for the two systems is practically
the same, but in the Browne system there is the disadvantage
of having the whole process done while you wait (133)."

Pennock noted, "This objection seems to me to have
little force, because a large part of the books returned in a
busy time are needed to go out again as much as the envelopes are needed for charging them (129)."

W. R. Maidment discussed the problem fully and gave
several suggestions for delayed discharge (134).

Any attempt to improve the charging system must therefore seek to obviate some or all of these disadvantages:
by reducing the delay to the reader; by releasing qualified staff at busy times; by reducing, if possible, the overall cost in staff time. The first two objectives are a-
chieved by any system of "delayed discharge" - the work
to be carried out while the reader waits is less, therefore the wait is shorter and fewer staff are needed....
The immediate purpose of delaying the work of discharging books is to make it unnecessary for the reader
to wait for his ticket. There are at least three ways of
doing this:

(i)   At busy times the reader may be given a temporary
      card when he hands in a book and the normal work
      of discharge and subsequent charge may be post-
      poned.
(ii) The tickets issued to readers may be made in such
      a form that they are expendable. Since the individ-
      ual ticket is not used again, there is no need to
      wait for it.
(iii) The process of charge may be altered so that the
      reader is required to produce his ticket but not to
      surrender it. As it remains in his possession, he
      obviously never has to wait for it.

The first method is seen in the "cloakroom ticket" system which was devised by Mr. L. R. McColvin. It is intended to deal with an unusually long queue such as may
be caused by some interruption of the service or by sud-
den illness of the staff. An issue tray is kept at the
counter, containing a series of dummy charges, each consisting of a book pocket, boldly numbered, containing a
book card bearing the same number. [See earlier reference to this method, no. 126]. Since the normal work
of charge and discharge have to be done in addition to the
"marrying" of temporary charges, there is an increase in
total work and the system is justified only for emergency
use.

The second group of methods - those using an expend-
able ticket - has not been widely exploited, but a possible
technique may be indicated. Instead of receiving tickets
when he joins the library, the reader would be issued
with a book of coupons, each coupon in the book bearing
the same number which, of course, identifies the reader.
The charge is made up of one coupon inserted in a pocket type book card and may be filed as in the Browne system. When books are returned, readers are not required
to wait for their tickets, but merely hand in the books.
There is no need to staff the counter for maximum traffic;
the work of discharge continues at a steady pace, ignoring
the minute-by-minute fluctuations in the rate at which
books are received. The costs of such a system are less
than might be supposed, and, if new books of tickets are
issued in the same way that cheque books are issued by
banks, there is considerable saving in the labour of re-
registering readers.

A more widely used method of "delayed discharge" is
that in which the reader retains his ticket all the time.
This, of course, means an adjustment of the charging
process, since the filed record must identify the reader

without using his ticket for the purpose. The simplest
method would involve copying the reader's particulars
from the ticket, which he is required to produce, on the
next vacant line of the book card. In practice mechanical
means of copying are used, as, for example in the Dickman system.

In 1901, this modification of the Browne system was
suggested by C. D. Johnston (135).

The book envelope is a common coin envelope (with the
flaps turned in) 7.5 x 12 cm. in size, made of the stout-
est stock which could be secured....
No date is stamped on the book-envelope, unless the
book becomes overdue, when the date of issue is written
on, or if renewed, it is stamped renewed with date....
The advantages of this system are of course true of
the Browne system, if the borrower carries the pocket
when not in use; but the substitution of the small card,
which can be easily carried in a purse or card case, is
a great convenience to borrowers.... One must be careful in taking a book-envelope from the charge tray for any
reason, as they are not dated, and could be easily misplaced... although the number of issues of a book may be
found by the dating slip, there is no record of the borrowers to whom it has been issued....

Newark System

The Newark Charging System was based on two other
card charging systems which had been used elsewhere (8).
John C. Dana crystalized the working of his Newark System
and released it to public scrutiny as part of the ALA Primer,
appearing in Public Libraries, 1896 (105).

The suggested equipment and charging procedure was
given in this manner (136).

On the inside of the front cover of every book in the library paste a manila pocket.... On this manila pocket,
at the top, write the call-number of the book. Below this
print information for borrowers. In this pocket place a
book-card of heavy ledger paper, or light cardboard. On
this book-card, at the top, write the call-number of the
book in the pocket of which it is placed, and at bottom of
reverse side author, short title, and accession number.

To every borrower the library will issue a borrower's card. This card is made of heavy, colored tag-board, and will contain borrower's name and address, his number in the series of borrowers' numbers, and important rules about lending books. The rest leave blank for dates.

The librarian, before delivering a book to a borrower, takes from the pocket the book-card, writes on it the number found at the top of the borrower's card, and after it, with a dater, stamps the day of the month. At the same time he stamps the same date on the borrower's card.

The borrower's card he places in the book pocket, the book-card he retains as a record of the loan, and the borrower takes the book away. The book-card, with all others representing the books issued on the same day, he places in a tray behind a card bearing the date of the day of issue. All the book-cards representing books issued on a certain day are arranged, first in the numerical then in the alphabetical order of their call-numbers.

At the New York Public Library, "variously colored book cards are used to indicate various classes.... [After charging] book card is dropped in proper slot in desk (ten slots indicating the ten classes). [In filing], book cards for foreign books are arranged alphabetically after book cards in English.... System has many exceptions, one of which is to write reader's card number on dating slip as well as book card. Others are the writing of Special or Sp. on book card opposite card number to indicate the privilege of extended time to special card holder, as well as on dating slip. In this case, call number or accession number is written on card (presumably reader's card) and the use of branch initials on reader's card to show card issued from a branch other than from which book is borrowed." Pratt Institute Free Library was reported to have used different ink pads for fiction and non-fiction (137).

S. C. Van de Carr, in discussing the lending department which uses the Newark System, recommended a special charging technique: "Ordinarily charging dates are stamped in red ink; novels less than one year old are charged with blue ink to distinguish them, as only one of these may be charged on a card at a time. Black ink is used for charging books at branches; green ink at stations; and purple ink in the children's room; so that books not issued through the lending department may easily be recognized at once (138)."

The charging of non-book materials is dealt with briefly by this same writer (139).

(a) Music. When there are several parts in one musical
composition, a borrower must take every part; an elastic
band holds the parts together - and the number of parts
is written on the pocket and slip of the first part. Make
only one charge on the borrower's card for all the parts;
and write after the charge the number of parts....
(c) Pamphlets. To charge a pamphlet or leaflet which
is not provided with a pocket and slip, make a temporary
charging-slip; write at the top of a manila slip, in pencil,
the number of the general class to which the pamphlet belongs, the author, if any, and the catch title,...also on
the front or title page of the pamphlet, write the class
number, and make a light pencil mark under the author
and first word of the title selected. Charge the pamphlet
in the usual way, but stamp the date and write the borrower's number near the outer edge of the inside back
cover of the pamphlet instead of on a pocket. In arranging the circulation, place such slips before all other slips
of the class noted, and in alphabetical order by authors
or titles. Destroy the slip when the pamphlet is returned.

Dana discussed the discharging of books in this manner (140):

When a borrower returns a book the librarian can learn,
from the date on the pocket, whether or not a fine should
be paid on it; if not, he can, if in haste, immediately
take out the borrower's card from the book pocket, stamp
the date of its return at the right of the date on which it
was lent, thus cancelling the charge against the borrower,
and lay the book aside and look up its book-card later.

The ALA Committee on Library Administration added
more information. "Libraries retaining borrowers' cards at
the library discharge at their leisure. Where the Newark
system is used (with the exception of the New York Public
Library) an incomplete discharge is made at the time of the
book's return - consisting of the stamping of the date of return on reader's card. It is obviously impossible to delay a
reader while book is checked off (141)."

The problem of discharge as evidenced by libraries in
1927 was summarized by Flexner (142).

Even with so definite a process as the discharge of books, an entire lack of uniformity in practice is indicated. Some libraries use different colored inks for charging and discharging; other libraries place any stamp opposite the date due or through the date of charge; and others cancel the charge with a bar stamp without any date. Many libraries justifiably feel that the date of return is an important part of the borrower's record and use only a stamp bearing the current date....

An attempt is often made to discourage the return of books without borrowers' cards since these deviations require additional records. When this occurs, however, a receipt must be given the borrower for the return of the book. A special form or slip incorporating the necessary information is issued by some libraries to be returned with the borrower's card to cancel the charge.... Many libraries file them in the same way as borrowers' cards. ... In some libraries the receipt takes the form of a temporary borrower's card on which a limited number of books may be drawn. By thus incorporating two records, this card saves duplication and creates in the mind of the borrower an impression of the library's willingness to meet an emergency.

The procedure for dealing with overdues was discussed in this manner by Dana (140):

The borrower's number, written on the book-card of any given book in circulation, will give, through the register of borrowers, the name and address of the person having that book. Overdue books are automatically indicated, their cards remaining in the tray, behind the card indicating the date they were lent, after the day for their return has been passed.

Helen Geer remarked that overdue postal cards are written from this information and sent to the borrower (143).

Renewal of books is possible under the Newark System but as devised by Dana the book must be brought to the library for renewal. Van de Carr wrote (144):

When a borrower has had a book for one month he may have it renewed, that is, charged again for another month, unless some other borrower has asked to have the book reserved for him, or unless the book has been out on the same card for three consecutive months. To be renewed,

a book must be returned to the library; it may not be renewed by mail, by telephone or by presenting merely the
card on which the book was charged.... At the end of a
month a book should be inspected for repairs.... To renew a book discharge and slip it in the usual way and
charge it again.

Helen T. Geer mentioned a later policy on book renewal (143).

1. If the book is returned to the library, the first charge
is canceled in the usual manner and the book is treated as
a new charge.
2. If the book is not brought to the library, the following
method is used.
    a. Author, title, and call number of the book, the
    borrower's card number, and date due or date of is-
    sue is given by the borrower to the desk assistant.
    b. Book card is taken from the circulation file and
    stamped with the new due date. Letter "R" or abbre-
    viation "Ren" is added in pencil after the date.
    c. Book card is filed under the original date, in cur-
    rent day's date, or in a special file.

In 1896, Frank Hill used the following plan for dealing with reserves in connection with his system, which was
very similar to that used at Newark (145).

Any book in the library (except fiction) may be reserved
by the payment of two (2) cents. The second volume of
a novel may be reserved in the same way.
    When a request for a reserve is made, a postal ad-
dressed to the applicant is filled out with the necessary
information....
    The accompanying "reserve" slip (red) is then filled
out and placed with the regular book-slip in the charging-
tray.
    When the book is discharged attention is at once called
to the "reserve," and the postal-card notice is completed
and mailed to the applicant - the book being placed on the
"reserve shelf."

Geer recorded that with the Newark System the circulation file is searched for each book to be reserved. "Clip
or signal tab is placed on the card of the book to be reserved. Each copy of the book should be tabbed in this manner (143)."

A differing opinion as to the stamping of the date in charging was held by **F. M. Crunden** among others. Stamping of the date on which the book is due, was desired by Crunden, who believed this "feature can be applied to any charging system; and common sense urges its universal adoption. The reader wants to know, not when he 'drew' the book, but when he should 'return' it (106)."

Flexner considered this factor in the following way (146):

> Since the period of loan of the book and the date of its return are of such importance, the best method of indicating when a book is due has never been finally established. This question involves the convenience of the borrower and the effectiveness of records, the speed of charge and discharge, and the expeditious return of books to the shelves. ....With these variations [of 7, 14, 28 days] in the period of the loan, it is necessary to indicate to the assistant how long each book may be kept. This is most commonly accomplished by the color of the date slip or a statement printed on it. In the actual charging it is accomplished by the use of rubber stamps showing the date involved in the transaction, ... The date for which they are set involves a question of library procedure....
>
> The question is: (1) Shall a book be stamped to show the date that it is due? or, (2) Shall it be stamped with the date of issue, requiring the reader to compute when it is due?....
>
> The size of the circulation of the library may conceivably be the governing factor in the choice. In large libraries the stamp set for each assistant [with a symbol to show responsibility for the charge] and the placing of the responsibility on readers for computing dates due are labor and time-saving devices of such importance that the date of issue is commonly adopted. Smaller libraries may allow the convenience of the borrower to be the primary consideration and stamp books with the date due.
>
> In libraries limiting the number of books of fiction allowed, the position of the stamp on the borrower's card may be made to differentiate between charges, non-fiction being stamped in one column and fiction in another; or a pencilled check or initial may be used as a symbol. This method is useful in charging new books and magazines when the number to be drawn is limited.

E. F. Corwin felt that a date-due slip in the back of
the book should be dated with the date the book is due and
numbered with the borrower's card number. He did not suggest the use of a borrower's card for the recording of books
borrowed. "There is no complete record in one place of the
number of books a borrower has out. This is the only essential feature of the original charging system that this one
dues not cover. But what of it? We have not found a single
borrower taking advantage of this fact, and we do not care if
they do. The borrowers worry over this feature more than
we do (147)."

At the University of Missouri Library the Newark System was combined with the slip system which was formerly
in force. A borrower's card was not used. The student
merely signed his name (148).

When the Newark System was adapted for use at the
Elkhart Public Library, E. F. Corwin desired that the borrower's card be kept at the library and "when once properly
filed is not disturbed, except when corrections in the address
are necessary (149)."

Flexner was concerned with the loss of the borrower's
card and the failure of the patron to bring with him his card.
She mentioned several adaptations which were incorporated into the charging systems when librarians were faced with this
situation (150):

(a) No reader's card. In some very small systems the
reader's card is omitted altogether. The registration
cards filed alphabetically must be kept close at hand and
consulted for the borrower's number each time a book is
lent. Registration records when used for this purpose
may be filed vertically to save space. There are disadvantages: (1) to the reader having to wait to learn his
number, and (2) to the assistant having to ask the reader's
name repeatedly.
(b) Identification card. In some systems the effort to
obviate these disadvantages has resulted in the issue of an
identification card to the reader, giving his name, address
and registration number. Books are charged to this number on presentation of the card. This method simplifies
charging and discharging by eliminating the stamping of
the date on borrowers' cards. However, the borrower
has no record of the number of books drawn and no receipt for books returned, nor has the library any method

of knowing or limiting the total number of books taken by
the borrower. It is difficult to curtail the reader's use
of the library even though he has many books overdue if
he presents his identification card each time he draws
books.

E. A. Lansden suggested using merely an identification card, stating the following: "The purpose of a reader's
card are twofold - to identify the reader as one who has
signed an application card and thus promised to take care of
library property, and second, to bear the reader's number
(151)."

At Colchester, England a method of registration and
issuing of the borrower's card was used, which may have
solved one problem (152).

As is well known the borrower's register is an integral
part of the Newark System. The frequent reference to
the borrower's register constitute a drawback to this and
other systems, and to eliminate this compilation and to
facilitate rapid reference, a revised type of enrolment
voucher has been introduced.
    The voucher now consists of a card 6" x 5" perforated
into two parts each 3" x 5", the bottom half consisting of
the usual borrower's form and the upper portion consisting
of the borrower's name and address only. The borrower
is required to fill in both parts of the voucher, the top
line being completed by the staff as usual; the one portion
bearing name and number and the other number and name,
and the parts are then filed in two sequences arranged alphabetically and numerically respectively. Thus the usual
borrower's register in the form of a bulky ledger has been
eliminated and the public do some of the routine work
previously required of the staff.

A variation of the Newark System was tried by C. B.
Clement at Manchester, New Hampshire Library. He said
that it combined the good points of the Browne with the modified Newark (153).

The distinctive feature of the new card is that directly under the registration number there is a slot through which,
in charging a book, the number is copied on the book card.
This method reduces to a minimum the possibility of mistakes in copying and keeps the numbers uniform in size,
and in even columns on the card. Blank pockets are used

to keep request slips with book cards, date slips with overdues, and for recording fines and indicating vacation
charges.

J. L. Woodruff modified the method of card stamping
in his system "resulting in a considerable saving of time in
the issue of books, and no apparent disadvantage to the service (154)."

The "Returned" column on the reader's card has been
done away with, the "Date due" being the only stamp
used so long as the card is in active service. At the
head of the columns is printed: "A book is out on this
card and due on the last day stamped below, unless same
is followed by the word Checked." When the last book is
returned and no other drawn, the word "Checked" is
stamped under the last date. If the book is to be renewed,
the "Renewed" stamp follows the last date due, with the
new date under the same. If a fine is due and the card
is held for payment the words "Overdue ___ days" are
stamped under the last date, and when the fine is paid
the "Checked" stamp again follows this. In every case
the "Checked" stamp with no date following it is prima
facia evidence that the record is clear.
The mere knowledge of the actual date of return has
never been of any service to us. By this new method the
handling of one stamp (except in the comparatively few cases indicated) is all that becomes necessary in checking
out books, an advantage that will readily be appreciated
by desk attendants.

Van de Carr believed the two advantages of the Newark
System were its simplicity and elasticity (155).

In charging, three dates are stamped and two numbers
written. One assistant can charge on an average eight
books a minute. In discharging a book, one date only is
stamped while the borrower waits; the book is then laid
aside to have its slip looked up later. As many books
as are needed may be borrowed at one time; or the number may be limited. From the borrower's card it is
easy to see if he has charged to him any books that are
overdue, in which case his card is held until the books
are returned and the fines paid.
It is possible to charge books without a borrower's
card and this is frequently done.

A few more advantages were apparent to Wood, who stated, "any number of attendants may give out books at the same time, puzzles may be solved at odd moments and not while the reader waits; statistics are easily kept, and from the book card the librarian may learn just how popular a book is and who has had it (156)."

Speed and accuracy were noted by F. M. Crunden: "one issue clerk and three runners [to acquire books from the stacks] can issue 300 books an hour, while one receiving clerk can credit the return of many more than that number.... The accuracy of the method is, I think, apparent. The book card shows who has the volume and when it is due. The borrower's card informs him that he has a book and tells him when to return it.... Every return of a book is credited on the borrower's card. The card is the arbiter of all disputes (157)."

However, in 1955, Helen Geer wrote that the routines "are slow, time consuming, and cumbersome.... There are at least 28 places in the circulation tray to look for a given book: each day's circulation (an average of 26 places) and overdue and renewal files (158)."

Corwin's modifications resulted in what he felt was "the simplest charging system yet devised.... The chief advantages are: First - It saves time. The record is made in only two places instead of three, and the necessity for the constant filing and refiling of the cards is done away with. Second - It saves money; viz., the salary paid for filing cards and the price of thousands of borrowers' cards (77)." But he saw that it was frequently necessary to ask the borrower's name if he does not have a card to present when charging books (159).

We find, however, that our borrowers take pride in remembering their numbers, and the majority of them will give their number when handing in their books to be charged, or if we ask the name will give their number. I sometimes fear that we shall come to know them by their numbers alone.
The disadvantages are mostly in the librarian's mind, and fade away when the system is thoroughly understood. We have found this to be true, and while not a large library, we have over 8,000 borrowers and circulate over 100,000 books per year.

Several possible disadvantages were noted by Wood, who said (156):

However, there are certain things that must be looked out for. 1) See that the stamps are set carefully each day, using the "due date," not the date of issue. In setting stamps two weeks ahead holidays are sometimes overlooked. 2) Be sure to copy the reader's number correctly, and make the figures clear and plain.... 3) In discharging put the right card into the right book.... 4) Have the reader's card and the book card the same size, so that both fit into the book pocket.

One of the difficulties was touched on by E. W. Gaillard. Greater accuracy in transcribing the borrower's number might be possible (160).

I am looking for some sort of mechanical device to obviate this difficulty. I have had in mind some such plan as this, but this has serious objections. I would have a series of numbers for a rubber stamp prepared, one after the other, on tapes of 500 or 1000 each, and when a new reader is placed on the list, cut from this tape his corresponding number and glue it on his card. When he takes out a book use this for a stamp and stamp the book card directly from the rubber stamp on the reader's card, and date in the usual way. This plan would be easy, cheap, and mistakes would be impossible, but the readers' cards would be very bulky to file, and the ink from the stamp would mar the flyleaves of the book. In short, it would be unclean and in the way.
Some such plan would, I am sure, be adopted by all libraries using the regular card charging system.

In 1899, soon after Dana's system was adopted, an article appeared in the Library Journal which outlined a charging system which would combine "the excellencies of the two most generally approved systems then in use, the Newark system, perhaps more used, and the Browne system, devised by Miss Nila E. Browne (161)."

In the proposed system: no writing by either reader or loan clerk is required to make the charge, no date need be stamped, though one may profitably be, any number of different privileges may be easily provided for, of the outfit but one item at most is used up, and the reader need not wait for the consultation of a file at the issue of

the book unless he chooses to keep his card at the library
when no book is charged upon it, and need not in that
case wait for the consultation of a file at the discharge..
..

The essential feature of the proposed system is the
substitution of a reader's card for the reader's library
pocket of the Browne system, and of a book-charge-envelope or card-case to be kept in the book-pocket when the
book is on the shelf instead of the book-card, of the
Browne system. The reader's card, which he may carry,
need not be large, as it is to receive no dating; it must
bear either the reader's name or library number, with
his address, date of expiration, name of library, and a
few extracts from the rules.... The card is practically
a ticket, each entitling to one book. Any number of cards
desired may be issued to each reader.

The book-charge-envelope, or case, in which the reader's card is kept, in file while the book is out, should be
small enough to be kept in the book pocket when not in
use, and large enough to hold the reader's card, when in
the file, say 5 x 11 cm......

The envelope, for purposes of reference when in use
(that is when the book is out and the envelope, containing
the reader's card, is in the file), should be so cut as to
give a central perforation about 3 x 6 cm., making it a
kind of miniature photograph frame, with wide enough
margins to receive the book call number and author and
title. The central perforation permits the borrower's
name and address on the book card to be read without
removing the card from the envelope.

If a book record is kept in the charge file, a color
time-indication scheme, such as is used at the Albany
Y.W.C.A.library may be adopted by having the opposite
sides of the envelope and the opposite ends of each side
of four different colors, with call-number on each of
these four places. Then a different color can be placed
facing the loan clerk in the charge file every other week,
if the usual period of issue is two or three weeks, and
charges overdue more than one week can be taken out and
placed in a separate file at the beginning of the fourth or
fifth week, when it will be necessary to recommence the
succession of colors. This will make it necessary to
look in but two files at most, to find where any given
book is and nevertheless delinquencies will never pass
unnoticed more than one week after the book is due.

The charging process in the proposed system is as
follows: On receiving a book at the loan desk the loan

clerk takes the book-charge-envelope from the book-pocket
and the reader's card from the borrower or from the file,
stamps date, or date due, on the dating slip, issues the
book and places the reader's card within the envelope.
That is all that need be done at the moment. The book-
charge-envelope with the reader's card within it may be
filed when opportunity occurs, either by the call-number,
or first by the date of issue and second by call-number,
as preferred.

Discharge: When a book is returned the reader may
either leave it at the receiving desk and depart, or may
wait until the book-charge-envelope is found in the file
and receive his card. The loan clerk has only to find the
book-charge-envelope, remove the reader's card, and replace the envelope in the book-pocket, and either hand the
reader's card to the owner or file it, at her convenience
....

Renewal, if permitted, is accomplished by a mere re-
versal of the position of the envelope in the file, if book
account is kept, or shifting of its place, if time account.
"Reserves," if permitted, can be provided for by inserting an extra temporary slip with note to that effect in the
book-charge-envelope, and memoranda of fines similarly.

Many variations in the system are possible, and its
flexibility makes it adaptable to a great variety of conditions. It can be modified to suit any free library, from
the large city library with great circulation to the smallest village library.

Visible Record System

In 1917, Jeanette M. Drake viewed the system then in
use at her library and "reckoned the cost of the supply of
readers' cards, the salary of the person filling out the cards,
the constant filing and refiling of the cards, the space required for this record, as well as the annoyance when the
cards that were brought in during the day had not been filed,"
and decided that some changes should be made (107).

With the system which she adopted, the following procedure was used (162):

The regular application blank is used [with] ... space for
the reader's name, number and address at one end. These
application blanks are arranged alphabetically in the file
where the readers' cards used to be kept. When a book

is charged the attendant asks the reader his full name
and address; the reader's name is then looked up in alphabetical file, his number found and the charge is made
in the usual way, the date stamped and the number written on the book card, and the date stamped on the dating
slip in the book. The application cards are always in
this one file and there is no chance for loss as in the
other system. They are never removed except to change
an address, or to be withdrawn from use.

Mrs. R. S. Roth developed in greater detail the purpose of the visible borrowers' record (163).

An original idea developed in our library - that a fan
shaped visible delinquent file might be enlarged and used
at the charging desk as a visible record of all borrowers'
names. There a very complete record could be kept on
each borrower's card of fines, fees, etc. Colored cards
were used as follows: salmon color for juvenile, cream
for adults, blue for country borrowers, and white for
transients.

At the Sioux City Library a card for each borrower
was filed in a cabinet placed in front of the loan desk. "If
the borrower does not remember his card number he looks
it up for himself before presenting his book to be charged.
The cards are held in by a rod. They are neatly typed with
the borrower's number at the top, and after that his name
by which the cards are alphabetically arranged (164)."

A note appearing in the Wisconsin Library Bulletin,
1920, mentioned that the "original plan was to use the applications as a charging file, but it seems better to use a plain
card for that and file the applications by number, doing away
with the borrowers' register in book form (165).

As with the Newark System, when the book is returned
the book card is withdrawn from the file and placed in the
book (164). Renewals are dealt with in the Newark fashion,
but Roth added, "We clip a colored strip of paper over groups
of book cards loaned to country patrons who have the privilege
of renewals. Likewise to teachers in the public schools.
There is nothing like a little color to designate locations (166)."

Drake admitted that there are "drawbacks to this system, but after using it for over two years," she writes, "we
know that it is a saving of time and money. Time thus

gained is more profitably spent in assisting patrons in the
selection of books (167)."

In another article, she gave a more detailed picture
of these advantages and disadvantages (162).

Finally, the advantages are:
1. Eliminates constant talk and argument as to where
   readers' cards are and constant explanation about
   bringing them each time a book is taken out, etc.
2. By asking addresses each time, these are kept up to
   date.
3. Card is always in the library in its proper place.
4. Saves time of assistant in filling out readers' cards
   in the beginning and the duplicates and the temporary
   cards.
5. Saves cost of readers' cards.
The disadvantages:
1. Readers have to wait while their number is being
   looked up.
2. Necessity of asking reader's name each time.
3. Reader will not have a receipt for his book, which
   he never had, anyway, under our old system.
4. Have to take patron's word as to number of books he
   has out.

Mrs. Roth listed the equipment which was purchased
for the system as adopted in her library. It was bought
with fine money (168).

The cost of our equipment:		
1	Posting tray	$ 7.35
25	Panels at $1.60 each	40.00
25	Separator guides at 15 cents	3.75
2,500	Cards in 4 colors	9.00
	Total	$60.10

Roth observed that "this new system has reduced routine operation to two-thirds the work at the main desk and has
saved one-half of the time of both librarian and patron (169)."
The 1933 article in Kansas Library Bulletin noted that the
system was "a great time saver for librarian, and annoyance
saver for the patron (164)."

M. H. Murdoch contrasted this system with machine
charging by remarking that with the visible file "two assistants can charge at the same time, one on either side of the

file." Murdoch believed that the saving was considerable because the following operations were eliminated (170):

> (1) numbering applications, borrowers' cards and numer-
> ical cross reference cards with numbering machine; (2)
> typing information on borrowers' cards, and typing, filing
> and withdrawing numerical cards; (3) changing borrowers'
> numbers into names for overdue notices; (4) lost card
> procedure; (5) making temporary borrowers' cards; (6)
> maintaining a separate blacklist."

The following observation appeared in Wisconsin Library Bulletin, 1922 (108):

> In the smaller libraries, where names are well known
> and files small, this consultation is rapidly done. But
> in larger places, names must be asked for in most cases,
> and may be difficult to catch, especially in a community
> with many foreigners. The files become bulky and it is
> hard for more than one person to work with them. Some-
> times various schemes are tried to avoid turning to the
> files each time, resulting in a system which is no simpler
> than the full Newark.
> The Detroit Public Library has secured all the advan-
> tages of dispensing with the borrower's card, without
> these disadvantages, by the use of a small identification
> card.

Detroit System

The Detroit Charging System, as devised by Ralph A.
Ulveling, was based on a similar operation in government
banks. Ulveling reasoned in this manner (171):

> In banks, which, like libraries, are used by people of all
> levels of education and the entire gamut of nationalities a
> parallel was found. For years their customers have
> made out deposit slips before approaching the teller's
> window. Though hundreds of dollars are sometimes in-
> volved, only a bank clerk's verification in each case has
> been needed. Based on this principle the new Detroit
> Charging System was evolved.
> This method of book charging was first tried in the
> Monnier Branch of the Detroit Public Library.

As stated earlier [see reference no. 109] the system was a

simplified version of the Newark Charging System.

The big difference, as far as supplies are concerned, is the introduction of date cards instead of date due slips. An article appearing in the Illinois Libraries, 1930, contained this information (172):

> Date cards of inexpensive manila stock may be used, with a different color to indicate seven day books, or by stamping the manila card with a red "7 day book" stamp. Both sides of the card are used and they are interchangeable in all books....
> Most of the equipment now in use may be utilized as the only change is the substitution of the date card for the old date slip, and the provision of pencils for the use of patrons.

R. Comstock recorded that their "expense for supplies was approximately $70.00 which included pockets, book cards, date cards of three colors, dater, pencil and chain, and charging tray with date guides (173)."

The charging operation as outlined by Ulveling is as follows (174):

> The system is very simple. The borrower writes his own number on the book-cards. When leaving the library he merely shows his books and identification card to the desk attendant. She sees that the number has been copied correctly, keeps the book-card with the day's circulation, and slips the proper date-card into each book-pocket.
> Date cards are stamped by a page during dull hours, in number corresponding to the circulation expected. These are kept in piles at the desk. To reduce the possibility of error in selecting the appropriate date-card, colors are used, each color indicating a loan period. Thus when a green book-card is withdrawn from a book-pocket, a green date card is inserted.
> Book cards are not stamped at the time of issue. Guides in the file trays date them sufficiently until they become overdue when those remaining are stamped....
> By placing a small table near the door for verifying, the crowd is divided and the usual confusion at the charge and discharge point is removed.
> In addition to this, due to her proximity to the exit, the verifier is in effect a guard as well.

At Ann Arbor a verifier was not kept at the exit during the stack hours, according to a notice appearing in Library Journal, 1931 (175).

> The main desk is close enough to take care of patrons during these times. We need better equipment and space in order to work the System to its fullest extent.

In the Children's Department at Edmonton Public Library, "any of the assistants who are out on the floor doing reference work can check the books without returning to the desk as it is easy to carry with them a few dated blue cards (176)."

Variations in the charging methods were reflected by one Special Library. "The client, ready to leave with his book, needs only to remove the card, jot down his name, department number and date, and leave the card on the charging desk. If the librarian is busy helping someone else, the client encounters no delay in waiting for book cards to be stamped. 'Out cards' for file material and simple charge slips for unbound journals likewise encourage self service (177)."

At the Evanston Public Library a change was made in their stamping procedure (178).

> We discontinued dating the book card, but resumed it, the chief reason being that at later periods we want to know the frequency with which the book has gone out.... This date also assists in knowing whether a book should be replaced when withdrawn.... The dating of the cards can be done after the patron leaves or all together when circulation is filed as one of those in-between jobs for the desk at the door which does not take time from productive work.

P. I. Field did not shorten his process of charging as much as the Detroit System does. He explained, "we use the borrower's card which we stamp, we use the dating slip which we stamp, but we follow the rest of the rules. We do not stamp the book card until it becomes over-due, but we simply file it in our trays until its proper date (179)."

Ulveling dealt with the subject of dating the book cards in this manner (180):

Difficulties arising from this are almost negligible. With
staffs trained to pencil in the date on every card that for
any reason must be taken from the slip tray, the smooth
functioning of the system is not impaired.... The history
of the book's circulation...may be obtained readily when
inventory is taken. By drawing a line below the last
charge, the year's activity of the volume is apparent at
a glance.

At Ann Arbor the problem was handled in this manner: "We
date our books on the page after the title page showing the
month and year the book went into circulation. As inventor-
ies are taken, we propose to pencil on the book card with
red or blue pencil the year date. When a new card is made,
the number of circulations on the old card can likewise be
penciled in on the new card, if desired (181)."

An article appearing in the Library Journal, 1929,
gave the following reason for the value of low book pockets
and date cards to discharge procedures: "This is necessary
to avoid loss of time when the books are returned. On busy
evenings the book cannot be slipped at the time it is returned.
Hence it is just checked by the clerk to see whether it is
overdue or not and is slipped later (183)."

Overdues are handled in the same manner as were overdues under the Newark System, except that the book card
is now stamped at the time the book becomes overdue, as
mentioned in [reference no. 174]. According to at least one
writer, "Renewals are made in the usual manner by pencil-
ing the renewal date prefixed by R on the book card and refiling it under the original date (183)."

Ulveling, in viewing the system, saw several advantages. He was pleased that assistants could now devote more
time to "floor service" (184).

... the Detroit library did not foster this plan for purposes of reducing its staff. Rather it was tried in the
hope that a more advantageous use of assistants' time
would be made and a better service to patrons result....
in actual practice staffs are spending less time on detail
and more in directing and advising, particularly at crowd-
ed periods when this service is at its greatest premium..
..
For the most part people accepted [the system] gra-
ciously and co-operatively....

In another article Ulveling wrote about savings in this manner (109): "Let it suffice to say that this system of book charging has functioned successfully while 250,000 books were given out in one month through 16 agencies, that in Detroit it has proved a time saver, and that it can be installed in new or established libraries easily, quickly, and at little cost (185)."

The librarian of the Monnier Branch of the Detroit Public Library reported in the annual report for 1928-29, "As a time saver the system is a distinct success and as to the errors our fears predicted for it- well, they simply did not materialize (186)."

The Library Journal article entitled "Charge your own" gave a list of conclusions and possible advantages and savings (187).

The conclusions arrived at:
a. The system is practical for the large branch as well as for the small branch.
b. Patrons do not object to it....
c. Foreign groups can handle it as readily as the English speaking peoples....
d. It is a saving over the old method and over the charging machine method which is being so generally taken up.

Advantages and Savings
1. All writing of card numbers by assistants is eliminated....
2. Ninety-nine percent of book card stamping is eliminated....
3. Stamping of date slips is done during the quiet hours instead of during the rush periods. Also, the actual time required for this kind of stamping is considerably reduced....
4. All pasting of date slips into books is eliminated by the use of a card date due slip.
5. Less danger of transposition of numbers results because one person, the patron, writes the number and another verifies it. Under the old system there was no check on the person doing the writing.
6. As to legibility and care in registering the number, the patron measures up well as compared to the attendant working under pressure and in face of a wait-

ing line.

7. Books are neater and more attractive looking without the pasted-in date slip, which was usually a mass of red or green ink giving a daubed appearance.

8. It reduces the amount of book card stock used as well as the time in retyping book cards because the elimination of dates on the book card doubles the number of charges which may be put on a card.

9. Automatically there is close supervision of the doors without entailing the expense or giving the appearance of having a guard.

10. Because of the time saved in the actual charging, long lines of patrons waiting to have books charged on busy nights have been practically eliminated.

Field also recorded a saving of time. "We had thought we would save time but we were very much surprised to see how much time! Our attention could be concentrated on the discharging, and for the first time in months there were no lines, although we were in our busiest months (188)."

At Ann Arbor "within a year, out of a staff of ten, eight college graduates (seven with library school training) were ready to give service to the people of Ann Arbor. This produced a problem of trained assistants versus routine work .... Trained assistants object to using their time in stamping book cards, date slips and borrowers' cards (189)." They adopted this self charging system and recorded the following results (190):

From the library viewpoint, we started out to eliminate routine for assistants and found we were able to take care of a twenty percent (almost one per capita) increase in the circulation in the last year with the same staff, each member far less tired and a great deal happier at the end of the day. We find that our overdues are less in spite of an increased circulation and that patrons are paying fines more promptly. Voluntarily on the part of patrons they state that, since they write their numbers on the cards, they feel they must get their books back on time and pay up fines promptly. They feel an added responsibility.

E. G. Baker remarked on their success in this manner: "Over a month has passed and to date there have been no serious hitches in our experiment. We are glad that it has proved a success for it leaves us with more time to devote to the many and varied reference questions that each day

brings (191)." At the Galva Public Library, "It was all so
simple that at first we felt that we were distributing the
books broadcast and they would be lost to us forever, but we
haven't had any difficulties except in getting people to remember to bring their cards. This is the only snag we have
found. We can, of course, look up the number, and we allow them to take out books, but we make them as uncomfort-
able as possible and next time the card is likely to be in evidence (192)."

        Ulveling mentioned that for a time after the system
was first begun snags "showed an increase. Without special
effort they gradually diminished as the system settled down
to a rhythmic routine until now there are fewer than under
the old method (193)."

        As to snags, Ann Arbor library staff had this to say:
"Of course our entire stock of books is not yet equipped with
new pockets, but we seldom have a book returned without the
date card. When we do we find it was because of the old
style pocket [too wide, cards fall out] (181)."

        When posed with the question of the value of the con-
tact between library assistant and patron, T. R. Brewitt answered (194):

    Our experience with the Detroit system does not indicate
    that it makes a barrier between the charging desk assist-
    ant and the patron. On the contrary, the contact between
    the desk assistant and the reader can be less rather than
    more mechanical when the assistant is able to bestow on
    the reader the attention which would otherwise be given to
    writing the borrower's number. Some library assistants
    may be able to discuss books intelligently, think up some-
    thing clever to say about the weather, keep one eye on a
    waiting line, and at the same time get a long number
    down without transposing figures. However, if I were for-
    turnate enough to have such a person on my staff, I would
    consider her talents too valuable to be spent in charging
    and discharging books!

        Wright dealt with the problem of the division of staff
occasioned by the need to maintain a verifier near the door
(195).

With us, up to rush hours, two people were formerly at
the main loan desk. Now one is at the main desk and one

at the desk at the door. Sometimes one is over busy and
at other times, less frequently, the other one needs assistance. Neither can help the other, for if one of the
purposes is that of guard duty, the desk at the door must
never be left vacant. In other words, team work, so essential at the loan desk, is impossible.

This separation of the assistants means that the load
for the one at the main desk is much heavier than formerly. She has to discharge all of the books, try to help
the public in the stacks, as well as instruct them in charging books even though it is five months since the system
was inaugurated. Practically no time is left for her to
assist readers and her partner at the door is not in a
physical location to be of assistance.

To offset this loss in reading guidance from the main
desk we have placed a reader's advisor's desk in the
stacks. Thus, rather than reducing the number of assistants, which is offered as one of the advantages of the system, it has made necessary an increase in the number of
assistants available to the public at one time....

Our chief objective in instituting the system was to provide a purposeful means of checking books taken out of
the building, rather than to have a police guard. This
the system does and less expensively than a guard, for
there is much which an attendant at the door can do in
between times that a guard could not do....

Since through the desk at the door an added function -
that of guard - is accomplished, it is reasonable to ex-
pect that it should involve additional expense.

At the Gary Public Library a modification was introduced which took care of the lack of a borrower's record.
R. R. Shaw described the method (196).

It therefore seemed desirable to develop some method by
which the shortcomings of the identification card could be
overcome while retaining its advantages. To do this we
have ruled the back of our identification card into 120 one-
fourth inch squares. Each time books are withdrawn the
transaction requires a single entry in one square regardless of the number of books taken; when books are returned a second transaction results regardless of the number of books returned. This method can be used with
any charging system in which identification cards are used.
It works as follows: Previously prepared date cards are
used, just as in the Detroit or Gaylord charging, but one
additional step is required. When the borrower brings

books to the issue desk they are checked, date cards are inserted, and the total number of books drawn at that time is written in the first square on the back of the identification card with ink or indelible pencil. Thus, if the borrower draws four books the numeral 4 is written in the first square of the card. When he returns these four books the 4 is stamped out with a special rubber stamp, pencil eraser size. A different stamp is used at each agency so that some indication of place of return is given. If he returns three only, the 4 is stamped out and 1 is written in the next square. Then if he draws two more books, the 1 is stamped off and 3 is written in the next square. The last number indicates the number of books charged to the borrower at any given time. If an unpaid fine stands against his record that is written in the space provided on the face of the card; thus keeping the square on the back available for a maximum number of transactions.

This gives an accurate record of the number of books outstanding regardless of the number of branches at which the card may be used. Books borrowed at one branch may be returned at another and the card bears evidence of this process; the borrower knows how many books he is charged with and has a receipt for books returned. The time required for entering and stamping of circulation on the identification card is much less than that required with the borrower's card, on which each volume circulated requires two entries and requires the comparing of dates to make sure that the right book is discharged.

It tells the borrower and the library how many books the borrower has; and it records fines and lost books, but so far, this system does not indicate when books charged by this method are overdue.

To complete the record we developed a simple convention which can be applied semi-annually, quarterly, or even monthly. The dates on which we check are January 1, April 1, July 1, and October 1. On January 1, for example, a circle is drawn around the number representing books outstanding. During January, two sets of numbers are carried, one for books out before January 1 and the second for books drawn after January 1. When books are returned, those drawn before January 1 are deducted from the circled number. Books drawn are added to the uncircled number and those drawn after January 1 are deducted from the uncircled number when they are returned. If on February 1 there are still outstanding books represented by a circled number, we know that the borrower has books overdue.

We have experimented with this minor modification of
the Detroit charging system at two branches to date. A
considerable saving in time has been effected without de-
creasing control over issue at one branch formerly using
the Newark system. At the second branch using the Detroit charging system, the brief addition manipulation required has caused no noticeable delay at the charging desk,
and needed control has been effected. At both branches
patrons have expressed satisfaction with the new charging
method.

N. D. Bassett recommended the Detroit System by revealing: "It has been declared one of the greatest forward
movements in library practice in twenty-five years. Because
it insures accuracy, saves your time and the time of your
patrons (197)."

Dickman System

In 1919, an ALA Committee reported on library administration, making the following plea (198):

Any review of short cuts and eliminations in circulation
methods is bound to bring to mind the often expressed
longing that some accurate mechanical device may be invented for the rapid charging and discharging of books,
one that would reduce to a minimum the use of human
beings in a process that is largely mechanical and rather
deadening, in order to set them free for intelligent, expert, educational service, at once helpful to readers and
stimulating to the mental growth of library workers. Is
not this, perhaps the time for the ALA to seek a solution
of this problem, by putting the matter clearly before the
library world, asking for working plans of a mechanical
device, and if results are not forthcoming within the profession, taking the matter up with some inventor.

The year before, E. W. Gaillard had written about an
attempt he had made in this direction (199).

Jennie Flexner, in 1927, revealed that the "mechanical device" which would aid in circulation work was soon to
appear (200).

Every effort is being bent toward freeing the circulation

assistant from hampering details of routine in order to
give him greater opportunity for personal service to readers. The long-sought mechanical device for charging and
discharging books, which may do much toward accomplishing this, seems at this moment on the eve of completion.
Thus in general ways the methods of circulation grow
more effective for both the librarian and the public.

A memorandum, prepared by Grace Finney, of the
Washington Public Library, was read to the 1928 meeting of
the American Library Association. It outlined the workings
of the Dickman Charging System then in use at the Washington (D.C.) Public Library (201). This was the system selected by the U. S. Efficiency Bureau after research into the
problem of mechanical book charging. "It does everything
the old pencil-and-stamp method does - except that it does
not make mistakes. It guarantees absolute accuracy and legibility. Yet, like all great practical inventions, it is simple
in construction and operation.

"It was installed in the Washington Library and is in
use there now. After years of test, Dr. Bowerman states
the following about the Dickman Book Charging System:

"Mistakes in copying numbers are eliminated, dates
are legible and much time is saved. Library statistics show
that 35 percent of book losses are due to transposing figures
in charging. The Dickman Charger has been in use at the
New York Public Library for more than 18 months. Yet
Miss Johnson, in charge of circulation, reports that not one
mistake has been made by the Dickman Charger despite the
fact that withdrawals average more than 1,000 volumes daily,
with many individuals taking as many as six books....

"Note there is absolutely nothing to get out of order.
In addition to being infallible in records it is infallible in operation....

"Under this method slipping of books is speeded and
snags are eliminated. The legible, accurate records on the
Book Card prevent confusion, argument and loss of time due
to blurred or faulty charging (202)."

The machine used in charging was described in the
following fashion by L. M. Harrod (203):

The stamping machine, which is the only piece of mech-

anism required, is very much like a stapling machine,
but sprung in such a way that the arm remains, when
the machine is not in use, at an angle of about 60 deg.
from the base. This arm has on its under-side a wide
inking ribbon through which are impressed the date (the
date slide being inserted every morning) and the borrower's number. On the upper side of the arm is a rubber
cushion which the assistant strikes in order to bring down
the arm on to the base and so to make the record on the
book-card.

At Toledo two different machines were in use: "The
one at the registration desk is equipped with place for one
date. We use that of expiration of card three years ahead.
The other is at the charging desk, equipped for four dates of
which we use only two (204)."

H. G. T. Christopher wrote that the following supplies
were needed (205):

Reader's Ticket. This is a slip of manilla 2 1/4 x
3 1/2 ins., containing the usual particulars, attached to
which is a metal tag bearing the reader's number in embossed figures. This ticket is permanently retained by
the reader, being handed over to the assistant for charging purposes only, and is then given back to the reader..
..
The renewal of readers' tickets can be effected in the
same manner as now, and the tags can be used again, as
they are detachable from the tickets and have a fairly long
life....
Book-Card. Also of manilla, this card is similar to
those of other systems. It measures 2 by 5 ins., and
the particulars of the book are entered at the top, the rest
of the card being divided lengthwise into two columns, one
for the date, and the other for the reader's number. This
is kept in the book-pocket when the book is in the library,
and is taken out in the charging process, and kept in the
issue trays.
Date-Card. This card is inserted in a book when it is
being taken out by a reader. It is made of a fair quality
card 2 by 5 ins., and is so designed that the date is always visible without removing the card from the pocket.
A heavy line across the centre of the card on both sides
splits the card into four sections. One section is used at
a time, the stamping being done by the machine.
Book-Pocket. This serves the purpose, not only of

holding the book-card when the book is in the library, but also of holding the date-card when the book is out on issue. As is explained in Date-Card (above), its measurement is governed by the fact that the date must always be visible without removing the date-card, and for that reason the pocket portion will measure 2 1/2 by 2 5/8 ins.

It is advisable to have particulars of the book on the pocket, to aid the discharging process, and a suitable method is to extend the back of the pocket above the height of the book-card, making this part of the pocket 6 ins. high.

Date Tags. A series of date tags is issued for the whole year, and the appropriate one is inserted in the machine each day.

In addition to these materials, there is the Dickman Bookcharging Machine.

A detailed explanation of the charging procedure was given by this same writer (206).

The reader takes as many books as he requires from the shelves, and placing them on the counter, hands his reader's ticket to the assistant. The assistant inserts the tag in a slot on the right-hand side of the machine (the tag can be inserted in one way only, so there can be no question of a number being upside down), then removes the book-cards from the books, at the same time inserting date-cards in the pockets. The book-cards are then placed separately on the platform of the machine, and the knob is depressed, thus stamping the date and the reader's number at one operation. When the reader's books have been charged, his ticket is taken from the machine and handed back to him. The book-cards are then placed in the sorting trays, and the charging process is finished. It will be noticed that the reader's ticket is untouched during the charging process, whether he has one book or twenty.

Finney wrote of the stamping procedure (112):

We stamp the date due instead of the date of issue. Books are returned at one place, and issued at two places. The issue machines carry four dates - namely, seven-day, two weeks, four weeks, October 1 (summer vacation date). The machine at the return desk has only one date.

Large libraries use the date of issue instead of date due and small libraries can use one machine carrying one date.

One Massachusetts library reported owning the machine on which the date charger had four changes of position, E. C. Trudeau reported (207):

The date cards are stamped 28 days from present date, 7 days and 3 days, the first thing in the morning and again during the quiet times of the day. The time spent in doing this involves anywhere from ten to fifteen minutes in the morning and five to ten minutes again at several quiet periods of the day and allows for a circulation of eight hundred to a thousand a day.

The Toledo method of charging was given in the 1930 pamphlet put out by Library Efficiency Corporation (208).

... which involves the use of the Borrower's Identification Card with a combination of Date Due for the convenience of the borrower, and Date of Issues for the library record. Through the use of the number plate attached to the Borrower's Identification Card, the Dickman Book Charging System furnishes an absolute receipt to the library for each volume issued and protects the borrower against any possible error from transposing figures, eliminating the need for the double check obtained through the use of the ordinary readers card. Stamping the date card (which replaces the date slip in the back of the book) with the due date in advance, enables the library to use our single-date Model "A" machine for the only record to be charged under this method, while the borrower is at the charging desk - the book card. In this manner the reader obtains the benefit of the use of the date due, whereas the library, by filing the book card under the due date, obtains the same results.

Winifred Riggs filled in a few more details: "... the current date, used for 14 days, 7 day and rental books, and the 4 weeks date used for the few books that are charged for four weeks at the request of the borrower. Since the 7 day and rental book cards are all conspicuously marked, they are easily separated when the filing is done the next day. Four week charges are found when sending overdue notices and are then filed under the date due.

"The routine of charging as developed by the staff is reversible so that two assistants can work easily together. 'A' takes book cards from pockets and uses the machine while 'B' is putting date cards in pockets and removing book cards.

'A' puts date cards in pockets last and 'B' uses machine (209)."

    The methods of discharging were outlined in the memorandum written by Finney (201).

    The charging cards which have replaced the charging slips formerly pasted in books stand up far enough in the book pockets to permit of reading dates without removing the cards from the pockets until after the book card is removed from the charging tray.
    After the book card is removed from the tray the charging card is taken out of the pocket with one hand and placed on the desk while the other hand slips the book card into the pocket.
    Removing the charging cards from books keeps these charging cards in active circulation until filled, instead of a large number remaining in books in the stacks for an indefinite period. ...
    When a person returns a number of books issued on several borrowers' cards the charging card in each book on which is stamped date due and borrower's number shows at a glance on which card a book is stamped.

    K. Smith revealed the discharging technique used at his library (210).

    In a small library with Dickman the usual procedure is to permit the returned books to pile up for a while, thus enabling some work - overdues, reserves, registration processing or something - to be carried out in the counter itself with purely nominal interruptions. This may be considered bad practice - but with small staffs it is always attempted, and I have found at our own branches is well nigh impossible with Brown Charging. It can be done - I have done it - with Dickman. Then an intensive drive on discharging coincides with the periodic shelving and wastes no time at all.

    In comparing this system with the Browne System, Harrod expressed his impression of this discharging method (203).

    It takes longer for the staff to discharge books because they have to be examined in the presence of the borrower, put on one side if busy, and examined later on in order to be discharged.

On the matter of overdues, Smith found that a numerical index of borrowers was needed. The borrower's number must be looked up in a "register" before overdue notices
could be sent out. He thought this its "one real weakness."
With Browne the name and address could be taken from the
reader's card.

But the borrower's number becomes an item of great
importance in Smith's scheme of interavailability (211).

We have a charging system wherein a reader keeps this
unit [card] and could, in true interavailability, walk into
any library and use it without penalizing himself in any
way. Let us visualize a theoretical idealistic scheme with
a nation-wide Dickman charging system.... Let the authority on whose voting list the reader appears issue his
ticket. This ticket has as its number a mixed notation
similar to that of a motor car registration. The letters
would represent the authority, simple enough surely. The
numbers following would be the number of the particular
reader in the readers' register, e.g., NE 46321 where
NE had been agreed to represent Newcastle. ....This
reader we will imagine to be a commercial traveller. He
uses his ticket in the normal way to borrow a book from
Birmingham to read on his journey to Glasgow, and his
number (NE 46321) is stamped on the book card. He may
finish the book at his hotel in Glasgow and return it by
post to Birmingham. Everything is clear; everyone (even
the librarian) is happy.... It may, however, so happen
that our commercial traveller forgets that he has the book,
and it becomes three weeks or so overdue. Birmingham
cannot send its normal overdue to the defaulting reader,
but forwards it instead to Newcastle, as indicated by the
NE. Here the name and address of the borrower are
turned up and the overdue re-addressed to him. Not a
very involved process, and the reader's home library
makes itself responsible for the collection of the book.

Trudeau recorded the cost of his machine as being sev-
enty-five dollars because "the date charger had four changes
of position. The date of issue machines cost fifty dollars
(207)."

After the initial supplies have been bought the additional
annual expense is slightly greater than that of the old system.

McDougall gave a summary of the expenses incurred at the West Ham Public Library in England (212).

> It cost us to convert this library Ł70 on a basis of 10,000 readers, including all printing and supplies. We have since spent a like sum on structural alterations and replanning our counter.... We also found it necessary to augment our stock in the fiction and juvenile classes by a special expenditure of Ł700, but when we consider that our estimate for new books had been cut for several years by approximately Ł350 each year, that is not surprising. A-Against this expenditure we have to credit an increase in the yield from fines which, consistent with the increase of issues, has increased by 30 per cent, a matter of approximately Ł60 per annum. Annual maintenance costs are hardly affected except as they would be by an increase in issues, however brought about.

Another English library gave a more detailed picture. Christopher presented this analysis (213):

> We will therefore consider the cost only from the angle of an established library converting to the Dickman system. As has been shown the stationery is entirely different, and existing stocks must be scrapped. These, then, are the necessary requirements:-

Bookcharging machine	Ł 10
Date tags	Ł 2 per set
Readers' tickets and tags	Ł 6 per 1,000
Book-cards	9/- per 1,000
Date-cards	9/- per 1,000
Book-pockets	16/- per 1,000
Ticket-holders	28/- per 1,000

> For a library containing 20,000 volumes with 5,000 readers this would involve an expenditure of about Ł75. With regard to the recurring expenses, savings will be effected on readers' tickets, because only one is issued instead of the two or more of the multiple ticket system, and the metal tags can be used for a longer period than the tickets are in force. The recurring expenditure, therefore, even including the ribbon and other replaceable parts of the machine (against which can be balanced the replacement of materials under present systems), should not be much higher than at present.
> Also to be considered with the cost, is the labor nec-

essary to effect the change-over. This involves the re-
labelling of the stock, the writing of pockets, bookpockets
and readers' tickets.

Finney felt that an assistant with a minimum of instruction could manipulate the machines and reminded the
readers that there could be no mistake in copying the borrower's number. She gave the following list of advantages
(201):

Legibility of numbers and dates.

Speed at return desk in seeing at a glance on which
card a book was issued.

Speed at slipping desk by having legible dates on charging cards.

More speed in issuing books.

Speed and accuracy were acclaimed by Trudeau, who
wrote, "It takes a trained assistant approximately a minute
and a quarter to charge ten books. The value of the machine method is the speed and accuracy with which a book
can be stamped (214)."

The West Ham Public Library was reported to have
issued "with one machine at the rate of 603 volumes per
hour. In discharging, it enables readers returning books to
pass straight into the library without waiting, and renders unnecessary the practice of requiring readers to give their
names for the purpose of checking the ticket before handing
it out, a practice which readers object to very strongly (215)."

McDougall remarked that one assistant could issue
1, 200 books in three hours (216).

Some of the advantages to the library staff were pointed out by Smith who had used the Browne system (217).

For rather more than three years I was in charge of
that branch [which used the Dickman System], and from
my own experience I know that a bigger issue can be adequately coped with by a smaller staff - at one time two
of us regularly dealt with an issue of over two hundred
books per hour and remained sane and good-tempered. By
this I mean that we actually issued two hundred plus books

in one hour, taking in a corresponding number and answering the innumerable service questions in person and
by telephone, new registrations and the what-have-yous
of small lending library service.

... It will be seen that the day's issue takes up approximately one third of the space of the Browne system in
the issue tray. Another obvious advantage for (a) a much
larger issue can be exploited on the counter, and (b) the
discharging assistant can reach a wider range of issues
without moving - a saving in time and fatigue.

The West Ham system was analyzed by Harrod, who
wrote (218):

It is still rather soon to attempt an evaluation of the
West Ham experiment; this can be done more satisfactorily in a year's time. ...

Some things are quite evident already, however, [after
2 months use]. To the borrower, the system is less ir-
ritating because of its apparently smoother working, it is
quicker, and offers an extended and more flexible service.
To the staff, it reduces the possibility of error, but it
makes more work, particularly at the exit counter, compared with the usual English system. To the library
authority, it entails a greater expenditure of money to
supply an adequate selection of books and the provision
of a larger staff to deal with the admittedly increased
work, for the same number of borrowers.

It is the freedom from many restraints in book borrowing which appealed to McDougall. "The Dickman book
charging system simplifies the procedure of multiple issues
of books to the irreducible minimum, it clears away irritat-
ing and anomalous restrictions and makes the library really
free to the reader in that sense, making it unnecessary for
him to take special steps to enjoy its privileges. Everyone
has the full benefits according to his undivided needs (219)."
However, he admired the record keeping potentials of the
Dickman System with which a permanent record was made of
all persons borrowing any particular book.

Christopher dealt with some of the complaints which
had been voiced by English librarians (220).

Naturally, until proficiency in the use of the system is
acquired the Dickman system is much slower, but after a
short period the difference in time taken by this and other

systems of charging is very small. Nevertheless, this combined with larger issues, is sufficient to cause queues inside the lending department, and the assistant in the charging counter must always be on the alert, to prevent this happening....

The possibilities of an assistant being released for other duties would not appear to be as advertised, because of the increased issues, with more books to be discharged, shelved, and charged....

Great objection has been raised against the use of numbers for readers, but although under present systems argument may have proved them unnecessary, the numbering of readers under the Dickman system is essentially a part of the system. Not to use numbers would mean having a costly metal tag containing the reader's name and address, and also book cards of sufficient size to hold these particulars. It must be understood that the reader's ticket is not retained, and that some record must be kept. Because of this use of numbers, the numerical register must be kept to allow for cross-reference from numbers to person in the use of queries and overdues....

The success, or failure, of the system must be judged by the results. The object of the system is to provide almost unlimited facilities for every reader, and the result of the policy can be seen in the statistics of the various Dickman libraries. Three of the libraries show startling increases in all classes. In the other library, the Muswell Hill Branch of the Hornsey Libraries, the statistics reveal a different state of affairs. The number of non-fiction issues over all classes was greatly increased in the first month of working, but after a short time these issues dropped almost to the normal of the previous system. Besides this the fiction issues showed enormous increases, forming 90 per cent of the total increase.

... This is a special problem, in what might be termed a "special" district [upper middle class, where women have plenty of leisure to read novels], and the failure of the readers to appreciate the system, cannot be accepted as an indictment of the system as it might be applied elsewhere....

In connection with this particular problem is the broader one of whether the ordinary stock of a library will stand up to the draining effects of such a system.

Another advantage is the interchange of books which is possible. Books taken from one branch may be returned at any other library in the system.... This is

possible because the reader has no ticket, and the books
can be sent back to the appropriate library to be discharged at any convenient time.

The Toledo Method of the Dickman Charging was
judged superior to the ordinary Dickman Charging in the following way (221):

The economies which can be effected with the use of
the Toledo Method are very substantial.
The triple charge of the Newark Card System - book
card, date slip and borrower's card - are reduced to just
one while the borrower is at the charging desk - the book
card.
All discharging on the borrower's card is eliminated.
Inasmuch as the average life of a reader's card is approximately three months, the identification card will save
an average of four replacements per year per borrower.
Thirty-three and one-third percent of the original cost
of the machine installation will be saved by substituting
the single date Model "A" for the four date Model "B"
machine, which is ordinarily required for use with the
Date Due Method of charging.

Riggs explained that the "Three columns of dates are
used and as each column reaches the middle dividing line it
is cancelled by a line drawn through it.   There is no waste
in the date card stock except the few dates that are stamped
on cards in excess of the number used for the day."   In addition, she records two advantages which were appreciated at
Toledo (222).

3. Simplicity of operation.   We have been much interested in the fact that the borrowers are not inclined to
talk over the desk when the machine is in use and on this
account the charging can easily be done by responsible
pages, thus releasing the assistants for more important
services.   There seems to be nothing to get out of order.
4. Saving from eye strain and fatigue. .... After the
first week or two, this release from eye strain was given
by the staff as the leading factor contributing to the reduction of fatigue.   Since we began using the machine for
charging, the circulation has been the highest in the library's history and yet it has been carried by practically
the same staff with less confusion at the desk and with
less wear and tear on the staff.

Smith admitted that "There are odd minor snags I know - worn numbers, interchanged date cards, the possibility of a reader taking out more than his allowance of fiction. ... But these abuses and the normal results of human frailty happen in every system and every sphere, and prevent life from becoming very drab (210)."

Of those who found such "evils of the machine" apparent, McDougall wrote in descriptive terms (223).

Only over their dead bodies would mechanical systems be allowed to enter their libraries. One would think that this evil thing picked the readers up in its maw at the entrance, carried them through a process, and discharged them, loaded up with the right books and breathless, at the exit. All lending library technique is apt to be mechanical in the sense of doing the same thing over and over again in precisely the same way, and is, therefore, apt to become monotonous.

Gaylord Charging System

An electric charging machine was introduced to librarians by an article which appeared in the 1931 Library Journal. Sara Patterson wrote (224):

Each operation performed by the machine is done better and more accurately than by hand. Printing done by the machine is always legible - handwriting is not.
There is less fatigue or nervous strain on the desk attendants during "rush" periods, and it is unnecessary for them to be relieved as frequently when charging is done the automatic way. The desk attendants can answer questions while making a charge, and still accuracy is assured.

The machine was described by Marietta Daniels as being absolutely accurate. "Working on a charge plate basis it definitely identifies the borrower.... In the top of the machine are two slots into which the borrower's card and the book card are inserted in order to charge the book. ... A date holder consisting of a piece of metal on which are attached four embossed date plates is also in the machine. These four date plates allow for charging on the current date, or on any date the book is due. ...A small dial on the left side of the machine controls the date to be printed on the book card.

Borrower's card contains a metal embossed number plate (225)."

In a descriptive pamphlet put out by Gaylord entitled Mrs. Brewster's Inspiration, published in 1938, it is mentioned that "the cost of the machine is less than ten cents a day (226)!"

According to Patterson "Borrowers take better care of cards on which a number plate is inserted, and they are also more likely to have their cards with them when borrowing books." The book cards should be plain, measuring 7. 5 x 12. 5. Those in use at the library may be used until the supply is exhausted provided that they are this size. When the card is placed in the charging machine (113)

a corner of the book card is cut off. This causes the card to be placed a little further down in the slot the next time it is inserted. Thus the machine always prints in a space just above the previous printing so that no space is wasted. After the lower half of the card is filled, the upper and lower half of the reverse side are filled. About forty-two charges may be made on a borrower's card and book card.

It is more practical to use date cards rather than date slips with this machine. If a record of the date and borrower's number is desired on the date card, this card may be inserted in the machine when the book is charged. The date and borrower's number will then be automatically printed on it. If this record is not desired, a number of date cards may be stamped at one time for use later.

The charging procedure was recorded by Daniels. She found it to be "less fatiguing motion than in inking stamps and stamping dates, and a greater saving in time (227)."

... To charge a book, the borrower's card and the book card are inserted in the two slots in the top of the machine. The machine, operating automatically, prints the date and the borrower's card number on the book card. Each time the book card is placed in the machine a corner is cut off, permitting the card to be placed a little further into the slot the next time it is inserted.

Gaylord Bros. asserted that "there is great saving in time, not only in the actual charging of books but also in the time spent in determining fines due, number of books charged out to a certain borrower, where to file book cards in the charging trays after they have been removed for any reason, etc., etc. (228)."

Patterson explained the first point by saying "There can be no question as to the fines to be imposed because the date and borrower's number are plainly printed on the book card (224)."

With Gaylord, book cards are normally filed according to date as in the Newark system, but Washington University maintained a classified arrangement attaching signal tabs to the cards to designate the date due. This altered his overdue procedure (227).

.... There are twelve colors available in these tabs, one for each of the twelve days during each two-week period that the library is open. ...On the morning following the date the books are due, all cards bearing the color for that date are removed and transferred to an "overdue" file from which recall and overdue notices are sent out.

The advantages, according to Gaylord Bros., are speed and low cost (229).

Speed... Reports from libraries using the machine prove that 3 to 5 charges can be made in the machine while one is being completed by hand.
Cost.... Since your charging system is not changed, but only the method of charging, the actual installation expense is kept at a minimum. The yearly rental fee for the machine is comparable to that for a telephone.

In another pamphlet appears this note (230):

Accuracy is assured.
There is no possibility of transposing figures.
The dates and numbers are printed on the cards automatically.
Saves time and confusion ... and eliminates errors.

On a bookmobile, Gaylord fills a need, according to the users, who wrote: "A fast acting, automatic charging

machine is almost a necessity in accurately handling such a
large circulation in the limited time available on a bookmobile schedule.... There is no question about its value in
speeding up the charging of books and in eliminating argu-
ments with students. We have a bookmobile staff of three.
The biggest one-day circulation handled by them was 1059 at
one school in a five and one-half hour period (231)."

Chapter 3

Double Record Versus
Single Record Charging Systems

The charging systems accepted by most public libraries were not often acceptable to college, university, and technical libraries where more information was deemed necessary.
Frederick Kilgour gave the following description of the basic
loan records which were often kept (232):

> To make books available, university libraries have devel-
> oped three kinds of loan records, which may be used in
> any combination. The most important of these is the book
> record file, in which the charge slips are arranged by
> call number. The book record, indicating the location of
> any desired book, is the fundamental loan record in a un-
> iversity or research library.
>   The book record file is often supplemented by a "date
> due" record. The primary function of this record is to
> make it possible for the loan librarian to recall books as
> soon as they become overdue. The recall of overdue
> books increases the availability of books to all borrowers
> and, when there is a large demand for a comparatively
> few specific books, this record is indispensable.
>   A third record that university libraries sometimes
> maintain is a borrowers' file in which are recorded the
> books lent to individual borrowers. This record has six
> primary functions; it shows what books are charged to
> each borrower; it serves as a means of identifying bor-
> rowers; it makes possible the limitation of the number of
> books lent to each borrower; it is useful to ascertain
> whether or not men leaving the university still have li-
> brary books charged to them; it is a convenient file in
> which to record fines owed and paid; and it is often the
> source of such information as borrowers' addresses. In
> short, the borrowers' record supplies unessential but
> sometimes convenient information. The majority of li-
> braries do not keep this record.

In the nineteenth and early twentieth centuries, in univ-

ersity libraries, if circulation privileges were extended to
students, the record was usually kept on book cards or temporary slips. [See reference 53.] But often these libraries
were open merely for reference. In 1893, Lodilla Ambrose
referred to a study which had been made of college libraries.
She wrote (233):

> I have not noted any college whose library is not a cir-
> culating one for its faculty. The major part of those
> who give any information on this subject state that stud-
> ents may draw books for home use. Several large insti-
> tutions limit students to a reference use of the library,
> but these provide long library hours.... One college per-
> mits a student to take a book out if he deposits the value
> of the book.

T. W. Koch made the following comment after book circulation privileges had been granted to students at the University
of Michigan in 1906 (234).

> In the one semester during which we have been loaning
> books to students we have found that the extension to un-
> dergraduates of the privilege of borrowing books has cost
> us next to nothing in the way of additional service at the
> desk; it has not interfered with the use of the library by
> the faculty, and we do not believe that there is a single
> professor at Michigan who would vote for the abolition of
> the newly granted privileges.

The double or triple record systems see reference
no. 1 were adopted by these libraries which desired proper
book control. In 1946, J. E. Wright stated, "This system
of recording loans has been in use for a good many years
now and it has proved very satisfactory. It is probably very
largely due to the accuracy of the records that in general reminders receive a prompt reply and that very little friction
occurs between the library and its users (235)."

Attempts were made at simplification. Slips were
backed or interleaved with carbon. [See reference no. 122]
A perforated card was adopted to make procedure easier.
[See reference no. 100]

M. Hood noted the prevelance of double record systems but also the problems (236).

There is some indication, however, that libraries are

looking more and more with favor on the methods used in
a single record system and are adapting visible charging
schemes and machines to their own special requirements.
The single record system is economical of time and material and helps to reduce the possibility of error which
exists in a double record system. On the other hand, the
single record system requires a greater degree of cooperation from library users in filling out the call cards
completely, legibly, and accurately.

It was believed by H. G. Bousfield that as "librarians
began to experiment with new methods, circulation procedures, particularly in college and university libraries, became
characterized by a high degree of dissimilarity.... This was
not the case in areas of cataloging and acquisitions, where
procedures were, to a great extent, standardized (237)."

Helen Geer made a comparison of charging systems
used by college and university libraries. She observed (238):

It can be seen that all of them, with the exception of the
Double Record Charging System, utilize a single charge
file. Some use call slips or book cards, and only one requires a machine. Date due slips are used in all except
one, which has a transaction card as a date card, and
filing is done by call number except in the Accession
Number Charging System.

Ralph H. Parker reminded us that to a limited extent,
"the development in circulation control procedures applied
both to college and university as well as to public libraries
(239)."

But the need for more flexible controls in collegiate libraries limited the usefulness of the charging machines
and the prevalence of closed stacks reduced the value of
self-charging systems....
In all systems requiring two or more types of circulation files (class, date, borrower), the time consumed in
handling the clerical details of circulation is indeed great.
A two-card record is more than twice as expensive to
maintain as a single-card record because all operations
must be performed twice, and some operations, like making dummy cards, must be added to this doubled routine.
Historically, the problem of the collegiate library has
been to find a single-card charging system which will ren-
der all the information.

In a later article he wrote of the possible trend in this "second great period of experimentation" toward punched, notched, or tabbed call slips in college and university librar- ies and to a transaction card in public libraries (240).

The adoption of an indefinite loan of books was sug- gested by McGaw and Komidar [See reference nos. 399-400]. Harvard University's Lamont Library devised their accession number charging system.

The reason for the advent of the great number of new methods of charging are dealt with by A. H. Trotier in this manner (241):

> If librarians have made significant progress in recent
> years in the direction of mechanization of library opera-
> tions, it has been not only because more machines and
> appliances suited to library applications have been avail-
> able, but because increasing costs of library services
> have focused attention on ways and means whereby these
> services could be carried on at costs they could afford to
> pay, and also because the growing problem of maintaining
> the staff required for accomplishing the essential functions
> of the library necessitated the substitution of machines for
> personnel wherever possible.

A suggestion was given by W. H. Jesse and E. E. Goehring for those who were faced with making changes in circulation procedures (242).

> ... the first factor to be determined before deciding upon
> a new system is whether a call slip or a book card should
> be considered the desirable minimum; that is, whether
> most of the Charges will be paged from the stacks or tak-
> en from the shelves (stack or open) by the reader. If a
> call slip must be made out for most of the books, the
> key-sort or punch-card type of system may be used, thus
> reducing the amount of writing for a majority of the bor-
> rowers at least. Many libraries, however, will find that
> the greatest number of their charges are from open shelves
> or open stacks and that, consequently, a bookcard must
> be considered the desirable minimum. It is these librar-
> ies which are faced with a specific problem needing a
> rapid and satisfactory solution, i. e. how to get overdues
> out of a classed file....
> Since the problem is thus reduced to one of finding a
> suitable sorting device, possible solutions begin to present

themselves; for example, a mere pencil mark placed on
the book-card would permit sorting by means of a photo-
electric cell, or a small nonprotruding steel clip would
allow for sorting by means of an electro-magnet.   To
these could be added other devices evolved from fundamental physical principles, but at this point the problem
should be turned over to technicians who will probably
have to be found outside the profession.

Jack Dove discussed in detail the problem of arrangement of records - a problem with which these technical libraries also are concerned (243).

The obvious first question to ask is why do we maintain
records of books on loan at all?   Presumably for a variety of reasons, including (i) to know what books we have
on loan and to whom; (ii) to have a statistical record of
their number; (iii) to safeguard public property; and (iv)
to ensure that books are not retained too long by the
thoughtless and careless.
Are these reasons really justifiable?   In my opinion
all except the second are....
This brings me to the methods used of arranging the
issue.   They are numerous.   The inner forms, to coin a
term, might be as follows:
i.   Strictly class order for non-fiction; alphabetical order for fiction.
ii.   Alphabetical order by author within main classes
for non-fiction; alphabetical order for fiction.
iii.   Alphabetical order for non-fiction and fiction alike,
in separate sequences.
iv.   Alphabetical order for non-fiction and fiction in one
sequence.
v.   Class order for non-fiction, accession order for
fiction.
vi.   Accession number order throughout.
The outer forms may be:
i.   Individual date order throughout.
ii.   Individual date order for books up to say four
weeks overdue, others in monthly sequence.
iii.   Weekly cumulations.
iv.   Fortnightly cumulations.
v.   Monthly cumulations.
vi.   Monday to Thursday issue cumulated; Friday and
Saturday separate owing to their excessive numbers or
variants of this method.
We need a revolutionary change of method and it may

well be that an electronic contraption, recently described
by W. H. Stock of the Royal Academy of Music at the
last London and Home Counties Branch Conference, will
be the solution. Wellsian, maybe, but it will have to
come for I cannot believe that photocharging is the sole
answer.   Until that invention is patented, and it is a part
of our routine that a mechanical device is capable of handling, how to arrange these book records?   Whether we
use the Browne or Dickman methods is immaterial.

I have been giving a trial to the cumulation of a fortnight's issue into one alphabetical sequence....   It is
speedier to discharge books and reserved books are more
quickly traced.   In both cases, the assistant has to look
in not more than two places for current books and the
Saturday morning queues are more quickly dispersed.   In
an issue of 493,000 from the Central Lending Library with
13,000 reserved books in a year, the tracing of reservations is speeded up considerably.

The biggest disadvantage is the actual filing of the current day's records into the main sequence....   Overdues,
of course, present another problem and need a fresh approach from the staff.   A visual chart has been prepared
showing the fines due on any particular day within the
past three months.

.... Reverting to overdues, it will be seen that there
is no record of the actual date on which a book is due
for return.   Hence, notice cannot be despatched in daily
batches.   Rather, a whole fortnight's loans have to be
written for at one time.

In the early stages, it is likely that there will be a
greater number of errors in book discharging.   Each book
must have its own identification number and this would be
the key if ten Nevil Shute's Round the Bend were together
....

The larger the issue, the greater need for some control over the public.   This can be done by using hanging
signs indicating at which part of the counter readers
should present their books for discharging....

.... I am sure that it is [worth the risk], particularly
if your issue does not exceed 400,000 at one service
point....   If you want a record of your precious non-
fiction and fiction separately, use some Samson Novelty
Tabulators as I now do, and as Hampstead does.   They
are only 30/- each and will save the time of someone re-
ligiously counting the charges each day....

Mr. Latham of Swansea proposed a revised issue system for non-fiction records in the Library World of Sept-

ember, 1949, and in November of that year, Mr. Barlow of Nuneaton told how he had gone even further. He is now keeping his Monday-Friday issues in one sequence and the Saturdays to themselves.... My own impressions are that, up to 400,000 issues, the system would work quite satisfactorily. Over this point, however, the cumulation of the current day's issue into the main sequence is a very lengthy process. But for reservations, tracing books quickly and staff convenience, it is to be recommended.

Circulation records show the number and classes of books which were used but O. V. Cook recognized that they do not show why a book was used or if its use filled the need (244).

Another part of good service occurred to William Randall who insisted that the librarian should charge the books (245).

The details of charging and discharging books may be delegated to student assistants, but it is a risk to do so. As in a public library, so in a college library the best personalities of the staff should be placed where they will serve the public. In a small library the librarian will be the most experienced member of the staff, and he should spend much of his time in public service. He will be of greater value to the institution if he establishes valuable contacts with the members of the college than if he prepares, for example, a first-rate catalog for their use.

Double Record System

The Double Record Charging System, which was popular with university libraries, was based on earlier card and duplicate slip systems. [See reference nos. 43, 44, 56].

The Oberlin College, in 1912, reported using a duplicate record system (246).

Book pocket contains two cards, one white, one pink with author's name, title of book and call number and accession number. Borrower signs name on both and leaves on desk. Dating slip with date of issue is put in book pocket. Assistant stamps both cards with date of issue - filing white cards by call number under date and pink card under borrower's name. These are ultimately divided into two files, the "day file" and the "long file," the latter including books drawn by professors and others privileged to retain them more than two weeks.

T. G. Schwartz, of the College of the City of New York, believed that the date due was more important than the date of issue because "the date-due on the book charging card renders it possible to inform inquirers whether it will be worth their while to reserve a book, whether the book may come too late to be of service, or may never be returned because it is charged to a delinquent borrower (247)."

At the Illinois State Library, A. L. Smith remarked, the patron must write name and address on one card, only his name on the other card. Both cards are stamped with the date due (248).

When a book was returned at the Oberlin College Library, the dating slip was taken out and saved for future use. The book was discharged by finding the book card in the file and checking the borrower's name. The pink card was then withdrawn from the borrower's file. At the University of Kansas Library a similar system was maintained with classified file and borrowers' file. The borrower's record was found behind a card bearing his name. This card had not been signed or dated when the book was charged as was the card for the class file (246).

At the Illinois State Library loans were made for two weeks with the privilege of a two-week renewal. Collections loaned to communities were checked out for longer periods and no date due record was kept for them (248).

Geer remarked that the Double Record Charging System is a slow and cumbersome process. She added (249):

.... The importance of knowing at all times where a given book is, whether it is on the shelves or in circulation, in order to give this information to faculty members, has made college librarians reluctant to experiment with other methods for charging out books.

Files often become of such great size that some solution must be found. C. J. McHale recommended the use of a "Grandstand file" composed of three sloping front units which hold all the cards needed in double record filing systems (250).

The time involved in the filing of book cards as well
as that expended in the actual charging became a problem at
the Memphis State College Library. H. F. McGaw recorded
the following methods which were adopted (251):

> Our industrial arts department made for us, according to
> specifications, four metal boxes, just wide enough to hold
> a date card, high enough to conceal about two-thirds of
> the card, and deep enough to provide for two compart-
> ments to hold, say, fifty or a hundred cards each. These
> boxes were placed on the circulation counter. By each
> box we have a sign.... One sign reads: "14-Day Books.
> Follow Directions on Box." On the box (equipped with
> card holder) are these directions: "14-Day Books. Sign
> book card and place it in front compartment of this box.
> From rear compartment take date card, which is already
> stamped, and place it in book pocket. Write nothing on
> the book card except your name."
> There are corresponding signs and directions for a 7-
> day box and a 3-day box. [The fourth box is for books
> be read in the reading room only].
> To provide for a date-due file, the following routine
> was established. On a blank book card...stamped at the
> top with the date the particular books are due, the call
> numbers of all 14-day book charges are entered. Like-
> wise, on another card, the call numbers of 7-day book
> charges, etc. At the end of the day these cards (each
> card will accommodate thirty call numbers) are filed be-
> hind the proper guides. Four days after a particular
> date the date cards are pulled and the cards of all books
> listed thereon, are searched for in the loan file. Those
> not found represent books already returned. Past due not-
> ices are sent on the others, ...card is scratched through
> indicating that the books are in....

D. M. Cooper was faced with a similar problem at
the University of Washington. She described the modifications
which were tried (252).

> For a period of a month...we took the pencil stamps and
> the ink pads off the desk, and substituted previously
> stamped date-due cards for each of our five pencil stamps.
> ...
> The procedure failed to give the results we wanted and
> brought a variety of headaches with it that we had not

known before. It saved no time because it only substitut-
ed for stamping the notions of picking up the date-due
card and putting it in the book pocket. We found it much
more difficult to pick up the correct card quickly and put
it in a book pocket than to handle a pencil stamp.... We
were constantly having to make special charges of one day,
overnight, five days, and so on for students having per-
mission to borrow reference material for special lengths
of time. It was impossible to provide previously stamped
date-due cards for all conceivable dates needed in a day's
work, and even so it was impossible for the clerk later
counting the circulation to know which date we had used
for each special charge.

We came then to our ...alternative, that of ceasing to
require the borrower's signature on the book card. This
meant that we were to be wholly dependent on the slip
record for the identity of the borrower.... Call slips
are easily lost and often accidently destroyed; book cards
more rarely so. In spite of this seeming risk, we felt
that if the new system saved as much of the patron's time
as we thought it would by cutting the charging time, a
higher book loss would be a cheap price to pay.

On April 1, 1947 we initiated the new charging routine.
Books moved across the desk with an ease and quickness
that were amazing.... As quickly as the book, card, and
slip could be stamped, and the student body card checked,
the patron had his book.

In September, [when inventory was taken] only four
cards appeared for books lost as a result of the new
charging system.

.... We feel that even if our losses are tripled the
improvement in service amply justifies them.

The more technical libraries were not eager for these
short-cuts. J. Thomas felt that the duplicate charge was
necessary because it tells at a glance which books and how
many an individual has. Often this information was asked
for (253).

An example of the more complicated records required
by specialized libraries was discussed by Leonard W. Duck
of the Henry Watson Music Library (254).

There are two distinct sides to the activities of the Watson Music Library. One - with which we are not here
concerned - is the lending of music and books about music to personal borrowers. For this purpose, ratepayers',

students' and subscribers' tickets are issued, and normal
lending library procedure followed. The more unorthodox
though equally important service is to supply sufficient
copies of choral and orchestral works to meet the needs
of music societies, choirs and orchestras, the period of
loan being normally three months. ....As over 24,000
items out of a stock of 318,200 are normally on issue at
once, it will readily be appreciated that the machinery for
recording these issues must be accurate, flexible and
reasonably foolproof. It must reveal the following information - and it must reveal it in a minimum of time, as
many short-distance requests are received by telephone
and the last-minute emergency call is so common as to be
almost a matter of routine:

(1) The number of copies of a work immediately a-
vailable.

(2) The number of copies of a work available at any
specified future date (and conversely the earliest date upon which a given number of copies will be available).

(3) In the case of orchestral parts, which are borrowed for every imaginable combination of instruments, a
detailed breakdown showing the number of parts available
for each instrument in a particular work.

(4) The number of sets on loan to each society, with
the date for return.

....In addition it must be possible simply and effectively to reserve music for a future date - six months ahead
is the working maximum.... Finally, it is necessary that
the borrower shall have some record of the transaction,
both as a reminder of the date of return and as an arbiter
in occasional disputes regarding the non-return of odd
parts.

The apparatus by which this information is marshalled
is as follows. ....a separate record is kept for each
transaction. This method has been adopted because no
two loans are alike....

Each batch of music issued at one time is therefore
entered on a white flimsy, a duplicate in blue being produced at the same time. This records the name and address of the borrower...the date upon which the music is
due for return, and full details of the items issued. It
is filed under the name of the borrower, the blue duplicate
being sent with the music. As a further check, borrowers who call personally for their music are asked to check
over the contents and sign the back of the issue slip before leaving. The whole array of white slips, clipped to
borrower's tickets and filed in alphabetical order of their

names, forms the record of issue proper....

Every morning the slips from the previous day are assembled and the information transferred to the appropriate 5 by 3 card, one of which exists for every work on issue. These cards supply all the information enumerated in desiderata (1) to (3) above, and form an indispensable part of the system. Filed in classified order, they act as combined issue and reservation cards, and are set out in columns as under:

Composer, title No. of copies in Library							
Issued				Reserved			
Borrower	No.	Due	Back	Borrower	No.	Date	Period

Each item is crossed off as it is cleared. The number of copies available is ascertained by totalling the numbers of sets on issue not "due back" before the required date, adding those reserved for the relevant period, and subtracting the result from the total number of copies in the library. The earliest date upon which a given number of copies will be available is found by adding together the number of sets to be returned and not already reserved until the required total is assembled, and noting the return date of the completing set.

The record of orchestral parts is simplified by the use of a rubber stamp, which in a rectangle measuring 2 1/2 in. by 3/4 in. contains the abbreviated names of all the more common musical instruments, with space to enter the number issued against each. This stamp is used both on the record cards and on the issue slips.

When a request is received and confirmed by reference to the record cards, details are entered on a temporary slip and filed until the following morning, when all "orders" are withdrawn from stock and placed on a reserve shelf, the temporary slips being then filed in date order. These slips automatically come to light on the required day and notify the staff that the order has to be entered on an issue slip, and either despatched or kept at hand until called for. The interim period on a reserve shelf, while not being absolutely necessary for the workings of the system, provides a double check and renders it virtually impossible for one work to be reserved for two people at the same time.

It will be seen that the procedure is basically one of

double entry, with machinery for long term reservation, and a record of each transaction for the use of the borrower. When music is returned, the relevant slip is taken from the issue and stamped "returned" with the date. Morning routine includes crossing off those items on the record cards which correspond with these cancelled slips, entering new items taken out the previous day, and taking fresh orders from stock and either placing them on the reserve shelves or entering them on the duplicate flimsies for immediate use. Weekly routine entails going through the issue for overdues. This is the one process in which details are not automatically provided, - this could only be accomplished by systematic triple entry, and it is calculated that the time taken in doing this would be more than is involved in the weekly scrutiny for overdues.

Voos and Costello mentioned the problem of security with which they were faced at a government research library (255).

All personnel using the library [Army ordnance technical center library] must be checked for their security clearance so that we do not circulate documents to those who do not have a "need to know." This in itself slows up the circulation process, but because regulations require a receipt for all classified documents borrowed, we have had to set up a three-card system.

The Atomic Energy Research Library made use of a quadruplicate record of loan. M. Gosset wrote (256):

The loan records are kept in quadruplicate, each copy being a different colour, white, yellow, pink or blue. The white copy is sent with the publication with a request to the borrower to sign and return it. The yellow copy is filed under the catalogue heading of the work, the pink and the blue under the date due back. When the white slip is returned it is filed under the borrower's name and is returned to him when the book is returned. Each day the blue and pink slips under that date are moved to the front of the drawer, the pink slip is used for calling in the loan, the blue remains as a record of a loan outstanding. If the first recall is ignored, a second recall requesting the immediate return of the borrowed item is made using an appropriate form. When this fails the librarian intervenes, generally with success.
Loans [of reports]

The borrower's name is entered on the back of the main card. All security classified reports are issued with a numbered receipt. The duplicate receipt is filed in the library under the borrower's name until the signed receipt is returned by the borrower. A dispatch book is used and is checked each day to see that all receipts have been returned. Declassified or unclassified reports are treated in the same way as published documents.

A master file was thought necessary by E. W. Browning (257).

.... The book card was taken from each book stored in the attic and filed at the charging desk. Now if an attic book is called for, the attendant has only to look in her file. If the book card is not there, the book is not in, and she has no useless trip to make.

Mrs. P. A. Marvin described the experience she had with a master file and the modifications which were made (258).

All books shelved in the reading rooms were listed in this master file of location. Those not listed were automatically known to be stack books... a small periodical file was appended to this file. The file not only answers questions of location, but indicates what volumes are currently at the bindery....

While the master file worked independently, it was still necessary to check in the numerical book-card file to determine if a book were charged out.

The final and most ingenious development in the system was the consolidation of the date-due file of call slips with the master file. By filing the call slip directly in front of the master file card for the book it became possible to determine - by checking only once and in only one file - the location of the book, whether or not it was charged out, to whom the book was charged and when it was due so that it would be available for the person desiring it.

An attempt was made to simplify the charging procedure for the patron of libraries which maintained double or triple records. Woledge and Page described briefly one method which eliminates much of the writing involved (259).

Card charging is not usually employed in universities; the number of books which may be borrowed by each reader

would make it impracticable. The borrower fills in his
slip for each book, and the slips are filed in triplicate
under borrower, book borrowed, and the date when due
back.   It is great economy in labor to have the slips folded and backed or interleaved with carbon, so that the borrower himself makes the two additional copies required..
.. It is useful to have a slip inserted in each book, pref-
erably at the end, on which the assistant issuing it can
stamp the date on which it is due for return....

In very small libraries, loans may be satisfactorily
entered in a ledger; but it will generally be found more
satisfactory to have a 5 in. by 3 in. voucher filled in for
each loan, and returned to the borrower when he returns
the book; carbon copies may be used for keeping records
under date due and name of borrower as well as under the
book borrowed.

In 1939, **F. A.** Sandall commented on the system being
used at the Massey Agricultural College at Palmerston North,
New Zealand.   "A piece of cheap, stiffish, coloured cover paper or card 8 in. by 3 in., is perforated across twice at dis-
tances of 5 in. and 6 1/2 in. from one end.   "After the borrower fills out one section of the card the book is charged.
This section serves as the book record in a triple entry filing system.   Writing is not eliminated but merely transferred to the library staff.   "The two remaining sections of
the card (which are also marked 'for use of library staff only') are, of course, for the borrower and date record (260)."

At the Kodak Research Library, a triple record is
made possible by having it recorded on a continuous band of
perforated paper.   **M. D.** Gauntlet believed this system which
produces carbon copies, more successful than the former
triple record system which made use of the interleaved carbon technique (261).

One type of form produced for commercial use seemed
promising.   It is supplied in flat packs of interfolded
forms, each pack containing up to five sets in different
colours, according to the number of carbon copies required at one writing.   The forms, normally used for orders, requisitions, receipts, etc., are obtainable in several sizes, the smallest of which is 6 to 6 1/2 inches
long and 4 to 4 1/4 inches wide.   The pack is loaded into
a "register" in which successive forms are guided between fixed sheets of carbon paper into position under a
window exposing a single form.

The register may be a large desk model holding both the pack and the completed forms or a small, portable model in which the paper is ejected and the forms torn off as required. This portable type seemed suitable for our purpose. At the time (1948) there was only one on the market. This measured 8 x 5 x 1 1/2 inches and held fifty sets of 4-5/16 x 6-inch forms in duplicate or triplicate. This form size is convenient in that, if two loan forms are printed on each, the 4-5/16 x 3-inch half-size forms can be filed in ordinary catalogue drawers. It was necessary for the manufacturers to print the required wording for us and also to make double the usual number of perforations. The fixed carbons do not extend to the full height of the 4-5/16 x 6-inch form, since the top normally carries a manufacturer's letter heading. Therefore, the top half of the window had to be covered so that writing was always carried out on the form in the lower position.

From 1948 to 1951 we used 200 packs, i.e. 20,000 loan forms, for recording an average of thirty loans a day. This first register proved generally satisfactory but had two minor disadvantages in the special circumstances of a library where the borrowers themselves fill in loan forms. Firstly, the sets of forms were merely pulled on by hand and had a tendency to get out of register when pulled by a careless borrower. Secondly, the carbon papers, which were in the form of small sheets held on pins at the bottom of the register, sometimes tore away from the pins owing to the friction between them and the band of paper.

By 1951 there were available other portable registers of slightly different design, but most of them suitable for our type of work. We selected W. H. Smith's "Alacra" in which the paper is moved by a sprocket wheel which engages with holes along the margin and thereby ensures correct register. Supply rolls of carbon paper are held at the side of the "window" and carbons are pulled across at right-angles to the direction of the paper movement when a new surface is required. The loan card size is 4-5/6 x 3-1/4 inches.

With both makes of register the forms were supplied in triplicate sets of white, pink and yellow. The register is kept on a small sloping platform on the assistant's desk and borrowers themselves complete the loan forms and eject them from the top of the register. At intervals during the day the assistant removes the continuous band of completed forms and accumulates them for the following day's filing.

The white, pink and yellow forms are filed by author, date, and borrower's name respectively. The method of recalling overdue loans within the organization is more economical of staff time than the usual method of written reminders. A pink form corresponding to an overdue loan is sent through the works' post in an envelope bearing a duplicate request to return the overdue material, or, if a renewal is required, to return the form in the same envelope. The borrower usually responds within a few days and the envelopes, which are not sealed, are used repeatedly, until the space for writing names is completely filled up. Few borrowers fail to respond to such reminders but in order to keep a check on these few a coloured paper clip is attached to a yellow slip as the corresponding pink slip is despatched. The colour is changed weekly and a visual picture of overdue loans is thus presented. The few unresponsive borrowers are reminded by special letter, telephone, etc.

Gauntlet noted the convenience of this system for loan records after several years of use, but he had much to say about the cost, the one drawback to its adoption by the small special library (261).

.... Neither the register nor the individual packs are costly, but each manufacturer stipulates the ordering of a minimum quantity of forms, usually 10,000 or 20,000, i.e., 20,000 or 40,000 half-size loan forms. Only by insisting on such a minimum can he quote a reasonable price to cover paper and printing. We have recently purchased a minimum stock of 40,000 loan forms which will last some six years and which cost in 1951 about ₤70. It is understandable, however, that many special libraries would hesitate to commit themselves to an untried system for many years ahead and to put a large expenditure on a single year's budget. One Aslib member has already suggested that a possible solution would be for a manufacturer to print a large quantity of standard loan forms which could be held in stock and sold to libraries in small quantities as required. Unless this could be done, the method is probably only of use to a library with a large enough loan service to justify the outlay required.

Tab Systems

We are not to feel that there is a best charging system, reminded Carl Vitz in 1927. "Different systems are
suited to different types and sizes of libraries. That system is best for any particular library which combines most
effectively simplicity, economy in cost, convenience, accuracy, and speed, taking into account both reader and library
(262)."

He remarked that the time record could be kept in
connection with other records "by various devices common
in business. Dated tabs or metal clips on book cards may
indicate the date of return and facilitate the discovery of overdue books in the book record (263)."

An early discovery of the value of these devices was
recorded by Melvil Dewey in 1878. He tried the use of colored date stamps, but these could not be seen without checking through the cards. Using different colors for the different days of issue proved difficult. Fourteen distinct colors
could not be found and cards could not be sorted easily. He
then turned to a date tabbing method (264).

.... The problem was to get a difference in form, so that
each day for four weeks could be made perfectly distinct
in the check-box, though the slips were all in one package.
I think I have solved the difficulty by cutting away nine
tenths of the upper 2mm. (1/16 in.) of each slip, thus
leaving a projection 2 mm. high and five broad. The
Monday slips have this projection at the left, the Saturday
slips at the right corner. Tuesday has 9 mm. at the left
and 36 at the right. Wednesday has 18 at the left and 27
at the right. Thursday, Friday and Saturday have the
right half of the slip divided in the same way. This leaves
an open space nearly as large as the projection between
each row of projections as the slips are put in a package.
The result must be plain. All books issued on any Monday can be taken out in the dark as readily as in the light
.... A glance through the check-box shows the comparative issues of different days in the week. They eye rec-
ognizes at once the very distinct colors used for each of
the four weeks in the month. At the hour for sending
notices, e.g., on Wednesday, all Wednesday slips of the
color which expire that week are delinquent, and the projection at the left of the center indicates each Wednesday
slip as plainly as if it were tipped up with projecting corner. An extra color may be used, so that the delinquent

slips may be left in their proper box.... By having an extra color the blue need not be used again for issues until a week later, by which time the delinquents will be so nearly in that no difficulty will be found in making a list of the few left, or in giving them to the proper person to send for the book.

.... The whole matter is made simple by using in charging the color that expires on the desired day, e.g., if blue were issued for four-week books two weeks ago, then blue would be the color for two-week books today.

(Date Tabs)

Marjorie Hood and Guy Lyle commented on the simplicity of the supplies used with the date tab system at Woman's College library (265).

In changing from a double record system to a single record system, it was necessary to devise a simple and quick way for an assistant to check through the class file each day in order to withdraw the overdues. The new form is printed on a stiff white card (3 x 5 inches) and takes the place of both the call slip and the book card. The essential feature of the system is the date tab, which extends above the top of the card. Tabs are numbered 1-31 and fall in six locations across the three-inch top of the cards. There is, of course, some overlapping of numbers, e.g., numbers 1, 7, 13, 19, 25, and 31 have the same location, being first on the left-hand side of the card. However, this is not confusing in actual practice since most charges clear every two weeks and it is seldom that more than three of these overlapping dates are in the file at the same time.

M. Peebles described the charging slips used with their system. Books are due on only three days of each week (266).

.... Our call slip is a 3" x 5" white card with one-half inch tabs extended at the top. These tabs are cut into thirds so that our call cards have three tabs, a right hand tab, a middle tab, and a left hand tab. The return date of the book is stamped on these tabs. This use of three date tabs was made possible by making books due on Monday, Wednesday, and Friday. Books due on Monday are checked on cards with left hand tabs, Wednesday books use the middle tab, and books due on Friday use

use the right hand tab....

This call card did not meet all of our needs however.
As a result our out file has taken on color. We have
used inexpensive, plain 3" x 5" cards without tabs in
green, blue, tan and yellow. On these cards we make
charges to reserve, browsing room, staff and personal
reserves. By having colored cards we can withdraw any
group of charges we wish for checking. Bindery charges
to other departments in the building are made on regular
call cards.

"Books are charged by the assistant who verifies the
call card with the book and stamps the date due on the date
slip," Hood and Lyle explained. "At frequent intervals the
cards are arranged for filing and counted for statistics (267)."

More mechanics are involved in the charging procedure as outlined by Peebles (268).

.... The call card is filled out by the borrower. The
book is brought to the desk by an assistant who adds the
accession number to the call card and checks the card
for accuracy. He then dates the book and the tab, initials
the call card, tallies the charge on the statistics card, and
files the card in the out file by classification number. This
completes the book charge.

Hood and Lyle related the following method of discharge (267):

Books are now discharged in one operation. The charge
is removed from the class file and placed in front of the
book. After the call numbers on the book plate and call
card are verified, the book is sent to the stacks and the
card thrown away.

The file, which is arranged by classification, serves
also as a date due file, according to Hood and Lyle. With
tabs for identical dates in the same location "it is now a
simple matter to withdraw overdues by checking only the column in which a given date appears. As a double check the
date due may be stamped on the top of the card so that if by
any chance a card remains in the file for a month or more,
there will be no question as to how long the charge has been
overdue (269)."

Peebles advocates one thing more. "When overdue

notices have been sent, a red tab is attached to the call card
with Scotch tape.   This takes very little time and shows at a
glance all the books that are overdue.   Old overdues can then
be withdrawn by pulling the red tabbed cards.   A green tab
is placed on books reported lost (266). "

The following method was used by Hood and Lyle in
dealing with renewals.   The borrower presents a new call
card with the book; "a letter R is written by the date on the
date slip and on the charge.   The book is counted as a new
circulation and the first charge withdrawn when the renewal
charge is filed (267). "

Reserves, faculty loans and other special charges
were dealt with by Geer in her book, Charging Systems (270).

Records for reserves, bindery, carrels, or other special
location charges are made on 3" x 5" cards without tabs
and placed in the regular two-week file.   Being without
tabs, these cards will fall below the date tab cards and
therefore cannot become confused with the regular call
cards.
Faculty loans can be treated in the same manner as
student loans or placed on a colored card in a designated
position (e. g. 12) with the tab left blank.   Date of issue
must be stamped below the tab.   If faculty loans are
made the same way as student loans, a duplicate record
on a 3" x 5" card is made for all overdues and placed
in a file arranged by classification number.   The original
call card is placed in a special file of faculty loans arranged alphabetically by name of borrower.
Undated cards with tabs in a designated position can be
used for student loans falling due on one certain day, such
as at the end of the semester.   Cards with undated tabs
also allow for other types of charges.

The following claims were made by Hood and Lyle
(271):

An evaluation of the system should be considered in terms
of time, accuracy, and economy.   As for time, four facts
stand out: (1) with only one record to make a book is
charged and renewed more quickly; (2) since books are
discharged in one operation, they are slipped in one-half
the time formerly required; (3) overdues are withdrawn
from the file in much less time than was formerly required to check the date due record with the book record;

and (4) most important of all, book cards and book pockets are entirely eliminated.   There is a considerable saving in expenditure for clerical help and supplies in both the Catalog and Circulation Departments.

When it comes to accuracy, there has been no cause for alarm.   In no instance has it been impossible to decipher handwriting and the few inaccuracies in call numbers have been solved quickly by consulting the shelf list. Errors in filing are not cumulative because all charges are withdrawn when they become due regardless of how poorly a charge has been filed.

Geer listed several disadvantages of the system which she saw (272).

1. Call cards with tabs are more expensive than those without, and can be used only once, since they are actually call slips.
2. Said to be less flexible in its adaptation to varying loan periods and reader categories than other systems.
3. Illegibility of borrower's handwriting could cause confusion.

Peebles remarked, "We save book cards, book pockets and fine slips.   We find it almost twice as fast as the old [double record] system (268)."

(Signal Tabs)

The Signal Tabs Charging System was introduced at Bethany to facilitate the checking for overdue books.   Nick Shumar mentioned that the system as used there was based on one due-date each week with books coming due only on Fridays (273).

.... Technically, a book may be kept out for two weeks, but actually, it may be kept out for twenty days.   For example, if a book is charged out on a Saturday, it becomes due two weeks from the following Friday....

The advantages of this system are apparent: (1) the date-due stamp is changed only once a week; (2) the circulation file is checked only once a week; (3) students know books are due on Fridays; (4) work schedules may be arranged for additional help on Saturdays to shelve returned books.

Metal tabs serve to designate the due date, according

to Shumar (273).

The metal tabs are standard library signal tabs, priced
at approximately $1 a hundred, and may be purchased
from any library supply company. Four colors are used:
green designates the first due-period, blue the second due-
period, orange the third due-period, and red designates
overdue books.

At Washington University, Sister Helen informed us,
a self service method of charging is in effect. The borrower writes his name on the book card and stamps his book
(274).

Shumar described the charging procedure at his library where it is not self service (275).

The student, to withdraw a book, simply signs his name
on the book card.... The desk assistant stamps the date-
due on the card and places it in the daily circulation file
by class number. A slip of paper is stamped with the
date-due and placed in the pocket of the book.

After circulation has been counted and statistics recorded, Sister Helen explained, "...clips of the proper col-
or are attached to the book cards. The cards are then filed
into the book record file (276).

According to this writer, discharging consists of a
single operation. "The assistant removes the card from the
file, crosses out the charge, removes the clip, and replaces
the card in the book (277)."

At Washington University overdue notices are sent
twice a week, therefore the color of the clips is also changed
twice a week. "After overdue notices have been written, the
colored clip is replaced by a black one, clipped to the top of
the card, and the cards are refiled (277)."

Shumar advocated another method for dealing with overdues (275).

Instead of sending out post cards for overdue books, once
a week (Thursday) a list is compiled of all the students
who have overdue books, who have books due the following day, and those who have pictures and records due.
These notices, typed with an original and three carbon

copies, are posted on the main college bulletin board, in
the women's dormitory, the men's dining hall, and the
main corridor of the library building, where they remain
for one week - until the new notice is ready. This system is highly satisfactory since it keeps the names of
those who have overdue books displayed, and the advance
notice of those who have books due the following day is
better, it is believed, than waiting to notify the students
that their books are overdue.

He described the following method of renewal (275).

A student may renew a book by filling out a mimeographed
renewal slip and dropping it in the designated compartment
of the daily circulation file. Space has been provided on
each renewal slip for the student's name, the date, and
the call number. When the daily circulation file is
checked, the desk assistant makes the necessary change
on the book card in the classified circulation file and
changes the metal tab to the color representing the new
date-due period.

Sister Helen found this system advantageous at Washington University Library. She wrote (278):

Student assistants can do the work in less than an hour a
day, and the time required for discharging books is reduced by more than half. The clips do not scratch the
hand, spoil the cards, or catch on adjoining cards. Neither do they add appreciably to the bulk of the file. They
are quickly and easily attached and removed. Any desired
statistics can be compiled, and all sorts of information indicated, as the possible combination of colors, sizes and
shapes are practically unlimited.

Shumar further stated, "Bethany's library has been
operating efficiently and at a minimum cost under this system. Its simplicity is an asset to a small college library
that must depend on student assistants for the bulk of the
circulation work (275)."

A variation of this system was advocated by E. J.
Belton in South African Libraries. It combined the use of
colored signals with the Browne system's borrower's pocket.
Belton described the system in this manner (279):

With this system, books are stamped, as before, with the

date on which they are due back - in the majority of cases, fourteen days after the date of issue. Both call slip
and book-card are now placed in the borrower's pocket,
with the blue book card in front to show clearly the author's name, by which the charge is to be filed, and to
these is added, behind the book-card, a thin pasteboard
signal.

These signals are 5 in. tall, 2 in. wide at the base,
and 1 in. wide at the top, so that they are not too unwieldy, but have a wide enough base not to fall sideways
and disappear behind the book-card, and are sufficiently
tall to show above it. Signals of seven different, distinctive colours are used, and one colour is used throughout
each week, so that all issues of one week, although due
back on different days, have signals of the same colour.
The pocket and its contents is filed into the one alphabetical sequence by author, and, of course, in time all the
colours are intermingled. On return of a book, the whole
charge is found under the author. The pocket and the
cancelled slip are returned to the borrower, the book-
card is returned to the book, and the coloured signal
dropped into a box, whence the different colours are later
sorted out for re-use. The book is then immediately
ready for issuing again. The filing of issue into the main
sequence and the discharging of books is thus very much
quicker, since in each case there is only one operation
instead of two.

The number of books issued on Saturday mornings is
very small, and these are stamped with the same date as
those of the Monday following, so a new colour becomes
"current" first thing each Saturday morning and remains
current until the following Friday evening. Overdues are
written on Saturday mornings, the colour in each charge
indicating the week during which it was issued and therefore when it was or will be due back....

The above systems do not apply to issues to members
of the academic staff but to the much larger number of
issues to students. In the case of staff, books are issued
for an indefinite period and are checked half-yearly for
renewal or return. No system to reveal overdues is
therefore necessary. A slip for each book is signed, and
these are filed under the name of the borrower in a special staff issues sequence. The book-cards are date
stamped, marked with the borrower's name as a cross
reference to the staff file and then added to the main alphabetical sequence....

Charges for books taken out for the whole vacation

were given white signals, the only necessary adjustment being that, at the end of the first week of term, first notices must be sent for "white" charges as well as for those overdue in the normal sequence.

.... In all, the system's slight delay in writing overdues and rather greater care needed in working the colour sequence correctly and checking for overdues are far outweighed by the considerable saving in staff time at the desk in the mechanical process of book charging and discharging.

(Scotch Tape Tabs)

The use of "Scotch Tape Tabs" to indicate the date due of a charge was begun at the University of Michigan, according to Horace Tollefson. He traced the early beginnings of this method, commented on its use and described in detail the supplies which were needed (280).

In 1942 William Patterson Reid, then associate circulation librarian of the University of Michigan general library, very carefully planned an efficient one-card charging system and put it into operation. Basing it on the standard book cards already in use, he incorporated one feature, the use of Scotch tape tabs, which as far as can be determined was new....

The Reid one-card system is based on the standard loan periods of one and two weeks, excluding overnight circulation and indefinite loans to faculty, which must be handled separately. It is applicable to the system of any library which uses a book card for home charges, and is working as efficiently at Rollins College as it has at much larger Ann Arbor. At Michigan, some material circulates for one day, which fits into the system.

The only equipment necessary is a roll of half-inch Scotch tape and a Scotch tape dispenser. The sides of each roll should be red-inked before use, so that the tabs will stand out more clearly in the circulation file....

.... Pieces of tape approximately one inch long are folded over the edges of the book cards so that a tab projects about 1/4 inch beyond the edge of the cards.

A tabbing guide is arranged by date and by the length of time the book is to circulate. Positions may be printed on the edges of the book cards when new stock is ordered, but this is not necessary. It is necessary that these positions be drawn on every tabbing guide which is prepared.

Dorothy Cooper gave this further bit of advice (281):

After a short trial we discovered that colored Scotch tape
is more effective for tabbing than the ordinary transparent variety used at Michigan. The coloured tape is more
easily seen in the indicator file, it does not smear the
cards with gum, and different colors can be used to indicate a wider variety of charges than in the original tabbing guide.

Tollefson wrote of the procedure of charging used at
Michigan and at Rollins (282).

(1) The date due is stamped on the book card after the
borrower has signed it.
(2) A tab on the card from a previous circulation is
cut off, the new one placed in a predetermined position so
that it will be pulled from the circulation file when the
book is overdue. Then the card is filed by classification
number.

He also described the mechanics involved in tabbing
the cards and filing them in the classified file (282).

The week is divided into two periods, Monday-Wednesday
and Thursday-Saturday (Sunday circulation with the first
period). During the Monday-Wednesday period, cards for
14-day books will be tabbed in one position, 7-day books
will be tabbed two positions preceding the 14-day position,
material circulating for 1 day will be tabbed two positions
preceding the 7-day position. For example, when cards
for 14-day books are being tabbed in position 6, cards for
7-day books will be tabbed in 4, and those for 1-day material in 2.
During the Thursday through Saturday period of the
same week, tabbing positions will move forward to 1, 5,
and 3, in clockwise rotation, on Monday of the following
week to 2, 6, and 4, on Thursday of the following week
to 3, 1, and 5, etc.
Overlapping avoided.
The six positions, with two positions used each week
for each type of circulation, are necessary to prevent overlapping of tabbing and to ensure, when the overdues are
pulled from the circulation file, that the cards for overdue
14-day, 7-day, and 1-day books can all be withdrawn at
one time. . . .
From 150 to 200 book cards can be tabbed in 30 min-

utes.   When the book cards have been tabbed and counted,
they may be returned to the charging desk for filing.
Once in the circulation file, the one-card charge is a
book record by classification number, as the home charges (plus the bindery charges, carrell charges, display
charges, etc.) are all filed in one shelf-list order.   The
charge is also a date-due record because of the Scotch
tape tab on the book card.   The cards for books on loan
to members of the faculty are not tabbed unless for some
reason the loan is limited.

    Serves special purposes.

    Special tabbing guides must be prepared at the end of
a term, when all books charged to students are due by a
certain date, and for periods when the library is closed
for longer than three days but for less than fourteen days.

    The over-due and find card routines must be closely
coordinated with the tabbing system.

    At the University of Washington, Cooper mentioned an
adaptation had to be made of the filing procedure used at
Michigan (281).

    .... The month charge and the three month faculty charge
used in this library are not allowed for in the Michigan
system, and we have had to make certain adaptations to
care for them.   Month charges are tabbed in the same
position as two week charges and then retabbed for two
weeks when they are pulled from the file with over-dues.

    To tab for faculty charges, we have added two posi-
tions to the original six on the book card - one below position six, and one below position one.   These positions
are tabbed in blue and red, and their use alternated according to the first and second halves of each quarter.
Daily during each period, we pull faculty overdues and
send notices for them, then retab the card for the current
three month charge.   This ensures that all faculty members are reminded of their books once each quarter so
that they can renew them when necessary.

    Tollefson remarked briefly on the overdue procedure
as used at his library (282).

    (3) The first overdue day after the book is due the book
card is pulled from the file and the tab is cut off.   After
the notice is sent to the borrower, a metal clip is placed
on the book card which is returned to the circulation file.
(4) On the next overdue day the book card is again pulled

from the file, a second notice is sent, and a second clip
of the same color is added to the card which is again returned to the file.
(5) One week after the second notice, the card is again
withdrawn from the file.   The metal clips are removed,
a fine card is written, "See Fine Card" is stamped on
the book card, and it is returned to the circulation file,
where it stays until the book is returned or is listed as
missing.   All further action is taken from the information
on the fine card.

Overdues were dealt with in a slightly different fashion at the University of Washington.   Cooper wrote (283):

.... Twice a week we pull from the file those cards having metal clips in a given position which indicates that
they are nine days overdue. [1st notices were sent after
5 days overdue].
We send an overdue notice, and type a duplicate slip
record which gives call number, author, title, and the
name and address of the borrower.   If the book is returned before the fifteenth day overdue, a bill for the
fine is sent and the slip record destroyed.   On the fifteenth day, book cards for the remaining slips are pulled
from the file, and bills for the maximum fine and the
book price are sent.   The over-due clips are then taken
from the cards, the tabs cut off, and a "missing" notice
stapled on each.   The slip record goes into the "missing
books" file where it remains until the book is withdrawn
from the collection at the end of a year.

The advantages of Mr. Reid's Scotch Tape Tab System were obvious to Tollefson, who said (282):

(1) The book card fulfills the function for which two
separate records have usually been necessary.   It is a
record by classification number of the home charge, and
it is also a date due record.
(2) The system, simple to operate, is inexpensive.
Any library which uses standard book cards can use the
system.   Time is saved in charging because the tabs can
be placed on the book cards much more rapidly than it is
possible to write and file a second record for each home
charge.   The discharging procedure is also simplified.
(3) The handling of overdues is much less complicated.
At Michigan, after the system was put into operation,
time was cut from 18 hours to 6 hours a week.   Further-

more, as the overdue assistant does not have to compare
call numbers when pulling overdues, chances for error in
this procedure are cut appreciably.

Cooper saw that the tabbing operation was extremely
simple and fast (283).

.... The position of circulation clerk, which includes other work as well, has been cut from full to three quarter
time. We have estimated that the tabbing system saves
us twelve hours a week in this position alone. Several
related routines have speeded up, and we find a greater
degree of accuracy in the discharging and revising of
books.

Greater savings were expected by this writer in the
future (284).

We hope in the future to eliminate the book card altogether, and use as a charge the call slip with which the borrower asks for the book. This would speed the service
at the circulation desk because the patron would not have
to sign a book card; it would reduce the library's supplies budget, and save time in the preparations divisions
by eliminating the use of book cards and book pockets.
In short, the Michigan tabbing system can be made to of-
fer the same advantages as many mechanical charging
system at a lower cost, and with no chance of mechanical
breakdowns.

(Inked Tabs)

The Inked Tab Charging System was explained by
Arthur Hamlin and Walter Wright. They described the supplies needed in this manner (285):

The call slip ... is similar to those in use by many university libraries, and files by call number to give a complete book record. The unique factor is a color application, so that an attendant can pick up a hundred or more
cards, riffle them endwise and in a moment determine
which books are overdue.
At Pennsylvania some books are charged for one week
only, but the majority of loans are for a two-week or a
month period. Books are stamped to fall due on Monday
or Thursday....
This coloring of the ends of the cards constitutes a

visible record of date due. The color and its position on
the card are determined from a schedule drawn up long in
advance following a regular pattern.   There are four
(imagined) positions along the short edges of the card,
making sixteen in all, counting top and bottom, recto and
verso.   Only 13 positions are used to indicate date due,
and these multiplied by four distinct colors of ink (red,
blue, green, and brown) give us 52 dates before it is
necessary to repeat colors and positions.   Since there are
two days each week on which the books fall due, the system theoretically runs just 26 weeks before it repeats itself.   In practice, we contract and expand the loan period
occasionally to conform to vacations or to graduation dates.

Shows nature of loan.

Of the three positions not used to indicate date due,
one is used to designate faculty charges. The color for
this position is changed annually on April 1.   Books
charged to faculty members are recalled or renewed in
June and July, when every professor must clear his old
charges with the circulation desk.

Another position on the card is used to indicate books
charged within the library building, particularly to carrells and library offices. This color changes every six
months.   Still another position is used to key the loan of
books which the library usually keeps in special locked
cases or over which special control is exercized.

Book cards and pockets have been abolished, according to Hamlin and Wright. The due date is stamped on a
strip pasted in the front of the book, opposite the book plate.
"The date due stamps are self-inking in four different colors
of ink: (1) black for reading room use, (2) red for one week,
(3) blue for two-week charges (the normal period), and (4)
green for one month charges to graduate students and faculty
(286)."

When a book is loaned, the assistant initials the call slip
and stamps the date due on it as well as in the book.
The accumulation of call slips is picked up several times
during the day and sorted into piles: one week, two weeks,
one month, and faculty charges (which though stamped one
month are without limit of time).   Each group of cards is
then taken, blocked square on the end, and spread out by
a shifting motion of the opposing thumb and fingers, leaving a 1/16 to 1/18 inch margin showing at the end of each
card.   Placed flat on a blotter, the exposed edges of the
cards are then swabbed in a predetermined position with

colored ink.   A rubber tipped moistener is used for this
purpose, and quick blotting is required or else the ink
will run.   The cards are then ready for counting and filing.

These two writers had other comments to make which
were concerned with renewals, overdues and reserves.   They
gave what they felt were the advantages and disadvantages of
the system (287).

With this coloring arrangement it is seldom necessary to
annul a color.   When an overdue charge is pulled to notify the borrower, a new color is added in the next position.   Only when a book has been renewed for 6 1/2
months do the colors interfere, as a result of the color
progressing from one position to another around the card.
The procedure then is to fold a narrow strip of white
gummed paper over the end, thus obliterating the colors
in all eight positions on that end.   In the case of isolated
errors, one ink sometimes goes over another with sufficient clarity, or the word "no" is written in pencil below the incorrect color to invalidate it....
Overdue notices are sent out regularly twice a week.
On Wednesdays and Saturdays an assistant goes through
the circulation file, thumbing about 100 cards at a time
and looking for a particular color in a particular position, which represents overdues, and sets them aside for
overdue notices.   The cards are then recolored in the
next position to sort out in another two weeks, and refiled.   A second card notice is sent if necessary, followed two weeks later by a letter.   If there is no response
to these three invitations to return a book, the borrower
is barred from his library privileges and disciplinary
action is taken by the dean's office....   A complete record of notices sent and transactions relating to each
charge is kept on the call slip.
Books are callable from anyone after two weeks, even
though charged for a longer time.   In case of a request
or a reserve on a charge not yet due, the second call
slip is stapled behind the first.   Before refiling, the original charge is recolored to sort out earlier, if it is a
one-month charge.   On a two-week charge, no recoloring
is necessary.   If the book is already due or overdue, it
is called in immediately, and the charge (with the reserve stapled to it) is recolored so that it will sort out
again in two weeks if it still has not been returned....
It is noted that this system provides no borrower's

record.   Ordinarily the need for this record comes up
only at the end of each term, prior to graduation exer-
cises.   Nearly 700 students were expected to graduate
last winter.   It took one staff member three days to go
through the circulation files looking for charges by any
one of these 700.   Certainly this labor charge three
times a year is cheaper than the maintenance of the extra record.   When a student drops out in mid term, his
name is listed by the assistant who sends our overdue
notices.   After an interval of two weeks or one month, if
no overdues have appeared against his name, his record
is clear.

The University of Pennsylvania library wanted a circulation system that would involve a minimum of records
and would be swift and accurate.   We had no wish to an-
alyze reading habits or circulation to any particular groups
within the university.   Our one card, with color sorting
for overdues, certainly gives us a minimum record, and
it is speedy.   Fortunately, no one in the department is
color blind.

So far as accuracy is concerned, there are cautions.
The initial stamping must be accompanied by a careful
checking of call number and legibility.   The desk attendant has to be on her toes during her two-hour period at
the front, after which she retires to other duties.   This
work cannot be done by just any new and careless student
assistant.   We do use some students for this work, particularly in the evening, but only after there is good evidence that they will do it well.   Full-time attendants in
the department are non-professional and often without previous library experience, but they are college graduates
and are paid top wages for non-professional library assistants.

We place much emphasis on obtaining intelligent and
personable young women who will be alert, responsive,
and sympathetic to the varying problems that come to a
busy circulation desk.   They are proving the prime factors in the operation - even more important than the mechanics of an improved circulation routine.

Geer recommended this technique in this fashion (288).

In college libraries, it is necessary to be able to locate
books at all times, even when they are in circulation.
This is difficult or impossible with some of the newer
equipment and procedures used by public libraries.   The
tab charging system, by reducing the book and date due

information to a single file, has made it possible to install and maintain an efficient and simple system.

Tab-Pocket System

This system, which was devised by Felix E. Snider, according to Helen Geer, is adaptable to libraries having a fairly small circulation (289).

R. D. Rogers described the charging pocket method as it was used at Columbia College Library (290).

Books are charged on white 3 x 5 cards already in each volume. These charges are then dropped in a bin for filing later in the day. When this arbitrarily-set time comes (at a slack period) an assistant takes all charges for one week and slips them in standard book pockets which have been altered by the punching of eleven holes three-sixteenths of an inch from the bottom and by the use of three staples. The first two staples prevent the charges from going so far into the pockets that they would interfere with the holes, and the third restricts the shifting of the charges from right to left.

Notice... that the sixth hole from the left is cut entirely out to the margin. Each pocket bears a number which corresponds to the number of this notch. ...Numbers six to eleven are used for week-book charges. [Each notch is used for two days in succession]. With six notches devoted to week charges, it will be readily apparent that there is no need to repeat the sequence for at least ten days.

Pockets with No. 1-5 notches would be used respectively for: (1) binding charges; (2) special location charges, e.g. in exhibits; (3) faculty charges; (4) interdepartmental charges; and special holiday charges extending more than one week....

All charges would be filed in specially constructed trays... with perforated ends corresponding to the eleven holes in the pockets.

We would insert a small steel rod in the No. 6 hole of the tray, pass it through all the charges, invert the tray and all No. 6 pockets would drop out, and conversely all pockets without the No. 6 notch would remain in the tray by virtue of the 3/16 inch margin which holds them on the rod. Overdues may then be sent for all charges which have dropped from the tray, after which

they may be placed in pockets with a No. 7 notch, so that
they will drop out on Wednesday, if they are not returned
before.

When the time comes to file week-book charges, an
assistant merely refers to the calendar, takes a supply of
the proper pockets from the drawer, slips the charges in
the pockets at the rate of thirty per minute, then proceeds
with the filing as he normally would.

Discharging. We attempt to discharge all week-books
at the time of return. Pocket and charge are removed in
one motion. An added second per book discharged is
needed to remove the charge from the pocket and to drop
the latter into a drawer in the filing tub. Once a day,
these accumulated pockets of all types are removed and
sorted by the use of the steel rod used in removing overdues. If an extra tray is used for this sorting, 300 pockets can be sorted and put away in 6 minutes.

Comparison of Statistics.

The Columbia College Library circulates from 1,500 to
2,000 non-reserved books per month for one week periods.
When overdues were sent three times a week under the
old system, fifteen hours per month were required for
checking charges. The present system requires four
hours and forty-five minutes, a saving of over ten hours
per month.

According to an interview H. F. McGaw had with
John H. Berthel, the librarian at the Butler Library, Columbia University, the system was given up in 1943 in favor of
the "more conventional type of book charging." McGaw further stated (291):

The chief reason, according to Berthel, for the staff's
abandonment of the system was that the equipment, being
homemade, eventually reached a state of disrepair which
resulted in the dropping out, during the sorting process,
of unwanted cards. The principle itself, however, seemed
to be regarded as sound.

McGaw suggested the following modification of the
Rogers system (292):

Instead of using an ordinary book pocket, or one which is
similar in type, as the one the pattern of which is shown
by Rogers, let us suppose that a specially designed pocket is used. (Since the economy of repeated use is to be
enjoyed, an extra initial expense might be justified.) The

pocket would be, say, 3 1/2 inches in width, calling, a-
gain, for an extra expense - that of securing new filing
trays.   The front and back of the pocket, along one side,
to a depth of almost half-an-inch, would be sealed together allowing just enough pocket area for a snug-fitting book
card.

Instead of boring holes in the charging trays (as was
done in the case of the Columbia College installation), and
sorting the pockets by inverting the trays, the 3 1/2 inch
pockets would be removed from the files in groups, just
as marginal punched cards are removed, for sorting with
the conventional type of needle.   By perforating the long
edge of the pocket instead of the short edge, not only can
four holes be added (for the coding of other useful classifications) to the eleven which Rogers used, but the pockets, when sorted, cannot lose their cards, because of the
snugness of the fit and because of the support of the opposite edge of the pocket.

The provisions of a pocket 4 inches wide, sealed and
perforated on both sides, would, of course, double the
coding capacity.

If one of the marginal punched card manufacturers
should make available a standard-form pocket of, say,
the latter type, perforated with 15 holes on each side
(the holes coded for both direct and indirect sorting), a
number of libraries might be interested.   Simply at the
expense of changing their filing trays, and of ordering one
or two tumblers and hand slotters and a few thousand
marginal punched pockets, they could consolidate all of
their files into one, yet continue to require, on the part
of the borrower, no more information than is furnished
under their present system....

The expense of providing trays of sufficient width to
accommodate 3 1/2 inch pockets would probably be little
more, and perhaps even less, than the expense of adapting the library's present trays for use with the Rogers
system.

This feature would answer one possible objection to
the Rogers system, that is, the dislike which many wom-
en assistants would have of handling the heavy charging
trays.

.... The writer has recently learned that Superior Business Machines, Inc., 307 Fifth Ave., New York 16,
N. Y., has put on the market a machine which will readily change an ordinary file card into a marginal punched
card.   Since "any kind, size or thickness of card stock
...may be used," there is no reason why a card pocket

cannot be treated in the same way as a card.

Notched and Punched Cards

R. H. Parker noted the present-day trend toward
notched and punched card charging systems. [See reference
no. 239.] But in 1898, a negative feeling existed. According to an article by M. J. Voight, the views on mechanization were worded differently by one librarian. "If a new machine comes to be wanted very badly, it will be produced;
but let us wait for an imperative demand, instead of cogitat-
ing how we can, by clipping off the corner of a card, or
sticking in a new pin, or even by calling an old spade an
agricultural implement, secure fame for ourselves as original inventors (293)." Now, M. J. Voight reminded us, "librarians clip and stick pins in new ways with their punched
cards (293)."

According to James N. Perry there are two types of
cards which may be called "punched cards" (294).

The term "punched card" is applied to a card on which
numerical or alphabetical information may be represented
by slots on the margin of the card (the Keysort, Cope-
Chat, or E-Z Sort types of cards) or by holes punched
over the area of the card (the Hollerith or Powers types
of cards).
The basic feature of punched cards (this term will be
used generally to designate both edge-notched and overall
punched types) is their susceptibility to sorting operations
directed either to any one or to a combination of notches
or holes.

R. H. Parker distinguished between marginally
punched and notched cards and the cards which have holes
punched on their surface. According to him, punched cards
are "cards with holes punched in predetermined positions to
represent various data, used to actuate machines to sort or
select the cards, to print or calculate. As here used, the
term does not include marginally punched and notched cards
sorted by manual insertion of a needle (295)." He said,
"There are two makes of punched card machines: the Hollerith machine manufactured by IBM, and the Powers machine,
manufactured by Remington Rand, Inc. (296)." These two
punched card systems can be considered simultaneously because, as Helen Geer wrote, the equipment is similar, "the

only difference being the manner in which the holes are
punched (297). " However, the equipment and procedure involved in the charging by marginally notched cards differs
greatly from these machine sorting systems. [See reference
nos. 300, 313].

Notched Card System

Eva W. Ramsey gave a brief background of the
Notched Card System as it was derived from forms of statistical analysis (298).

It is interesting to note that, although the first patent was
issued in 1896, it was not until 1920 that the marginal
punch card was used to practical advantage by Dr. Alan
Gregg, who conceived the idea of using individual survey
cards in tabulating the results of a bookworm survey in
Brazil. He experimented with cards upon which information was coded by cutting notches around the border by
hand with scissors. For group separation these cards
were placed against the sharp edge of a ruler which fitted
into the notches and forced the unnotched cards to a higher level. The separation was then made by picking out
the unnotched cards.
A few years later Drs. Hackett and Soper adapted essentially the same system to other disease surveys, this
time using a punch which "bit into the margin of the card,
transforming the hole into an open notch. " Rods or wires
were run through a pack of such cards at any of these
holes, whereupon the notched cards would fall out, while
the others would remain suspended.
In the meantime the system has been developed, improved, and perfected to meet the requirements of every
type of statistical analysis.

The history of this system as it applies specifically
to libraries was summarized by Howard F. McGaw (299).

The McBee Company developed its marginal punched card
system on the basis of the patents of Alfred Perkins, of
England. In his 1925 patent Perkins exhibits cards pre-
punched along the edges with small, symmetrically placed
holes. A rod or wire can be easily passed through any
given hole in a pack of such cards. Then, on the raising
of the sorting instrument, any cards previously notched at
the given hole will fall from the pack, the other cards re-

maining impaled.   Thus a sorting takes place instantan-
eously.

Perkins points out that two kinds of notched systems
may be employed.   In the first, a given hole is assigned
specific significance....   In all such cases "direct" coding is possible in the sense that the operator moves directly from an observed fact to notching the hole marked
as corresponding to that fact....   Perkins also provided
for "indirect" coding.   Under this system meanings can
be arbitrarily assigned to a series of numbers and the
coding of any of these provided for through the notching
of one or more holes.   By arranging the figures, 0 to 9,
in one position on the card; then, just to the left, one or
more similar "fields,"... we may designate the first
group as "units," the second group as "tens," and so on
....

But even this arrangement was capable of improvement
as Perkins' 1929 patent reveals.   Here it is shown that
each field can be reduced from 10 to only 4 holes, as indicated below:

Additional fields	0000	0000
here as desired	7421	7421
	tens	units

Frederick Kilgour described the McBee equipment
used in the Notched Card System (300).

The essential feature of this method of keeping circulation
records is the Keysort card itself ... on which the book
record and the date due record are combined.   The cost
of these cards, including the charge for the wax plates
from which they are printed, is approximately three times
that of the printed cards formerly used.   The size of the
card, Harvard's being 3" x 5", the amount of printing
and the number of cards printed are all factors that determine the cost of each order.   The notching and sorting
of these cards is done with McBee equipment.   A treadle
punch ... notching as many as 200 cards in one operation
is rented for $4 a month.   In addition a small hand punch
... used to notch only a few cards at a time is rented
for $1 a year.   The McBee Company furnishes free of
charge the sorting needles and angle irons ... to facilitate
sorting.

An article printed in 1940 clarified the use of the

notches (301):

>This notch establishes the desired classification just as a
>Yale-type key is notched along the edge to identify it with
>a particular lock.

K. M. Stokes described the desirable size of the
cards (302).

>The McBee Company's regional representative suggest-
>ed that the card be 3 1/4" x 5" instead of 3" x 5" size
>that Harvard uses, because the company's machinery is
>adjusted to produce the larger card at the minimum price
>. . . .
>A considerable saving is effected in ordering cards by
>100, 000 lots. For each newly designed card there is an
>extra charge for the electroplate from which it is to be
>printed。

She also listed several variations that were in use
(303).

>Of the other university libraries which have adopted Key-
>sort cards for circulation records only one, Iowa, uses
>the inexpensive 3 1/4" x 5" size. Harvard and Brown
>have the standard 3" x 5". Georgia uses a 3 1/4" x 6"
>card and Tennessee a 3" x 6", in the latter case because
>"this gives space at the bottom of the card for a location
>report to the borrower who requests a book not on the
>shelves. " (Letter to author from Dorothy E. Ryan, Un-
>iversity of Tennessee, Nov. 27, 1946)。

McGaw showed how one school was able to get double
use from one card (304).

>By using both inner and outer rows of holes; by providing
>rather narrow spaces for call number, signature, etc.;
>and by omitting the conventional request for author and
>title information, Ohio Wesleyan is able to make double
>use of its call card; the top half and the bottom half are
>identical.... It does not matter which end the borrower
>uses first, but after that end has served its purpose, it is
>"scratched" (with a large crayon) and the other end is then
>used.

Stokes showed how the cards and the holes were labeled (305).

.... Holes were numbered or labeled on all four edges
at first, but later only on the two sides and the bottom
of the card.   The labeled holes include those for charges
to the Reserve Book Room, (R.B.R.), binding, and several departmental libraries as well as one to be notched
for "missing" books.   The numbered holes can be assigned in any way desired and are so coded in a manual kept
at the circulation desk.   Nine holes were labeled for due
dates.   Three more were labeled for faculty charges:
1 Sem. ... and Summer Session (S.S.).   Spaces marked 1,
2, 3 were left at the bottom of the card for the stamping
of the original due date and two possible renewals.

     Stokes noted variants at several schools (306).

Harvard, Brown and Indiana have a form listing a number
of possible locations printed on the backs of their cards
for the same type of information.   This requires a second
electroplate and increases the cost of the printing.   If it
is desirable to keep the cards inexpensive, the single notation usually necessary could easily be jotted on the back
of the call card in pencil by the attendant who handled it,
taking a little longer than the check mark necessary on
the printed form.
     Iowa's card has a printed form at the bottom for re-
cording fines or lost book charge.   The same information
is mimeographed in the library on the back of Tennessee's
card after a charge becomes overdue.
     University of Georgia.
     The University of Georgia's card has been planned to
serve almost the same purposes as the Hollerith card
Mr. Parker used with the I.B.M. equipment at Texas.
The card is the 3 1/4" x 6" size and has holes along all
four edges.   On the left side are the holes for due dates.
In a letter of Nov. 25, 1946, to the author, he states that
the bottom, "which is used only for specific studies and
is not normally notched in day-to-day operation," has five
holes representing graduate students and the four classes
and four holes numbered 7, 4, 2, 1, where the school
classification of the student borrower can be coded.   This
is a departure from direct coding or assigning a single
meaning to each hole.   If the digits 7, 4, 2, 1 are assigned to four consecutive holes, called a "field," any
number from one to nine may be indicated by clipping one
hole, or a combination of two holes such as 1 and 2 for
3.
     At the top of Georgia's card are two sets of holes,

each numbered 5, 4, 3, 2, 1 and labeled respectively for
tens and units.   Here locations in departmental libraries
are notched according to an assigned code.   On the right
side of the card four sets of holes are similarly numbered and labeled, with the two extra fields affording space
for coding hundreds and thousands.   If a charge becomes
overdue, the individual borrower's number is punched a-
long this side.

Stokes and Chapin made note of several early difficulties in this system, the manner in which they were solved,
and the usage of various notches of the card (307).

The original card design, used for four years was eventually found to be inadequate, the main objection being that
the holes were on all four margins.   The top holes soon
were worn and frayed - especially for those charges
which were in the file for a long time.   This made the
mechanical sorting of the cards difficult.   Another reason
for the new design was to change the physical layout of
the old cards.   The new one had space for the flash-
board number which notifies patrons when their books
come from the stacks; two, instead of one line for the
book title; and boxes to clarify college status by checking
undergraduate, graduate, assistant, faculty or other.
The 18 holes on the right hand side of the original
card were designed to pull overdues twice a week, with
a nine-week interval before repeating the same holes.
This plan was never put into effect, however.   After the
new card arrived it was decided to sort the overdues
only once a week.   There is now a sorting cycle of 18
weeks before repeating occurs.
The bottom of the card is set up for recording long
term records such as books to departmental libraries,
missing books, and books at the bindery.   The 13 holes
here can code all the above charges.   When sorting for
the missing book, a series of three holes are used.   The
cards are dropped out by use of a mechanical sorter which
was purchased from the McBee Company after hand sorting proved unsatisfactory.
The holes on the left hand side of the card denote semester, carrell charges, and faculty charges.... [We]
assign one hole on the card to each letter of the alphabet
and punch each faculty charge with the initial of the borrower's last name....   To facilitate dropping out all faculty charges at once, one hole was labeled "Fac."   This
hole has been used only once, and has proved unsatisfact-

ory.]

Believing that it might be necessary to drop out all charges for a semester of a summer session prompted the assignment of three holes to "SS 2 semester 1, " but these holes have been used only in connection with missing books.... Any hole could, of course, be reassigned by simply noting the change on the code sheet which was set up to guide the clerks.

The hole labeled "Car. " has been used for coding all charges to carrells, for graduate students or faculty members. This hole is needled only once at the end of the academic year when an inventory check of carrell charges is made.

Another type of coding design is discussed by M. L. Hocker (308).

The card is quite simple, and many of its printed items are self-explanatory. The "Do not write below" space at the top is used for the date due. Enough room is left here for renewals. Sometimes is is necessary to recall a book for reserve or other reasons and space is so designated for that. The "Hold for" space is used for recording a reservation on a book, with enough space left for name and address of person for whom the book is to be held. It is the holes around the edges of the card which give Keysort its flexibility and make the one-file system both possible and practical.

At the beginning of the school year, each week of the semester is numbered "Week 1, " "Week 2, " or "Week 3" in consecutive order. This record is kept on a calendar at the charging desk. The holes for Weeks 1, 2, and 3 are used because the regular loan period is for two weeks .... The "Week 4" hole is used for irregularities in charging periods which result from school vacations....

The hole for 1 may be used for a special temporary recreational book shelf; or the hole for 2 may be used for a temporary history collection. A code of such designations of special charges is kept attached to the charging desk calendar. When books have been lost and paid for, such recording is made on the charging card and the "Paid for Books" hole is punched and the charge refiled until later when the withdrawal is noted on the shelf list ....

So far, the holes with the alphabet are not used for anything, but they, too, can be designated for any other special charges needed.

Stokes remarked that the cards may be notched for special charges and longer than normal withdrawal periods (309).

Personal Record.

Because faculty members are usually given the privilege of keeping books out for a semester, and of having an unlimited number of books at any one time, a personal record is essential for them....

At Penn State, faculty charges are notched "1st sem.," "2nd sem." or "S.S." All faculty charges are dropped out at the end of each term and notices are sent out asking that the professor either return the books charged to him or renew them....

Indiana punches a faculty charge as a regular two-week loan, but adds a punch at the bottom of the card for the borrower's initials. If the card falls out in the sorting at the end of two weeks, it is put back in place. If it falls out again in the sorting two weeks later, "the time punch is covered up with a card saver sticker and the card refiled without further attention." (letter, Jan. 15, 1947, from E. L. Craig, ref. librarian.)

This method is not entirely satisfactory because a sort for one faculty member's charges drops out a number of others under the same initial. Georgia grants unlimited loans to faculty members, but notches an identification number into the faculty member's charges by numerical coding. It is then possible to check any one man's charges if it becomes necessary - for instance, if he accepts a position in another university and his record needs to be cleared.

When a student charge becomes overdue, Georgia notches the coded student number into it so that any student's overdue charges can be dropped out if clearance is necessary. The arbitrarily assigned location code 55 is notched into the top of all charges for seniors and near the end of the session these charges are dropped out "so that special follow ups may be made," according to Ralph H. Parker, director....

Special Forms and Economies....

Iowa, Brown and Harvard have special forms for carrel charges, or charges to graduate desks. Each consists of the usual form printed in one strip with a longer form to be detached and left in the book being charged. Brown's and Harvard's additional form is of the same card stock and is attached to the usual form with perforations where the two may be separated. Iowa has its additional form

printed on thinner stock and attached to the usual form by
a slight line of glue at the bottom.   The principle behind
carrel charges is that they shall be made out in duplicate
so that one part may be kept in the book to insure its retention in the carrel, while the other part is filed as a
charge in the location file at the circulation desk.

G. Upchurch indicated several variations and additions
to those given by Stokes (310).

.... Nine holes are set aside for regular one-week and
two-week dates due, with three more for semester and
summer school charges.   Holes are labeled for books in
Recreational Reading Rooms (R. R. R.), Reserve, Reference, bindery, etc.   The seventeen numbered holes can
be assigned to various uses, such as special exhibits, and
changed as needed.   A key to these is kept at the loan
desk.   Holes at the bottom of the card are notched for the
names of faculty borrowers, with the idea that the personal file for faculty loans may later be abandoned.

McGaw showed the manner in which various universities used coded holes to show the date due.   "Texas College
provides direct-coded holes for the six days, Monday through
Saturday.... Cornell, Georgia, and Illinois use five weekly
periods in connection with their charging systems (311). "

McGaw also noted that variations in the cards, rather
than variation in the notches, were used to handle other
types of special charges (312).

Brown University, in addition to notching its cards to
correspond with the respective locations, also uses differently colored cards.   While the card for regular charges
has a black strip across the top, the cards for New Books,
Desk Reserves, and Shelf Reserves have strips colored
green, brown and blue, respectively.   A card with a red
strip is used for Lost Books, Replacements and Reservations.   (Letter dated April 28, 1949, from Helen Thompson).
Georgia records its departmental charges on a card
which is unprinted except for the marginal coding, and
which is just like its regular call card except that it has
a black "slug" along the right edge; and the clipped corner instead of being at the upper right, as is true of the
regular call cards, is at the bottom right.   These differences make it possible for the two groups of cards to

"...be filed together or separately and yet be readily selected each from the other." (Letter, dated April 30,
1949, from Evelyn Fritz).

Kilgour has recounted the actual charging process
(313).

.... an assistant charges the book to the borrower by
stamping the date due on both the call slip and a date slip
glued on the inside of the back cover of the book. After
giving the book to the borrower, the assistant drops the
charge in a drawer.
        Another assistant removes the charge slips from the
drawer every hour and separates them into two groups,
one for books charged for one week, and one for those
charged for two weeks. At the same time she counts the
number of volumes circulated. Using the treadle punch,
she then notches one of the holes on the side of the slips,
determining the specific hole to be notched by consulting
a prearranged schedule which lists the holes corresponding to the various dates due. This notching operation
which requires only a few seconds, produces the date due
record on each slip. In this connection it may be pointed
out that books are charged to fall due on three days only
of each week - Monday, Wednesday, and Friday - instead
of the six days that the library is open.... The books
being due on only three days a week simplifies the sorting procedure described below. The sorting is done only
three days each week instead of six.
        After the slips have been notched, they are filed by
call number in the book record file. This record actually consists of two files which have been termed "active"
and "inactive." The former is made up of Keysort cards
for books charged for outside use, and the latter of cards
for books in cubicles, in the reading rooms, at the bindery, and those charged to department and special libraries. In general, all charges are put in the inactive file
if the Circulation Department does not keep a record of
the date due. It is possible, of course, to combine the
active and inactive files by recording the inactive charges on Keysort cards.

A variation on the normal Keysort principle was described by Hocker (314).

1. Borrower fills out charging card with call number,
author, title, signature, address, telephone no. and cam-

pus status....
    2. Desk attendant checks card, especially for correctness of call number, stamps date due on both charging card and date slip in book, and drops card in temporary charging box.

    Stokes illustrated one manner in which the filing of the cards is done (302).

Charges for books which do not circulate but are used in the building are filed in a separate "Room Use" file. Since these charges do not need to be notched, a small saving is effected by making the backs of such cards serve as magazine charges by having them printed locally as magazine call cards.

    Stokes later added to this procedure a discussion on the single versus divided file (315).

For libraries which have in their location files a great many inactive charges - charges for reserved books or for books in departmental reading rooms - sorting by hand with a Keysort needle of a single file incorporating both active and inactive charges would be a long, cumbersome process. For this reason some libraries have separated the two files so that only the active file has to be needled for overdues three times a week....
    .... Brown has a single file, but Mr. H. Glenn Brown, supervisor of readers' services there, points out that "one of the advantages of the system may become one of its annoying disadvantages. The master file necessitates a concentration of services; books are called for, charged and discharged at the same location. If you wish to distribute service along a counter, it is impossible to do so without losing one of the big advantages of the Keysort System, the single file. (Letter to Douglas W. Bryant, Nov. 22, 1946.)
    Harvard had two files at the time Mr. Kilgour wrote about the adoption of Keysort cards, but now has a single file. Perhaps this explains why Harvard's books are now due on only one day each week. Needling the combined file probably takes no more time once a week than needling the active file three times weekly....
    The single file is particularly desirable not only because it lessens the clerical work involved in charging and discharging books, but also because only one checking is necessary to find the location of a book not in the

stacks.... However, a study of all requests at the University of Illinois circulation desk revealed that about 50% can be filled by sending the call slips directly to the stacks without the customary preliminary checking.

Since this checking has been abandoned, half of the patrons are served faster than they could be by the old system. The unlucky other half have to wait longer than when the preliminary checking was done, for the book must be searched for by the page and then checked in the location file. Most libraries would be able to fill much more than 50% of their requests immediately. The situation at Illinois is complicated by the fact that the complete collections of thousands of books in departmental reading rooms in the general library are only charged to those reading rooms.

... A study of the individual library's percentage of requests which could be filled without necessitating any checking would probably show that little inconvenience would be caused by a divided file, if preliminary checking were eliminated.

Stokes and Chapin went on to say that they had hoped to use "unpunched cards for long-term records." However, "Experience showed that the loss in time and convenience resulting from having to stop to think what hole meant which item on the unprinted back of the card, nullified the economy in using cards twice (316)."

Another unexpected difficulty was noted by Stokes and Chapin (317).

There was was a daily increasing file of Keysort charges, but there still remained the huge file of long-term call slips. To check two files for information about a book not on the shelves, was a nuisance. One file was decided upon, in spite of the disadvantage of having to needle thousands of inactive charges to extract the overdues from the active ones.

The catalog department was stamping core collection locations on the shelf list or catalog cards of most of the books being kept in departmental libraries. This made possible the discarding of location cards from the location file .

....But the files at Illinois were still big, approximately 100,000 cards, for only two departmental library core collections had so far been stamped on the shelf list and not so great a proportion of the books in those librar-

ies were considered core items as both the catalog and
circulation staffs had expected. Instead of the half hour
daily that had been estimated for sorting overdues, sorting the 100,000 records which were on punched cards required three hours. Such a long operation was boring for
any clerk, especially when the sorting dropped out only a
few cards. During one typical two-week period, the 100,
000 cards were needled four times (twelve hours of work)
to drop out 121 overdues.

That problem was solved during the 1949 Christmas
vacation by transferring most of the departmental charges
in the files to the public shelf list. The Keysort cards
were trimmed to standard catalog size, punched for the
drawer rods, and filed immediately behind the matching
shelf list cards. Now the students can check the shelf
list before requesting a book from the stacks and know,
in most cases, if the book belongs in the Bookstack collection or in another library unit.

Transferring these charges has cut the files down from
38 feet to 11 feet. A corresponding reduction in the number of cards in the files has solved the sorting problem.
One clerk can now sort all overdues in less than two hours
a week.

To keep the shelf list up to date the departmental librarians now fill out a card designed for filing into the
shelf list, for all books which they will have for more
than six months. Books which are to be in the departments for less time are handled on Keysorts at the circulation desk as before.

. . . .

Still another considerable, unexpected expense was
$308 for twenty-two new file boxes at $14 apiece.

The merits of the one-file system and the divided file
system were discussed by Hocker (318).

The one-file system has definite advantages in discharging
and checking for the location of a book not on the shelves.
However, the divided file makes it possible to eliminate
approximately half the cards to be needled each week.
Since faculty charges are often for longer than the regular
two-week loan period, these are placed also in the inactive
file. All faculty charges are clipped at the hole marked
"Faculty"; thus, it is easy to needle these out of the inactive file when the time comes to check. In a similar
manner all special collections are checked from time to
time by needling out such charges from the inactive file.

This includes all end of semester charges, mending, binding, and any special designations that have been made. Thus, the entire inactive file can be checked by "installments," eliminating the necessity for "tearing down" the whole file at one time.

Kilgour described the process of discharging a book (319).

Upon the return of a book, there is only one operation in canceling the charge. The assistant at the book record file removes the slip from the file and places it in the book. After the call numbers on the book and on the charge slip have been verified, another assistant sends the book to the stack and throws away the slip, providing the book is not overdue or does not have a waiting list. In the case of an overdue book, the assistant keeps both the original charge and a fine slip for entry in the fine record. If the fine is not paid when the book is returned, the charge is set aside and a notice of the fine is sent to the borrower.

The method of finding overdues was told by Kilgour (320).

The date record notched on each slip is obtained by a sorting operation in which an assistant removes about 300 cards from the active file and runs a sorting needle through one of the holes. She then raises the needle, and the cards notched on that hole drop out, falling out in the same order, in which they were filed. The entire active file is sorted in this manner, the assistant replacing the cards not sorted out. An inexperienced operator can make sorts at the rate of 60,000 per hour, an experienced operator about 90,000. From the cards separated from the active file by this process, the assistant sends out overdue notices to the borrowers. Before she refiles the slips in the book record file, she notches them again so that they will drop out one week later, if the borrower does not return the book. When an assistant has sent a second overdue notice for a book, she again notches the slip for a week in advance. After a third notice has been sent, it is not necessary to renotch the slip as the original notch serves the purpose. If the borrower does not return the book now, the slip will drop out weekly to call attention to the delinquency. Notching different holes changes the period of time between overdue notices.

A specific illustration of this method of keeping the date due .... The date due is January 20. The assistant sorting the file on January 21 runs the needle through the hole marked Week C Fri, and when she raises the needle, the card drops out. Having sent the overdue notice she will notch this slip Week A Fri. If the book is not returned within a week's time, the slip will drop out again on January 28, when a second over-due notice will be sent, and the slip renotched on Week B Fri. Until the borrower returns the book, the slip will now drop out every Saturday.

Since the officers of the university have unlimited loans subject to recall if the book is in demand, the Circulation Department does not send them over-due book notices. Instead, the assistant sets the slip aside to file back into the active file without renotching it. This slip will sort out again three weeks later at which time the assistant enters the record on the officer's personal card and files the charge in the inactive file.

From a letter by Luanna H. Stahlecker is learned the Iowa procedure of handling overdues after the second weekly notice has been sent (321).

The second time the card falls out, the oldest punch is covered by a card saver. In this way the card will be needled one month later. At this time it is checked with the shelf list and shelves. We do not check our shelves or shelf list prior to that time as the few errors compared to number of overdues does not make it profitable. After checking at this time to see positively that it is not some error on our part, the card is returned to the file until it is needled again another month later. At this time the patron is sent a notice saying that the records have been transferred to the business office and all payments must be made there. Our ... card is then stamped at the top "Lost." All punches except number 16 (... the punch for lost (books) ...) are covered and the record at the bottom of the card shows the amount of fine due, the cost of the book and the amount of the processing fee. A duplicate of this card has been sent to the business office. When records are cleared at the business office we receive the report and mark the original card "Pd. at B.O." with date of payment. If a book is returned within two years from date of overdue, the cost of the book is refunded, as well as processing fee if the book has not been reordered.

A variation is employed at the University of Arkansas (310).

> Instead of using the cards themselves for checking and sending of overdue notices, copies are made and the original charges returned at once to the location file. In this way the cards are never away from the loan desk, while the assistant sending overdues is free to take the duplicates for checking in the stacks or go somewhere else to write the notices. Record of notices sent is then kept on the duplicate records, and these make up a personal file for late books.

Additional equipment is used to designate overdues at North Carolina (322).

> . . . clips supplement Keysort in designating overdues. After 1st notices have been sent, each card ... is clipped with one of the three colored clips representing overdue days.... When second notices are sent a second clip, of the same color as the first, is attached to the card. When bills are sent a third clip is attached and books are declared lost if no acknowledgement of bills is received. (Letter, dated May 12, 1949, from George F. Bentley) Cards are not perforated along the top edges. Therefore, there is room for the clips.

Renewals under this system, according to Kilgour, are made in the following manner (232):

> To renew a charge, the assistant at the circulation desk obtains the original charge from the active file and stamps the new date due on both the charge slip and the book. Before the slip is notched a second time, a blank Keysort card is stapled to the back of the slip, cancelling the first notch so that the charge will only drop out of the file on the day after the renewal date due.

The process of reserving books is dealt with by Kilgour (319).

> .... The waiting list, in the form of the original call slips with which the borrowers requested the book, is stapled to the back of the charge in the active file. Therefore, the assistant checking the call numbers discards only the current charge and sets the book aside with the waiting list in it. Another assistant then notifies the first bor-

rower on the list that the book will be held for him at the
circulation desk for two days.

Stokes relates a variant of this method (302).

For personal reserves a Keysort card made out by the
patron who wants the book is kept in a separate "reserve"
file until the book is returned.   The charge already in the
location file is stamped "Personal Reserves."   When the
book is discharged, the stamp indicates that another card
from the "reserve" file is to be inserted in the book. The
patron is then notified and when he calls for the book the
original request card becomes the charge.

Ohio Wesleyan, said McGaw, used a slightly different
procedure; "the borrower fills out a notice form (a postal, if
it requires mailing), which is sent him when the book becomes available; and he does not fill out the call card until
he gets the book.   In this way he has to fill out only one card
at a time... (323). "

Also at Ohio Wesleyan, McGaw discovered another use
for the cards (324).

Books in the reserve room are on closed shelves and are
arranged by department, then by instructor, then by auth-
or and title.   Because of this arrangement the student is
asked to call for the reserve book by supplying the above
classifications on the call card.   In addition, he furnishes
signature and address, and checks his college status.
     ... the system provides for several shortcuts. ... the
library found that in only nine instances would there by a
possible complication if only the first two letters of his
department were used on the call card....
     Instead, then, of having to write out, under depart-
ment and instructor, Fine Arts - Stewart, Political Sci-
ence-Strachan, Physical Education-Strimer, or Zoology-
Stull, the student is required to supply only "Fi," "Po,"
"P. E.," or "Zo," respectively along with, in each of
these cases, "st."....
     On the author and title lines of the reserve room call
card, the student needs to furnish only the briefest information: The surname of the author and only a few words
of the title....
     Finally, in respect to the signature, address and
class, ...the borrower's registration number may be sub-
stituted for the three items named....

At the time the assistant gives a reserve book to a student, the assistant indicates on the call card the first three numbers of the Dewey classification, the copy number if necessary; and the time or date due. In order not to slow up the lending process, none of the coding is done until after the borrower receives his book, and most of it is delayed till after the book has been discharged. Then the name of the borrower, his college status, and the call number of the book are notched into the card....

Statistics on Reserve Room Use.

At the end of each semester the reserve room furnishes to each instructor a list of all the books which he has had on reserve, indicating the author, title, number of copies, "period" (i. e., whether the book has been on reserve for 1-, 2-, or 3-hour loans, or for 1-, 2-, or 3-day loans), and number of circulations.

McGaw felt that it was possible to use these notched cards to compile statistics, but "In general, college and university libraries have no further use for the call card if the book is returned on time (325)." Librarians have given two reasons for not using the cards for statistical purposes. "Some libraries are handicapped by staffs too small to undertake such studies.... Other libraries may conceive ambitious plans for the obtaining of information on book use, only to have such plans canceled by other considerations (326)."

In appraising the Notched Card System, Kilgour found that it had several inherent advantages (327).

An evaluation of any system of loan records should be based on three points: (1) the time required to use a record for any one book; (2) its accuracy; and (3) its cost.

As far as time is concerned, the necessity of checking the requests in both active and inactive files has slightly, but only slightly, increased the period required to obtain books from the stack. When it comes to accuracy, it is somewhat improved with the Keysort method; all records of one loan are on one card. Number of renewals, number and dates of notices sent, reports of misplaced books, waiting lists, and all similar information is kept on the original charge slip. Filing errors are not cumulative because all charges are sorted from the file the day after they become due, no matter how badly the charge has been misfiled. The decisive factor is the total labor cost of maintaining the Keysort System. At Harvard the staff has remained the same size as under

the triple-entry system. But the volume of circulation
for the first six months during which the new method
was used was 24.5 per cent greater than that for the
same period in 1937 when the previous high record had
been set. Because of this increase, it would have been
necessary to add at least four people to the Circulation
Department to maintain the triple-entry method. Even if
more assistants had been employed to work with the former method, it is doubtful that the records could have been
kept up to date; each record would probably have been a
day or more behind time, and the sending of overdue notices would have been a week or two late. As it is, all
work is up to date, and there is reason to believe that
the present system is operating at considerably less than
full capacity. Even though full efficiency has not been
attained, the new method has already reduced annual expenses about $3,500.

Upchurch noted several advantages (310).

Use of the McBee Keysort cards has eliminated the date
due file entirely.... One advantage is the elimination of
the confusion and rush at the end of the day, when duplicate records had to be made for the date-due file, and
that file cleared of charges for books returned during the
day. Another is the lessening of chances for mistakes
through the making of only one record when a book is
charged and the canceling of only one when the book is
returned.

The Keysort cards, claimed Stokes and Chapin, gave
definite advantages in the field of accuracy. "One of the
problems to be solved in 1947 was to cut down inaccuracies
in copying and filing charges. Keysort has been successful
in this respect. There is no more copying of charges, and
the punched cards provide for a systematic plan of removing
dead or misfiled cards (328)." Likewise, she saw distinct
financial gains. "The saving in labor would cancel the cost
of the Keysort cards and there would remain a saving of at
least the cost of present supplies $189.96 (329)."

An article in 1955 also noted financial advantages,
but one problem might arise from the situation (330).

.... A saving of one full-time clerical position has already been effected (about $3,000 a year)... The primary
disadvantage lies in the cost of supplies, according to

Mr. Blasingame.   The library estimates that it will use
$800 or $900 worth of punched cards per year.   Though
this cost compares very favorably with the saving in personnel time, it still may present a problem in convincing
budget authorities that the added expense is worthwhile.

Having used a two card system in the past, then
changed to Keysort, Hocker was able to compare the two
systems.   In regard to savings, she was able to state, "The
entire circulation procedure under Keysort consumes much
less than half the staff time used with our old charging system, and such a saving as this compensates many times over
for the rather expensive charging cards (331). "

N. S. Boardman, in a letter to McGaw, was more
specific in the amount of time needed and saved by the new
system (332).

Far more time is needed to make out and address the overdue notices than is required for the sorting, arranging,
and filing put together.

However, Hocker noted one place in which the system
failed to function as smoothly as hoped (333).

Keysort has been in use for almost two years.   Its one
disadvantage is a certain cumbersomeness when a student's library record when withdrawing from school has
to be cleared....   Since the only record for Keysort library charges is the classed file, it is still necessary to
check through the entire student part of the classed file.
This cumbersomeness can be eliminated by clipping each
day the initials of the borrowers' last names, which would
thus reduce such checking to one letter of the alphabet,
which could quickly be needled.   However, thus far, withdrawals have been so few that the additional clipping each
morning is not justified.   Withdrawals average less than
one a week, and, by actual record, the average time for
checking a withdrawal is 10 minutes.   The extra time,
which would be spent if the initials of borrowers were
clipped during the morning routine, would be much more
than this.

Stokes discovered a variation of the notched card system, which adapted notched cards to a different type of library (334).

Galesburg's revolutionary plan should be very attractive
to small libraries which do not need a call slip system
because their books are on open shelves instead of in
closed stacks.... Besides making it possible to use each
Keysort card nineteen times, this method eliminates the
disadvantage of having handwritten call numbers in the location file, with all the attendant possible inaccuracies.

This variation functions as follows (335):

At Galesburg Undergraduate Division of the University of
Illinois Library the Keysort book card has the author,
title and call number typed on it and is kept in the book-
pocket when the book is not circulating.   When it is taken
out the borrower signs in one of the 19 spaces ruled on
the front and back of the card.   The due date is then
notched into the card and it is filed until the book's return.   When the book is discharged, the card is put
back into its pocket.   The next time the book circulates
the due date to be notched into the card may fall on the
same hole as the previous notch.   If not, that notch is
closed up by a correction sticker and a new notch punched
.... the one card forms a triple entry circulation record;
it acts as the location record, the date due record and
the borrower's record.

J. M. Mullendore noted several reasons for the development and form of this book card variation (336).

After a comparison of several forms used by other libraries, a book card on the order of those used by the University of Illinois at Galesburg was designed for books and
bound periodicals.   Since the stacks are open and patrons
help themselves, call slips are not used.   Therefore a
combination call slip and charge card would have effected
little or no saving in time or materials.   Book cards
previously prepared eliminate the inaccuracies of charges
when written by the borrower.   The patron needs only to
sign his name, and much time is saved in filing and discharging.

According to a letter, dated June 2, 1949 from
Louise Stubblefield and an interview with her on February
10, 1950, McGaw found that a variation upon this book card
existed (337).

The Galesburg and Chicago cards are identical except in

two respects: 1) while the former card provides for 19
circulations, the latter card, by adding extra lines for
addresses, accommodates only 14 circulations... 2) at
Galesburg, three direct code holes in "the top row ... indicate (respectively) whether the book is being used by Staff
(or) whether it is a Reference or Browsing Room Book. "
The corresponding holes on the Chicago card are for Reserve, Faculty, and Missing. The holes along the bottom
edge of the Galesburg card are used for the last nine months
of the year, January, February, and March being coded
in the center holes at the top of the card.

The Mayo Clinic, according to Mullendore, uses the
following procedure (338):

.... A blank form was designed for unbound periodicals.
The marginal printing on both forms is identical. The
card as it is designed permits the sorting of any group
of cards within a few minutes. The top of the card provides for seven of these groups: binding, study table
charges, interlibrary loans, long term loans, missing
books, theses and room charges. Two spaces at the top
have been given to a type of charge new to this library:
location cards, or duplicate book cards for books on the
new book shelf and for books that are temporarily on the
reference shelf. By this method the location of any book
not found in the place indicated by the catalog card may
be determined quickly.
Nine spaces at the upper part of the left margin of
the card are used for making dates for overdue notices..
.. The bottom and lower left hand side of the card has
a space for coding the classification number.
.... Having the main catalog entry and the classification numbers punched would be useful, however, and the
only extra time spent on such a record would be at the
time the first book card was made. Correctly punched,
these items would never need changing, and each new
card could be punched from the old one. A sample card
could be punched for periodical titles and the daily charge
on hand-written cards quickly punched from this form.

McGaw made note of a difficulty in reusing the book
cards, but, he felt the problem can be surmounted (337).

... if the card becomes too bulky with stickers, many of
them are torn off, and new ones, providing sufficient cov-
erage but consisting of only one sticker to each unwanted

notch, are added...

Boisen, at Butler University, observes that in using a card over and over sometimes there is a little difficulty in superimposing the "card savers." Whenever this happens it is a simple matter to retype a new book card. [Letter, dated April 27, 1949]

McGaw related "...a suggestion made by Young. He indicates that the cards in use can often be converted to this (system)... since only the margins are used leaving the center area undisturbed [Young, Library Uses of the Marginal...."] However, he also received a letter containing doubts about the system's concrete value. "The staff at the Chicago undergraduate division feel that the ... system compared relatively well with the typical charging systems, but (the staff members) are wondering if it has genuine advantages over the Keysort call card system or I.B.M. or photocharging methods. [Letter, dated March 13, 1950 from David Maxfield (339)]."

Mullendore, however, saw a number of advantages (340).

Our correspondence with other libraries about the system revealed that many thought the cards expensive and that the chief complaint was the use of the card savers (mending stickers) needed to change the date for overdue notices when the book was renewed or circulated again. While the initial cost of installation is somewhat expensive if large quantities of cards are reordered, the cost is only slightly higher than that of other cards. The expense of the cards is offset by shortening the time needed to answer questions and to discharge the books. We have found that the processing of the daily charges (punch the date due, mend any previous punches with card savers, retype book cards on the new forms) is easily completed in two hours of clerical time. Much time also is saved in sorting cards for the overdue notices which must be sent three times each week.

Comment

In conclusion, punched cards have been found to be a reliable and economical means of maintaining circulation records.

I. Strom wrote of a European variation of the notched

card system (341).

At large research libraries it is often necessary to register loans under author, borrower and date of loan or
return.   This can easily be done with edge-notched cards,
but a purely edge-notched card system requires a considerable amount of work during the actual attendance on
the client.   In order to speed up the attendance on clients,
the system under consideration has been modified to the
extent that the primary work is done on book cards on
which the author's name, title and other permanent data
concerning the book are already filled in beforehand.   In
addition to the book card, the library clerk fills in an
edge-notched card of the same size, which is coded for
all data pertaining to the book and the loan.   The edge-
notched card is filed with the book card alphabetically under the author's name in one file.   The edge-notched
cards can be easily separated from the book cards and,
if required, filed under borrower's name or date.

F. E. Orton told of another variant (342).

Instead [of accepting punched cards] we devised a system
for which the equipment could be made quite inexpensively
in the university's workshop and the cards could be run
off for us by our regular commercial printer, [a change
from two card system to one card].
The essential equipment consists of a sorting box
measuring 7" long and 3 1/16" wide on the inside, with
fourteen 1/8" holes properly spaced and about 1/2" from
the bottom in each end of the box: two slender rods for
inserting in the holes; and a device for punching the two
necessary notches in the lower edge of the call cards.
The call cards have seven 3/8" spaces on the bottom edge
marked off in each half, which serve as guides in the
notching of the cards.   The series on the left half of the
card start at the left edge, extend nearly to the center of
the card and are numbered 1 to 7.   The series of spaces
on the right half are placed by starting at the right edge
and running back toward the center of the card.   These
are lettered A-G.   The numbers 2 through 7 are assigned
to the six days of the week on which books may fall due.
The letters B, C, D and E are allocated to an ever repeating cycle of four weeks.   The number 1 and the letters A, F and G are reserved for various codings such
as faculty charges, books sent to the bindery, etc.   From
predetermined schedules we notch (3/8" wide by 5/8" deep)

a call card in one space in each half of the lower edge of
the card, and then by placing two rods in the proper holes
in the box it is possible to drop out that call card from
a group of dissimilarly notched cards. The initial step
in sorting out the overdue cards is accomplished by placing a few inches of cards at a time in the box and shak-
ing it. Those cards with notched spaces coming directly
over the rods, and thus being unsupported, will slip down
onto the rods. By means of a third rod run through the
holes near the top of the cards it is possible to remove
all the cards except those which have dropped down, leaving these, the overdue cards in the box.

If we redesign this equipment we quite likely will place
a scale or guide on the punching machine so that the
notching of the cards could be done more accurately and
the necessity of printing the letters, numbers and mark-
ers for the notches on the lower edge of the cards would
be removed. An electrically vibrated sorting box would
simplify and speed up this sorting operation. We have
seen such a box which was developed independently by the
Zatocoding Company (see L J, May 15, 1948, p. 794) and
which they use to do a sorting operation similar to that
done by our equipment.

McGaw also explained an adaptation of the marginal
punched card (343).

.... after using Keysort for more than ten years
The new call card, which is 3 1/4 x 4 inches in size,
and which is filed, as was its predecessor, according to
call number in a central file, has no perforations at all,
and hence does not require the use of a sorting needle.
A notch is made along the top edge of the card to correspond with one of the letters as shown in the pattern
below (the letters are not printed on the card but are
shown here simply to indicate the coding arrangement):

A C DE FG

The letters A to G are notched in continuous rotation
to designate the respective weeks during which certain
classes of books are due. For instance, the schedule in
June, 1950, called for the notching of position "B" for 1-
week books charged June 5th. Such books would be due
June 12th and would be removed from the file (by hand)
on June 19th for overdue followup. The same position
(i. e. , "B") would also be notched for "Day books charged

June 12th, since such books would likewise be ready for
overdue notices after June 19th. [Letter, dated May 20,
1950, from Morrison C. Haviland; letter dated June 23,
1950, from Robert H. Haynes.] The coding and notching
system used with this kind of card may be identical with
that used with a marginal punched card. The essential
difference between the two types of cards is that one is
perforated and the other is not.

The following reasons have been given for the shift to
the new system on the part of Harvard College:

1) We can print our own cards more economically.

2) The Keysort system has never saved us as much
time as we anticipated, for we have found that what we
saved in one respect we lost in another, e.g., making renewals under the Keysort system takes more time and is
more of a nuisance.

3) Going over the file by hand gives us constant opportunity to do the supremely important job of keeping the
file in order. [Haynes (letter)]

In answer to Haynes's comments, the following points
should be brought out: Statement No. 1 goes unchallenged;
plain cards are less expensive than perforated ones. As
to Statement No. 2, we have to take Harvard College's
word for such an experience, but the testimony of librarians generally is that their marginal punched card system
is more efficient than was the superseded system. As
for the example which has been chosen - the making of
renewals - Harvard's new system does not seem to require the patching up of the original date-due notch. The
same procedure could be followed with marginal punched
cards, but, whether with the one type of card or with the
other, the time saved by not using correction strips must
be compensated for by having to sort out from the fallen
(or extracted) cards the unwanted ones - the ones still
notched at the original due-date position.

The advantage of going over the file by hand (Haynes's
Statement No. 3) is not to be slighted, but careful desk
work day by day should make such a procedure unnecessary except perhaps on a once-a-quarter or once-a-sem-
ester basis.

Regarding Harvard College's present setup we are reminded that it "... is new with us, is more or less in an
experimental stage, and we are not ready to make a definite prediction as to how we are going to like it. "
[Haynes (letter)]

Kilgour gave the details of a triplicate punched card

of the McBee type with inserted one-time carbons assembled in a "Snap Easy" form. The Herlin Press of New Haven manufactured the forms....

When the borrower fills out this charge slip, he automatically makes out a first and second overdue notice. Before the charge is filed, the circulation desk attendant notches the hole corresponding to the date on which the volume will be due. If the borrower does not return the volume on or before the date due, the form drops out when the attendant sorts the file. She then removes the post card on the back of the form to mail it to the borrower, renotches the form so that it will drop out one week later if the borrower does not return the book, and refiles the form. The second overdue notice goes out in a window envelope, and the third or higher is a form letter....

These charge forms are wide, thick and expensive. Their horizontal dimension of 6 3/16 inches would make them impractical for a large library, but in this library the charge file has not exceeded four tub trays with outside dimensions of 6 7/8 by 15 1/2 inches. The forms cost $12.75 per 1,000 in an order of 50,000; our previous 3- by 5-inch paper charge slips cost $1.66 per 1,000 for 150,000. We have used the new forms at the rate of 36,000 per year so that the total increase in cost has been approximately $400.

With the former systems, however, the circulation desk attendant only had time to send out overdue notices during the academic recesses. During January, 1955, 1,419 overdue notices were sent to borrowers with no increase in staff although the desk attendant has been heavily burdened at times. Of the volumes overdue at the time of the first notice, 62 per cent came back between the first and second notice and 34 per cent between the second and third leaving 4 per cent for which it was necessary to send third notices.

...Volumes charged for outside use in 1953/54 and 1954/55. The abrupt increase of 28 per cent (only 9 per cent was due to renewals) that began one month after overdue notices started to go out clearly demonstrates the additional available volumes. This one-fifth increase in service has been achieved at relatively low cost.

Punched Card System

Punched card charging was mentioned in a Library

Journal article in 1936.   E. M. Fair suggested exploring
the possibilities of using "an extension of the electric sorting machine by which a properly punched card such as a
'Hollerith' card might convey all the necessary records to
the final human or mechanical recorder (345). "   Ten years
later, in 1946, an Englishman was encouraging consideration
of "the Hollerith which, if it could be adapted by some ingenious librarian for the sorting of charging cards, would be
a great boon on the charging desk (346). "

At the First Session of Monticello Conference of the
Association of Research Libraries in 1955, Lloyd Morey,
President of Illinois, suggested, "Punched card systems and
other mechanical devices need to be considered, particularly
for book distribution, microreproduction, and other duplication work.   Fines and alternate methods of hastening the return of books are yet another field in which discussion of
standards might be undertaken with some hope of agreement
(347). "

Punched card charging has become useful in solving
some circulation problems, according to Helen Geer, who
wrote: "IBM equipment utilizing punched cards is best suited
to large university libraries which necessarily have large
circulations.   The endless possibilities for punching various
types of information on the cards and the sharing of these
machines with other departments of the institution have made
it possible for many university libraries to purchase this expensive equipment.   In the public library field, probably in
only the very large institutions could the purchase of these
machines be justified.   However, it is possible for the routines done on the expensive machines to be performed at a
local IBM office.   It is interesting to note that the two public libraries in which IBM equipment is used - Detroit and
Stockton - vary greatly in size of circulation, but can still
use the same machines for charging purposes (348). "

(Punched Call Card Method)

The punched call card method provides several advantages over other punched card methods which Parker felt
should not be overlooked.   "By using a call slip printed on
a tabulating card, and retaining this card as a receipt for
the delivered book, it is possible to eliminate all other cards
and yet maintain complete circulation control.   With this
single record, the library can achieve all the advantages of
a triple-card charge system without the disadvantages (349). "

This method was started at the University of Texas Library in 1936 and later recommended in this fashion by R. H. Parker for use in other libraries (349):

When a book is issued, the date due is stamped on a date slip in the book and on the tabulating card call slip. Books may be issued for any length of time on the same form of call card simply by using a different date stamp for each loan period. During the day, cards for books issued are kept in a temporary charging tray, sorted approximately in class order. Books returned to the library during the day on which issued are checked in from this temporary file.

At the end of the day, the cards are sorted according to the date on which books are due (this has probably been done by placing all seven-day books in one compartment, all four-week books in another, etc.), and are then placed in the magazine of a duplicating punch, a gang-punch, or a reproducer. The code for the date due, using the last digit of the year and the numerical code for the month and day, is set up in the punch; and on their being run through the machine, date due is automatically punched into the cards.

The University of Florida Library included more punched information on their cards in spite of the fact that "The policy has been to punch a limited amount of information on the IBM cards in order to conserve the labor of the IBM operator. The following information is punched and printed on the cards in the current file: date due, first five digits of the call number, the Cutter letter, type borrower and type loan. The semester file contains cards punched either with symbols for location or type borrower only (350)." There is no end to the type of information which could be included, R. H. Parker knew, but he explained the reason for omitting much of this information (351):

The punched cards are then arranged and filed into the general circulation file by call number. This operation can often be done more economically by hand than by machine, for machine filing entails manual coding of the call number into each card. When a book is returned, the card for it is removed from the file and destroyed, or returned to the borrower as a receipt.

Concerning the borrower's name he suggested (351):

A large portion of all books lent to students are returned before due; thus, a great saving in time can be achieved by punching the borrower number when the overdue notice is sent. The library desiring to maintain a complete borrower record may punch the card completely at the time of issue.

With the Powers-Samas punched card available in England in 1946 records are made on a "card measuring 4 3/4 inches by 2 inches. The shape and material of the card are standardized, but the layout and contents of the card are at the discretion of the user, providing that he accepts one or two limitations imposed by the design of the machines which will handle the card (352)."

Parker knew that a great number of cards which must be kept on file deal with material to which reference is seldom made. "Most large collegiate libraries also have sizable files of cards for books charged to divisions of the library. These would, of course, be kept on tabulating cards with the location coded and punched, and may be interfiled with the personal charges if desired; but the advantages of a single file are to some extent offset by the extra time needed to search overdue cards in the larger file (351)." At the University of Florida Library (353):

Different color half-inch striped cards are used in the master card file for books not shelved in the stacks, but which are temporarily loaned elsewhere, such as reserves, carrels, browsing, etc. ...Each such group has its characteristic punch so each group of cards can be mechanically selected for inventory purposes.

Margaret Duer revealed the decision at the University of Florida as to the filing (350).

Because of the frequent handling and sorting of the IBM cards, it was necessary to establish two files. Cards in the current file are passed through the sorter on an average of thirty-four times a month. The semester cards, loans to faculty, staff, location cards, and binding records that are handled extensively over a period of months become frayed and cause stoppages in the IBM equipment.

R. H. Parker continued his discussion of the charging method by a consideration of overdue searching procedures

(351).

To obtain the equivalent of a time record the entire circulation file is run through a sorting machine or through
a collator which selects those cards containing the desired
punching without disturbing the sequence of the remaining
cards. It is not necessary to search the file more often
than overdues are sent. In fact, some libraries make
books due only two or three days each week, so that
searches of the file are not necessary each day. The
time necessary to accomplish this object is small indeed,
since both the sorter and the collator select cards at the
rate of approximately 400 per minute.

...When the cards for overdue books have been selected, notices are sent to the borrowers and a hole punched
in the call card to indicate such notice. A column for indicating that a first notice has been sent should be set a-
side on the card, and a code used to indicate date of notice. Before cards for overdue books are returned to the
circulation file, a rubber stamp should be used to mark
clearly the overdues. Such a procedure makes discharging returned books much less strenuous, for it is not necessary to watch the due date. Another method of checking on returned overdue books is to place the cards for
all returned books in a receptacle as they are withdrawn.
At the end of the day, they are run through a sorter to
select overdue cards on which fines should be assessed.
Should the book not be returned after the first notice
is sent, the charges for which a second notice is needed
can be selected from the file by setting the sorter to pull
those cards punched in the "First Notice" column. After
sending the second notice, another similar punch should
be inserted in the appropriate column of the charge card.

In reference to renewal of books the University of
Florida Librarian recorded, "To renew a book, the borrower must fill out a new card (354)."

Pratt saw that it becomes a simple matter to locate
a book for reserve when you maintain a record in shelf list
order (353).

At the University of Florida Library these three types of
record are combined on one card which is filed by call
number in the master card file. By consulting this file
one can readily determine the location of desired books.
By mechanically sorting the cards at the rate of 225 per

minute, one can determine what books were due on a designated date or what books, if any are checked out to a borrower.

Parker believed this one important advantage of the punched call card method is worthy of note. "Since each book issued is represented by a tabulated card, all analyses and studies of library use are brought within the reach of accomplishment. A study of the distribution of circulation by class of book and type of borrower, made at ... University of Texas Library in 1934-35, which required about two thousand hours of clerical time, could now be repeated far more thoroughly, with the machines in 125 hours (355)."

Margaret Duer believed this system provided a solution for definite needs. She wrote: "The single charge card system, ease of handling overdues, and the value of statistical studies are all in favor of the IBM system of book charging. The cost of the operation is reasonable for large college or university libraries (350)." The following information as to costs was given by Duer for the equipment used at the University of Florida Library (350):

2 steel files	500. 00
Printing punch and Sorter, yearly rental	960. 00
IBM Card Circulation (year's supply)	225. 00
	1, 685. 00

The fact that the printing punch and sorter are also being used by the order and serials departments makes the use of the equipment more economical for the library.

A problem which has caused some difficulty is the frequent breakdown of the equipment which necessitates the sending of the IBM cards to the Administration building where IBM equipment is also used. ... it does require fourteen months to fill an order for new equipment.

T. E. Callander believed that the Powers-Samas machines possessed advantages because of their "infallible accuracy, and the speed at which they work (356)."

Four advantages were given by Parker which he saw in the procedures (357).

1. Conversion from other systems is simple since there is no book card, there are no new records to prepare upon changing to the system, and there is no neces-

sity for card pockets.

2. Duplicate and triplicate file records for dates and names are eliminated; high speed selection of call cards in class sequence produces all desired results.

3. Fine procedures are simplified.

4. Research studies in library use are made possible.

A variation of the punched call card system was suggested by J. R. Sharp. This writer suggested using the "Automatic Key Punch" to make two cards - a book card and a record card - containing date, book number and the borrower's ticket number. When the book is returned the book cards are machine sorted into date order, then book number order. The Interpolator matches book cards with the identical record cards. These cards are destroyed. The unmatched record cards are for books which are still on loan. These are saved for overdues (358).

Another approach to Punched Call Card Charging was put into effect at one government library where a triple record was needed. It was described by Legare Obear (359).

After a decade of study, the mechanization of the Library's charging system has been started. The new plan, devised with the assistance of the International Business Machines Corporation and involving punched card charges, gives the Library the necessary control over the material on loan and at the same time makes it possible to prepare overdue notices almost automatically. The Loan Division began preparing Government charges on punched cards on a trial basis in July. By the beginning of October, it was evident that one punched card operator could handle even more than the highest volume of Government charges, which has varied from 200 to more than 400 a day. It is possible to prepare punched cards for as many as 750 items a day. Plans to initiate the punched card charging operations for other categories of borrowers have been made.

The new system calls for the manual listing of author, title, imprint, call number, and borrower's code on a master card. This information is then punched and duplicated in three sets of cards - one for the Discharge File; one for the Borrower's Account File, arranged chronologically; and one for the Central Charge File.

Delinquent loans, the perennial problem of any book lending operation, have been lessened by the prompt request for the material at the expiration of the loan period.

Overdue notices can be prepared as frequently as twice a month with a minimum of manpower and lists can be furnished to borrowers at any time regardless of their length, since the machines can tabulate as many as 120 items per minute.   Individual recall forms are also being developed. It is hoped to have recall operations on a current basis in the near future.

(Punched Book Card Method)

R. H. Parker recommended the Punched Book Card method by saying, "It is possible to utilize a punched card to achieve many of the advantages of the punched transaction card method and all of the advantages of the punched call card method, and in addition, to be able to sort and file records of loans by machine (357)."   The procedure he suggests is as follows (357):

If a punched book card is used containing call number, short author and title, and the desired additional information (which may be duplicated from the shelf list), the record of a loan is made by having the borrower write his name and address on the card; an embossed plate, like that used by department stores, may be used to impress the borrower information on the card.   A date due card is inserted in the book.

The completed records are mechanically sorted by call number.   At this point, the date of issue and transaction numbers are reproduced and interpreted.   The duplicate deck is now filed by collator into the loan file; the original deck with signatures or stamped borrower identification, is filed intact behind a date guide.

Upon return of a book, the duplicate card is withdrawn from the loan file and is inserted in the book as the new book card.

For overdues Parker mentioned a simplified method (357).

On each due date the deck of original cards is matched against the loan file.   The collator is set so that it will select the original cards for books not returned.   Since the cards contain all information necessary for notification of the borrower, notices may be prepared without reference to other files.   One possible method of preparing notices would be by photostating the loan record for insertion into window envelopes. ...

The original loan cards for books returned before due
may be destroyed or held for special studies.   Those for
overdue books are held for subsequent notifications.

Another variation of the punched book card method
has been used at Walthamstow Branch Library, in England.
Eric Leyland described his method in this manner (360):

1. Each borrower retains his reader's ticket permanently, as a type of season-ticket guaranteeing him entrance into the department and the right to borrow books.
2. This ticket is in the form of a small block of wood
measuring some 2 1/2 in. x 1 1/2 in. and is about 1/4
in. thick.   On one face is pasted the usual label bearing
name, address and number.   On the under side - the
thickness - is carried the reader's number embossed in
metal.
3. Each book on the shelves carries in a specially designed pocket, pasted in the back cover, two cards, one
orange in colour, the other blue.   The pocket has been
designed to cover the cards entirely except for about 1/4
in. which protrudes at the top.   This ensures that the
cards cannot fall out.
4. Each of these cards bears the number of the book
in coded punched holes.   The cards are identical except
for the colours.   The orange card is known as the charge
card; the blue as the discharge card.
5. When a reader takes out a book, the orange card
is taken from the pocket, and his borrower's number is
stamped on it, using his specially designed wooden ticket
and a date-pad.   This ensures both rapidity and accuracy.
The date-label of the book is stamped with the date of return as usual, and this date is also stamped on the top
edge of the blue discharge card, which remains in the
book while the borrower has it in his possession. . . .
6. The orange charge cards are kept until the next
day. . . .
7. When the reader returns the book the assistant has
only to open the cover, check that the blue withdrawal
card is still in the pocket, and pass the reader through.
If there is a fine there is, of course, a slight delay, but
only in such a case.
8. Mechanical Operations.   Before any book is returned
to the shelves, the blue withdrawal card is taken from its
pocket, placed in a Reproducing Punch and from it is rapidly and accurately reproduced (in one operation) two new
cards, orange and blue.   These are placed back in the

book.   The blue withdrawal card used for this reproducing is kept aside, forming a record that the book has
been returned.

Sorting and Counting.   Orange charge cards, representing a particular day's issue, are sorted into classes mechanically, and counted, using a Sorter.   They are then
placed in strict numerical order by the same machine.
This machine operates at a speed of 400 cards a minute.

The resulting file is placed behind a date-guide bearing
the date stamped on the date-labels of the books issued on
the same day.

Leyland further stated that only a certain portion of
the circulation file must be searched for overdues (360).

The blue withdrawal cards representing books returned on
that same day, are first sorted into dates (by mechanical
means ...)

Each pile bearing a date corresponding to an overdue
date is then sorted into strict numerical order by the
Sorter.

These piles are then run against the charge cards behind the corresponding date-guides, in an Interpolater.
This machine will mechanically marry like card to like
card, throwing the pairs into one bin, rejecting unlike
cards.   These ... still remain in their original numerical order and are returned behind their date-guides.
Married charge and discharge cards are destroyed....

Overdue cards give some trouble, for only the reader's number appears on the charge cards, and names and
addresses have to be looked up in the records.

Reserves proved a problem until the Walthamstow
Library decided on this novel scheme (361):

...each shelf, tier or case in the department bears a
blank label upon which is written the author and title of
reserved books which, when placed in correct order, will
appear on the shelf, tier or case concerned.   Before the
assistant shelves each consignment of books, the label is
first examined and any book about to be shelved appearing on it is put aside.

The Walthamstow librarian was pleased with the method, but offers these deductions: "Counter staff can be cut
by at least 60 per cent in a large department having 30,000
books on issue at any one time. ...The system serves little

purpose in a department under a certain size. One cannot
reduce counter staff below a certain level. ...My own opinion now is that the system would not justify installation in
any department which has less than 20,000 books on issue at
any given moment.

It should be pointed out, however, that in a system
containing a central library and branches it is quite possible
for all discharging work to be done at the central library,
which would, therefore, entail the installation of the main
battery of machines in a single building, with a reproducing
punch only in each of the branch libraries (362)."

Parker said that the system was particularly applicable to college and university libraries but acknowledged that
it may also apply to public libraries. He listed the following advantages (357):

1. Loan records are kept in class order by machine.
2. Less work is required of the borrower than in the
call card system.
3. Transfer of books to reserve or special collections
is simplified, since the record of the loan and auxiliary
catalogs may be reproduced from the book card by machine.
4. Completed transaction records may be used for statistical studies with a minimum of manual punching, since
all items except borrower identification are punched automatically.

(Montclair's Method)

By way of introducing this novel method of charging,
a few remarks by R. H. Parker can be mentioned. "A system, which combines the complete control envisaged in the
'perfect' system, with completely mechanized preparation and
cancellation of the record, has never been offered to the public, but a trial installation made in the Montclair Public Library in 1941 is still in use. For two reasons it will probably never be widely used: first, the expense involved in
the preparation of a punched identification card for each book;
and second, the fact that it is feasible only in large units,
and not in small branches (363)."

This method, according to Margery Quigley, was intended, not so much to decrease expenses, but to fill more
definitely the need for library surveys and studies. This

quality can be represented in other punched card methods,
but was more fully developed at the Montclair Library as revealed by the detailed work done (364).

> ... the shelf list is retained. An additional card, which
> is a punched card called the "master book card," is being
> made for each book. The master book card contains, in
> the form of punched holes, practically all the information
> on its Library of Congress shelf list card and in addition
> some combination of punches to describe the contents of
> the book. If the book is non-fiction, it is described as
> one of the four following types: (1) aesthetics and belles
> lettres; (2) popular appeal or current interest; (3) schol-
> arly and philosophical treatises; (4) textbooks. If the
> book is fiction, there is a punch on its master card say-
> ing that it falls into one of the following classes: (1) ad-
> venture; (2) detective or mystery; (3) fantasy; (4) histori-
> cal; (5) humor; (6) individual or group studies; (7) roman-
> ces; (8) short stories; (9) sociological studies; (10) animal
> stories....
> The book card now used under the Newark charging
> system is replaced by a punched book card which dupli-
> cates all the information to be found on the master book
> card.

Quigley explained that the borrower's card is also a
punched card, "which gives certain information over and beyond the borrower's name, address, and card number. This
information has to do with age, sex, color, descent, occupation, residence zone, marital status, education, and reading
interest (364)."

The procedures of book charging are begun in the
main room of the library, but the mechanics are carried on
elsewhere, according to the article by Quigley. "One of the
important advantages of the punch-machine system for libraries is that it takes certain files of cards, and the work connected with them, from expensive and often urgently needed
public areas of the building to less expensive work areas behind the scenes (365)."

At Montclair the actual charging of a book was conducted in this manner (366):

> When the perforated book card and the perforated borrow-
> er's card are inserted side by side in the machine at the
> desk, a button is pressed and the two cards are repro-

duced in the basement where IBM equipment is installed,
on a single "transaction card." The machine in the basement automatically files the transaction card as it is
made. When the book is returned, only the book card is
inserted in the machine at the desk and a return card is
produced. Then a machine in the basement with unbeliev-
able speed, automatically removes from the files the particular transaction card made at the time the book was
charged.

In 1952, Quigley wrote that a solution for the branch
libraries which had no tabulating equipment was found in pre-
punched, prenumbered cards, which are ordered from the
factory in pairs, one of which is perforated to become a
stub (367).

The consequent advantage of running the "outpost" and the
automatic types of book charging under different circumstances in the same system is that every loan is now discharged, or, if still outstanding, it may be traced mechanically in the Tabulating Room.
.... All steps in the circulation cycle with the exception
of the actual charging, the application for a library card,
and a request for a reserve - each of these three involving the borrower's presence - are carried out in the central Tabulating Room.
.... Through the stub card it has been possible to
charge and discharge away from machines. ... Through
stubs it is easy to charge unaccessioned, uncataloged, or
ephemeral material.

In 1941, this librarian wrote, "By sorting these transaction cards in various combinations it is believed that many
uses incidental to the primary purpose of the system will become evident and that the numerous facts thus gathered may
add to our present inadequate body of knowledge about reading interest, habits, and trends (364)."

Three years later, on studying the surveys which had
been made, F. E. Hirsch had these comments to make:
"...as the reader studies the twenty-three statistical tables
more thoroughly data gathered by machines during a whole
year and uses his imagination, his efforts are rewarded beyond expectation. He finds that the business machines have
spread before him an amazing wealth of sociological, educational, and professional information, certainly more conclusive evidence than is usually gathered together in strenuous

and costly 'surveys' (368)."

Quigley brought out a totally different efficiency angle
on the use of the punched card machine system by noting
that "this modern method of handling library routines keeps
each book and its card always together, reducing the time
lag between return and re-issue of the book (369)."

In another article, she wrote in greater detail of the
overall savings (370):

> ... even in a library such as the Montclair Public Libra-
> ry, where the volume of loans is relatively small (annual
> circulation approximately 300,000 and staff the equivalent
> of 28), there are actual net savings as well as obvious
> acceleration of service in using the punched card machines.
> According to Dr. Watson O'Dell Pierce's study for the
> Public Library Inquiry (in which this library is designated
> as Library B), the "misassigned time" of the Montclair
> Library's professional staff has been reduced since the
> installation of the machines from 37 per cent in 1939 to
> 22 per cent in 1948.

In 1936, Parker generalized on the implications for
the library world by saying, "When a few modifications in
models are made to meet needs peculiar to libraries, the
day will not be far off when library attendants help borrowers and supervise, while a completely automatic charging
machine both makes and files all charges (371)."

Along a similar line, E. L. Beeler remarked, "Frank-
ly, I fail to recognize the extreme importance of a human el-
ement in such technical routine services as the charging of
books. Future librarians may even find an infallible robot
(of congenial appearance, of course!) entirely satisfactory
for such chores. It seems to me far more important that
we release trained staff members who are qualified to give
personal service where and when it is needed (372)."

W. J. Hand described the special library of the future,
drawing back "the curtain on the panorama of the year 1975"
desiring that we "pay a visit to the library of the Nuclear
Corporation (373)."

> The books are charged by means of a punched card sys-
> tem. When a book is borrowed, the borrower's card and
> the book card are placed side by side in a small control

machine at the desk.   At the press of a button, a charge
card, which duplicates both the borrower's pattern and
the book's pattern, side by side, is mechanically produced on a machine in the workroom.   The book card is
replaced in the book pocket.

Accession Number System

According to Helen Geer, the Accession Number System is "based on the general planning principle of removing
all barriers between students and books" and "should give
quick service and free access to the library shelves (374). "

Philip J. McNiff applied this system in Harvard's
Lamont Library in the following manner (375):

.... Each book is given a circulation number.   This number appears on the book pocket in the back of the book
and on the verso of the title page....   The numbers 1 to
29, 999 were set aside for books in the reserved book collection. The numbers 30, 000 to 99, 000 were assigned to
books in the general collection....
After the borrower has selected his book, he must fill
out the necessary information on one of the charge slips..
.. At the top of each slip there is a series of five
blocks provided for the writing of the circulation number,
a block for each figure.   The book collection will always
be limited to less than 100, 000 volumes and thus the five
blocks will continue to be adequate.   The arrangement of
a separate block for each figure makes for legibility,
which in turn speeds up the filing and canceling of charge
cards.   In addition to the circulation number he fills
in the author, title, his own name and address, and his
status in the university.
The borrower then presents the book and charge card
to the attendant stationed at one of the combined inspec-
tion and charge points at the exits.   After checking the
charge card for accuracy, the attendant writes the circulation number on a predated date-due slip which he slips
into the book pocket.   This transaction completed the borrower is free to go.   The date-due slips have the same
block arrangement as the charge cards and are printed so
that each card can be used four times.   A white slip is
used for books in the general collection and a colored
slip for books in the reserved book collection.
The charge cards are arranged by circulation number

under the date due.   A separate file is kept for required
reading books which circulate for one night only; these
are considered overdue on the following day and steps are
taken to retrieve them.   Books from the general collection are always due on the same day of the week.   A
book borrowed on Wednesday is due on the next Wednesday; a book taken out on any other day is due one week
from the following Wednesday.   Filing by date due automatically segregates the overdue books.   Making books
due on one day each week reduces to four or five the
thirty sections in the charge file which would result from
having books due every day.   This system serves also to
spread the work load during the week.   The heavy week-
end circulation of required-reading books means a busy
Saturday and Monday; the next peak load comes on Wednesday, when books from the general collection are due.
    .... It is now possible to handle twice as many books
in about one-fourth the time previously required.   The
library attendant removes the date-due slip from the returned book, checking to make sure that the number on
the slip agrees with the number on the book pocket. After
this simple operation, the book is ready to be returned
to the shelves.   The date-due slip is used to cancel the
charge card; this is a clerical transaction and the book
can be in use while the canceling process takes place. If
the date-due slip has been lost or destroyed, a note can
be made of the circulation number and the book sent along
immediately.

    McNiff saw several advantages inherent in this system
(376).

The Lamont charging system is simple; it requires no
machines; it allows the combining of charging and inspec-
tion, with consequent saving in time and money; it gets
returned books back into use with as little delay as possible.   Its chief value, however, lies in the increased
efficiency with which books are made available to the students.

    Geer, however, noted one disadvantage: that the sys-
tem was applicable only to "fairly small circulations (374)."

    A variation upon this system was described by T. R.
Adams (377).

The library uses a horizontal C-slip, 2" wide and 3" long

for charging, with places for copy number, author, title,
and borrower's name....

Charging books to student: (1) student fills in C-slip;
(2) student assistant (a) inspects the C-slip for accuracy,
(b) stamps the date on the C-slip and the date due slip in
the book (date is changed once a week), (c) C-slips are
filed by copy number at the end of day after circulation
is counted.

Student returns book: Student assistant checks copy
number of book in C-slip file, removes C-slip and crosses off date.

Adams went on to list several advantages gained with
the variation (377).

(1) less time needed to process books - no book card
or pocket; (2) no slipping of books; (3) very few snags;
(4) economical - backs of old programs and other scrap
paper can be used to make C-slips; (5) record of unpaid
fines on overdue books is kept on C-slips and filed by
name of student; (6) as the copy number is the same as
the accession number, reserves and any other books
checked out can be located through the card catalog; (7)
simple to teach the new student assistants; (8) Date Due
Slip gives record of use of book; (9) any material can be
checked out on C-slips; (10) C-slips are used by the
teachers to check out library and other books to students
from their rooms; (11) a reading list of each student
could be made by filing the used C-slip by student name.

Conversely, he saw two disadvantages (378):

(1) student borrowers must help more in charging process; (2) no classified breakdown of circulation statistics.

Double Call Slip System

(Missouri's Method)

The history of Missouri's method was given by Geer
(379).

One of the most recent methods in the college and university library field is the double call slip system.   Its
chief characteristic is a slip which is divided into two
parts, one becoming a charge card for the book and the

other a date due slip or transaction number record.
Based to some extent on the McBee Keysort punched call
card charging system, the double call slip system was
used first at the University of Missouri Library in 1951
under the direction of Ralph H. Parker, and later, with
slight changes, by the St. Louis University Library. In
1952 the Circulation Department of the Columbia University Library developed the method further, but made considerable changes in the Missouri pattern.

Geer also made note of the supplies and procedure of
this method (380).

Necessary equipment
   1. Call slips - with space for the title, author, and
      call number of the book, and the name and address
      of the borrower - specially designed with a perfor-
      ated stub which is torn off to form the second rec-
      ord. This stub may be at the left of the call slip
      as at the University of Missouri Library, or at the
      bottom as at St. Louis University Library. It has
      space for the call number, volume, and copy num-
      ber of the book.
   2. Centamatic Multiple Punch which has movable slugs
      that can be set to punch out designated numbers.
   3. Metal rod or needle.
   4. Flag-it stickers and round stickers to cover up the
      holes for the renewal routines.
   5. Fine record slips.
   6. Stamp and ink pad.
   7. Guide cards for circulation file, which is arranged
      by classification number.
   8. Circulation statistical sheets.
   9. Overdue notices.
Optional equipment
   1. Time clock for stamping call slips.
   2. Date due slips.
Charging routines
   1. Double call slip for book to be withdrawn is filled
      out completely by the borrower.
   2. Information written by the borrower is checked by
      the desk assistant.
   3. Call slip may be stamped in a time clock at this
      point if the time of the charge is necessary.
   4. Call slip is sent to the stacks.
   5. Copy number, accession number, year, or edition
      of the book is added to both parts of the call slip

by the assistant when the book is brought to the
desk from the stacks.

6. Perforated stub is torn from the call slip and
   placed with the date due slip in the pocket of the
   book.   If date due slips are not used, the stub in
   stamped with the date due and placed in the book
   with the date due at the top.   This completes the
   charging process.

7. Call slip is placed in the proper section of the
   charging tray for filing.

8. Call slips are punched in the following manner:
   the punch is set to stamp out each of the numbers
   on the line except one.   The number not punched
   out is the code number for a given week, representing the date the book is due.   Books are due
   on one day a week, usually Friday....

9. Call slips are counted and stamped with the due
   date.

10. Statistics are entered on record sheets.

11. Call slips are filed in the circulation tray by the
    classification number.

Discharging routines

1. When the book is returned to the circulation desk,
   the date due slip and the stub end of the call slip
   are removed from the book pocket.   The book is
   ready for shelving unless it has been reserved....

2. Stub end of the call slip is matched against the call
   slip in the file.

3. The matching slip is removed from the file, thus
   indicating the return of the book and clearing the
   borrower's record.

Renewals.   When the book is brought to the library, it is
treated as a new charge if it is to be renewed.   When the
book is not brought to the library the following procedure
is followed:

1. The call number is given to the desk assistant by
   the reader.

2. The call slip is pulled from the circulation file.

3. A sticker is placed over the hole indicating the original date due and the call slip is repunched for
   the new due date.

4. Call slip is placed in a temporary file of the day's
   charges.

Reserves.   A call slip is made out by the borrower wishing to reserve a certain title.   These are filed separately
by date of reserve and a flag-it sticker is placed on the
original call slip of the wanted title.   When the desired

book is returned, the flag will indicate the reserve and
the waiting list file can be checked.

Several advantages of this method were seen by Geer
(380).

Advantages
1. Circulation routines performed with speed, accura-
     cy and efficiency. One slip is used to give the
     book and date due information, thus providing a
     single file in which to look for this information.
     Confusion and rush at the circulation desk are re-
     duced to a minimum, thus allowing the borrower
     to be taken care of more quickly. Overdues are
     handled easily and quickly by means of a sorting
     device. Filing errors are not cumulative since
     all the charges are sorted from the file on the day
     after they are due.
2. The system is simple and inexpensive to install.
     No machine is necessary and the supplies are not
     costly.
3. Less manual labor is required of the desk assist-
     ants since the sorting and filing are done mechan-
     ically.

Disadvantages
1. It is not possible to give a faculty borrower a list
     of the books charged to him.
2. Occasional difficulties arise from the failure of
     the desk assistant to record on the stub and call
     slip the copy numbers of the books withdrawn.
     This disadvantage can be eliminated by using pre-
     numbered call slips with the same number on both
     the stub and the main portion.
3. Some faculty users may object to the amount of
     writing necessary, when withdrawing many books.
4. Careful checking of call slips is necessary to
     avoid inaccuracies.

(Columbia's Method)

In an article published in 1953, Stubblefield detailed
the procedures and disadvantages of the system which needed
to be replaced (381).

The Loan Desk at Columbia was divided into two sections
called the Delivery Desk and the Charging Station. At
the former the reader presented his call slip...and re-

ceived his book.... If the reader used the book in the library, he returned it to the same section; if he wished to
take it home, he went to the Charging Station where he
signed his name and address on the permanent book card
in the pocket of the book and where the attendant stamped
the date due in the book. It was at this point that he returned the book when finished with it. At both Delivery
Desk and Charging Station he was required to show identification as borrowing privileges are not extended to all
users of the Columbia Libraries.

Handicaps
(1) At peak periods, such as after term papers were
due and before examinations books would be returned
by the thousands. They piled up waiting to be slipped
....
(2) Daily or weekly sending of overdue notices was impossible. Notices were sent only at the close of each
semester - three times a year.

Fred Forrest visualized the system that was to replace the old one (382).

The proposed system eliminates the book card. Instead,
a double call slip is used, the upper portion of which carries the same information as the call slip in use now and
which is, like the book card, 3 x 5 in size. This portion would be filed in the location, or charge, file. The
lower portion, 3 x 3 in size, carries only call number,
author, and title, and would function as a date due record.
Perforations make it easily detachable. Another card
would be involved in the charging process, a transaction
card (3 x 5) with space for date charged, date due, and
transaction number.

The system, as it was finally adopted at Columbia,
was somewhat different from that seen by Forrest. Stubblefield described the changes (383).

The call slip, which also serves as the charge card, is
a fold-over type of card with carbon on the back in order
to make an impression on the fold-over portion. The
face, or original... carries the same information as the
old call slip... It is the customary library size, 3 x 5,
while the fold-over portion, or carbon copy ... is only
3 x 3, thereby eliminating from this portion the information about the library client. The reason for the size of

the carbon copy is that the tube system at Columbia is quite small and will not take a regular library size card in a sufficiently heavy paper stock.

The method of charging was also described by Stubblefield (384).

The reader fills out the call slip-charge card and presents it at the desk. The desk assistant, after the call number has been checked in the location file, tears the two portions of the card apart, keeps the original at the desk, and sends the carbon to the appropriate tier. When the book comes to the desk with the carbon copy in it, it is matched with the original. The desk assistant takes a pre-dated transaction card...showing date charged and date due and stamps on it in the space designated a transaction number by means of a Bates numbering machine. With the same machine set at "duplicate" he stamps the carbon copy with the same number. The transaction card is slipped into the book pocket and the charging operation is completed.

The procedure for filing was detailed by Stubblefield, who also noticed a problem and its solution (385).

The original is stamped with the date of the operation and placed in a box for filing in the location file. The carbon copy is also dated and it is filed in a transaction file under the date by transaction number. At Columbia we have two charging desks, one at the Loan Desk and one at the stack exit. That means that for each day we have a separate series of transaction numbers for each date. In order to avoid any confusion in case of duplication a different color of ink pad is used in the Bates machine at the stack exit and a different colored pad is used when dating these charges.

Stubblefield also described how special charges were made under this method (385).

....Some books are non-circulating material and thus marked. The assistant at the Delivery Desk uses for these a transaction card on which only date charged is recorded. A slip reading "For use in the Library" is placed in the book and it must be returned on the date borrowed. The same procedure is used for charges to persons who do not have borrowing privileges. The car-

bon copy is also marked making it easy to determine the
next morning if all these charges have been returned. A
charge to a departmental library or faculty member follows the same procedure except that no "For use in the
Library" slip is placed in the book.   For the convenience
of the desk assistant a transaction card of a different col-
or is used for those on which only date charged is indicated.

The process of discharging books took place in the
following manner.   Stubblefield explained (385):

When a book is returned at the Return Desk an assistant
removes the transaction card from the pocket and places
the book on a truck to be returned immediately to the
shelf.   The returned transaction cards are arranged by
date and transaction number.   From these cards the carbons in the transaction file bearing the same transaction
numbers are removed.   These cancelled carbons are
then arranged by call number so that the originals may
be pulled from the location file and the two parts destroyed.
The charge cards of a day's charges are kept at the Return Desk throughout the day so that books used only in
the library may be discharged before they are filed in
the location file.   The charge cards remaining at the end
of the day represent the charges for home use and they
are filed in the location file after they have been counted.

Forrest dealt with the means of renewing books (386).

When a reader gives a desk assistant a list of call numbers of books he wishes renewed the assistant will pull
the cards from charge file and write "ren." and stamp
date of renewal below last date.   The card may then be
placed in tray with the day's charges for re-filing.

The method of reserves and recalls was also described by Forrest (387).

The reader may reserve a book by writing his name and
address on verso of call slip.   As in present system, the
person assigned will collect the cards each morning. The
double card is torn apart, the lower portion to be kept in
date sequence just as the call slip was formerly; the upper portion will be filed in call number order in tray
marked "Outstanding Reserves."   The lower portion will
be checked against charge file and the outstanding charge

card pulled and notice sent if the two weeks period has expired. The lower portion of the request and the upper portion of outstanding charge will be stamped with the date the notice was sent. The outstanding charge will then be returned to the file and the lower portion of request filed under date for second notice. When the notice is sent the reader is requested to return recall card with the book. The assistant at return desk will place such books in a designated place.

....The person in charge of recalls will collect the books at intervals, discharge them, pull requests from "Outstanding Reserves" file, and place it in the book ready for the notice to be sent. A lower portion can be filled out at this point so that the book is ready for charging when the reader calls for it. His request card will serve as a charge card without further signing. If the reader returns the book before he is sent the notice or if he returns the book without the card, the Return Desk assistant will not know that it is a reserve and it will go back to the stacks. When the charge card is pulled then it will be apparent that a request has been made for it. It will then be necessary to go to the shelf for the book. (Some modification was made in the reserve procedure during the course of the experiment.)....

Reserves, as expected, provided some problems. Making the charge on the same slip as request saved the reader time, although there was some confusion at first because of reserves outstanding under the present system. The usual method of dealing with these was for the assistant to fill in the new call slip and ask the reader to sign it. If there was a second reserve on it the charge was made on the book card. The "Outstanding Reserves" file was not kept; instead the upper portion of request card was clipped to outstanding charge in file, the order of reserves being noted by pencilled numbers. This method perhaps saves time, but there is still some question as which would be the better system. Some books, as anticipated, reached the stacks before the reserve was discovered.

Stubblefield has noticed that occasionally the reserve system does not function to perfection. She writes (388):

Some books which have been reserved by other readers are returned before they are due. These books go back to the shelves immediately as we do not know until the book is discharged from the location file that it is re-

served. One must then go to the shelf for it and occasionally it has already been charged out by another reader.
If we recall a book we request the reader to return the
post card with the book. In that case the book is placed
in a designated place so that it may be checked in the
file for the reserve. We have found the readers willing
to cooperate with us in this matter.

The way of handling overdues was described by
Stubblefield (385).

The carbon copies in the transaction file which remain
for a certain date are the overdues (that is, excepting
those charged to departments or faculty members). The
original is pulled from the location file, the shelves are
checked, and the overdue notice sent. It has been found
that this type of card photographs well in the photo-clerk,
although to date only third notices have been photographed.
When scheduling difficulties of the photo-clerk are ironed
out the photographing of all overdues would undoubtedly be
practicable.

In analyzing both the new system and the purposed experiment, a number of tests were made. Forrest described
these in general (389).

Before the experiment began time studies were made of
the routines under the system in use during the course of
the experiment. Time studies were made again using if
possible the same desk assistants to carry out the studies.
Any comparison of time on routines is somewhat arbitrary
as there is no direct parallel in most cases between the
two systems.

The conclusions drawn from these tests were given
by Forrest (390).

The time studies strongly suggest that more efficient
work could be done with the present staff time if the proposed system were put into effect. (One cannot say that
the proof is absolutely conclusive as the data is necessarily fragmentary; further study of the overdue routine
which could not be accomplished before the writing of
this paper should clear up several points.) The complete
charging operation would be completed at one point at the
Delivery Desk while the assistant at the Return Desk
could accomplish the cancellation procedures. When the

latter desk functions as a Charge Desk much of the assistant's time is wasted which could be utilized.   The staff
time saved from slipping could be used in overdue work.
The person at the special Stack Entrance Desk in the aft-
ernoons has extra time that could be used in dating transaction cards and even in cancellation as the date due file
is movable.   The increased efficiency of the overdue
method would be an immense gain.   At the same time it
can safely be estimated that increases in costs at some
points would be balanced by savings in other directions.

        Forrest showed that the new method contained several
disadvantages (391).

The advantages and disadvantages anticipated were largely
borne out by the experiment... The disadvantages are:
    1. Readers at the Circulation Desk must fill out more
information.   Advantages to the reader should more than
offset this drawback, and reader reaction gave evidence
that it is not a major disadvantage.
    2. The fact remains that the person having stack ac-
cess will have to write considerably more than under the
present system.   Many stack users, however, fill out, or
partially fill out, call slips before going into the stacks.
It is believed that they would cooperate willingly if they
were explained the purpose of the new system.   The a-
mount of writing he would have to do could be reduced by
having him fill out the upper portion only; the assistant
at the Stack Exit Desk could fill in call number on lower
portion later.   Author and title would not be necessary on
this part (these are asked for at the Delivery Desk as
they may prove useful to the page in locating the book).
Another suggestion has been a fold-over card on which
the information on the lower portion could be reproduced
by the use of a wax preparation on the back of that part
of upper portion.
    3. The reserve system under the proposed change is
perhaps less efficient although not to a striking degree.
Whether the service to readers by a reserve system justifies the time expended is questionable and is to be studied further.
    4. The assistant handing out books at the Delivery
Desk has increased duties.   The staff does not feel that
this routine is too difficult considering the advantages
gained.

        However, Stubblefield was able to show that these

were not insoluble (392).

> Slight improvements have been made in the procedure
> both during the experimental period and since the system
> was permanently established; however, no major changes
> have been made in the basic features of the system.
> Trial runs have been made on two types of call slips, in-
> terleaved and spot carbon. Spot carbon causes some
> smudging in the file but not to the extent of making any
> charges illegible, and it was found that spot carbon makes
> a better impression and eliminates the extra procedure of
> tearing out and disposing of the carbon. For this reason,
> the spot carbon call slip is now being used.

She found, however, a problem in having the readers
fill out the cards (388).

> Legibility is sometimes a problem as the readers fill out
> the call slip themselves in pencil. They are naturally
> not as easy to read as a typewritten book card would be.
> We do have the author and title on which to double check
> if the call number is not plain.
> This system requires very accurate work on the part
> of the desk assistants. Such accuracy in the matter of
> volume and copy numbers may be slighted in very busy
> periods when one is working under pressure. Lack of
> complete information can be cleared up by checking shelf
> list and shelves, but that is time consuming.

There were several advantages revealed in a comparison of the new system with the old (388).

> It should be apparent that the limiting factors which were
> major considerations in the designing of the new system
> have been observed. This is not an expensive system.
> The only piece of machinery used is the Bates numbering
> machine which costs about eighteen dollars. The same
> card trays, guide cards, and overdue notices are used.
> The increased cost of the call slips is somewhat offset
> by the elimination of the book card and the time taken in
> preparation of the latter. The transaction card replaced
> the date due slip and the transaction cards formerly used
> at the Delivery Desk. No changes had to be made in the
> cataloging preparation for the books already in the collec-
> tion. The new system is operated with the same circula-
> tion personnel as the old. Some routines have been added
> but old ones have been dropped; the new routine at the

Delivery Desk is more complex but the Charging Desk is entirely eliminated; discharging from two files is compensated for by the elimination of the extra sorting and handling of the books in slipping under the old system.   The changeover was easily made as old charges could be slipped as previously without interfering with the new discharging routine.   A permanent feature of the Circulation Department, the location file, has been retained.

Forrest also listed the advantages found with the new system (393).

The advantages (both anticipated and unanticipated) to the reader are:
1. Charging is completed at one point.
2. Identification is shown only once.
3. Name and address is written only once.
4. All books are returned at one point.
5. Books are returned to the stacks more quickly. During peak periods under the present system some books do not reach the shelves until two days (37 hours of library time) have elapsed.   Under the proposed system the most time required would be four hours.
6. More books will be available because of systematic system of overdue notices.   (Still an hypothesis.)

Other advantages affect the Department more directly than the reader:
1. Elimination of Charge Desk routine.   The two separate routines of charging and discharging are entirely separate, making routines more efficient and more easily learned.
2. Slipping eliminated.... Under the proposed system the Desk Assistant takes book from reader, places it on truck; all other steps are eliminated except the removal of the truck to the sorting area.   The congestion at the file is eliminated and one truck instead of eight is needed in the Circulation area.
3. Easier compilation of faculty records.   (Still an hypothesis).
4. Control strengthened by the systematic overdue routine.
5. More accurate statistics kept without tally sheets.
6. More accurate charging with transaction card.
7. More accurate information on charge card (made from catalog card).
8. Easier check on slips sent to tiers (also an advan-

tage to the reader).

     After the system had been in operation for a longer
time Stubblefield found more advantages (394).

     There have been other minor advantages which have been
of help to the department:

     (1) All information is on the face of the card making
checking in the file easier.   Under the old system one
might have to pull the card from the file and turn it over
if the signature was on the back.   If photographed for overdue, two exposures were necessary for one card.
     (2) Author and title are copied by the reader from the
card catalog.   Under the old system, desk assistants had
to make new book cards when the old one was filled or
the book had none.   As the bibliographic background of
staff members is somewhat limited, they could not always
make them accurately, especially for languages such as
Russian.
     (3) It is now possible to make a check of faculty and
departmental charges from the transaction file without
going through the location file.

     Stubblefield gave the results of the tests (388).

     The test of the new system is whether it has eliminated
the drawbacks of the old without generating proportionately greater ones.   It should be obvious that this system
has cleared up the sources of reader irritations.

     Stubblefield also claimed: "After eight months of use,
this charging system now used at Columbia has proved to
have sound basic principles which make for effective circulation control and which may be easily and effectively adapted
to other libraries (395).

     And Geer felt that the Double Call Slip System was
"a solution to university librarians seeking a way to charge
out books without using expensive equipment (396). "   She
added, however, that there was much clerical work involved.

Indefinite Loan System

     A single record system is possible if there is no
time limit put on the loan of a book, because a date record

need not be kept. J. S. Komidar introduced his comments on the possibility of this system with the following remark (397):

> The collection must be a large and comprehensive one which permits a reasonable amount of substitution of titles and provides more than one copy of the titles most in demand. Regardless of the excellence of the book collection, however, the factor which controls the success of the indefinite time loan system is the accessibility of the student body. A system of recalls is essential, and the efficiency with which the recall system operates depends on whether or not the students can be reached easily by telephone or campus mail. Unless it is possible to have a book returned within a day after notification, the plan cannot operate satisfactorily.

H. F. McGaw also recognized the importance of having the students "within easy reach (both as to distance and time)" but felt that this system would prove "superior to the one in most common use at the present time." He described the mechanics of the charging procedure (398).

> The borrower (Fred) selects his book from the open stacks, writes his name on the book card, and drops the card in a box provided for this purpose. The circulation assistant, when a number of cards have accumulated, stamps them with the date loaned, secures the necessary information for circulation statistics and reader's records, and transfers the cards to the charge file.
> Fred is guaranteed a 7-day loan period. He may keep the book for a much longer time, without any penalty, but once someone else demands the book, Fred must surrender it on one day's notice, or pay a fine. If another student (Margaret) asks for the book, the assistant sends Form I to Fred's home room.
> The time and effort usually spent by the library staff on maintaining a date-due file, in sending overdue notices, and in renewing books, are conserved for more worthwhile duties.
> A different emphasis is placed on circulation. Books are called in only if they are actually needed, not just to recover them to fill up empty shelves.... When the librarian requests a book, the borrower knows that it is desired for the use of a fellow student, and this knowledge furnishes proper motivation for returning the book.
> The fine is sufficiently heavy to discourage both the in-

different student's forgetfulness and the selfish student's practice of "buying" an extension of time.

A technique for dealing with the designating of books which are being recalled was suggested by Komidar (399).

To facilitate checking of returns, a black metal tab is fastened to the top of the card of the volume being re-called. Tabbed cards are checked at eight o'clock each morning and notices sent for overdue books. Black tabs are exchanged for orange ones to indicate overdues. Fines for overdue books are the same as those for reserve books, 25¢ per hour per title, beginning at 8:15 A M the day fol-lowing the date due.

McGaw went into detail in his remarks on the so-called problems involved (400).

Critics may point out that the indefinite loan will result in the retention of a book until the borrower receives Form I. This will sometimes happen, of course, although the writer is convinced that, on the whole, students will return books as soon as they finish with them. The stu-dent would otherwise accumulate so many books that they would appropriate his entire desk space, both at school and at home. The student is also aware of the likelihood of misplacing a book.... The most important influence operating on him is his recognition of the fact that anoth-er student's demand may limit his use of the book to only seven days.
    It will be acknowledged that books, by their mere pre-sence on the shelves, induce students to read them. How-ever, the indefinite loan plan doesn't imply that all the books are always out.... Furthermore, the suggested system, by its nature, will encourage a student to place reservations on books, to the end that he gets the best books for his purpose (selected from the entire holdings of the library).
    .... The library will not collect enough fines to take care of rush orders, miscellaneous supplies, etc. This charge is easily met by our recalling that the ideal cir-culation system should operate in such a manner that the fine box is always empty.
    .... In case a reader wishes to read a book in the library, he still signs for the book, but instead of desig-nating his home room, he writes his table number. This not only provides helpful statistics as to the total use of

the book, but obviates the necessity, on the part of the assistant, for searching the shelves and the charge file, and perhaps all the tables - even (especially in a rush period) giving the report of "missing" - for a book that is being used somewhere in the reading room. (A different box is provided for self-charging these books.)

Charging of Reserve Books and Nonbook Materials

(Reserved Books)

Under some of the various charging systems as attempt is made to show method for dealing with reserve books or "room use" books as often called. [See reference nos. 97, 116, 173, 198.] However, a basic plan was set forth in the December, 1887 Library Notes for dealing with "restricted books" which were needed for class assignments (401).

Each professor is invited to send in lists of books which he wishes withdrawn for a time from circulation and kept in the reading room, so that each student may be sure of opportunity of consulting them....

...we went back to the common device of putting the books behind the loan desk, and issuing them on call. Instead of the common call slips we made first green call slips printed thus: -

The new feature here was the hour line and the record of the fine to be paid for failure. The clerk drew a line between the hours between which the book was taken out, thus showing how long it had been out if called for by sum [sic] one else. On its return the charge was canceled by a line between the hours of return. The objection of this plan was, of course, the delay in writing even the briefest title or call number of the book when calls came in great haste.

We then adopted a long slip (7.5 x 25^{cm}) five times the size, and heded [sic] thus:

Under this hed [sic] ar [sic] 30 lines on the face and and 40 on the back, or 70 in all on the card, which is thus good for 70 issues without rewriting a number or title. The top is fild [sic] out like any book card with author, brief title, and call numbers. The student wishing it signs his name (or initials, for we recognize all our readers by their initials only) on the first blank line. The clerk puts the nearest hour in the colum [sic] "issued, "

and cancels the charge when it cums [sic] back, by the
nearest hour in the colum [sic] canceld" [sic]; e.g. from
8.30 to 9.30 all entries are markt [sic] 9.
    While the book is in use the long card stands in the
book's place on the shelf behind the loan desk.   When the
book cums [sic] in, the card is laid inside it and projects
from the cuvers [sic].
    ... we are trying the long card because it is more
prominent as a special kind of book.   It is also of choco-
late color, while other book cards ar [sic] white.   Finally,
the long card holds twice as many issues, thus giving a
fuller record of the recent use of each book....

    J. D. Rideout commented on the method used at the
University of New Hampshire where books were all on closed
reserve but of two kinds: Two-hour and three-day (402):

    Two-hour and three-day reserve books are shelved togeth-
    er in a closed workroom.   They are distinguished from
    one another by book cards of different colors, yellow and
    blue.   The blue card states: "You may keep this book for
    three days.   The date when it is due is stamped on the
    book pocket.   A fine of 25¢ is charged for each day the
    book is overdue."

    The University of California in 1929 used a rental col-
lection to supplement the reserve book collection charging
three cents a day.   Coupons were purchased from the business office which were used instead of cash (403).

(Non-book Materials)

    In the 1941 volume of Wilson Library Bulletin, Azile
Wofford gave a description of the method often used in charging pictures, periodicals and vertical file material (404).

    Pictures
        In the first place, pictures on various subjects may
    be checked out at one time by the reader....   Also the
    reader may have several batches of pictures out at the
    same time and there is consequently much opportunity for
    confusion in their return.
        Pictures in the Greenville Public Library are mounted
    on cardboard 10 by 14 inches, unmounted pictures being
    kept in brown folders of a slightly larger size.   They are
    filed by subject headings penciled on the upper right-hand
    margin, the mount or folder to be filed the long way.   All

pictures circulate for two weeks, without privilege of renewal, and a fine of five cents per day on each package
is charged for overdues.

Unmounted pictures are circulated to adults at the
discretion of the library assistant, but not ordinarily for
use in schools.... If pictures are circulated unmounted,
they should be so charged.

Pictures are circulated in folders, about an inch larger than the mounts, made of heavy brown wrapping paper
with generous folds on all four sides. On the top side is
pasted down a date due slip headed by the printed rule as
to length of loan and fine charged. A limit of twenty-five
pictures, ten on a given subject, may be borrowed at
once, though the reader is asked to borrow less if the
supply is limited.

The charge is made on a P-slip with a carbon copy
for each. The reader's name in order for filing is lettered by the assistant at the top of the slip and his library
number, if used by the library, is added below. The
pictures presented are assorted by subject, and so listed
with the number of each subject. A total of the pictures
borrowed is indicated at the bottom of the list. The date
due is stamped on the original, the carbon copy and the
date due slip. The reader then writes his name and library number beside the date due on the date due slip.
The carbon copy of the charge slip is clipped on the inside fold of the brown folder and the reader cautioned to
keep it there and to return it with the pictures. The original slip is held for count and for filing alphabetically
by the reader's name behind the book cards for the corresponding date.

When the pictures are to be returned, the reader identifies the wrapper by his name and has a record of what
pictures he borrowed for each date due. If the returned
pictures tally with the charge in the file, the two slips
are checked and discarded. Otherwise, they are clipped
together, with indication as to what pictures are yet to be
brought back, and returned to the file to await the return
of the missing pictures or to be treated as overdues. All
returned pictures are examined, and the reader charged,
for damages beyond those of normal wear before they are
returned to the file. "Damage noted" is stamped on the
back of picture mount so that future borrowers may not
be held to account for that damage.

Pictures

In the Greenville Public Library, the last three months'

issues of all magazines may be circulated for a period of
seven days without the privilege of renewal and a fine of
one cent per day on each periodical is charged for overdues.... At the circulation desk is kept an alphabetical
file of cards with the name of a magazine lettered at the
top of each....

When the reader presents a magazine, or as is usually the case magazines, to be taken from the library, the
assistant draws from the file a card for each magazine
title represented.   On the card she writes in the date of
each issue being taken and has the reader write his name,
library number or both, according to library policy, below
the list of issues.   The assistant then stamps the date due
beside the name on the periodical card and on the slip
pasted on the back cover of the magazine.   The periodical cards are then held for count and for filing in the
date due file alphabetically by the name of the magazine.

When the periodicals are returned, the card is found
by the date due and a check is made that the charge on
the card tallies with the periodicals returned.   If all have
been returned, the date due is scratched on the back cover of each magazine.   The periodical card is returned to its
place in the file on the desk and the magazines are routed
for return to the shelves.   If only part of the magazines
are returned, the card, with indication as to which issues
are still out, is returned to its place in the date due file
to await the return of the others or to be handled as overdues.

Vertical File Material

For circulation of material from the vertical file, all
large envelopes in which periodicals and pamphlets are
delivered to the library are kept at the circulating desk.
Cards similar to those used for periodicals, except of
another color, with the heading "Vertical File" are kept
on file at the desk.   In the Greenville Public Library, all
material, except that marked not to circulate, may be
taken from the vertical file for a period of seven days
without privilege of renewal.   When the reader presents
material from the vertical file, a list of the subjects with
number of clippings or pamphlets on each subject is made
on one of the vertical file cards.   The reader is then
asked to write his name, library number or both, according to library policy, below the charge.   This charge is
repeated on one of the brown envelopes, selected to correspond in size with the material being taken, and a circle drawn on the envelope to enclose the charge.   The

date due is then stamped beside the name of the reader
on the vertical file card and within the circle on the envelope in which the material is taken.... The vertical
file cards are held for count and to be filed in the date
due file for the corresponding date.

When the vertical file material is returned to the library, the assistant searches under date due for the vertical file card on which the charge tallies with that on the
envelope. If all material is present, the card returns to
the file on the desk and the material is routed for filing
in the vertical file. Otherwise, the vertical file card,
with indication as to what material is still to be returned,
goes back into the date due file to await return of other
material or to be treated as overdue.

Lucile Fargo mentioned that in some schools different
colored cards are used for different types of non-book materials. "This adds to ease in filing and discharging (405)."

In special libraries, periodicals often form the bulk of
the material circulated. Lucile Jackson dealt with the two
main methods of routing these in her Technical Libraries
(406).

There are two main systems of routing periodicals. The
first consists in having each individual pass the journal
on to the next name on the list either directly or by inter-
office mail, with the understanding that each issue is to
be kept no longer than three days or some other specified
period. This hand-to-hand routing provides no control by
the library, and requires a clientele inclined to be voluntarily considerate if it is to operate successfully. The
other method involves the return of each journal to the library, from which it is sent out anew to the next person
on the routing list. The advantage of this latter method
is that the location of all circulating issues is always
known, and it is therefore not difficult to find a particular
one in the event that there is need for it. It is obvious
that this system of circulation may take most of one staff
member's time if many periodicals are routed. Moreover,
it may also take longer for a journal to reach the last
name on the list, particularly if special messenger service is not used.

D. J. Campbell wrote that he had made use of a
visible index, the Lampel "Synoptic" system used in Europe.
This makes it possible to suspend in a frame the permanent

cards for all periodicals with temporary cards showing order,
receipt and circulation of all issues to the public.   The method of circulating these periodicals is given below (407).

> Circulation is also controlled by means of the temporary
> cards.   Each individual or department to whom journals
> are circulated is designated by an initial.   The periodic-
> als spend the first week on a rack and then are circula-
> ted, in an order recorded for each on the back of its
> permanent card.   There is no need to record the first
> routing, since it follows automatically a week after re-
> ceipt.   Periodicals are returned to the library staff after
> each routing which is only possible because circulation is
> kept to a minimum.   Subsequent routings are each re-
> corded by an initial and brief date in the remarks column,
> each entry automatically cancelling the previous one.
> When circulation is over, a dot is placed between the vol-
> ume and part numbers and the parts are placed on a sec-
> ond rack labelled "Not to be removed until (one week a-
> head)".   People who wish to borrow them then put their
> names on the labels, and all subsequent removals from
> the library, including those for binding or loan to another
> library, are recorded in the loan record, which having a
> page for each periodical, requires only the briefest pos-
> sible detail.   Periodicals not circulated, which go straight
> on to the second rack, have a cross on the temporary
> card by the part number.   Library users are educated to
> look for the spot or cross, and the circulation symbols,
> if an issue is not in its usual place.
>   Periodicals are thus displayed twice, and can be lo-
> cated at any time by means of the two records mentioned.

Punched cards were used in the system described by
Harvey Bumgardner which was used at the Detroit Edison
Company Library (408).

> ...This system does away with the involved and tedious
> hand method of record-keeping and route-list preparation
> ....
>   All of our punched cards and circulation lists are pre-
> pared by another company department which handles cus-
> tomers' accounts for electric service.
>   Magazines are returned to the library only after the
> circulation to ten names has been completed.
>   He noted the discontinuance of the sending of a list
> of magazines to some 1,050 employees once a year for
> checking those publications desired during the following

year.

The Company serves an area of about 7,600 square miles, with many offices and employees stationed in outlying districts. Presently approximately 1,050 employees, regardless of work location, are receiving magazines upon request. The total number of magazines-per-employee circulation handled last year was 192,000 (number of copies x 10 x average number of issues per year)....

In 1940, when we had 8,500 company employees, magazine circulation required one hundred man-hours per week to do the job, or the equivalent of two and one half employees. In 1951, after we had completed all of the changes enumerated above, and with approximately 11,600 employees, this work is being done with only thirty man-hours per week being required.

One of the latest advances in the matter of routing scientific journal material was described by V. W. Clapp in 1955 (409).

An interlibrary facsimile communications hook-up between the Library of Congress and the National Institutes of Health.... Its use by the Library of Congress and the Institutes represents the first attempt in this area to use facsimile as a substitute for the time-consuming loan of scientific journals.... A "flying spot" of light scanned the article transmitted; the blacks and whites of the printed page were converted by photo-electric cells to electrical impulses, which were sent over special telephone line and reconverted to print in Bethesda at the rate of 15 inches each minute. Scientists receiving the copy were enthusiastic over the speed of the service. And since they could keep the copy at hand, rather than returning it to a library at the end of a borrowing period, they were freed from the usual "overdue" notices. From a library's point of view, there are similar advantages; workers at the lending library need not be deprived of books that are borrowed for the usual lending periods. "This enables us", said Mr. Clapp, "to have our cake and eat it, too. We can give a much wider service without having the books leave the library."

Chapter 4

Circulation Control -
The Transaction Card System

As mentioned by Maurice Tauber, among others, the introduction of Transaction Card Charging Systems was designed to reduce the amount of professional and clerical time spent on the mechanics of circulation (410).

Ralph R. Shaw, by whom the idea of Transaction Card Charging was first conceived, put the idea into effect at the Gary, Indiana, Public Library where it was used with the Recordak Charging Machine. In 1941 he made the following explanation (411):

> The installation of photographic charging at Gary illustrated that on the experimental level, at least, it is not necessary to make any changes in the materials or records used in any library which uses self charging or mechanical charging with predated date due cards. The only change required is the numbering in consecutive order of date due cards. The charging system in use at Gary for more than a year employs no elements that are new or differ greatly from those customarily used, but this description is not, of course, intended to preclude possibilities of great improvement over this first experimental installation. The camera replaces the mechanical charging machine or the manual charging process, the supplies are date due slips, which are identical with those used for self charging except that a serial number is stamped on each; either borrowers' cards or identification cards may be used, and book cards may be used or may be replaced by the book itself. The slips are numbered with an automatic numbering machine.

This new photocharging system was mentioned by T. A. Bailey, who went on to trace the later developments of the use of the transaction card with other mechanisms of charging (412).

Later other systems embodying the principles of the photocharging system were developed by Remington Rand and
International Business Machines Corporation and recently,
Stewart Smith, at the St. Louis County Library, adapted
the principles to a new audio-charging system, using dictating machines... All these methods have in common
the transaction card which is the key to the systems.

The actual procedure involved when books are circulated by the insertion of serially numbered transaction cards,
was described in this manner by Bailey (412):

These transaction cards may be plain serially numbered
cards or they may be punched cards. Transaction cards
are numbered serially one to any number sufficient so
that cards will not be reused in less than three months'
intervals. When a book is lent, a transaction card is
placed in the book, and when it is returned, the discharge
is made by simply withdrawing the transaction card.
These cards are sorted in numerical order, and the missing transaction cards guide the overdue clerk to the proper position on the microfilm, photocharger paper, or to
the dictating machine disc for the name and address of the
borrower, and the identity of the book.

A Mr. Smith at the July, 1955 California State Library Workshop mentioned the following three methods being
used in this type of charging (413):

1. What might be called the "hand-operated" method,
which was conceived by Walter Kaiser of the Wayne County, Michigan, Library.
2. Photographic charging, which was invented by Ralph
Shaw while he was at Gary, Indiana, Public Library and
which is now used with Recordak or Diebold cameras and
the Photocharger. The latter device was invented by Mr.
Shaw and is manufactured and distributed by Remington
Rand.
3. The "audio-charge" method as invented by Stewart W.
Smith, of the St. Louis County Library, using an audible
rather than a visual record of the transaction. Through
the medium of commercial dictating machines such as
"Sound Scriber," "Gray Audograph," or Edison equipment.

During the last few years the Brodac and Bookamatic
systems have been devised which make use of the transaction
card method. See reference nos. 556, 567.

The advantages and disadvantages of Transaction Card
Charging Systems were revealed by Mr. Smith (413).

1.   Speed of both charging and handling return and low
labor costs.
2.   Speed in arriving at circulation figures....
3.   System can easily be adapted to name and address
charging as opposed to borrower's number charging. This
results in greater economy in sending overdues and makes
possible the elimination of the numerical registration file
at least.

The disadvantages of transaction charging are:

1.   More difficult processing of reserves than with book
cards.
2.   Relatively high investment in mechanical equipment
and occasional need for service.
3.   Inability to make daily analysis of circulation statistics - must use sampling technique.

In 1955, Herbert Goldhor criticized many charging
systems which were in vogue and attempted to direct attention toward simplification by listing the criteria of the "ideal
circulation system (414)."

If we estimate conservatively and in round figures that it
costs five cents to charge and discharge a book, the total
cost of public library circulation is about $20,000,000 a
year or roughly one-third of the total expenditures for current operations of all public libraries. This is about the
percentage of total expenditures that various surveys have
shown the cost of circulation work to be in individual public libraries.
     The work of making and cancelling the record of loans
is not only costly but, for the most part, without any use
or value providing information on books kept out longer
than the authorized period.
     We may get some workable idea by considering absurd
systems, such as having patrons borrow books without a
record of the loan and solely on their honor (would more
books be kept out than under present systems?). Or using a type of ink which would fade, triggered somehow by
the return of the book. Or developing methods for detect-
ing "overdue prone" borrowers (how much do we know a-
bout what kinds of books are kept overdue for how long
and for what reasons?). But it is more likely that the

problem will yield to a rational and systematic analysis.
In an effort in this direction, here are twelve criteria
for an admittedly ideal circulation system for a public library:

An ideal circulation system should be economical to install and to operate. In general, machine systems have
high capital and low maintenance costs; and hand systems
have low capital and high maintenance charges (since they
usually take longer, and time means salaries)....

The system should be easy to understand....

It should reduce to a minimum the possibility of error
in making records, in filing them, or in cancelling them
again.

It should take as little time as possible for each transaction, to minimize the time required of the patron and
to maximize the number of patrons who can be served by
one clerk....

It should require as few operations and as few support-
ing tools or forms as possible....

It should be proof against mistakes in the operation of
the system by staff members or patrons. This would involve built-in devices to prevent or at least detect breakdowns in machinery, to arrest errors, and to foil attempts to steal books by changing or falsifying records.

It should readily lend itself to use in all types of agencies (branches, departments, schools, bookmobiles),
with all types of materials (books, pamphlets, unbound
magazines, phonograph records, films) and other variations (such as multiple loan periods with both juvenile
and adult borrowers).

It should allow for the centralization from all library
agencies of as many of the operations as possible, to
facilitate their standardization and mechanization and to
free personnel in the branches for service to patrons.

It should be as easy, convenient, and effective a system as possible for both patrons and staff. For the patron it should allow him to return to any library agency
a book borrowed from any other agency. He should not
have to produce a card or other form when he borrows
or returns a book, and he should have some indication in
writing in the book as to when it is due. For the staff,
an ideal circulation system should be truly automatic and
operated completely by the patron (as is a dial telephone
in a pay booth). The more inconspicuous a circulation
system is and the less attention it needs or draws, the
better it is.

It should do supremely well the one most important

thing needed: to identify the items which are overdue
and the borrowers who have them.   Since only relatively
few items are kept overdue, the record of other loans
should be handled as few times as possible....

It should facilitate and at least make possible the exe-
cution of four subsidiary functions of a system of circulation records: to renew any item, to place a reserve a-
gainst any item now on loan, to count the number of items
circulated by various categories, and to produce a record
of the use of each book (for consideration in discarding
and book selection for studies of reading)....

It should facilitate or at least not constitute a barrier
to the use of a new or different classification scheme,
such as one based on readers' interests; to changes in
the length of loan period or in other circulation rules; to
the transfer of books between agencies; or to changes or
innovations in other areas of librarianship.

L. T. Dinnan, responded to the article by Goldhor assuming that it was an attempt to advocate transaction card
charging. She writes (415):

In a small library... the question of book control becomes a vital reference consideration, and is the real
weak point of all transaction number systems....until a
system is devised which really meets the needs of the
small library and does for it what the book card system
now does and the transaction number systems do not do,
the small library would do well to stick to the book card
system, aided perhaps by the Gaylord or some other machine, but fundamentally using the available labor of its
desk staff, which must be on the job anyway. The old
adage that a bargain is only a bargain if you need the
goods still applies, and in spite of ideal systems or criteria for them, time is only money if you have a market
for your time.

Since the suggestion was made to discard the borrower's card, H. C. Bauer gave an opinion in support of the
use of cards (416).

There are cogent reasons enough for supplying patrons
with library membership cards, but even if there were
not, good public relations would be the clincher. The
truth of the matter is that people like to register and receive membership cards if the amount of red-tape involved is not excessive. To have a special card made

out in one's own name inflates the ego. A patron of a library likewise would presumably have a greater affinity
and attachment to a library with which he is duly enrolled
and officially authorized to carry a membership card.

Bernard Van Horne described the condition which existed at Portland, Oregon, Public Library when the decision
was made to discard transaction card charging (417).

The Library Association of Portland, Oregon, has discarded the transaction card for charging and gone back,
or as we like to think of it as gone forward, to hand
charging.... Of the two basic requirements for a charge
system - title accountability and an overdue record - the
transaction card fails completely on the first and does the
second only moderately well. The savings and the disadvantage of quick return to the shelves, while real, are
not nearly so great as were believed.

Needless to say, long consideration and study were
given the problem. Alternatives were exhaustively studied. We have long been troubled by the cumulative effect
of transaction cards on our ability to produce a desired
title or any information about it. Our library, like many
others, has been plagued by rising book losses....

Our experience since the abandonment of the transaction card in November, 1957 has been short but startling.
For one popular title, old but still popular (Gone with the
Wind), on which we had assumed we were giving good
service, only 5 copies of the 22 on the shelf list could be
accounted for.... Of 100 reserve cards in one week, 17
titles could not be found. With hand charging these are
reported to the departments and notices are sent to those
who left the cards. With transaction cards they might
have been in the reserve file for months. Multiply these
episodes by the days of the year and the number of readers!

The board of directors accepted the fact that the abandonment of transaction cards would mean more personnel.
This cost proved much less than we had anticipated. A
better report on costs will be available with longer experience since we are now in the busiest months and we have
had to cope with the legacy of the transaction cards in an
unwieldy delinquent file.... It will be difficult to isolate
charge system costs because of the concurrent sharp rise
in all aspects of the use of the library but we can, even
now, be sure that they are less than anticipated....

We have lines, yes, but they move quickly and they are

not frequent. ...Reserves here are heavy and the readers
have expressed strong approval of the speed of reporting
on them.   Our total number of reserves on file has greatly decreased.

We are using the hand charge as a point of departure
for improvements in the charge and registration systems
.... We file our book cards and send overdue notices on
a weekly basis. We will next try a two-week basis since
this will reduce the number of files for searching.

We have no qualms or regrets about the decision to
drop transaction charging. We hope that further developments in the application of machines to charging will be
found but we are convinced that to be acceptable to us
they must provide information in a 24-hour period on the
state of stock as well as due-date accounting.

In the periodical Odds and Book Ends for fall, 1957,
it was recorded that "All of the transaction card charging systems eliminated the filing of circulation records and the carding of books. Most of them simplified the overdue process.
However, none of them have really solved the problem of reserved books as yet (418)."

Photocharging System

As explained by Shaw the photocharging systems make
use of a camera, date-due slips, identification or borrower's
cards and a book card or similar record.   See reference no.
411

The Recordak Microfilmer was described by Corbett
as being "a machine which will photograph documents on a
200-foot roll of 16 mm. panchromatic film at a reduction of
26:1, and which will reproduce same for viewing on an incorporated projector with a magnification of 24 times the film
frame. Dimension: Height 36 in., width 20 in., depth 22 in.
(419)." At Youngstown Public Library modifications were
made on the camera equipment (420).

We use Recordak Model J C - 1 cameras with a few local
adaptations. We disconnected the left-hand control button
and use the right one only; took out the tray in the photographing area and replaced it with two pieces of plywood
which serve to make a flat surface and to fix the spacing
bar permanently at five inches; installed in the desk at
the left of the operator an ordinary mercury switch for

controlling the camera on and off. This is more convenient to reach than the one provided in the camera, doesn't
wear out, and is quieter in operation.

We use the reader in the camera at the two smaller
branches, the Recordak reader at one branch, and a Rem-
ington-Rand model F075A at the main library where we
handle also the overdues for the book trailer. Where
there is considerable film scanning, there is much to be
said for having a motorized reader, on which the film remains constantly in focus.

The Diebold Portable Flofilmer was chosen by the
Free Public Library of Philadelphia according to a pamphlet
published by Diebold Incorporated. "This is a high speed
microfilm camera, small, attractively styled and simple to
operate. Forty-seven Diebold Portable Flofilmers have been
installed throughout the system (421). " According to another
pamphlet (422),

.... The camera does successfully the same microfilming
job as done by cameras ten times the size and ten times
the weight.

Microfilms faster than any operator can feed letters,
bills, checks, statements, cards or other documents.

E. M. Bowen gave a useful description of their machine (423).

The camera. The camera chosen was one of those marketed by the Flofilm Division of Diebold Incorporated, of
Norwalk, Connecticut. This company manufactures three
microfilm cameras, a portable model and two office machines. The 9600 Portable Flofilm Camera was chosen
for use, some of its main recommendations being its
cheapness and its small size in comparison with the microfilm cameras marketed by Kodak and Remington Rand
....

The 9600 Portable Camera is neat and compact, standing 12 inches high, and weighing 20 pounds. When open
it takes up 2 square feet of counter space. It will photograph copy of mixed weights and sizes up to cardboard
thickness, 11 inches in width and any length, at a reduction of 24:1 on to 16 mm. film. It uses magazine loaded
film, which is easy to insert and remove, and may be
handled safely in any light. Illumination control is obtained by a switch which can be set as desired to light,
medium or dark. The electrical components are integrat-

ed into a compact electronic pack which can be removed
and replaced as a single unit when necessary. The camera is simplicity itself to operate; the material to be photographed being guided to the rollers which carry it
through the camera in a matter of seconds.

The Remington Rand Photocharger differs from the
other two machines in that it is a camera which exposes sensitized paper rather than film. This fact was mentioned in
a 1947 Library Journal article (424). By way of advertise-
ment Remington Rand, Inc. released the following information
(425):

The Photocharger can be installed in any library in five
minutes. It is the only charging system which requires
no changeover in equipment, borrowers' cards, book identification or in any other supplies. All you need do is
plug in a Photocharger, number some date due slips consecutively with a numbering stamp and you are ready to
start photocharging.
The Photocharger is the most accurate charging system known - the camera cannot transpose a number.
The Photocharger requires no reading machine. It provides a complete record giving all pertinent information in
a size easily read by the unaided eye. Economy is combined with convenience by using photographic paper which
is much less expensive per square inch than film, thus
making possible the production of a readable copy at low
cost.
The Photocharger can take care of approximately 300
records per hour, far in excess of actual needs in charging books.
Easy to operate.
The Photocharger requires no previous experience to
operate. It can be fitted into any charging desk or can
be mounted on a table or typist's stand. It is low-slung
and will not obstruct supervision.
The Photocharger automatically cuts off strips of paper
18" long containing ten charges and drops them into a
light-proof container attached to the camera underneath
the charging desk. The Photocharger can be equipped
with a receiving spool to pick up the entire 350' roll.

Another piece of equipment was suggested by Remington Rand as a "rapid, convenient way to read the Photocharger record." This Photocharger Reader has a reading frame
which "holds the photo-record in position for rapid reading

and easy concentration. The Photocharger Reader saves time in the preparation of overdue notices (426)."

M. Bloss favored the use of film rather than the paper negative, for a record of the transaction. He gave two reasons for this (427).

.... With the film you can photograph the book information directly from the book pocket, rather than the book card or book slip, thus eliminating what can be a very troublesome piece of paper. Furthermore, the film cost is about one-third that of the paper negative. The paper negative record costs about $2.25 a thousand "charges," plus whatever it costs you to develop the photographic paper in your own library. The microfilm would be about 75¢ a thousand charges, developed. Recordak has a new camera out which would triple the number of exposures per 100 feet of film, lowering the film cost still more.

The date due cards can be printed in various colors, according to Charlotte Matson, which indicates "the length of issue and matches the color of the book slip. To prevent possible errors in dating, we use a separate rotary dater for each length of issue, the handle colored to match the date card.... For convenience in reading the film, we distinguish each length of issue by the location of the serial numbers on the date due card, since colors do not photograph. "Rental" is stamped on the date due card of rental books, which are dated as of the current date, when the charge begins (428)." At the University of Illinois Library, Marianna Andres recorded, two colors were chosen for the transaction cards (429).

We chose the colors green and white for the transaction cards and had them made a little longer than the book cards, partly for economy - we felt we could use them longer - and partly so that they could be removed from the book pocket more quickly without pulling out the book card also.... The choice of whitet ransaction cards proved to be unfortunate because they looked too much like our new wide book cards with the accession number at the top. A number of times during the first few months of 1953 books were found shelved with the transaction cards still in the book pocket.

At Youngstown Public Library six complete sets of these transaction cards were used; each was designated by an initial prefixing the number on each card (430).

Series	Use	Number of cards
O	One-day loans	2,000
S	Seven-day loans	16,000
F	Fourteen-day loans	15,000
T	28-day adult loans	35,000
J	28-day juvenile loans	35,000
V	Vacation loans	1,000

These cards will be used over and over again until the
"date due" spaces are filled up (allowing normal use, a-
bout ten years).   In addition, there are two other numbered sequences of transaction cards used for charging within the system, for example from the main library to a
branch.   These are used once only and are so printed
that they may be used by the library on the receiving end
of the loan as a temporary card.   By filling the necessary
book information in on the transaction card, the charge
can be made manually.   These transaction cards, like the
others, are filed in sequence when the loan is completed,
but when a series is filled in (no missing numbers), the
cards are thrown away.   There are two sequences in use:
"C" for "one-circulation" from one agency to the other, -
and "L" for "long-loans", within the system for an extended or indefinite period.

These transaction cards resemble others in use, with
one important (to us, at least) difference.   The transaction
numbers are printed in bold face type three-eights of an
inch high.   This is the same kind of numbering you see on
a baggage check in the railroad station, in fact, that's
where we got the idea, and we had a baggage tag maker
print the cards.   These larger numbers make scanning the
micro-film much easier.

One other feature of the transaction cards: the sequences are printed in colors to correspond to the loan period
stickers to help get the right card in the right book.   The
color scheme also applies to the daters,   and to the book
cards in the ten other branches where manual charging is
still in use.

Three types of transaction cards can be used with this
system according to Corbett: cards requiring manual filing,
punched cards, and notched cards which he referred to as
Cope-Chat.   He briefly compares these three types (431).

Summing up the various methods of filing transaction cards
one would say:
1. Even manual filing represents a saving in time as

compared with the filing of Browne "charges." It is, however, a boring job and requires the strictest accuracy if
overdue notices are not to be sent out in error. Even in
the best of systems, the occasional mistake is almost certain to occur.

2. Undoubtedly, machine-fed cards can be sorted in the
least possible time, and with strict accuracy. The cost of
the cards including punching, might well be prohibitive,
and at best their life can be estimated at no more than
half those of the conventional type. Bearing these two
factors in mind it will probably only be in large systems
where a cheaper punching cost can be obtained that this
method will in any way be economical. Only in exception-
al circumstances would the purchase of machinery be war-
ranted. In some instances cheap use of another department's machinery, given adequate time for its use, may
possibly be justified.

3. Cope-Chat cards cannot approach machine-fed cards
for speed. On the other hand, they reduce manual filing
by half and the work can be done locally in each library.
While not designed for large-scale work, they do appear
to be ideally suited to the number of transaction cards
any one service point may be called upon to file each week.
While the cards cost three and a half times conventional
transaction cards, this is less than the cost of machine-
fed cards when punched, and they have a life equivalent
to the former and twice that of the latter.

Shaw remarked that the numerical registration file
could be eliminated since the charge records give the name
and address of the borrower. He makes one further point.
When a borrower forgets his card it is not necessary to look
up his number or make a temporary card to charge a book,
"his Social Security card or any other identification may be
photographed in place of his borrower's card (432)."

The book card may be used, according to Shaw, or it
may be eliminated by pasting the identification of the book in
the upper right hand corner of the inside of the back cover
(424).

At Youngstown Public Library the "Transaction cards
are stored in ordinary metal trays on a two deck table. They
are sorted in a wall-mounted set of pigeonholes (10 each way)
(420)." The tray for the cards and other items of equipment
were made by the janitor for the University of Illinois Library
(429).

One of our janitors made a wooden tray with two compartments to hold the two kinds of transaction cards.   This
was done much less expensively than purchasing one read-
y-made.   Another homemade product, and one for which
we had no pattern, was a strip-winder.   A contraption
like this was necessary for referring to the photostrip
more than one time.   One was built to hold the roll for
the two-weeks books and one for the four-weeks books
while making overdue notices.   A third piece of homemade
equipment was a straight board with two rows of overlapping book pockets.   This was needed to hold reserve post
cards.

The charging procedure was given by Shaw, reflecting
the way it was done at the Gary Public Library (433).

In order to charge the book, the borrower's card, the
book card, and date due card are photographed on about
one-eighth of an inch of 16 mm. film by simply pressing
a button; then the date due card and the book card are
placed in the pocket of the book, the next book card is
placed in the machine, the button is pressed, and it, together with the date due card, is placed in the book; until finally with the last book charged on any card, the borrower's card also is picked up and placed in the book, and
the process is completed.

Later at Gary when the Remington Rand Photocharger
was installed a modification was made (434).

At one side of the Photocharger a stack of pre-dated date
due cards (stamped with date-due for patrons benefit) is
placed, and a maximum of 20 cards (at one time) are
placed on the cardholder of the Photocharger.   These
cards are serially numbered at the head, the lowest number being on top of the pile.   The charging desk assistant
places the book card which has been removed from the
book pocket, on top of the serial card and just below the
serial number.   The borrower's identification card is
placed last just below the title.   Then by stepping on the
foot pedal the Photocharger records all these items on a
small portion (2,000 charges for 350 ft. roll) of photographic paper.   The book card, identification card and
date due card are all picked up in one operation and placed
in the book pocket.   The speed of operation is increased
with experience.

When Wandsworth's library experimented with photo-charging, four charges were photographed at once with the Recordak. Appropriate pairs of charging cards and transaction cards are placed in the book pockets and the "ticket" is returned to the reader (435).

H. D. Martell believed that the "key to multiple charging is simultaneously photographing one serially numbered transaction card with from two to seven book cards. At the Bacon Memorial Library, Wyandotte, Michigan, the following routine was worked out using a Diebold Flow Film Camera (436).

> Charging: 1. The patron presents his books and identification card to the circulation clerk. The clerk opens each book, removes the book card from the book pocket and stacks the books open to pockets. 2. The clerk arranges the book cards so the information on each card is exposed, places one serially numbered transaction card in front of the book cards, and places the patron's identification card in front of the transaction card. The information is ready to photograph. If more than four books are to be charged an acetate template is used to keep the cards aligned while photographing. 3. After the cards are photographed the identification card is returned to the patron. The transaction card and first book card are placed in the proper book. Additional transaction cards are taken in rotation and one placed with each book card in the proper book pocket. 4. The charging operation is completed. . . .
> The average issue at Bacon Memorial Public Library is three books per patron. By multiple charging we use one-third less film and do the charging twice as fast.

In 1956, Corbett reported again on the experiment being conducted at Wandsworth. He had found that the book card could be discarded (437).

> By experiment it has been found that if the book number is printed at the top right hand corner of each flyleaf and the transaction cards permanently housed in a dispenser on the bed of the microfilmer, all an assistant has to do is hold the book in the machine against the dispenser and place the reader's ticket at the right of it. He then presses the exposure switch (by means of a foot pedal) and the record is taken. The top transaction card is removed from the dispenser and placed in the pocket of the book, the ticket returned to the readers, and the process is thus

completed。   With this method book cards are not required
....   One card only, therefore, goes into each book on
issue and the simplicity of the arrangement is such that
the whole process can be completed in 3-25 seconds, which
is significantly quicker than Browne.   It may, in fact, be
possible to fit the camera with an instantaneous release device, so that as the book touches it the exposure is automatically made, and thus saves even a few more fractions
of a second.
    One may wonder why such an obvious method had not
been tried before, but I think all experiments had been
based on resting the whole book or a specific part of the
book on the bed of the microfilmer for filming, whereas,
it is only necessary to hold the top right-hand corner of
the flyleaf under the camera.   The book never leaves the
assistant's hand.

    The Norwich Central Lending Library in England made
use of pressure-button photography.   P. Hepworth reported
that the "photograph is taken as soon as the book is laid on
an operating button, no manual or pedal work being necessary
(438)."

    Corbett recorded that tests had shown that this instan-
taneous press-button release switch is no speedier than a foot
pedal.   He gave this advice to those who felt it easier to operate, "If it is used the assistant must always remember to
place the membership card on the microfilmer first, before
bringing the book on to the exposure switch, otherwise the
photograph will consist of the assistant's hand instead of the
membership card (438)."

    A borrower's card is not used with the charging meth-
od at the Tulsa Public Library.   Mrs. A. B. Martin explained (440):

    Each patron signs his name and address on a scratch slip
    (the Tulsa Public Library uses L.C. proof sheets cut in
    half).   The date due slip is inserted in the book pocket on
    which are typed the author, and title and call number of
    the book.   The borrower's name is placed beneath the au-
    thor and title of the book and the button is pressed record-
    ing the transaction on film.   If the borrower takes more
    than one book he signs his name only once.   The slip with
    his signature is used until all books charged to the individ-
    ual have been recorded.   The signature card or slip is
    then destroyed. . . .

Each borrower fills out an application card which is
kept in an alphabetical file near the charging desk. No
numerical record is kept and borrowers are not required
to present identification of any type.   The signatures and
addresses of the patrons have been adequate as a means
of locating overdue and missing books.   There have been
only seven instances in which the names were so illegible
or in which such inaccurate information was provided that
it has been impossible to reach the borrower in the nine
months since the system was begun.   The average patron
signs his name and address while the date due slips are
being inserted in his book so there is no delay at this
step.   Borrowers are spared the irritation arising from
failure to bring identification cards or from lost cards.
The expense of numerical registration and identification
cards is eliminated.

In English libraries where interavailability is practiced,
photocharging can be adapted to allow loans on tickets of other authorities.   Corbett, in 1955, explained that "Photography
is as usual but the transaction card only is placed in the book.
The ticket and the book card are retained and all such 'charges', regardless of date, are filed in one numerical sequence
of accession numbers (444). "

Later, in his book, entitled Photocharging, he dealt
with this subject extensively (442):

Loans on tickets of other authorities....
There are two classes of readers to consider, (a)
those using the tickets of another branch library in the
system, but which is still on Browne, and (b) those using
tickets of other authorities.   In turn, class (a) divides into two further categories.   (i) Those habitually using the
photocharging branch, and (ii) those only occasionally using
this branch, and borrowing in the main from the library
at which they were originally registered....
Category a-(i) is easily dealt with by re-registering the
reader at the library he habitually uses.   In the case of
category a-(ii), however, if a reader's ticket is to be
withdrawn from him against each book borrowed, then he
is in fact being penalized as compared with other residents
using a photocharging library.... The answer to this problem, therefore, obviously is to photograph the reader's
ticket in lieu of a membership card, and then return it.
Category (b).   From this stage it is but a short step
to convince oneself that the reasoning holds good with the

tickets of other authorities.   All such tickets should be
treated in the same way as normal photo-charging membership cards, and thus preserve one method of charging
for all loans except inter-library loans, which must be
treated somewhat differently, due to the need to return
the books within a month.

Andres complained that at the University of Illinois
they had found no practical way of charging magazines, pictures, and clippings (443).

It would be unsafe to clip a transaction card to such material, and since it is impossible to put pockets on all of
it, we continue to charge it by hand.   Charging phonograph records at the main charging desk was found to be
a very awkward procedure, as quite a bit of space is
needed for this and our new charging desk is not large
(less than 10 feet long). ... They are charged in the Art,
Music, and Film room, in which they are located on the
second floor....

At the Vancouver Public Library, these non-book materials were dealt with in the following manner (444):

Pamphlets taken out at one time are all issued on the
same TN card and placed in an envelope which is marked
with TN number, number of pamphlets and date due.
When more than one pamphlet is issued a record is kept
of the number of additional pamphlets and added to the
daily count.
Clippings and pictures are recorded on a card - number issued, subject matter, etc. , - they are placed in an
envelope which is marked with TN number, etc., like a
pamphlet.
Hand charging is done (1) in cases of power shortage;
(2) while film is being changed; (3) for all Deposit borrowers, since the card must be clear before money is refunded; (4) for Branch loan; (5) for holiday loans.

H. S. Hacker in describing the procedure used on the
Erie County Bookmobile with the Remington Rand Photocharger, revealed the method of handling the sensitized paper after
a number of charges have been recorded (445).

The blank paper record in the Photocharger is so arranged
that as soon as eight charges (borrowing records) have
been snapped, they are dropped together in a light-proof

envelope to be developed by a library helper or by whatever other arrangement is found most convenient. Since
neither handling of the basic photocopying equipment nor
the developing requires special training or particular skill,
the whole job is generally handled by the regular staff in
about half the time formerly required.

If the Photocharger is used, the photographic record,
when developed, can be placed into a separate box or tray
for each day's charges as a 1947 Library Journal article ad-
vised (446).

Once or twice a day sort the 7-day and 14-day date due
slips returned into trays or pigeonholes containing the
photographic record corresponding to their numbers, keeping the 7-day and 14-day cards in separate packs.

Shaw gave the following procedure to follow when discharging a book (433):

When books are returned the only process that is necessary to discharge them is to take the date due slip out of
the pocket and put it in a drawer for later filing, returning the book to the return shelves for shelving immediately. Each day the date due cards returned are sorted into
piles by serial number, which process takes approximately
ten minutes per thousand cards.

In the same article, Shaw continued giving the method
for dealing with overdues (433).

Then, when the books for any date which have not been returned are a week overdue, all the accumulated date due
cards are put in order by the serial numbers stamped on
the card and missing numbers are noted; this process
should not require more than fifteen minutes a thousand.
These two steps replace all of the filing of cards and carding of books that was previously necessary. Thus, if
books issued on June 1 used date due cards numbers 1 to
1000 and the file of date due cards is complete, that
means that all the books have come back, and consultation
of the film is unnecessary. If numbers 50, 100, 150, and
200 are missing, the film reader is turned to these numbers on the film, which, of course, occur in consecutive
order; and the typist sitting at the reading machine at her
typewriter types off the overdue notice, making a carbon
copy which is to be used for later notices, and mails the

typed overdue notice to the borrower.   All books returned
automatically discharge themselves, so that we police only
4 or 5 per cent of books issued instead of policing 100
per cent of them as is done in conventional charging systems.

A slight modification was adopted at Gary Public Library to aid in caring for overdues (447).

Once a week the cards for the books which will become
overdue in the following six days are arranged numerically.... At this point missing numbers for each date are
recorded on a plain card and placed in front of that day's
pack.... Any missing transaction cards which are returned before notices are written are interfiled by hand
and the number scratched from the list of missing numbers in front of each pack.

Bloss said that at Youngstown Public Library, in the
final sorting "a blank red card slightly over five inches long
is put into the empty pigeon holes; when the cards are assembled the missing ones are automatically flagged in the files
(420)."

Martell, who suggested the method of multiple charging [see reference no. 32], gave the following instructions
for locating the overdues (436):

Missing transaction cards indicate overdue books, and
microfilm is checked for the title of the book and borrower.   If a patron has been issued five books and returns
all but one book the missing transaction card indicates the
overdue book.   The clerk searches the microfilm for the
transaction sequence in which the missing number falls.
For example: The patron withdrew five books and the
transaction card photographed was number 351.   This indicates that the patron has number 351-352-353-354-355.
If all transaction cards are returned but 354 the clerk lo-
cates the transaction sequence, 351.   As the book cards
and transaction cards are mutually in sequence the overdue title is found by counting the photographed cards
starting with number 351.

At the District of Columbia Public Library a Remington Rand Photocharger-Photoclerk system was adopted.
Short-cuts were revealed in the overdue procedures as an
issue of Pioneer indicated.   Other libraries have used the

Photoclerk for overdue routines with photocharging but have
had some problems.   The article noted this but gave some
advice (448).

Some libraries have reported much difficulty in getting
suitable facsimile photographic reproductions of photo-
charges with the Photoclerk for mailing purposes.   The
simple solution to this problem is using a typewriter with
larger type in preparing the original readers' cards, as
the Photocharger reduces the typing by 40 percent and
small type becomes barely legible.
    It is interesting to note that the use of the Photoclerk
for overdues has resulted in a considerable personnel
saving.   Prior to its installation, a typist in the Central
Library Circulation typing pool could type approximately
50 overdue notices and about 35 bills an hour.   The latter
required longer time because it was necessary to insert
the amount of the fines and other charges.   Production
with the Photoclerk is dramatically higher.   A clerk now
photographs about 300 an hour.
    A further saving is accomplished through the use of
window envelopes which eliminates the need to type the
readers' names and addresses for mailing.

    Shaw advised that all date-due slips should be retained
as they may be used over and over again (446).

Missing date-due slips should be replaced by numbering
another slip.   This may be done by numbering machine
or in pencil or black ink.   Date-due slips for 7-day books
should not be reused for at least three weeks to avoid confusion of series; date-due slips for 14-day books should be
held for six weeks.

    At the Free Public Library of Philadelphia centralized
overdue control is used, according to the pamphlet printed
by Diebold, Inc. (449).

The overdue operation for the entire system is located in
a separate office in the Central Library.   The film from
each branch is sent to central overdue.   The branches are
relieved completely of the problem of controlling overdues,
mailing notices, etc.   With the use of Diebold electric
readers, three girls can handle overdues for all 44 agencies in the Free Library System.

    Wandsworth's library avoided much of its overdue rou-

tine, according to Corbett, by sending only one notice, at the
beginning of the 10th week of issue (441).

> These overdues will now be sent in weekly batches instead
> of daily.   The file of returned cards, carrying the approp-
> riate week's identifying letter, will be filed in serial num-
> ber order (or they can be presorted).   Any omission from
> the complete run of serial numbers will denote overdues. .
> .. The number of overdues is quite low as a result of
> leaving notification for this relatively long period, but sta-
> tistics previously kept (Record, May, 1955, p. 201-2) re-
> vealed the soundness of this practice.

Matson wrote that, with regular renewals (with card
and book present) "the date due card is removed and a new
transaction photographed, the due card being marked 're' or
'trans,' as the case may be.   The matter of repeated renewals or transfers is controlled because there is a record of
the previous renewal or transfer on the dummy in the returned file or on the date due card (450). " When the book
is not present or when renewal is made over the telephone
another policy is usually followed.   Shaw remarked that all
that is required to make a renewal is the serial number on
the date due card.   He continued (451):

> However, since most libraries will not renew books for
> which reserves are waiting, when making renewals over
> the telephone it is usually necessary to ask for the same
> information that is required in the conventional charging
> systems in order that the reserve file may be checked be-
> fore the renewal is made.   The information is entered on
> a slip or card, preferably of a different color than that
> used for date due cards, and it is thrown into the tray
> among the date due cards returned that day.   When the
> cards are arranged for recording of overdues, the num-
> bers covered by renewals are represented by renewal slips,
> and thus overdue notices are not sent until the renewal
> period is over.

At Tulsa Public Library, Martin revealed, most of the
books circulated for 28 days with no renewals (452).

Reserves may be handled in any one of several methods, according to Shaw, who explained (432):

> A Linedex listing each title on reserve may be kept at the
> return desk where the book can be checked against the

waiting list and sent to the reserve assistant if there are reserves waiting, or dummies may be put on the shelves, or a Linedex list may be maintained at the return shelves or at the charging desk.

Martin gave another helpful note: "A red 'Flag-it' on the pocket of books on which there is more than one reserve serves as an additional reminder (453)."

At the Queens Borough Public Library the Remington IVI desk was used as a visual reserve file. Charlotte Murray wrote of this, giving the alterations which were made on the stand (454).

An extra flange was put on the inside edge of the frame to correspond to flange on the outer edge. The grooved channel was removed from the center of the frame and the clips at the bottom of the frame were made larger. The library's bindery department made binder's boards to fit into the frames. These boards have inter-fitting pockets of library buckram, two rows of twelve pockets or twenty-four pockets to a board. The boards are then slipped into the frames and the reserve postals are filed in the pockets, giving a secure and easily consulted method of checking returned books for reserves.

The counting of circulation is simple, Shaw said, since "the first and the last numbers on the date due slips give the total number of the date due slips used each day, and that corresponds with the number of books charged out. To get the total it is necessary only to add to these the number of books renewed, if renewals are to be counted in the circulation, and you have your total (455)."

At the Tulsa Public Library, Martin explained, "A tally sheet is kept by the photocharger on which the first and last number in each series of numbers (28-day, 7-day, and rental) is noted. A record of fiction, non-fiction, and periodical circulation is kept by the simple device of a tally mark on this sheet for each book circulated (453)." Blasingame, quoting from Susan Smith, described a similar means of keeping track of circulation. "A sloping board with a hole at the top rested on the desk. Different colored marbles to represent the various classes, fiction, history, biography, literature, etc., were dropped into the hole as each book was issued and the take counted the next morning. A resourceful librarian could make quite a game of this (456)."

Bloss did not advocate the count of circulation by classes or the record of the use of the individual book, but saw that if they were needed they could be had at probably less time and expense than with book card charging. "The film can be read and tabulated in any way that is desired for almost any kind of circulation study that one would wish to make. As to the record of use of individual titles, the book could be stamped each time it is returned to the shelves, as a part of the sorting and shelving process (457)."

At Wandsworth an automatic adding machine was used to give "total Adult Non-Fiction, Junior Non-Fiction, and Junior Fiction issues (441)." H. E. Tucker described the electric counter which was wired to the switch of the Remington Rand Photocharger and activated electrically (458).

The unit consists of two micro-switches at $1.59 each, a four-digit non-reset electric counter at $4.25, a small amount of wiring, and a holder for the switches and counter, manufactured of wood by the library's carpenter shop. [connected with Remington Rand Photocharger]

In operation the lower quantity of circulation in a branch, whether adult or juvenile, is selected for counting. Assuming that juvenile is the lesser circulation, pressing a single button marked JUV actuates both the micro-switches - the one controlling the Photocharger and the one controlling the electric counter. Pressing the other single button marked ADULT actuates only the one micro-switch controlling the Photocharger. With the transaction card charging system the number of loans for any given period is automatically obtained by subtracting the first number from the last. A similar subtraction of first number on the counter from the last gives, in this case the number of juvenile loans. Subtraction of this figure from the total number of cards used gives the number of adult loans.

Counting by this method can be done on a daily, weekly, monthly, quarterly, or annual basis as desired. The four-digit counter allows a figure up to 9999 and can go far beyond this since the next number is 0000 and the series begins again. Being non-reset there is no chance of making errors in resetting; furthermore the reset feature triples the cost.

There is no limit to the number of switches and counters that can be used for counting a variety of types of materials.

Perhaps this is the solution to **M. J.** Mamalakis' request made in 1942 (459).

> Why not include a mechanism such as is found in cash registers which would automatically total the number of books circulated during the day? There could be keys to punch in the 10 classes which would cause an imprint on a roll of paper in the machine. This would provide a record of the books in each class. It would be a simple matter to tally the totals of each class from this record.

It at least seems reminiscent of a device described by **M. W.** Plummer in 1891 (84).

> The librarian has invented and has in use an ingenious device for registering the classification of books circulated. A set of buttons, bearing on the top the numbers of the classes, is placed in a drawer at the delivery desk. These are attached to numbering stamps, and each time the button is pressed a number is registered. At the end of the day, the last number under each button shows the circulation of that class.

At the Lakewood Public Library a charging machine was devised which performed the operation similar to the manner of the Recordak or Diebold. This charging machine operated successfully for three months but had to be discontinued because of the impossibility of obtaining film under priorities. O. Pragan wrote of this charging device (460).

> .... This apparatus consists of a 16 mm. movie camera adapted for this purpose and built into a machine made entirely of non-priority materials. The whole mechanism is built into the interior of the charging desk with only a glass plate and a press button visible to the public. The records to be photographed - borrower's card, book card, and date due card - are placed on this 5 x 9 inch glass plate. When the button on the desk is pressed, the light switch (four 100-watt bulbs) is turned on and, simultaneously, the shutter of the camera is released. All information necessary for following up the book is recorded in this one operation and book and date-due cards are slipped into the book pocket. (The borrower's card is returned to him after all his books have been charged.).....
> The daily routine consists only of winding the motor and reading the film and frame counter. The film counter indicates the amount of film already used; recording this

is necessary to determine when to reload the camera.
The frame counter gives the total of pictures made which
is the record of the daily circulation.

The significance of this library-owned and non-commer-
cial outfit seems to lie in its practicability. The camera
and microfilm reader can be used for other purposes.

A general consideration of the costs of photocharging
was made by Shaw in 1947. He wrote (461):

The Photocharger can stretch your total useful budget.
The Baldwin-Marcus study showed that the median cost of
charging books was 2 cents for labor alone. If that figure is adjusted for increased labor cost since 1940, for
vacations, holidays and other lost time, and for the cost
of supplies and equipment, the median cost is well above
3 cents per charge. Properly applied, photocharging can
reduce the cost to less than 3/4 of one cent for labor,
equipment and supplies, thus saving up to three-fourths
of the present cost of circulation work!

Furthermore, as pointed out in the Baldwin-Marcus
study noted above, circulation work consumes approximately 30 per cent of the average library budget. Thus, even
if the savings were limited to 50 per cent of the present
costs of lending, that would represent a 15 per cent increase in the total budget. Photocharging is the easy way
to stretch your available funds.

He gave a detailed picture of what the costs had been at Gary
Public Library for camera, reading machine and supplies
(455).

The camera in use at Gary is not owned but is rented for
a charge of $150 a year. Installation of this device is
not recommended for two reasons: (1) the cost appears
excessive for the simple task involved in the library. Experimentation has shown that it would be possible to use
almost any standard 16 mm. movie camera with single-
frame attachment mounted on a tripod above the desk to
do this job. Several agencies are now working on development of cameras to do this work, and it appears certain
that a camera costing in the neighborhood of $200 will be
available for purchase in the not too far distant future.
Since this camera would be good for at least twenty years,
it should mean a cost of only ten dollars a year for the
camera as against the present cost on a rental basis of
$150 a year. However, even at a rental cost of $150 a

year, this scheme would be economically feasible so far as total costs involved are concerned. (2) The second disadvantage is a more serious one, and that is that if cameras are rented at $150 a year, very few libraries could afford to rent spare cameras, and thus would be in a serious situation if a breakdown in the camera should take place. If cheaper cameras were obtained by purchase, it would be possible to have one or more spare cameras so that a breakdown in one camera would not necessitate waiting for a repair man....

The cost of film is $2.75 per hundred feet including developing and a hundred feet of film charges 7200 books so that film cost including developing is only a matter of some 38 cents for each thousand books charged. Labor costs are greatly reduced because of elimination of all the unnecessary carding, filing, registration work, etc. Insofar as the actual charging operation is concerned, we know that one machine with one assistant can handle more than twenty thousand charges a month and still have time for other work.

The staff at the loan desk over the twelve-hour day was reduced to one person at a time who also answered telephones, sent reserve notices, counted the circulation, arranged the cards in order for typists to handle overdues at the reading machine, and did a number of miscellaneous tasks in addition to charging books.

A cost study was conducted at the Glendale Public Library which revealed the following information as given by B. A. Miller (462).

Total costs under the manual charging system were found to be $22,025.97. The costs under photographic charging were $19,339.17. Thus it was $2,686.80 cheaper to operate a year under photographic charging. The manual system of charging required 11 full time employees in the circulation division; under photographic charging the circulation division was able to handle increased circulation with eight employees. The cost of salary was $.059 per volume circulated under the photographic system while it was $.075 per volume circulated under the manual system. The photographic system shows a high salary total; however, this is because salaries in effect were higher than during July 1946-June 1947. If the manual method of charging has been used during the period of the photocharging study, the salary total would be much higher as 11 salaries would have been needed instead of the eight re-

quired by the photocharging system.   The purchase price
of supplies during the period of July 1948-June 1949 was
also higher than during the earlier period.   With salary
and supply prices higher, the savings under photocharging
system are much greater than the $2, 686. 80 difference
which the study shows.
    The improvements in efficiency, speed, patron morale
and staff morale under photocharging are items which cannot be estimated in a cost analysis.   It is felt that photocharging is the most satisfactory and efficient method of
charging under which Glendale Public Library might operate.

    In April, 1958, **F**. Henselman reported on the stop-
watch studies on Remington and Recordak and cost analyses
which were made at one library where Recordak, Diebold and
Remington Photocharger were compared.   He wrote: "The
results showed that the two overdue systems Remington and
Recordak are almost even on elapsed time," reflecting an
"over-all difference of only 54 minutes per year in favor of
the Remington Photocharger."   He gave the following 1958
cost comparison for the operation of the system,   excluding
the purchase of the photo machine (463).

    The cost per roll figures given below include everything:
the original cost of the paper or film, tax, postage or
shipping charges, spools, envelopes, processing.   The im-
ages per roll are based on our experience and in the case
of Recordak may be too conservative.   Main reports
12, 000 pictures per roll as against 10, 000 per roll in the
branches.   We have used the 10, 000 figure:

Machine	Images per roll	Cost per roll	No. rolls needed for 1, 450, 000 cir.	Cost per year
Remington	2, 400	$7. 24	604	$4, 373
Recordak	10, 000	8. 63	145	1, 251
Diebold	3, 000	2. 69	483	1, 396

We own our Remington and Diebold machines.   We rent
our Recordak equipment for $420 per year per machine.
Something better will come along some day and we will
welcome it.

    Bowen showed the costs involved when Diebold equip-
ment was used at the Toronto Public Library (464).

The cost.   Preferential prices are quoted in Canada
for libraries, because of the educational aspect of their
work.

	Price to Industry	Price to Libraries
Diebold Portable Camera model 9600	$1195.00	$ 975.00
Diebold Portable Reader model 9204	420.00	325.00
Diebold Motorized Reader model 9202	1790.00	1500.00

The magazines of film, each of which contain 50 feet
of 16 mm. film, and which record 2,000 - 2,400 separate
transactions, cost $3.90 each, which includes the charge
for processing the film.

The cost of the McBee Keysort punched cards is not
high when it is remembered that each can be used to record 28 separate issues.

The cost of machinery and accessories compare very
favorably with those of the Kodak and Remington Rand
companies.

Conclusion.   It has not yet been possible to estimate
how much would be saved in a full year of operation, but
a library in California and another in Canada have estimated that they save at least $4,000 a year, and that librar-
ians are freed from much routine work, since that involved in a photocharging system can well be carried out
by non-professional assistants.

At the University of Illinois where the Remington Rand
Photocharger was used, the expenses were as follows (429).

The price of the Photocharger was $490 plus $10 freight
charges.   We purchased a six-month supply of photographic paper at $4.75 a roll.   We have found that we average
about a roll a week.   The charge to process one roll is
$2.50 and since we send them to Chicago to be processed
there is also a slight mailing cost to consider each week.
This usually amounts to about 24 to 38 cents depending
upon whether or not a metal container is used for mailing.
. . .

As far as the charging-out process alone is concerned,
after the purchase of the Photocharger and the photographic paper the only other necessary initial purchase was

50, 000 transaction cards at a cost of $150. 00.

At Charlotte Public Library "the monthly rental fee on the Recordak Junior camera was only $15 and on a 200-foot roll of film purchased for $6, a total of 8, 000 books could be charged. This meant that the film cost for one book charge was only . 00075¢ (465).

In 1946, Tucker wrote: "The cost of photographic charging is not great, especially in view of the staff time it saves. The rental of a Recordak Junior is $12. 50 per month. This combined with film purchases, processing and postage totals approximately $18. 20 a month, or about $220. per year. For one machine at a central library this is not too expensive, but it does preclude the possibility of using photographic charging in the smaller branches (466). "

At Glendale, California, E. L. Robertson found the following situation to be true (467).

Offsetting the annual cost of the system (rental of the present 5 machines and 1 separate reader, $960; film and development, $350; mailing charges between library and laboratory, $25; totaling $1335), plus $1000 for 100, 000 date-due (Keysort) cards which will last indefinitely, is the salary of at least one clerical employee and the goodwill of the public and staff. Keysort cards are being adapted to the remaining manual process of putting the returned date-due cards in numerical order, thus cutting the operation down from an hour to a few minutes a day.

The following prices were given in March, 1958 for the installation and running costs in an English library (468).

The Surrey County library committee have decided to include in their estimates for the next financial year the cost of installing a photo-charging apparatus in Woking Library. It will cost about Ł450 and running costs will be about Ł180 for the first year and about Ł96 a year subsequently. It will take the place of another assistant librarian who would have had a starting salary of Ł324 a year, rising to Ł560 a year.

In Publishers' Circular, 1955, a note was given of one English library's experience with photocharging (469).

It is not made specifically for libraries or book-charging

and can be used for micr..ilming any records up to foolscap size.   This secondary use should be taken into account
when considering the initial price of the machine, which
is Ł425. .... Thus, costed on an annual basis, the initial
outlay can be reduced to a very small yearly expenditure,
ie., Ł42 per annum on an estimated ten-year life, or
Ł25 per annum on a fifteen-year expectation.

The Recordak Microfilmer used at Wandsworth cost
Ł425, "but has an almost indefinite life and there is little
to go wrong with it.   On a basis of a 10 year expectancy of
life, which is very modest, this averages Ł40 per year,
which would be more than saved by economies effected in
staffing the counter, " according to Corbett.   He also said
they had invested in "one hundred thousand printed white
transaction cards (3 in. by 2 in.) at approximately Ł50 and
capable of being used for several times. "   At Wandsworth
the "cost of operation is small and would be offset by savings
in the stationery of the book.   A 200 ft. roll of film costs
Ł1 17 10   and is processed within 24 hours for 5   Twenty-
    s. d.   s.
six thousand issues can be photographed by the method explained (on the basis that two books are charged on an average
to each reader).   Thus a library issuing just under 7, 000
books per week would find one roll of film would last four
weeks.   Total cost Ł2 2 10   or   10 6   per week (470). "
                       s. d.   s. d.

At Wandsworth, savings of time were reflected by this
charging system.   When compared with the Browne System,
Corbett wrote (470):

Time and motion studies show that the average charging
time is 6 seconds as against 5 1/4 by Browne....   The
time taken in discharging is 3 1/4 seconds as opposed to
9 1/2 by Browne.   The approximate time for both processes of charging and discharging is thus reduced by 40 per
cent.
The time taken in counting and sorting the day's issue
is reduced by sorting transaction cards only by 40 per
cent.
If adopted each reader would be given only a ticket of
the season ticket type, as against four, thus reducing the
time taken in writing by 75 per cent and also effecting
economy in stationery....
The overall time spent in charging, discharging, counting and sorting the issue, and registration of readers, can
be reduced by 40 per cent.   This was calculated by time

tests, on five assistants, first with Browne and then with
the photocharger, and was worked out in terms of the annual issue. . . .

    In terms of economy in man-power it is difficult to
give an exact figure.   Obviously so much depends on the
existing staff.   In Wandsworth the existing staff is adequate but there is little to spare and, at the Central Library itself, issues have risen rapidly in the last three
years.   The photocharger would save the employment of
the extra assistant who is most urgently needed, and at
the two largest branches with a staff of ten, I am confi-
dent that photo-charging would save an assistant at each.
Whether or not staffs can be reduced in numbers depends
on local circumstances but, in any event, staff time can
be saved on counter work and used to better purpose.

    In another article, he wrote, "In my own experience
in libraries with staffs of eight, ten, and twelve respectively,
photo-charging resulted in the first instance of saving additional expenditure for an extra member of the staff, and in the
other two instances the establishment of each was reduced by
one assistant (471). "

    Hepworth revealed that photocharging produced an over-
all saving of staff time (472).

    Though the total staff at Norwich is at a modest provin-
    cial level (the usual staffing for a 10 a.m.-8 p.m. day is
    four in the morning, five in the afternoon and three in the
    evening), the Librarian and Sub-Librarian, and often one
    other member of staff too, can, for the first time for
    years, engage in real librarianship on every day of the
    week.   The behind-the-scenes jobs that had come to a
    dead stand are moving again, and the continual rises in
    issues, that were crippling our Saturday service, can
    once again be taken in stride.

    A shift was made from professional librarians to cler-
ical help for routine duties according to Andres (473).

    As far as personnel is concerned, the department former-
    ly operated with a staff of four professional members, but
    the work of one of these members was confined almost
    entirely to duties of a clerical nature.   Usually there
    were two full-time pages or clerks, and perhaps one or
    two part-time clerks.   . . . .
    With the new system, we have operated most of the

time with the help of only three professional staff members, but we now have three full-time and five part-time
people in our clerical section, or the equivalent of five
and a half people.   There is a chief in charge of this
section who has the responsibility of training the members
and making their schedules - no small matter.

Matson gave information as to costs and savings as
viewed at her library (474).

Rental of the machines, which are not sold, is moderate,
and the films, with postage and processing, cost about
$8.00 each.   We began to use the Recordak on January 3
and on July 3 we finished the sixteenth film, at a total
cost for rental, films, and incidentals of about $250.00.
We are saving about that amount every month in salaries.
The cost of the date due cards and the time spent in numbering them should be taken into account but that is hard
to compute.   They will last a long time and numbering
will not have to be done often.
Except at the busiest times, only one person is needed
to run the machine, but teamwork at the desk, opening
books and getting them ready, in which many patrons
seem glad to share, helps speed up matters.

On a bookmobile the Recordak is found to save time
and money, according to James C. Foutts (475).

The driver and one clerk handle all charging, discharging,
sorting, and registration, leaving the two librarians free
to work with the patrons.   Books returned by children
from a classroom can be recirculated in less than twenty
minutes.
Recordak cameras were chosen because the savings in
film cost between 16 mm. microfilm and paper film would
approximately pay the monthly rental for the camera.   The
second advantage was that we could speed up the charging
process and effect further savings by eliminating book
cards.

Murray reported a saving in staff time.   "It used to
take on the average of an hour and fifteen minutes of five
people daily to file circulation, now it takes two to two and
a half hours of one person's time to file date cards with
McBee Keysort .   It took two hours to send overdues - now
it takes thirty-five to forty minutes.   Reserves used to take
fifteen hours a week of three persons, now it takes sixteen

hours a week of one person's time.... The staff was reduced
by one person and there is still a lighter work load for the
rest of the staff (476). "

Savings of operational time were mentioned by Marjorie C. Donaldson in The Pioneer (477).

It has been possible to check out as many as 300 books
per hour during a busy period with one Photocharger.
With an average daily circulation of 1, 600 and a high of
2, 400 in the Adult Circulation Department, we have found
two Photochargers to be sufficient.   Even at the busiest
hours they carry the load rapidly and effectively.

Hacker remarked that the Photocharger processed up to 300
charging records an hour (478).

Robinson wrote that the lack of slipping of books was
a time saver (479).

This saves 55 1/2 hours per week on a circulation of
7, 000.   No filing of book cards.   Filing of TN cards need
not be scheduled since done with a Keysort Needle they
take less than one quarter the time of handsorting and can
be fitted into salvaged time.   No counting of circulation.
This saves 3 hours per week.

Bloss gave the following facts concerned with overdue
procedures (420).

Overdues work for the main library and the book trailer,
whose combined annual circulation is about 320, 000 volumes, takes less than the time of one assistant.   She does
the final sorting of the transaction cards, lists the missing numbers, searches the film, types the first, second,
and third notices, and handles the other details of overdues work in about 3 1/2 days a week.

An article which appeared in the 1940 Journal of Documentary Re-Production noted that "the cost of issuing overdue notices can be decreased from about 30-35 cents to 2 cents per
volume (480). "

The District of Columbia Public Library where Photocharger and Photoclerk were used reported that the personnel
cost of developing "photocharged and Photoclerk copies is almost negligible.   The continuous roll paper processor has

been placed in the duplicating section where the staff develops
charges while carrying out other assignments. At present, 5
rolls are being processed each day, and it is estimated that
it requires approximately 12 man-minutes per roll to prepare
solutions and start the processing operation. It takes 35 minutes for each roll to go through the processor (481). "

At Tulsa, according to Martin, the staff members handling overdues report that "the present method takes more
time than previously when signature charging was used. Some
eyestrain from reading film is reported, but considerably less
than when numerical registration was used (453).

Murray mentioned that "There have been no complaints
about eyestrain. No assistant has had to spend more than an
hour at a time reading. ...

"At first there was a slight problem of impressing on
the staff the importance of entering the transaction card number on all routine processes connected with over due and
messenger books. However, with time this is eliminated
(482). " At Charlotte it was noted by Bailey that constant use
of the microfilm reader in the searching for overdues caused
great strain on the eyes. "The eye strain led to glasses for
one clerk and later to the loss of another employee (465). "
Tucker felt that "eyestrain may or may not be a serious disadvantage, depending on the excellence of the camera and its
accessories in making a clear photograph, and upon the quality of the machine used for film reading (466). "

The main weakness of photocharging, according to Hepworth, is lack of application in recovering transaction cards.
"If the junior assistant recording gaps does not do so consci-
entiously, before preparing her overdue series, the record of
an issue is lost for ever. The remedy for this is (i) strict
staff training, (ii) hand or (iii) mechanically sorted punched
cards (438). "

Notched cards were adopted at another library for a
different reason, according to Bailey, who found the "process
of sorting and filing the transaction cards was entirely too
slow. The average speed of this operation was only four
cards per minute. " Filing these cards in Dewey Decimal order took an average sorting and filing time of nine cards per
minute and discharging - two books per minute. "This meant
that time was gained in one place and lost in another (483). "

Bloss made the following remarks about some factors which many had regarded as disadvantages (427):

> Our initial fears that users would be unhappy about not knowing how many books they had out, or about having no record of books returned, proved to be groundless as the new method became established. We experienced no difficulty whatsoever in using the microfilm record of circulation. Our overdue assistant has been on the job for more than three years; all of the people who work with circulation control are pleased with the simplicity and efficiency of the system. Large sized, easily read transaction numbers and a motorized reader are important factors.

Corbett saw little evidence of any unwarranted number of wholesale borrowing, but admitted that unless tokens were used there was no limit to the number of books that could be borrowed. He mentioned another possible disadvantage (484).

> There is obviously a limit to the capability of the machine; beyond this another would be necessary. Under the circumstances operating in Wandsworth Central Library, this limit cannot be ascertained and only a large library with very big peak issues is likely to find more than one machine necessary....
> Even the most reliable of machines is certain to break down one day. An emergency method of charging is necessary. Revert to Browne by slipping charges and ticket into a pocket.

As recorded in Minnesota Libraries, Matson made the following adjustment when equipment stopped working (485).

> We no longer worry about what would happen if the machine stopped working for a while, for we take it in our stride, and snatch at the daters that are always set up (just in case). Books are simply charged to the card number, the slips kept in the library and the proper date due cards marked to indicate that they were not photographed, inserted in the pockets of the books. It is all very efficient and beautifully simple. Incidentally, when one such crisis came on a busy afternoon, four people were required to do the charging manually that two had been doing with the machine.

The Remington Rand Photocharger used on a bookmobile had to be adapted to certain operating conditions, according to Dallas R. Shawkey, who wrote (486):

> For lighting of the picture area we use the two recommended 100-watt frosted bulbs. However, we have found that we must watch the lens setting. On particularly bright days the lens aperture must be very small, and on less bright days it must be larger, otherwise the film is too light or dark for easy reading. Good films are also dependent upon a good operating generator.

Robinson desired more speed and flexibility of his photocharger (479).

> In spite of reports to the contrary, we find photocharging slower than handcharging. The Recordak cannot be speeded up - books are charged only as fast as the machine will photograph cards. Nor is it possible, with one machine, to have more clericals stamping out in rush hours. We are reasonably fast, as the advertised "1, 500 books per library day" has been beaten by us many times in the past year. Overdues take no longer. We type our notices directly from the Reader. Reserves ceased to be a problem once we realized that our whole method of handling them had to change - that there could be no more tagging of book cards but that the books themselves must be found.

According to an article announcing the Shaw Photocharger, snags are possible (432).

> Snags, which are quite common in other charging systems do occur in photocharging when a book is returned without the date-due slip. When that happens a brief entry may be made on a slip and the book returned to the shelf immediately with the overdues checked against the snag slips before mailing. As each snag is identified, the snag slip may be discarded.

Andres found snags and other problems present where photocharging was used (487).

> In the first five months of 1953, 208 books were returned with the transaction cards missing in spite of the fact that there is a warning on the card saying not to remove it from the book pocket. This is not a very large percentage of all 45, 000 books which were charged by the Photo-

charger during that time, but it did cause quite a bit of confusion in the Circulation Department. Since searching on the photostrip for the names of patrons who had taken these books would have required too much time, they were not cleared until overdue postals for these books were ready to be written. In spite of our regular routine of checking on the bookshelves and on the snag shelf before writing the overdues, we received an average of two calls a day for the first three months from patrons notifying us that they had received overdue notices for books already returned.... Besides the 208 cards which were permanently missing, many cards which at first glance were thought to be missing were found being used as bookmarks.

Another way in which the new system does not seem to benefit the patron is the time taken in the charging of books. The patron feels that the purpose of a mechanical charger should be to save time for them too. Since the Photocharger can be used for only one book at a time, our patrons stand in line longer at busy times than they formerly did when there were more staff members who helped charge. When there are a number of magazines or pamphlets to charge by hand, the procedure is also held up considerably. We think the longest time anyone has had to wait is between four and five minutes. When an extra page is available, she is sent to the charging desk to assist with the handcharging at busy times, but when there are only two on duty this is sometimes impossible. We have not found it feasible for the professional staff to help charge at these times because that makes them unavailable for help in book selection and in the use of the catalog.

Finally, there are some difficulties in the photographic charging system from the point of view of the staff besides those connected with book reserves.... In the first place the professional staff members do not get to see the patrons' identification cards any more, as it is difficult for us to remember the names of the new patrons.... One of the disadvantages connected with any mechanical charger is that it may occasionally get out of order, and naturally ours has, more because of our inexperience than because something was wrong with the machine. Our chief difficulty, especially at first, was in changing the roll. This is not a difficult procedure, but when the chief of the Clerical Service Section was not on duty to change the roll, although the others in the section knew how, they did not always handle the mechanism with her gentle touch. And when some of the screws get a little off balance, the

Photocharger just won't charge.   Fortunately this seldom
happens anymore.

One film was returned with about one-third of it black-
ed out.   Others have had some black parts.   The Chief
of the Clerical Service Section reported as of the end of
May that there were no books lost since January 1953 due
to such blackouts, which is very fortunate because there
is no way of tracing a book not returned if the record of
its circulation doesn't register on the photostrip.   It may
be that we were to blame for some of these blackouts, as
on one occasion the roll was left exposed before wrapping
for mailing.   We also seemed to have trouble with the
roll if it was not mailed in its metal container.   Even
though this requires more postage, we are now mailing
them in the metal container and find that there is a decided improvement in readability.   Remington Rand had
told us that it would not be necessary to mail them in the
metal container.

Certainly it has gotten rid of quite a number of the old
problems, but a new system always presents new problems.
We hope that as time goes on more of the difficulties will
be adjusted.   After all, the system is still new and there
have been other changes in the library and in this department during the year which have demanded much time and
attention so that it has not been possible to concentrate to
a great extent on this one change.

Shaw believed that the "only possibility of error is
that which always occurs in any system using cards and arranging cards, plus the everpresent possibility of loss of a
date due card after the books are returned to the library;
however, our snag shelves show no appreciable number of
errors, so that elimination of most snags can be credited to
this charging system.   With ordinary care by the assistants
at the circulation desk errors should be far less than in other
systems. " He also saw that the system offered a number of
advantages (488).

Among the advantages offered are: a permanent record of
who borrows what or rather what card borrows what, reduction of filing, elimination of carding, reduction of overdue work, automatic discharging of 95 per cent of the
books without any filing of cards or slipping of books,
elimination of numerical registration and of branch registration, elimination of book cards, and increased accuracy.

Among the advantages listed by Miller for photocharging are four which should be mentioned (489).

> 1.   It is a speedier method of charging books and partic-
> ularly of discharging returned books....
> 2.   More accuracy is obtained when the borrower's card
> and book checks are photographed than when records are
> handwritten and hand-stamped.
> 3.   Patrons are very much pleased to be relieved of tak-
> ing part in the charging process....
> 6.   It reduces the work in sending overdue notices.   In
> the photographic system, all of the information required
> in sending an overdue notice is on the film and it is un-
> necessary to go to a numerical file to obtain the name
> and address of the borrower.

Robinson wrote that photocharging eliminated fatigue
and nervous tension to a great deal.   He also reported that
amount of printed supplies was reduced.   There was no need
for readers' cards or date slips (479).   Hacker saw that no
special space or handling problems existed in connection with
supplies when using the Remington Rand Photocharger.   "In
fact, on the last score matters were greatly simplified owing
to the fact that each paper photo-record is a complete record
that takes up less than six square inches (490)."

The installment of photocharging can affect the division of work among the members of the staff, according to
Corbett, who explained (491):

> The photo-charger can be a very potent factor in the divi-
> sion of staff into professional and non-professional grades,
> as anyone can operate it and it is largely foolproof.   By
> its employment, work other than the mere mechanics of
> issue and discharge can be banished automatically from
> the counter.

Bowen gave the advantages of photocharging by comparing it with the Newark hand charging system (492).

> ... it saves much time in marking books both in and out.
> Under the Newark System of charging, it takes a good as-
> sistant 4 seconds to mark out each book, if the borrower
> has written his library number legibly on both label and
> bookcard, and presents the book open at the correct place
> to be stamped, and 8 seconds if nothing has been done.
> More time is often needed, however, to check each num-
> ber carefully.   This speed, moreover, cannot be main-

tained for quantities of books.   On the return of a book,
the assistant has to compare the date due and the borrower's number on the book label with the borrower's card,
and stamp the latter to record the return of the book,
which has later to be discharged.   Using photographic
charging, it takes an average of 5 seconds to record an
issue, and of 3 seconds to check a returned book, by removing the transaction card and seeing that the correct
book card is in the book, which is then ready to go back
into circulation, if not required.   A good assistant, using
the microfilm camera, and relieved at regular intervals,
can charge out 550 books an hour with far less possibility
of error than can arise from the writing of six-figure borrowers' numbers at speed.

It is compared with the Browne System by Corbett,
who wrote in 1956 (493):

Hand sorting has not proved such a tremendous job as one
might think.   In any case it saves time as compared with
sorting Browne charges, inasmuch as it is a matter of
sorting a consecutive sequence of transaction card numbers
instead of the widely separated accession numbers of book
cards, and also because the highest number used is considerably lower than that on book cards.

In the book entitled Photo-Charging which was published in 1957, Corbett gave a more complete comparison
(494).

We are now firmly convinced that photo-charging is vastly
superior to Browne and can confidently recommend its
consideration, but at the same time, must stress that its
success or failure depends very largely upon the thought
given to its introduction, good staff training, and public
relations. . . .
Let us now try to show how the one photocharging
compares with the other [Browne System] on the grounds
of efficiency and economy.
1.   Registration and tickets.
Both Browne and photo-charging use an identical type
of form for registration.   Browne needs a number of manilla pocket-type tickets; with photo-charging, one membership card only.   The cost of stationery is approximately
the same, but if xylonite cards are used they will have a
longer life, and thus prove more economical in the long
run.   Three-quarters of staff time is saved in ticket writ-

ing with photo-charging as compared with a system normally issuing four Browne-type tickets.

Photo-charging may not be quite so adaptable to interavailability while the majority of libraries still use Browne,
and it gives greater freedom to a reader, inasmuch as
his ticket will not be withdrawn.   To the reader, at least,
this is an advantage. . . .

2.   Stationery of Book.

Both methods need a type of "rules label" and pocket.
Book cards are not required, nor are date labels essential with photo-charging, but the latter requires transaction cards which will take up to about twenty-four issues.
Financially they break about even in this respect.

3.   Operational equipment.

Browne requires issue trays, pigeonholes, and date
stamps only.   Photo-charging needs a microfilmer, film,
a transaction card cabinet, and a date stamp - obviously
expensive.   Say L 42 per year for microfilmer, estimat-
ing life at a very conservative figure of ten years, and
another L 50 for film, for an annual issue of 320,000 (this
includes developing).

4.   Filing of charges.

. . . . This is a decidedly easier sorting process and
single cards are more easily handled than tickets   and
book cards.   Photo-charging represents 40 per cent saving in time in this respect. . . .

One can truthfully say that providing no fine is due
(and the delay in this respect is the same with either
method) the discharge can be effected just as quickly as
a person can present her book open at the desk.   In other
words, the speed of discharge is the maximum possible.

Corbett also compares photocharging with the token
system.   See reference nos. 570-580.   Corbett gave this information (491).

There will be a natural tendency to compare the photocharger with Westminister's token system and without having any experience with the latter, I would say that the
most apparent differences are:

(a) The token system must be quicker for charging but
slower for discharging.

(b) Readers can be limited to a given number of books
with the token system; but, on the other hand, tokens
could be used with the photo-charger if required.

(c) There are no machines to buy with the token system and no fear of breakdown.

(d)   The photo-charger gives a complete record of issues, overdues can be sent and no irksome restrictions
are necessary to guard against the unauthorized "retention"
of books. . . .

(e)   Loans on other library tickets can be merged
more easily into the photo-charging system.

In the November, 1952 issue of Catholic Library
World, Shaw gave a suggested variation of the photocharging
procedure which would be workable in scholarly libraries.
The procedure is as follows (495):

In cases where it is necessary to search charge files,
photographic charging can obviously not be used because
it eliminates these files.

The large number of scholarly libraries which now
send call slips directly to the shelves should be able to
effect great savings in cost as well as more effective control and speedier service by the use of a Photocharger.
The discussion and procedure which follow, therefore refer only to this group. . . .

Thus current practice requires maintenance of three
or four files, ie., "room charges," a chronological file,
a call number file and a borrower's file for certain classes of borrowers, as well as a special file (or shelf list
record for long-term loans or indefinite loans).   There is
considerable time lag between the time when a book is removed from the shelf and the time when an appropriate
charge card is filed in the appropriate file or files, so
that it is not always possible to determine quickly where
every book is.   In general, the charging procedure in
scholarly libraries entails much greater costs than are
encountered in public library charging.

Photographic charging by the method outlined below
should:

(1) Effect greater savings in cost of charging.

(2) Eliminate all filing of cards and slipping of books
except for filing borrowers' records when they are maintained.

(3) Effect placement of books on the shelves immediately after return.

(4) Provide an immediate report on the location of a
book if it is not on the shelf.

(5) Provide absolutely accurate charge records (mis-
slipping and errors in copying numbers are eliminated).

(6) Control short term loans and room charges as accurately as long-term loans - with a single procedure for

all types of loans.

(7) Eliminate the need for registering borrowers in those libraries which now do that. The bursar's receipt or any similar identification will serve in place of registration.

(8) Eliminate the need for book cards if desired. Book pockets can be eliminated also.

(9) Make studies of "who reads what" easy, as the photographic record contains all the information.

(10) Make possible economical preparation of lists from the catalog - the camera will copy a catalog card as quickly and easily as a call slip.

Photocharging Procedure

Supplies required are:

1. Call slips in duplicate with carboned back on first slip so that a carbon is made automatically.
2. Pre-numbered date-due slips identical with those commonly used in public libraries except for a serial number stamped on top.

Steps in Charging

1. The borrower hands in the duplicate call slip.
2. Copies are sent to the stacks.
3. Page gets the book, putting one of the carbon copies of the call slip in its place. Use a dummy consisting of a strawboard the size of a book cover with a pocket to receive the carbon copy of the charge slip. (If the book is not in its place, the page finds a charge there, copies the name of the borrower to whom it is charged on the call slip and returns all copies to the loan desk.)
4. Page sends book and remaining copy of call slip to loan desk.
5. Book is checked with call slip by loan assistant.
6. Assistant photographs call slip and appropriate date due slip together.
7. Put date due slip in pocket and give book to borrower.
8. Files original in personal file if required or discards it.

In the same periodical Ambrose Burke gave another variation of photocharging which answered the needs of the library at the College of Steubenville, comparing it with the system suggested by Shaw (496).

This paper is a record of our application of the photographic methods which Mr. Shaw has perfected.   At the
College of Steubenville the emphasis is on developing a
technique for evaluating the use of the library.

In reading what follows it will be helpful to follow the
points of Mr. Shaw's article.   Where they fit in, our variations can be interjected.

"Loretto Plan" begun in 1945, then based on self charging claims attention because it provides qualitative evaluation of circulation and justifies the use of more techno-
logical means of charging such as photocharging, punched
cards, voice recording.   These means can record and present many more items of information than were here-to-
fore possible.

Basically, the "Loretto Plan" is founded on a classification system for the library clientele (faculty, students,
etc.) that is adaptation of Dewey's classification of knowledge.   It is this plus a set of symbols to classify the
type of use to which library materials are put.   The classification of the individual users of the library brings them
into groups according to their subject specialty, class
year, vocational objective, sex, and may cover any other
significant aspects of scholarly pursuit....

The plan can be used for the reference collection, reserve books and in either open or closed stacks.

In contrast to Mr. Shaw's "Photographic Charging in
Scholarly Libraries," the College of Steubenville practice
does not use call slips and thus would be ruled out of
profitable use of photocharging, according to his standards.
However, no charge file is maintained, either chronological or classified.   Eventually, there is a record of books
charged to each borrower, but it is not useful on a current basis.

A comparison with Shaw's listing of ten advantages of
photographic charging leads to these observations based on
our experience:

1. The circulation loan in a small college library alone
   is not enough to justify the cost of the machine.
   Savings in a larger library might be greater.   Our
   cost accounting shows that photocharging costs .6
   of a cent per charge.
2. Reserves in our library have special handling,
   though photocharging is used for them also.
3. The lack of call slips provides no means of immediate report on the location of a book not on the
   shelf.   That flaw is becoming more evident in our
   present practice for a day student body of 500.

Shaw's device of carbon call slips readily eliminates that flaw. In place of dummies pocketing the call slips for books in circulation, a pocket attached to the shelf might serve.

4. Accuracy depends on care on the part of the operator to get a clear picture.

5. We do not feel that we have worked out well enough the control of short term loans and reserves.

6. While registering of borrowers can be eliminated the "Loretto Plan" classification of borrowers makes it advisable. The library form is included with the registration forms as each new student matriculates.

7. We have eliminated book cards but not the book pockets which are placed on the back cover. Besides the call number, author, title, and accession number, our book pockets have date of publication and checking squares.

8. The study of "who reads what" is our chief justification for the use of photocharging. This is the chief point of this paper.

9. The preparation of lists, based on photographing catalog cards is not feasible where the photocharger takes only one copy 3" x 3", as is the case with ours. It could be done with two pictures per card.

Photocharging Procedure
(Open Stacks)

Supplies required:

1. Registration forms.

2. Borrowers' cards.

3. Temporary identification slips (for record of room use.)

4. Transaction cards (sometimes called T-cards). These are numbered in sequence and pre-dated. A different number sequence (say 4 or 5 figures) and variation of color of card is used for different circulation periods.

5. Borrowers' register (alphabetical listing of patrons).

A. Circulating books.

1. Borrower hands book and borrower's card to circulation assistant.

2. T-card is placed in book pocket, borrower's card below transaction number.

3. Dial attached to Photocharger is set to the symbol

by which patron indicates the type of use... (Fr-
Free choice for recreational reading, etc.)

B. Books used in the library (including reference and
bound magazines).
   1. Temporary identification slips found in trays on the
      tables are filled out (including borrower's number).
   2. Slip is left projecting from the book laid on the
      table. (Several may have used the same book).
   3. Books are collected periodically by library staff
      members.
   4. No T-card is used in photocharging. RU is the
      symbol dialed into the picture.
   5. Date (representing scholastic year) is stamped up-
      side down in checking square of book pocket.

C. Returning books.
   1. Remove T-card and drop in designated place.
   2. Stamp date (indicating scholastic year) in checking
      square on book pocket.
   3. Place book for shelving.
   4. Once a week file returned T-cards by transaction
      number. Books fall due only one day in the week
      (Friday).
   5. Make overdue notices for books covered by trans-
      action numbers that are missing. A record is kept
      of the transaction numbers for each date-due per-
      iod.

III. Behind the Schenes.
     . . .
     B. Procedure.
        . . . .
        2. When a suitable amount (those for one semester) of
           the photocharge strips has been accumulated, they
           are cut into the individual charges, sorted into lots
           corresponding to classification groups of library pa-
           trons, further sorted on a form divided into the
           elements to go onto the tabulation sheet, and finally
           reduced to the record for an individual....
        5. Tabulation of the photocharger will bring out as
           many facts as the library wishes to analyze. In a
           large system punched cards would be advantageous,
           and problably the best method.

The following outline was given by Henselman who
compared the three types of machines used in photocharging -

the Recordak, the Remington photocharger and the Diebold
camera (463).

Charging out books:
    Advantages of Recordak:
        Quicker to use (but not enough to matter greatly).
        Easier to use.
        Cards in wallets can be photographed.
    Disadvantages of Recordak:
        Size.
        Appearance.
    Remington had advantages of:
        Size and appearance.
        It is quieter.
        It is easier to load.
    Disadvantages of Remington were:
        Assistant must be more precise in arranging cards.
        All of the information recorded is in a 2 1/2" space,
           which necessitates meticulous arrangement.
        Sometimes it is impossible to group cards so that
           all of the information shows.
    Diebold advantages over the other machines were:
        Size and appearance.
        Speed with which film can be changed.
    Disadvantages of Diebold over both of the other ma-
chines:
        More concentration needed in placing cards.
        Cards in wallets cannot be used.

Audio-Charge System

      Stewart W. Smith described his system as follows
(497):

    This method, for want of an existing or better name,
may be called "Audio charge." The method is identical
with photographic charging, except that the record is audible rather than visual.

    The equipment required by his system was "a record-
ing device, (disc, cylinder, tape or wire), and a file of serially numbered combined date due and transaction cards....
The recording equipment is relatively low in original cost,
maintenance is negligible (497)."

    He added, however, that "the St. Louis County Library

has experimented with two different types of equipment: a
tape recorder and a commercial dictation machine using
discs as the recording medium.... Our present opinion is
that the dictating machine is better-adapted for book charging
than the tape recorder; advantage in the tape is fidelity of re-
production (498)."

Helen Geer reported in 1956 that it had been determined that two machines were found to be superior when used
with this system (499).

From experiments made in 1948 by S. W. Smith in the
St. Louis County Public Library, it was found that of all
the dictating machines and tape recorders on the market,
the Soundscriber and Gray Audograph were best suited to
the making of charging records.

L. M. Speer described the types of transaction cards
(500).

The consecutively numbered transaction cards are the
basic guides to books loaned and returned. We decided
upon three divisions, differentiated by series of numbers
as well as by the color of the cards. Thus, for the
adult books, loaned for one month, white transaction cards
are used with two series of numbers: 1-9, 999 and B1-B9,
999. All new books, magazines, pamphlets, and music
records, loaned for a fourteen-day period, are given blue
transaction cards, numbered F1-F9, 999. Juvenile books
have salmon colored cards numbered JI-J9, 999. Each
morning a supply of these cards is stamped with the date
due.

J. Archer Eggen showed the uses of the transaction
cards (501).

The transaction cards are expensive but we had the McBee
Company make them of a high rag content stock and hope
to use them from eight to twelve times. The T-card
serves as a date-due card. The estimated number needed
for a day's business are stamped with the proper due date
each morning. We've not compiled cost data but do know
that the T-card replaces five printed forms formerly used:
Date due slip, book card, registration card, borrower's
card, and another card filed alphabetically by borrower's
name.

The borrower's card was described by T. A. Bailey
(502).

> The identification card now used is printed on perforated
> sheets which are placed in the typewriter with a carbon
> and a yellow sheet of paper. The carbon copies are filed
> away as permanent records of users of the library. This
> type card has cut down on two duties which were once per-
> formed at the circulation desk, namely those of filing reg-
> istration cards and changing addresses. The latter, be-
> cause the patron, when charging a book, will hear and
> correct a faulty address.

The Cedar Rapids Public Library, stated Eggen, used
a variation on the identification card (503).

> ... we decided to eliminate borrower's cards and allow
> our customers to present any identification with name and
> address.

The charging process worked in the following manner
(504):

> Books were... charged audibly the same way they had been
> by the photographic process. The clerk read the borrow-
> er's name, address and telephone number, Keysort trans-
> action number, author and title of book into the micro-
> phone. This was slower than the photographic method.

Bailey noted two objections to this procedure (504).

> Staff members found two serious objections to this meth-
> od: first, they thought the process entirely too slow and
> second, they found that borrowers objected to having titles
> of their books read aloud. These two objections were
> eliminated when it was decided to substitute the accession
> number for the author and title of the book.

Another solution to this problem was discovered by
Speer (505).

> We now have overcome that problem by placing the micro-
> phone in a sound absorbent half-size telephone booth by
> which the assistant's voice is muffled.

The manner of using the microphone and machine was
pictured by Eggen (503).

Each digit in a number is read and the surname is practically always spelled out.

Eggen also detailed the process for special or unusual
library materials (506).

Non-book materials are "talked" out of the library, too.
If no pocket has been provided on a magazine or a pamphlet, the T-card or 3-day slip is fastened to the material by a paper clip.

Smith described the handling of records (497).

No processing of the recordings is necessary. When a
disc or tape is filled, it is simply removed from the machine and filed for future use when the books charged on
it become overdue.

The discharging process, stated Eggen, worked in the
following manner (503).

A returned book is discharged by merely removing the T-
card from the pocket and placing it in a discharge tray.
The book is then immediately ready for the next borrower.
These returned T-cards are sorted with the Keysorter into numerical order, and when a given series is a week
overdue it is searched for missing cards. A missing T-
card, of course, denotes an overdue book and the overdue
clerk gets busy.

The method of handling overdues was disclosed by
Bailey (504).

As an aid to the overdue clerk, the charging staff punches
the end key on the Audograph after every 10th transaction
number. This end key punches a hole in the index strip.
The first and last transaction numbers are recorded on
the index strip and the disc and the two strips are filed
together until they are needed for transcribing overdues.

Bailey also told the manner in which overdue notices
were sent out (507).

If the accession number is put on the overdue notice and
if the client cannot locate this overdue book and wishes to
know the name of the book, the accession records are on
hand so that a library clerk can immediately turn to the

record and identify the book.   There have been very few
such requests and not one has caused any trouble.... 。
   With the Audograph and using the Keysort transaction
card, it took 3-6 minutes per overdue notice.   When a
second notice was sent the same process had to be used
and the same time spent again.   Would it not be less expensive and time saving to type two overdue notices, a
tag for the "black list" and a tag for the Central Lending
Records office at one time?   A perforated sheet of overdue notices in quadruplicate was devised.   The message
on the backs of the first and second notices identifies
which notice it is, and gives all the needed information
for the client.   The typist can run these perforated sheets
of ten notices into her typewriter, type all notices and
tags for ten different persons before she takes the sheets
out of the typewriter.

   A variation on this procedure was explained by Eggen
(503).

   Overdues are typed in triplicate.   The original, with postage applied by the postage meter, is sent as a first reminder.   The other two copies are filed in place of the
   missing T-card which they represent.   Slightly longer than
   the T-cards they are easily located.   If the book is returned in response to the first notice, the remaining two
   are destroyed.   If not the second notice is sent.   The
   third copy has the transaction number, the book number,
   and the name and address of the careless customer....
   Only then is the title searched from accession records
   [in sending a form letter requesting the book] 。

   Speer recorded a few considerations and warnings involved with the processing of overdues (505).

   Taking off the overdue records is simple if the person
   who dictated spoke clearly and slowly.   Otherwise both
   titles and borrowers' names must be rechecked by the
   catalog and registration files respectively, which does
   take time。   Unless a second machine can be purchased
   for this playback process, the taking of the overdues
   from the one machine should be done when the library is
   closed or in a very, very slow period of the day, for,
   while this is being done, the machine is not available for
   charging.   We found it best to purchase a second machine, which is in readiness if the other one should break
   down, and which eventually may be used to charge books

in the children's room.

Renewals under this system were quite simple for both library staff and reader, according to Speer (500).

Telephone renewals are taken on buff colored transaction cards, the readers being asked to give the transaction number, which they have quickly learned to do, the author and title of the book, and their own name and address. Before the overdue notices are sent, these renewal records are checked....

Speer described the procedure of reserves (500).

.... A visible index of all titles reserved and kept at the circulation desk makes checking easy and if they do pass beyond the desk, searching the shelves daily from this index finds the books quickly. Also, a clip placed on the book pocket of any book which has several reserves on it, or on a new book as it comes from the catalog department, succeeds in catching many of the reserved titles, especially since the greatest number of reserves placed are on best sellers.

A variation upon the usual method was evolved for a set of special circumstances (508).

.... It was decided to eliminate the rental collection and use a free loan period of three days for currently popular books. This would give us a quick turnover and still make all books available free of charge. However, we anticipated an increased volume of business with this new collection and dreaded the thought of manual charging. Finally we hit on an idea for "talking" these three-day books out of the library, still using only one recording machine and one set of transaction cards for both loan periods.

A special form with blank spaces provided for T-number and date due was printed on the cheapest grade of paper available. A supply of these pre-dated with the date due, three days off, is kept at the charging desk with the regular T-cards. When a "three-day" book is presented for charging, the desk attendant places one of these forms (let's call them "3-day slips" for convenience) in the book pocket. She pencils in the next transaction number in the sequence in the space provided and places the corresponding T-card in a slot in the desk. She then runs through

the charging routine on the recorder as though it were a
regular 21-day charge.   Each morning the T-cards which
have been deposited in the slot during the preceding day
are stamped with the proper date due, arranged in numerical order, and placed in a special tray in the return side
of the desk.

When a "three-day" book is returned the 3-day slip is
removed and the book is immediately ready for circulation.   The returned 3-day slips accumulate in a tray during the day.   Each morning an attendant matches the 3-
day slips with the proper T-cards and places the T-cards
in the discharge tray with those from "21-day" loan period transactions.   These T-cards are then sorted to their
proper place in the numerical sequence and are eventually
used again.   The 3-day slip is then discarded.   Overdues
are simple.   When a series of T-cards in the three-day
tray become seven days overdue, the book number and
name of the customer are searched on the proper record
and the regular overdue notice sent.

The Three-Day Shelf went into operation January 2,
1952.   The first day tripled the normal Rental Collection
Circulation and this pace has held. . . .

Alta Parks also reported a variation using a slightly
different procedure and equipment (509).

Gary Public Library has now been using the Gray Audograph combined with the McBee Keysort cards for its
loans to branches and classrooms in schools from the Extension Department. . . .

Books requested by teachers are selected each morning
by a professional staff member and stacked on the charging clerk's table.   Keysort cards are predated for 8 weeks
according to the estimated day's need.   Using a lapel microphone on a long cord, the clerk moves freely from one
group of books to another.   As the Audograph also has a
foot pedal, 12-15 books can be charged per minute. . . .

Because the operator goes to the books rather than
having to bring books to the charging machine, something
resembling a production line technique is possible.

Smith reports savings from this system in two distinct areas (510).

Operations have been speeded up, particularly on the return process. . . . While the audio-charge may not be quite

as fast as the photographic, it is sufficiently speedy to
meet requirements on a bookmobile lending up to 700
books in a period of about five hours.

A third area for saving was noted by Bailey (504).

The cost of materials for charging with the Audograph has
been cut to a fraction of the microfilm cost.

Likewise, Speer has seen a number of savings in this
system (505).

A minimum of time is spent on keeping the record of a
book which has gone out and come back on time.   The
only process needed is filing the transaction card in its
numerical sequence.
Discs are inexpensive initially and can be reprocessed
many times at a cost of three cents apiece.
Above all, the public library is employing a machine
to take the place of a slow, hand stamping and writing
process.

A number of disadvantages have been discovered with
this system.   Speer noted (505):

The loss of the circulation count by classes is minor,
and a periodic checking could be made any time we wish.
With no book card or date slip the record of the
chargings on an individual book does not exist.   This will
be missed when it comes to discarding and replacing.

She also noted another which was partially compensated
for (505).

Since only one person can use the machine at a time, people have to wait a little longer than with the hand stamping method.   All mechanical systems, however, are the
same in this respect, and the wait is very short.   The
speed in discharging books also somewhat compensates for
this.

Eggen also noticed a few disadvantages, but these, too,
had compensations (511).

We've had our troubles.   Customers lose T-cards, reserves may be missed, electric current has been off; but
an efficient circulation department manages to overcome

each crisis as it comes. In any event audio charging is
new, it's efficient, it's business-like and business is
booming.

One anticipated disadvantage has not come up. "Throat
irritation, which we feared," says Smith, "has not been noted
(510)."

The advantages inherent in this system have been described (512).

Audio-charging eliminates several steps from the old orthodox routine: (1) the filling out of the application card;
(2) the filling out of a library card for the patron and a
duplicate one for the library, for reference in case the
patron forgets to bring his card; (3) the "due slip" in the
library book and the book's own "due" card which was
carried in the pocket in the back of the book.

Speer has seen several advantages also (505).

Discharging is simple and fast.
Slipping is eliminated, speeding the availability of books
for the next reader.
Arranging and counting daily circulation is eliminated
and circulation statistics simplified.
Two fewer records are made in the cataloging process:
i. e., book card and date slip.
The registration file is cut in half.
The charging is more accurate, there is no chance to
copy a reader's number incorrectly.

Geer sums up the influence audio-charging systems
have had and the attitudes toward them (499).

Librarians have found the audio-charging machines particularly useful on bookmobiles where they can be operated
by means of an inverter with 6 volt electric power systems. On the whole, however, audio-chargers have not
been popular in libraries, although reports show they are
used in some small and medium sized ones.

Wayne County System

W. H. Kaiser has given a definition of this system
(513).

The first installation of this charging system was made in July, 1949. Since then it has been placed in nineteen community libraries, thus providing sufficient experience for evaluation. It is enough to say here that results have been very satisfactory.

The Wayne County Charging system is one of several variations of what may be characterized generally as loan number charging. It differs from others of the same general type in that (1) no mechanical devices are required; (2) a charging slip which provides up to four book charges is used; (3) six colors of loan cards are used to identify quickly any overdue books; and (4) simplicity and economy of materials.

Columbia University in 1949 reported a system with many similar elements (514).

We have tried a multiple-use charge card which when filled out by the student provides the call number, brief author and title, borrower's name and address.

This card is presented with the book at the loan desk. The desk assistant slips a predated serially numbered card in the book pocket, enters the serial number on the charge card and permits the book to be taken. The charge cards are filed by serial number as the books are issued. When a book is returned a page slips the date card from the book pocket and returns the book to the shelf for reader's use. Later in the day, a clerk arranges these date cards by serial number and matches them with the charge cards. The charge cards which remain in the file after the matching process represent books which have not been returned. This scheme has greatly facilitated the use of books and has reduced the cost of charging and discharging.

The supplies necessary for the Wayne County system were described by Kaiser (515).

The Wayne County Library system requires the use of two items: (1) a transaction or T-card; and (2) a charge or C-slip. Six serially numbered decks of transaction cards, each deck a different color are required. Each deck must be stamped with the date before it goes into use (books are due one day each week). Each deck must be complete before it is put in use, no numbers missing. The number of T-cards to be used is determined by the highest weekly circulation figure.

White cards are used as temporary replacements for
missing cards in any deck.   Charge slips or C-slips are
filled in by patrons on both sides.

The process of charging books was summarized in
these words (515):

Charging Book to Patron: (1) Patron fills in a C-slip on
one side writing his name and address, and on the other
side giving author, title and copy number of each book,
using one slip for four or fewer titles.   (2) Attendant (a)
inspects the C-slip for accuracy; (b) inserts a predated
T-card in each book pocket; (c) copies the transaction
number for each book onto the C-slip in the box for that
title; (d) places the C-slip in container face down to preserve the numerical order.

Kaiser goes into greater detail in one particular area
of the charging process (516).

In the present Wayne County System the patron supplies
his current address when he gives his name and address.
The assistant checks the legibility of the patron's handwriting, which has proved legible with few exceptions, and
identifies him by sight or by other accepted identification.
We believe that in cases involving a dispute about charge
records, having a patron's signature is superior to having
his card number written by himself or by an assistant....
We believe also from our experience that a patron signing
his name feels that he is on his honor, that his name is
his bond, and that in signing his name he has committed
a responsible act.   During the early trial period while the
staff became accustomed to new procedures, there were
four or five cases of fictitious addresses uncovered. (Theoretically, this should not happen if adequate identification
is insisted upon in every case of questionable identity.)
Within the past six months, however, no fictitious addresses have been reported.

In 1957, Kaiser reported that additional information
was now required in the area of charging (517).

...The Wayne County Charging system requires that the
patron fill out a slip each time books are borrowed from
the library.   The patron signs his name, address, telephone number, school, if a student, and furnishes an
identification acceptable to the library....

The manner of handling special charges was noted in the following paragraph (518):

Magazines without pockets can be charged with this system in the following manner: Patron fills out C-slip for periodicals as for books.   Librarian stamps due date and records T-card number of periodical.   The T-card is retained at the library.   When such periodicals are returned, the proper T-card is pulled and placed with all other T-cards.
Pamphlets.   The patron signs a C-slip and fills in information about the pamphlet on the reverse side.   Place the collection of pamphlets in a large manila envelope that has a book pocket on it.   The T-card can be placed in this pocket, thus a circulation count is automatically added for each group of pamphlets.

The discharging procedure was described by Kaiser in 1950 (515).

Patron Returns Book: (1) Attendant removes the T-card. The color of the T-card quickly indicates whether fines are due.   (2) Attendant places the T-card in the deck tray of returned cards for sorting.   (3) The book is thus immediately available to the next borrower.   No slipping or discharging is required.

The search and care of overdues was also noted by Kaiser (515).

Discharging Records: (1) Returned T-cards are first processed by color sorting for due date.   (2) When a due date becomes "overdue" then the deck for that date is arranged numerically.   (3) Attendant then goes through the deck and wherever a T-card is missing, makes note of missing T-card.   C-slips of corresponding numbers are removed for that due date to discover which books are overdue and who has the books.

This system includes a registration file, whose function was analyzed by Kaiser (516).

Whatever other purpose registration serves, the essential one is to guarantee that trustworthy persons are borrowing library books.   This library's system meets this test eminently in comparison with the system previously used and one which is used by most public libraries.

He further thought (519),

... indeed, the greatest rush in registration occurs simultaneously with the circulation rush when there is also
greatest need for reader assistance. The time saved by
a simplified and adequate identification and accountability
process..., and the still larger amount gained by the institution of loan number charging, have given our librarians far more opportunities to work with readers.

To summarize our results, the Wayne County Library
loses fewer books under the present system than under
the old....

It is our conclusion that the new system offers tighter
control.

According to Kaiser, his attitude in this matter has
been justified (520).

The data of ten years reveal an amazingly consistent loss
factor. The central conclusion is that losses of books
through circulation procedures neither increased nor decreased as a result of eliminating traditional library and
registration cards.

The procedure for handling renewals follows one of
three courses (521).

Patron Has Book with Him
    Check the Reserve list....
    Remove L-Card. Have patron fill in new charge slip,
    as though he were taking the book for the first time,
    and insert current L-card.
Patron Left the Book at Home
    It is best to ask him to phone in as for Telephone
    (see below) OR
    If a patron can supply the information, note the author
    and title and patron's name, when the book was due
    and to what date renewed. Consult this record when
    processing overdues.
    When overdues are processed, this record should be
    transferred to the renewal due date along with the
    patron's original charge slip.
By Telephone
    Secure loan number and due date. Give patron the
    new due date and ask him to place in the books.
    Make a record of the above information, and place
    with C-slips for the date book which was due. When

overdues are processed this record should be transferred to the renewal due date along with the patron's
original charge slip.   All renewal charges made without L-cards should be added to the L-card circulation
count.

The Reserves are found in the following manner (522):

For books on continuing or frequent reserve, place any
distinguishing card or sticker in pocket to flag such books
for checking against the reserve list.
    Check the reserve list with the shelves regularly each
day or check with books before shelving, except for books
known to be "flagged.".…
    A visible index has proved useful when numerous re-
serves are involved.

Kaiser found that the system embodied several savings
(523).

Staff has more time to help patrons, and … economy of
materials.

The disadvantages of this system were enumerated by
Kaiser (524).

(1) We thought patrons would grumble at having to help in
the charging process.   From ten branches over a period
of several months, we have received but three outright
complaints.   (2) Reserves, too, have given us far less
trouble than anticipated; one librarian likes the present
system better than the old for reserving books.   (3) Small
children and old people, of course, must be assisted. Older children enjoy helping the younger ones to make charges.   If a date due slip in book is not used, some may
feel that is a handicap since it is not possible otherwise
to tell how often a given book has been circulated.   Upon
analysis this lack does not seem too important, and (5)
some librarians may wish to have a classified breakdown
between the types of books circulated.   However, it is
possible to do this with the new system, but again one
wonders just what is done with the information that can't
be done without it.

W. Bacon has written several criticisms of the system (525).

1.   Assume that the library has no limit on number of
books per borrower; will the more voracious readers
cheerfully or even willingly set down "author, title and
copy number" for each of the weekly dozen titles, adding
name and address for each four?
2.   If they do, what happens at the circulation desk
during the busy hours?
3.   The staff handwriting, we assume, is readable if
not precisely "library hand" yet mistakes creep in.   Can
we not be sure that mistakes will multiply with hundreds
of scribbled titles in dozens of unfamiliar hands?   Would
snags, then, be really "at a minimum"?
4.   How can reserve handling be "better" (i. e. more
efficient), with up to four titles on a single slip?   In the
case of this library, one to two hundred new reserves in
a week is not uncommon.   It would be simply hopeless
for us to attempt to handle them under such a system,
and previous experience with the intricacies of county-
library reserves suggests even more trouble there.
5.   If two slips (or cards) are used for each transaction whereas the modified Newark plan uses one (which is
reusable), how can there be economy of materials?
6.   Transaction numbers give a direct, unclassified
count of circulation, and the point is made that the information gained from the usual breakdown is not significant.
Granted, but if an unclassified count is all that is desired
(many librarians would differ), wouldn't it be simpler
merely to measure the cards with a ruler, or weigh them?
This, of course, could be done with any card system.
7.   How long would the extemporized "shelf list" thus
salvaged from the old book cards be a valid record of
holdings, in view of additions and withdrawals?   Or does
Mr. Kaiser propose to make new book cards specifically
for this purpose?
8.   Time spent in sorting circulation, keeping cards
in date file, is eliminated; but isn't this to some extent
balanced by the convenience of knowing at any time exactly where any subject material the library owns is located
without fumbling or long searching?   Certainly, if the library makes any pretense to being a reference center,
facility in locating materials is of first importance.
9.   One of the advantages held out for the new system
is the substitution of name-address charging for those
pesky borrowers' numbers.   Wouldn't it be simpler for
the small or medium-sized library simply to adopt signature charging with visible-file equipment, as so efficiently
practiced by every bank in town?

10. What are we after anyway - knowledge of what we lend, knowledge of who reads what, of what x reads - or maybe not knowledge at all, but just "saving staff time"?

In view of the foregoing, the new system suggests itself as mainly adaptable to libraries where there are (1) definite limits of number of books per borrower; (2) few reserves; (3) no interest in immediate location of a specific book; (4) no interest in class or other analysis of circulation; (5) conditions which permit the borrower to do most of the work. How many libraries would subscribe to such a system or find it practical?

Advantages, on the other hand, were described by Kaiser (523).

We have found the following: (1) No slipping of books. (2) No circulation to be counted or filed daily. ...(5) Overdue handling is easier, not having to look up the patron's name and address from the card number. (6) Registration process simplified. (See already published articles on signature charging). ... (8) Supplies branches with the equivalent of shelf lists by using former book cards.

A variation upon the Wayne County System was formulated in New Zealand. W. Benton writes (526),

Instead of a record on film of all the books on issue, our record consists of filing trays of serially numbered cards pocketed with reader's slips. Our requirements for the new system were some thousands of white cards 5 in. by 3 1/4 in., and same number of printed date cards 4 1/2 in. by 3 in., manilla pockets and sixty-four double wooden filing trays.... Issuing a book is a simple matter, a buff coloured, numbered, pre-stamped date-due card is placed in the pocket of each book borrowed, and the borrower's slip is filed with a white file card bearing the same number as the date card. Before the day's work commences, a day's supply of "issue units" (white numbered file cards pocketed with buff numbered date cards stamped with the date 14 days ahead, and filed in numerical sequence in trays) is placed at the issue desk. No date stamping is done at the desk. At the end of the day the record of issue consists of trays of white cards in numerical order pocketed with readers' slips. ... As books are returned, date cards are removed from book pockets and the books returned to the shelves....

Overdues are done when the books are 14 days overdue, and in order to find out which books are overdue,
"discharging" has to be done - this involves the pairing
of returned date cards with their white file cards....
When there is no date card to correspond with the file
card, a green overdue slip is inserted in the pocket and
the issue slip is not removed. Overdue date cards are
discharged each day. The units with green slips are extracted from the main sequence and transferred to an overdue sequence....
Advantages. ... (c) Discharging. When a book is returned, its date card is removed and filed in date sequence, and the book is ready to be shelved. All routines connected with the discharging of returned date-due
cards take up the time of one assistant each day, whereas
under the previous system at least three assistants were
continuously engaged in this work.

A second variation was described by John Pike in 1954
(527).

.... It can be done simply, effectively and inexpensively;
The only equipment necessary being one or more number-
ing-machine-date-stamps. These require five or six digits in the latter portion and be set to stamp the same
number twice. The only other requirement is a plentiful
supply of blank "slips" the size of the book cards in use.
The sequence of operation is as follows: a blank slip
is placed by the borrower in his reader's ticket before
he presents his book for charging out; this is done by
placing the book card in the ticket (as we do normally)
but behind the slip; the date and number are stamped on
this and on the label in the book. The charge is placed
in the order of stamping and no additional filing is necessary. When the book is returned the details on the
date label enable the charge to be located and the transaction completed, the slip being kept for use again.

L. R. Rift described a third variant in College and
Research Libraries (528).

One feature of the proposed system is the availability of
the charge cards for analysis of book circulation without
interference to the regular circulation routines. Overdues
and renewals require a small amount of extra work; but
the adoption of the system is urged on the premise that
this extra work is well compensated by work savings on

regular charges, which are greatly in the majority....

Similar to most transaction card systems except T number is stamped in book with date (no T card goes with book) and T number is checked with circ file on date due (not when book is returned) by maintaining a check list of T numbers from books returned. Processes are reversed.

The patron writes name, number, address, call no., author, and title on charge card.

Desk attendant stamps transaction number and date due on the date due slip and on the charge card (all on one stamp).

Desk attendant punches date due and transaction number code on the charge card.

He files charge card by call number.

Book is returned near circulation desk for discharging procedure (could be modified to return anywhere in the library).

The transaction number appearing on the date-due slip in the returned book and the corresponding number on the check list are crossed off. The book is immediately ready for shelving.

Once for each date-due code: All charge cards for books due are removed from the circulation file by means of the sorting key.

Act on and refile one month overdues (cards with tabs).

Charge cards are sequence sorted according to transaction number by means of a sorting key. Transaction numbers not checked off on the check list are overdues or renewals. Mark "R" on renewal cards. Attach tabs to overdue and renewal cards and refile. Discard balance of cards....

Overdues

Charge cards are automatically pulled on or after date due by means of the sorting key. Remove cards after sequence sorting as explained in discharging procedure. Act on overdues. Refile charge cards in circulation file.

Renewals

Mark transaction number on check list with "R".

Charge card will be pulled out of the circulation file on the original date due.

Mark charge card with "R", attach tab and refile in circulation file....

Makes use of "a numbering machine like the ones used in many libraries for accessioning. The machine is set to stamp the same number twice before it advances one

number.   Coupled with this numbering is a date stamp,
which is set to indicate the date due.   Used on date due
slip and charge card of each book . . . .

A punch very similar to a three-hole punch used in
most offices, but it punches out in a scallop pattern all
numbers except the one which we are coding. . . .

Date due is coded across the top with numbers 1-10.
T number is coded on side in thousands, hundreds, tens
and units. . . .

Card sorting is done by call no. manually, date due
(on date due) by card sorter and T number (on date due)
by sorter.

Final discharging procedure for most books consists of
pulling the charge cards from the circulation file by means
of a key for marginal punched cards. . . . This system is
the fastest card sequence sorting system presently used in
American business establishments.   The whole procedure
takes only a few minutes for each time the cards are
pulled from the circulation file.

Notched Transaction Card System

At the University of Toronto, M. L. Newton and R. H.
Blackburn reported a system combining notched and transaction cards.   In their words (529), "It involves the use of a
serially numbered card punched and slotted in such a manner
that they may be sorted into consecutive order with a sorting
needle."   They added (530):

In order that serial numbers might be as small as possible
and cards for different days be easily distinguishable, we
begin with six decks of cards, each deck numbered consecutively from one to 650 and each a different color - blue
for Monday, and so on.   Another series for busy days and
the special rushes that occur at Christmas and Easter consists of three decks, each numbering from one to one
thousand and the whole series numbered on the back from
three thousand to six thousand.   At the end of the fall
term the system was extended to University College Reading Room with six new decks of four hundred cards each.
Decks are distinguishable not only by color but also by a
special code of slots, so that a mixed pile of cards may
be sorted into decks quickly with the needle.

The method of using this system in the charging process follows (529):

.... The charging procedure begins with a student presenting a request-slip for a book he wishes to borrow.
When he receives the book a serial card is put into the
book pocket and the number of the card is copied on the
end of the request-slip which thus becomes a complete
record of the loan. ... The slip is put immediately into
a pigeon hole file at the desk so that the book may be accounted for quickly if it is asked for by another student.
About four hundred books a day are borrowed in this manner most of them between three and five o'clock, and
most of them are returned between 8:45 and ten o'clock
the following morning.

McGaw reports a variation in filing by sequence of issue rather than classification (531).

Since, in most cases, overnight loans are made only a
short time before the library closes, and are due back
within a very short time after the library reopens on the
following school day, the record of the charge, while necessary, of course, need not be one which is easily acces-
sible while the books are in circulation. ...
   The principle underlying the new procedure was developed by Shaw in connection with the charging system at
the Gary, Indiana, Public Library. As applied to overnight reserve books ... [it shows this one difference from
the system in use at University of Toronto. After charging several books,] the library, then, soon has a file of
call cards arranged in the order in which the books were
charged, which arrangement also corresponds to the serial
numbers on the transaction cards.

The discharging method takes place the next morning
(529).

Under the new system, a returning book is cleared immed-
eately by the removal of the serial card from the pocket,
and is ready to be shelved. For instance, on the first
morning of the spring term about 2,200 volumes were returned to the main desk and were cleared for shelving almost as quickly as they arrived; checking of records was
done later.
   As serial cards are withdrawn from returning books
they are simply dropped into a box at the desk. After ten
o'clock, the deadline for return of overnight loans, the
cards which have accumulated are taken away to a workroom and in a few minutes are put into consecutive order

with the sorting needle.   Cards which have not returned
show up readily as gaps in the deck...; these gaps are
listed and the corresponding numbers pulled out of a file
of request-slips, so that notices may be sent.   Thus we
check only the overdues, or about eight per cent of the
total issue, and make a net saving of about ten hours a
week.   The process of looking through the slips one at a
time to find slips for overdue numbers is the only close
work required by the system.

The procedure for discovering missing cards was u-
nique at Toronto, stated Newton and Blackburn.   They accomplished with it ... what other systems accomplished with
complicated machines or by hand.   Of course, plain cards
and hand sorting could be used for the whole process, as in
most photocharging systems, but would be much slower
though still not as slow as systems which use book-card (532). "

This procedure was described by McGaw.   It was, he
stated (533), "a special technique ... whereby the left-hand
margin of its card is printed in black ink, and the cards are
notched along this unperforated edge in such a manner as to
expose by jags in the otherwise solid black line, any missing
cards.   With this system it is possible for the library assistant to note missing numbers by glancing at the edges of the
cards ten at a time instead of having to look at each card
separately...."

He also saw an improvement on this process (534).

The detection of missing cards is made much easier and
faster, however, if, while the complete deck is held in
proper order, the entire patterned edge is pencilled in.
In other words, each card will have a black spot of 1/8
x 3/16 inches at the right hand edge of its left-hand margin.   With this arrangement any card missing from the
deck will show up as a white spot in the otherwise solid
black line, and hence call itself immediately to the attention of the library assistant.

Newton and Blackburn noted several advantages to this
system.   The cost of the system was quite low (529).

The needle is inexpensive and should last for years; the
cards cost less than two cents apiece and show so little
wear after four months of use that we think they may not
have to be replaced for two or three years.   Since the

cards paid for themselves, in time saved, during the first
three months of use, the principle advantages of the system cost nothing.

Other advantages were seen.   "The saving in eye
strain and headaches is worth mentioning.   The unexpected
but noticeable decline in the number of 'snags' and 'funnies'
has meant an additional saving of time and worry.   Time
saved, of course, is time released for other work, and so
amounts to an improvement in service to readers (529)."

There is a great saving of filing time where notched
transaction cards are used, as reflected by a time study conducted at the Wayne County Public Library.   The findings
were as follows (535):

The primary finding of this study is that in one hour approximately 1100 transaction cards should be sorted,
checked, and recorded for missing numbers.
A secondary and useful standard is that approximately
60,000 holes can be sorted in one hour, assuming the usual proportion of cards, requiring direct, breakdown, and
sequence sorting ....

One anticipated problem did not develop (536).

Loss and mutilation of cards, which we worried about at
the beginning, have not been problems: at the end of the
fall term, after a total overnight circulation of 23,769,
there were only six cards lost and only two that had not
been accounted for.

This system, Newton and Blackburn believe, is not
adaptable to all libraries, but it could benefit many (536).

Since it is necessary in a university library to be able to
locate any book quickly, book-cards for all our seven-day
and indefinite loans are filed in a single alphabet which
must be cleared as the books come in.   It would not be
feasible for us to use punched cards for those loans.   In
a public library, on the other hand, it might be possible
to dispense altogether with book-cards and most of the
work that goes with them....

McGaw predicted that the marginal-punched transaction
card system would become more widely adopted by academic
institutions.   "The fact that the same cards can be used re-

peatedly - hence the economy to be effected by purchasing
them in rather small quantities - is one of the advantages to
be noted.   Another advantage - the simplicity of the transaction card's design - makes unnecessary the purchase of a
specially prepared form.   When the speedy missing-number
detection system used by the University of Toronto Library
is added to the card's design, the system should find increasingly greater favor (537). "

Punched Transaction Card Method

        The Punched Transaction Card Charging System "re-
quires no book cards and no card punching at the time the
loan is made.   The basic feature of the system is the arrangement of the record of books on loan in the sequence in
which they were issued (538). "

        When circulation control is the main "need" to be con-
sidered then a record of the transaction is all that is necessary to fulfill that need.   To obtain that record, according to
IBM Corporation, this is the procedure which can be followed
(539):

> When the borrower presents the book and the loan slip at
> the charging desk, the library clerk inserts the loan slip
> in the IBM Book Charging Recorder which automatically
> prints the date of withdrawal and a transaction number.
>   This transaction number is a consecutive number. Start-
> ing with "1" each day, the Book Charging Recorder auto-
> matically advances by one as each loan slip is stamped.
> At the same time it also prints the due date, as well as
> identification of the branch or charging station. ...
>   An IBM transaction card is inserted in the book pocket
> to complete the record of the charge.
>   These IBM cards are prepunched and prenumbered with
> branch number, due date, and transaction number. Enough
> cards are provided to cover the maximum daily circula-
> tion.   The punched data in the card makes it possible to
> sort the cards automatically by use of the IBM Electric
> Punched Card Sorting Machine.   These cards can be used
> over and over again, year after year.
>   The preprinted, prepunched transaction cards are kept
> in consecutive order at the charging desk.   To charge out
> a book, the library clerk selects the next available card,
> compares its number with the transaction number printed
> on the loan slip by the time stamp, and places the card in

the book pocket.

The loan slip is dropped behind the one for the previous transaction so that the loan slips are always in numerical sequence. ...

When a book is returned the IBM Transaction Card is withdrawn from the book pocket and placed in a holding file for returned cards. The cards are held for each daily or weekly period. ... the book is ready for circulation immediately.

At the Los Angeles Public Library a system was devised which combined the use of Recordak for charging with IBM punched cards to aid in filing. According to that library the IBM equipment prepares punched transaction cards, sorts and arranges them as an overdue control (540).

The I. B. M. transaction cards (approximately 3 x 5 inches in size) are pre-punched and pre-printed by I. B. M. equipment in the Tab Room at the Central Library. A shorter card than is customary with I. B. M. is used so that it will fit into the book pocket without projecting beyond the book covers. In order to reduce the number of transaction cards needed by half, cards are designed to be used twice each year and between periods of use are stored in specially provided metal drawers in the library agency. On one end of the card the library agency number, a serial or transaction number, the month and due date are punched and printed. This same information, except the date is changed to six months later, is on the other end of the card. Enough consecutively numbered cards are printed for each day beginning with No. 0001 to take care of as somewhat larger than average day's circulation for the library agency. If this prepared deck is exhausted before the end of an unusually heavy day's circulation, the next day's deck may be used. The advantage here is to the borrower who gets an extra day's circulation. The decks of cards will be used over and over again every six months. Only lost, mutilated, and overdue cards will have to be remade by the Tab Room.

The pamphlet printed by IBM Corporation noted that it is possible to make a daily check of those books which have become overdue, but it is a saving of time when the circulation of several days can be checked simultaneously. The procedure for caring for overdues is as follows (541):

Books which have become overdue during the period are

determined through automatic arrangement of the IBM
cards by the IBM Electric Sorting Machine.

At the close of each cut-off period, daily or weekly,
the returned Transaction Cards for a specific due date
are sorted to transaction number. ...

After this automatic sorting, the cards are examined
manually or machine processed by sorting machine or collator to determine which numbers are still missing from
each day's file. These numbers represent overdue books.

As the missing numbers in the IBM Transaction Cards
are determined corresponding loan slips are withdrawn
from the loan file. ... These overdue loan slips, kept in
sequence as they are pulled, are filed in an overdue file.

When an overdue book is returned, the IBM card is removed from the book pocket. The corresponding loan slip
can be taken from the overdue file either at this time or
when the IBM card appears in the periodic check for overdue books.

... The loan slips for overdue books being grouped together, the typist simply transcribes the required information from slips to overdue notices.

Los Angeles uses centralized overdue control. It is
worked in this manner (542):

.... Each library agency sends its exposed film to Recordak Corporation for developing, and its transaction
cards from returned books to the Tab Room at Central
Library for sorting. The IBM equipment sorts these cards
just by date due and then about ten days after each due
date arranges them in numerical sequence by transaction
card number. The cards for each day represent all books
due on that day that have been returned. These are
matched against a master deck containing a complete sequence of transaction numbers. When transaction cards
are missing, the corresponding cards in the master deck
are selected by the machine and fed into a separate pocket. These cards represent the books that are overdue on
that particular day. For each overdue book two cards are
made: a pink-edged IBM card to be used as an overdue
record (showing transaction number, library number and
date due) and a duplicate of the missing transaction card;
these duplicate transaction cards for each day are merged
numerically into the transaction cards returned in books
due on that date, which have been sent to the Tab Room.
This produces a complete deck which is returned to the
library agency to be stored for use six months later.

The pink-edged overdue records ("Tab Checks") which
are also returned from the Tab Room are in transaction
card order under date due.   At the library agency the
roll of microfilm for the date for which overdues are to
be sent is selected from the file of developed film and
placed in the Reader part of the Recordak.   The transaction number on each overdue record is located on the film,
first by date due and then numerically.   The overdue notice is typed directly from the film, which gives all the
necessary information.   The overdue records are then
placed in the overdue file.   As over-due books are returned,   the transaction cards from them are matched a-
gainst the overdue records.   Matching transaction cards
and overdue records are destroyed, since the overdue
transaction cards have already been replaced in the permanent deck by the Tab Room.

As second and third notices are sent, needed information is added to the "Tab Check" (pink-edged overdue record) and the overdue file is cleared as overdue books are
returned.

The Stockton Public Library has used this method
since 1949.   At that library, the staff dealt with renewals in
this fashion (543):

Renewals can be made either in person or by telephone.
It is only necessary to give the desk attendant the transaction number and date from the IBM transaction-control
book pocket.   The corresponding slip is located.   If the
renewal is made by phone, the slip is marked "R," dated
with the new date, and returned to its proper place in the
file.   When overdues are run, it is eliminated from the
delinquent list since it bears a renewal notice.   A renewal in person with the book at hand follows the same procedure, except that the book charge slip is used over a-
gain, the book is given a current transaction card, and
the old slip is restamped on its reverse side and treated
as a new charge.

As observed by Klausner, the reserve system appears
to be a weakness of the system.   "There seems to be no substitute for the usual method of locating the wanted book card
and clipping or holding it until the book is returned and
snared.   But it is a costly method if a large circulation file
must be kept and searched constantly to insure control."
Stockton finds a partial solution in their visible file (544).

All reserves are made on postal forms which are filed in
shelf order in a visible file. This file is mounted on a
movable base and is a quick reference source as to what
books should be held from recirculation. ...
The reserve-book system, which has previously been
operated by a junior librarian (professional) was incorporated entirely into the circulation procedure and the librarian was released to do professional work.

In 1948, Klausner referred to overdue and reserve
procedures in this manner (545):

Previously it was not possible to maintain the overdue
procedure for the main library, but it is now being handled for the main library and seven branches. Reserves
are now part of the circulation procedure and the junior
librarian previously attached to this service does professional work.

Margaret Klausner pointed out several changes which
were brought about by her acceptance of this method of charging at Stockton: (1) "Termination of book-card purchases
spared the catalog department considerable typing, thus freeing clerical time for other tasks. Elimination of the book-
card also ended the slipping of books, a procedure that required a great deal of time at the circulation desk and was
evidently unnecessary if overdues could be controlled; 2 The
need for the daily breakdown, filing, and counting of circulation was avoided by the adoption of the 'IBM' system. The
numerically stamped book slips provide a daily circulation
tally, to which are added the number of renewals made. ....
3 It is no longer necessary to keep a double borrower's file
of name and number records, since only the borrower's
names are important (546)."

In regard to answering a "need," IBM proved satisfactory for this library. "Stockton chose the IBM method of
circulation control because of its simplicity, the possibilities
it offered to reduce operating costs and its flexibility. ...
The system is inherently flexible and certain variations can
be introduced in the operations. ... Where circulation loads
are heavy, Stockton uses both the punched transaction-control
cards and the automatic stamping machine. Where the branch
has a potential for heavy circulation but has not yet achieved
it, the IBM transaction cards are used as already described;
however, ... the charging assistant writes the transaction
number on the book slip. ... All card sorting is done at the

main library (547)."

Savings were also noted at the Los Angeles Public Library and credited to use of both Recordak and IBM (548).

> Photo-lending has been installed in the Central Library, 35 of the larger branches and 4 bookmobiles. The circulation in these agencies amounts to 88% of the total circulation of the L. A. P. L., or over 7,000,000 circulation annually.
> The cost of photo-lending including all IBM and Recordak equipment, films, currently made transaction cards, and salaries of tabulating operators amounts to approximately $2,550.00 monthly.
> The Circulation Department alone has eleven fewer people on its staff than in 1948, this saving being largely attributable to photo-lending. There is also a substantial reduction of clerical personnel in branches. This reduction in staff has resulted in a direct saving of over eight hundred dollars per month.
> In addition to the monetary savings photo-lending has increased efficiency and eliminated many repetitious routines. Work-loads have been greatly reduced in those branches where no personnel cuts have been made, thus releasing time to be used more effectively in direct service to the public.

A variation of the IBM system was adopted by the Mill Valley, California Public Library which illustrates, according to G. G. Young, the method as it is fitted to the less extensive installation (549).

> The IBM demonstrated a method that substitutes a slip of paper filled out by the borrower in place of the film and camera. This slip is then given a serial number (transaction number) standing for that loan. The IBM also suggested that the numbered date-due cards which are placed in the books be punched for mechanical sorting on the IBM sorters.
> ....No major changes in this system were made at Mill Valley. Modifications consisted of the selection of less expensive equipment, since the amount of work to be done does not warrant the IBM machinery. Four chief economies will be mentioned: (1) substitution of a numbering machine for the IBM time stamp; (2) use of a date-due slip pasted in the book rather than having the transaction control cards dated; (3) use of a once-a-week due date

rather than having books fall due daily exactly two weeks
from the date of the loan; and (4) sorting and arranging
the transaction control cards by use of the Perkins device
(Keysort) rather than by IBM sorter.

A fifth simplification was made possible.... With no
additional signature required, it was only necessary to include on the charge slips a statement to be signed by the
borrower, guaranteeing prompt return of the specific book
loans. In this way, it was easy to eliminate all registration of borrowers and still retain good legal control.

The numbering machine chosen for use at Mill Valley
Library, selling for approximately $20, is the type commonly
used for accessioning, numbering borrowers' registrations,
etc. In charging the... attendant stamps transaction number
on charge slip and inserts similarly numbered control card
in book pocket. " Young further stated (550):

By using date-due slips in the books, it is possible to re-
use the undated transaction control cards at fairly frequent intervals, and so reduce the number required. Eight
week intervals were chosen since that period would give
ample time for a two-week loan, a two-week renewal and
four weeks' overdue time in which to press for the return of the book. This plan has cut the cards required
to one-third that suggested by IBM.

A further advantage gained by using date-due slips is
that they provide a permanent record of the use made of
each volume which can be of considerable importance in
any program of weeding out unused books.

Under the IBM system a once-a-week change of due
dates permits a smaller initial investment for transaction
control cards by smoothing out circulation peaks. A set
of cards is used for a whole week, and therefore it is possible to predict more accurately the maximum number
needed with fewer extras purchased "just in case. " ...

Since the transaction control cards are not dated, it is
necessary to select some method to distinguish different
sets of these cards. A prefix number similar to that used
in metropolitan phone numbering is employed.... A six-
wheel numbering machine with provision for depressing
zeros, so they will not print, makes possible a five-figure
number with a space between the first and second giving
numbers ranging from 1 0001 on up. Each week for eight
weeks the next prefix number is used and then the series
is repeated....

At Mill Valley, the transaction control cards were pre-

pared to be sorted by Keysort ... These cards are 3"
x 5" in size and punched along two sides.... Punching
was done, a few at a time, as needed during the first
eight weeks of the new system. A Tri-Mee 303 punch
was used....

The code used was not printed on the cards as it is
in Keysort installations, but was considered simple enough
to be memorized easily....

Numbers were coded by notching units, tens, and hundreds in the fields indicated. ... Since the numbers do
not run beyond 1400 it is not necessary to have more than
one hole for thousands....

When books are returned, the transaction control cards
are taken from them and dropped into a bin. After the
cards accumulate sufficiently, they are sorted by prefix,
using a steel 12-inch no. 2 knitting needle.... Following
sorting the cards are stored in labeled drawers with others of the same prefix.

Once a week, when preparing to send out overdue notices, it is necessary to arrange all the returned control
cards for that particular prefix by Keysort procedure ....

Following arrangement of all the cards for a set it is
necessary to examine the set for missing numbers. These
gaps represent books that have not yet been returned, and
are either overdue or have been renewed by telephone.
To close the gaps for telephone renewals, a yellow renewal slip is filed in the place of the missing transaction control card. It bears the transaction control number, title
of the book, and new date due. It had been previously
filled out at the time the renewal was requested. All other gaps are filled by drawing the pink charge slips made
at the time the books were loaned. Overdue notices are
then prepared from these charge slips. As overdue books
come in, the transaction control cards are filed in place
of the charge slips and the latter removed. Second notices are sent to those borrowers still having charge slips
in the transaction control card file at a later date.

Arranging the transaction control cards, inspecting for
gaps, and filing charge slips in these gaps takes approximately an hour a week, considerably less than the three
hours or more previously spent arranging book cards.
Chief advantage of this new system, however, lies in the
elimination of the slipping process. All books are immediately ready for recirculation. Borrowers also appreciate
being able to check out books without having to carry "library cards." The staff time saved on registration work
is also appreciable.

Bookamatic System

In an article published in 1946, **G. G.** Young related the developments which led to the conception of the Bookamatic (551).

> To repeat and produce information many methods have been devised ranging from the transcribing by hand or typewriter, through embossed plates of metal, mimeograph stencils, direct and reflex photography and by means of punched cards. After discarding the hand methods as too slow and inaccurate, and the mimeograph and photograph as too messy, involving the use of inks and fluids and darkrooms as they do, and the punched card as too expensive, we have the embossed plate left as probably the most practical.
> This device has been used for many years in addressing regularly mailed matter and in the "Charge-a-Plate" system used in department stores to identify customers with charge accounts. It has been used to some extent in the Dickman and Gaylord Charging devices where an embossed plate is used for the number. However, these two latter devices represent only a beginning of what might be done. If we are to print anything at all, we might just as well print the entire information such as name, address, etc., about the borrower rather than just a number, and in so doing eliminate half the work of maintaining two registration files.

In the same article, Young suggested certain equipment which he felt was workable in the system (552).

> Among the various printers available is one called a Tagimprinter the Addressograph Model 60... Either one or two tags can be inserted under the ribbon, which is of carbon paper so that the tag does not become soiled with ink and a source of dirty fingers and books. The form to be imprinted is placed over the ribbon and a light tap on the printing arm makes the impression. The ribbon is advanced manually by turning a knob. The machine has a rear gauge to position the paper being printed. The Tagimprinter is 5 1/2" long, 4 3/4" wide and 4 1/8" high and weighs 6 pounds.
> If such a printing machine were to be used in a library that had provided one plate or tag for each borrower and one for each book, a transaction slip bearing complete

information about both book and borrower could be produced accurately and in a matter of seconds. An Addressograph tag, similar to the Army identification tag, but
a bit longer and measuring 2 1/2 by 1 1/4 inches, has
space for five lines of type with 22 characters to the line.
For the borrower's tag the first three lines could be devoted to his name and address.   This would leave two
lines for such information as sex, age, occupation, education, nationality, race, etc., which, if in code, should
not be particularly objectionable to the borrower.   For
the book tag, five lines of 22 characters would be enough
to list class and accession numbers and author and title.
Probably there would also be room for other information
such as date of publication, degree of readability, type of
book, etc.

The tags are small enough to be carried easily in any
wallet and are perforated at one end so borrowers could,
if they so desire, carry them on key rings, or among the
younger borrowers especially, on necklaces as was done
in the Army.   This same hole in the book tags could be
used for a rivet or a loop of stout cord fastened to the
book to prevent loss of the tag.   Book pockets and cards
would not be needed, but a date slip pasted to the front
fly-leaf would be used.

The method of registration would be accomplished in
the following way, according to Young's suggested system
(553).

The registration of borrowers would be much as it is now
in most libraries with the exception that more details
would be asked for....   Re-registration time for borrowers and controls on borrowers as to the number and type
of book permitted can be indicated by colors of tags since
they must be given a protective coating to prevent rust
after manufacture....
Perhaps a simpler method would be an annual, biennial
or triennial validation by embossing the decade and year on
the plate.

The charge a book, Young would have used the following procedure (554).

When a borrower wished to take out a book, he would present it with his tag to the attendant at the circulation desk,
who would put the book tag in one side of the printer and
the borrower's tag in the other.   A slip of paper 3 by 5

inches in size would be placed in the machine and the operating handle depressed. This would make a printed cop-
y of all the information embossed in each tag. ... The
date slip in the book would then be stamped with the date
due, using a self-inking rubber stamp dater, and both the
book and his tag handed to the borrower.

Young felt the need for a classified file (555).

The transaction slip thus made would have been previously prepared to indicate the date due. The preparation
would have been of two kinds. The first one would be
stamping the date due with the rubber stamp dater. The
second would be the selection of some device for indication in the files of those slips due each day. Transaction
slips could be filed just as book cards are commonly filed
under date due, but a single circulation file would have
certain advantages; and since the transaction slips would
be used in the time file but once, it would be possible to
graft one of several devices onto them. One such device
is the Perkins patent (commonly called Keysort) using
marginal perforations and notches. Another is the tab
slip as made by Remington Rand. Transaction slips of
different colors would probably be the least expensive, but
since there are a limited number of colors light enough to
be printed on it would be necessary to assign one color to
two or more days.... In this way a single master circulation file could be maintained rather than the twelve or
more now usually indicating books in circulation. If desired, new slips could be interfiled into the circulation
file as soon as they had been made without holding them
for counting since statistics could be determined from slips
that had served their purpose in the time record.
     When books were returned the transaction slips would
be drawn from the file. Since the slips would have served
the time record purpose and would not have to be fitted
back into a book pocket, this process would be relatively
rapid. When the period of the loan had passed far enough
to warrant sending overdue notices, all the remaining slips
of the appropriate color would be drawn from the file.

     The transaction slips would provide valuable informa-
tion and statistics for library studies (553).

The series of old transaction slips would form the raw
data for any statistical examination of the circulation the
library desired to secure.... The extent to which informa-

tion about the use made of the library was gathered would be limited only by the needs of the staff and governing body and the time at their disposal.

A further advantage of these old transaction slips would be in the preparation of mailing lists of names of people who have actually been interested in a subject to the extent of checking out a book on that subject. If, for example, the library has prepared a new book list on photography, it would be a simple matter to select old transaction slips for books on this subject and from them mail copies of the new list to borrowers who are presumably more interested than others and would use them.

Young's tabulation of costs is perhaps a good indicator of expenses for similar items in the later system as it was finally formulated by the Addressograph Company (556).

The largest item of expense is, by far, the initial one of supplying tags for all borrowers and all actively used books. These tags retail for $26.50 a thousand in lots of ten thousand or more. This is 2.65 cents each and with the cost of labor and rental (or interest and depreciation of a high-speed keyboard-operated Graphotype [which sells for about $300 if equipment is bought] it has been estimated by the Addressograph representatives that the finished tags will be run four cents each. The Gaylord Borrowers' tags cost $18.00 a thousand and must be inscribed with name and address and a double registration file must be maintained to keep a record of the borrowers' numbers. Therefore it might be that the cost of the tags for borrowers would not be much greater than that of Gaylord cards and possibly even a bit less. In addition, there is available, at one cent each, a leather pocket or case for the borrowers' tags. This case could be offered for sale to such borrowers as desire them at five cents each and help defray in some measure the cost to all the borrowers' tags....

Securing funds for the book tags presents greater complications since so many tags must be secured at the beginning of the system and will be used for many years following. Therefore, any plan for financing book tags should be spread over three to five years. .... A library of 50,000 volumes might easily pay for ten thousand tags a year (a matter of $265.00) and at the same time with no additional staff get them embossed. That same library attempting to do the whole process in one year would have to raise over two thousand dollars to care for both tags and labor.

Compared to the cost of the tags and their embossing the cost of the machine for printing is small.   The Addressograph Model 60 sells for $25.50 and should last for at least ten years, a cost of $2.55 a year.   Carbon paper ribbons sell for $.60 each and are reported to be good for at least 12,000 impressions.   Slips of paper suitable for transaction slips sell for about one-twentieth of a cent each.   Therefore, a library with an annual circulation of 100,000 could expect to spend $50.00 a year for transaction slips.   The labor cost of filing these in the circulation file would be no more than is now spent on the regular Newark type of file, but there would be an additional cost for the statistical filing.   This would vary with the demands of the library executives for figures on library use.

Though he had no concrete examples or statistics to work from, Young noted several advantages in his proposed system (556).

Lacking a history of actual use the book-charging method described here cannot be thoroughly evaluated.   However, certain advantages can be enumerated.   These consist of the following:

1) A single registration file rather than a double one.
2) A single master circulation file rather than twelve or more.
3) A record of the exact location of every book not on the shelves.
. . . .
. . . .
6) Rapid and accurate charging.
7) Rapid discharging requiring only reasonable attention to be accurate.
8) Extremely flexible raw data for any statistical survey of the use made of the collection.

In 1955, Geer stated (557),

The Addressograph-Multigraph Corporation of Cleveland, Ohio, has adapted its credit plate, used with charge accounts by department stores, to library circulation procedures.

The supplies required under this system were explain-

ed in a pamphlet issued by the Addressograph Corporation
(558).

    A. Emboss one permanent plastic book card for each
       book. (Card may be later embossed on opposite
       end of card should original book be discarded or
       withdrawn from circulation, thereby providing a
       double use of the card).
    B. Emboss and issue permanent plastic borrower's
       identification card for each borrower.
    C. Establish permanent sets of serially numbered and
       punched McBee Keysort or Punch tabulating date
       due cards and corresponding serially numbered low
       cost expendable transaction cards. Use a different
       color card or ink for each period of book issuance
       or to indicate branch or department from which
       book was charged out.

    The charging process finally formulated for this sys-
tem was discussed by this booklet (559).

    A. When a borrower presents a book to the charging
out desk, the charge clerk performs the following simple
operation:
1. Removes plastic book card from the book pocket and
   places it in the Addressograph Bookamatic charge imprinter.
2. The borrower's "Plastic Identification Card" is placed
   next to the book card in the Addressograph Bookamatic charge imprinter.
3. Charge out clerk pulls proper colored date-due card
   and transaction card, and quickly checks number to
   make certain they match.
4. Charge out clerk imprints both sides of transaction
   card in two quick motions, then places transaction
   card with other imprinted transaction cards of the
   same color.
5. The Plastic bookcard and the date-due card on which
   the return date has been stamped, are then placed in
   the book pocket and the borrower's "Plastic Identification Card" is returned to the borrower.

    "The return of books," states the pamphlet, "is equal-
ly simple (560)."

    B. When a borrower returns a book to the charging in
desk, the charge clerk performs the following simple op-

eration:

    1. The date-due card is removed and checked to determine if late charges are applicable.

    2. The date-due card is placed with other date-due cards of the same color.

      The search for overdues is accomplished in the following manner (561).

    At a later time, the date-due cards are mechanically sorted by means of needles or sorting machines into a numeric sequence. The missing numbers from each day's numerically sequenced date-due cards indicate which transaction cards represent overdue books and automatically provides a completely addressed overdue book notice for insertion into a window envelope. The top half of the transaction card is kept in an overdue file until book is returned.

    The operation of the Central Records Section is also simple.

    C. The two-piece, completely imprinted transaction cards are sent to the Central Records Section on a daily basis, by the charging out clerk.

    1. Pre-addressed numerically sequenced complete transaction cards are received and filed as to date due by Central Records Section. Cards are received in color groups and in numerical sequence so no sorting of In or Out filing is required.

      a. One-half of the form represents a pre-addressed past due notice that can be used as described above.

      b. The second-half of the transaction card provides the means for establishing a central file of books that are past due. These cards should be filed by title or Dewey Decimal number or by date due, whichever is best suited to each individual library's needs.

      The renewal procedure, states the pamphlet, "is easy (562)."

    The Transaction Card is taken from the numeric file, stamped "Renewed" and filed in the front of the tray of Transaction Cards for the new due-date. If the borrower has brought the book into the library when requesting renewal, the new due-date can be stamped on the McBee Due-Date Card. If the renewal is made by telephone, the borrower can be instructed to note the new date and the

clerk's initials, authorizing the extension. This keys the
Due-Date Card, so that the Transaction Card can be immediately located.

In finding reserves, "Books are quickly checked a-
gainst a reserve file and can then be returned to shelves
(562). "

Statistics may also be kept with this system (562).

The Transaction Cards pulled from the circulation file
daily can then be sent to the professional staff members
responsible for posting to circulation records or for re-
viewing purposes to determine which books should be re-
purchased and which books should be considered dead stock.
(The availability of these cards will also assist in taking
an accurate inventory.)

The Addressograph Corporation claims many advantages for its system (563).

100% accurate, legible records of charges prepared by
machine.
Faster return of books to shelves for recirculation.
Simple business like method for charging out books
with resulting improved public relations.
A simple "one source" procedure for checking over-
dues.
Professional and clerical duties are clearly separated
with the result that the public receives better service.
Different loan periods - 7, 14 or 28 days - can be ad-
ministered easily.
Fewer assistants are needed at circulation desk.
System designed for use in main library, branches or
bookmobiles.
Charging machines are low cost and require minimum
of counter space.
Eliminates need for numerical file of book borrowers'
cards issued.
Borrower's identification card is not needed for the re-
turn of a book.
It is possible to know at all times where a given book
is, to whom it is charged, and when it is due.
Machines required are simple to operate.
Transaction Cards provide complete and permanent re-
cords of all books withdrawn from library.
Patrons are not required to take part in any of the

charging process.
Extra charging machine, weighing less than 10 lbs.
may be moved between departments to handle peak loads.
Circulation desk is neat and free from clutter of un-
slipped books.
All handwriting is eliminated.
Typing of overdue notices is eliminated.
Counting of daily circulation is easy.
Permanent book cards eliminates need for preparation
of new cards.
Eliminates eyestrain and mental fatigue.

Geer felt that the system was expensive but "It would
seem that this charging system has great potentialities for
cooperation...between college or school libraries and other
departments in the same institution. One identification plate
could be carried by ... a student in a school or college for
registration, identification, and for withdrawing books from
the library (564)."

"This...book charging system was first installed in
Midland, Michigan," according to the Addressograph Corporation (565).

Harold O. Harlan wrote an appraisal of this new system in 1957 (566).

....The change to Bookamatic charging from modified
Newark hand charging has resulted in important savings
in staff time. Two especially important savings have been
in the elimination of registration files, both alphabetical
and numerical (since these are no longer needed) and the
elimination of typing of overdue notices.

Brodac System

In a pamphlet released by the Bro-Dart Industries, the
machine was described in the following manner (567).

Brodac .. works on any ordinary 15 amp. outlet. It operates on the principle of Thermography -- which is heat
reflection and absorption. When the material to be copied
is placed in the machine, a heat-sensitive paper picks up
the carbon in the ink or type and transfers it to the sensitized paper. This provides an immediate visible copy
without developing or further processing of any type. If

for some reason, the charge is not copied correctly it may be re-recorded.

Brodac is also capable of making a "copy of a copy." This means that the copy you have made can be transferred to another slip.

This system, in addition to the Brodac Machine, also lists book cards, reader's identification cards, and transaction cards among its supplies. The charging process was described by the Bro-Dart Pamphlet (567).

1. Book card - Reader's Identification Card - and Transaction card are placed in the machine.
   a. If reader forgets his card, a driver's license, social security card or other identification may be used.
   b. Numbered transaction cards are usually pre-dated with date due or date issued.
2. Two buttons are pushed - and Brodac copies the book's title, reader's name and address and the date. Charges are copied on a master roll of sensitized paper. As this paper moves through the machine, it is automatically cut into convenient slips. While Brodac is making its copy, the librarian is getting ready for the next charge. ... not a moment is wasted.
3. Book card and Transaction Card are put back into the book pocket - Brodac charge slips are removed from the machine at the end of the day. They are in numerical order and are put into a date file for reference at the end of the loan period.

The discharging process works in the following manner (567):

As books are returned, the Transaction Card is removed and filed numerically. Once the card is taken out, books are ready for shelving. No book slipping is necessary! Now books can be shelved immediately - ready for more circulations - with no hold-ups for further processing.

Lost Transactions Slips

If a book is returned without a Transaction Card, one of the following methods may be used:

1. A slip is made up with the book's title and the reader's name and address. This slip is checked against Brodac Charge Slips before overdues are sent.

2. The borrower is fined and given a receipt when fine is paid. An overdue notice is mailed automatically

and borrower must present his receipt as proof that book
was returned.

Overdues are handled without the need for typing (568):

1. At the end of the loan period... Transaction Cards are
    checked for missing numbers.   The missing numbers
    indicate overdue books.
2. The Brodac Charge Slip file is consulted.   The slips
    that apply to the missing numbers are removed from
    the file.   All other slips for that date may be de-
    stroyed... or kept for future reference if desired.
3. The Brodac Charge Slip and a special Overdue Notice
    are placed in the Brodac Machine before the next
    day's charging begins.   In a few seconds, an overdue
    notice is made... slipped into a window envelope and
    mailed.   The Brodac Charge Slips are kept until
    books are returned.   Second and Third Notices can be
    made from the same slip.

Because reader's name and address is copied onto each
charge slip - it is no longer necessary to refer to a numerical borrower's file.   In fact this file can be discontinued, eliminating a good deal of time and labor in the
registration of borrowers.

The reserves, according to the pamphlet, would be
found by using a visual file of post cards (569).   Renewals
are cared for by this method (568).

If book is brought in personally for renewal, the simplest
method is to make a new charge... using a new transaction number and filing the old transaction card as though
the book had been returned.

If patron phones in his renewal, he is given a new
transaction number over the phone, with instructions to
change the number on his Transaction Card.   The new
Transaction Card is put into a "Renewals" file until the
book is returned.   A dummy card is made up with the
original transaction number, to prevent the issuing of an
overdue notice.

The Brodac Charge Copy for the original charge is located and the original transaction number replaced with
the new number.   The Charge Copy is refiled according
to the new date.   When the book is finally returned, the
new Transaction Card is removed from the "Renewals"
file and filed in its proper position.

The Brodac machine is available with an attachment for aiding in circulation statistics, records, and book culling (568).

An additional feature of Brodac that many librarians will find especially helpful, is the ability to code the book card to show number of circulations.   While Brodac is making its charge copy, a dot is automatically put on the back of the book card.   The position of the dot is moved every week.   By observing the clusters of dots - the librarian can easily tell how recently and how actively the book has circulated.   One card can be dotted for three years... and if the ink color is changed... six years. The number of book circulations per day can be determined by using the first and last transaction number per day.

The cost of this system was outlined in the pamphlet (569).

The base Brodac Machine, ready to be inserted into a charging desk, carries a list price of between $750.00 and $900.00, depending upon the extra equipment attached - such as the Book Card dotting mechanism and the cutting mechanism.

The machine will be available on a rental basis at between $25.00 and $40.00 per month, depending upon what extra equipment is needed.   Rental price will include service.

The cost per charge will vary between $4.50 and $7.50 per thousand charges, depending upon the quantity prices of the charging paper purchased.   The cost of making an overdue notice is the same as the cost of making an original charge.

The pamphlet listed the following advantages (568):

Eliminates Book Slipping ... Book Card Filing ... Numerical Registration ... Locating Reader's Name and Address ... Typing of Overdues.

The Brodac System is a reasonably new development in charging operations. So the pamphlet states, it "is now being used experimentally in the main library of the City of Miami, Florida, where it is apparently working quite successfully. Bro-Dart expects to make ten additional installations during the latter part of 1957 and will shortly accept orders for delivery during early 1958 (569)."

Chapter 5

Selective Charging - Token System

L. R. McColvin, writing in 1954, showed how a new approach was made to the problem of operating libraries in a more economical manner. He gave the following account (570):

> In discussion of what charging system to adopt and how to restrict the number of books lended if a transaction card system was adopted, someone - Maidment, I think - said "Give them three tokens, one to be surrendered for each volume borrowed." And I said, "If you give them three tokens, why bother to keep any records. They can have their three books. Let them. If they bring them back they will take three others. In what way are we worse off if they don't return them? It is only they who will suffer." And this remark, intended to be frivolous, is the basis of our new Token system. It was only after long and thorough tests and many ingenious solutions of the contingent problems, in which we were helped (as regards the tests) by the Metropolitan Boroughs' O. and M. Team, that we arrived at a detailed scheme.

W. R. Maidment, a year later amplified this system with the inclusion of "selection" (571).

> Economies are made by reducing the work in each transaction and the small gain becomes important when multiplied by the number of times the operation is performed. There is, however, an entirely different approach by which a saving may be made: this is to reduce the total number of transactions by a process which may be termed selective charging. The "token" book issue method adopted at Westminster charges only books loaned on other library tickets, those loaned to Westminster readers are not recorded, but merely controlled by the number of tokens issued. Comparable savings would be made in many libraries if the token control system were used for fiction and the normal charging process for non-fiction. ....

However, he believed that there were some factors which must be taken into consideration (572):

Although selective charging seems to be a very simple solution to the dissatisfaction felt with the usual charging methods, the amount gained will vary from one library to another according to the percentage of fiction in the works loaned.

McColvin described the supplies that were used at Westminster (570).

The token system is simple - that is its justification. Every borrower is given a Reader's Card and three tokens. The Reader's Card is similar to a Brown pocket ticket and is valid for one year and must be shown every time a book is borrowed so that an assistant can check that it is still "in force."

Mrs. D. L. Mason, who observed "from the librarian's side of the Westminster charge desk while she was in England in 1954, described the tokens (573).

These were pieces of hard celluloid about 3 or 4 inches long and about 2 inches wide, blue and stamped with the Westminster coat of arms.

The process of charging books, according to McColvin, was as follows (570):

The borrower gives up one token for every book he borrows and is given one token for every book he returns. The date due for return is stamped on the date label - the only process to be undertaken - and fines are charged as usual.

Epsom and Ewell Public Libraries in England tried out a system combining the token and normal charging procedures (574).

...It involves the separation of the stock into "token" and "non-token" categories. The "non-token" category contains (a) all non-fiction; (b) fiction classics, (c) frequently reserved fiction titles and series, and (d) recent fiction until it has ceased to be reserved at all frequently. Groups (b) to (d) have been kept to the absolute minimum, but experience so far indicates that they could have been

cut out altogether. The "six-months" rule for the reservation of new fiction was already in operation. All "token"
books have been given a special date-label, printed in red,
the wording of which includes the information that reminder notices will not be sent for overdue fiction books. Other preparatory work included the provision of display panels for reserved "token" books; a new routine for dealing
with "token" books reported lost, and the introduction of
a standard replacement charge; the adaptation of ticket renewal methods to incorporate a follow-up of defaulting
readers; and the provision of a fines indicator, visible to
both staff and public, on which the dates are moved up
each day, making it unnecessary to use fine guides in the
issue trays.

   ... it had to be remembered that the scheme was experimental, and the possibility of reversion to normal
charging had to be faced. It was, therefore, not considered that re-registration would be justified at this stage.
At present, each reader is entitled to three general tickets, and a cumbersome but, it is hoped, purely temporary,
scheme has been worked out to leave him with full liberty
of choice in the use of these tickets during the experimen-
al period.

   A ticket handed in at the exit counter with a "token"
book is inserted (after issue-counting) in an alphabetical
file of readers' tickets, where it remains until the reader
wishes to use it for a "non-token" book or does not want
to take out a book. Other books are charged in the normal way.

   At the entrance counter, tokens (of normal pocket shape
and size but of distinctive colour) are handed out for each
"token" book returned, and the books are immediately
ready for shelving.

   The tokens, whether numbered or un-numbered are then
being used and re-used throughout the day. The un-numbered tokens, representing fiction issues, are counted in
batches of fifty and transferred to the entrance counter for
re-use. The numbered tokens and dummy book-cards are
available for re-use as soon as the transactions which they
represent have been completed.

   The reading habits of individual readers vary but little,
and it is found that nine books out of ten presented for
stamping at the exit counter match the tokens temporarily
held by the reader, and procedure is simple and automatic. For the tenth case a change has to be made, by taking a ticket either from the alphabetical file of readers'
tickets, or from the delayed-discharging filing tray.

McColvin gave the details of the overdue procedure (570).

> But no overdue notices are sent; indeed they cannot be
> sent as no record whatever is made of what books are
> borrowed.   We do not know who has what or when it was
> taken.   At the end of the year the borrower must produce
> three tokens - or pay ten shillings for each he cannot pro-
> duce - before he can renew his Reader's Card.   If he
> loses a token he may be required to pay ten shillings be-
> fore he can obtain another; and no borrower can "lose"
> and pay for more than three tokens in a year.   This rule
> is our safeguard against the "clever" borrower who hopes
> to build up a private library at our expense, we we do
> not propose to penalize the bona fide honest reader.

McColvin also described the renewal process (575).

> Renewals by post and telephone will be dealt with by main-
> taining a file of dated renewed book number cards.   Thus,
> if a borrower on returning a book says, "but I renewed
> that on the 15th March, " we can check whether such was
> the case.

The practice of reservations was dealt with in the following manner (575):

> At Westminster we only reserve non-fiction, and a clas-
> sified visible index of reserved books will be maintained.
> Before non-fiction books are returned to circulation they
> will be put in rough order and checked with this index.
> This index need include only "single reservations, " as
> books which are reserved by subsequent readers are
> stamped accordingly before issue.   Tests show that this
> indicator check takes less time than the present "stopping
> in the issue" method, but we realize that we shall have
> to watch for books that are not promptly returned and we
> are prepared to buy extra copies to avoid undue waiting -
> a small price for the other savings we shall effect.

McColvin amplified these ideas later (576).

> Firstly, as regards "reservations".... Tests show that
> this [visible index checking] takes no longer than the old
> method and is as efficient.   Much of the work is done in
> the little lulls that occur even at busy times - when
> queues are not allowed to collect.   But we are able, at a

little extra cost in time, to "panel" books not only at the
library of reservations, but at all libraries possessing
copies.   Borrowers get first copy to come back, and so
are generally better served than formerly.   If a book does
not come back within three weeks - and as, of course, we
cannot know when it was borrowed, or if it is missing,
lost, stolen or strayed - we normally buy an extra if it is
in print. . . . I would add that we have not had to make any
increased demands upon the L. U. C. and N. C. L. as a
result of the system.   Nevertheless, of over 43, 000 special requests for items not at the time on the shelves, all
but 0. 8 percent were last year supplied - by reservation,
special purchase, inter-branch loans and inter-library borrowing. . . .

Mrs. Mason had the following comments on the reserve system (573).

Reserves could be made for non-fiction only, and up to
three at a time at two pence each.   Since the books could-
n't be checked while out, they had to be checked coming
in.   This meant that all incoming nonfiction had to be
lined up in order on shelves behind the desk, and since
these shelves, two of them, were only about four feet
long, checking had to go on a great deal of the time.
While I was there, a temporary system of large sheets of
beaverboard with colluloid pockets stapled to them were
used, and into these pockets were inserted bits of different colored cards marked with the number, author, and
title of books wanted.   These were inserted in order of
course, and your method was to hold one of these huge
sheets and go over the shelved books.   There were three
drawbacks to this method: one, the cards were written
in ink and not too easy to read; two, when there were a
great many reserves they seemed to pile up more than
one in a pocket and slip behind so that they were not seen;
and three, at least once a week one of us would knock the
boards off the lower shelf with the result that all the cards
spilled over the floor.
      A card was supposed to stay on the board for three
weeks, and if the book was not back, interlibrary loan
came into play. . . . When I left, a permanent set of boards
was being attached to the wall and would probably be a lot
more useful.

McColvin suggested an alternate system (575).

But, of course, there are "complications" and "contingent problems".

Firstly, we issue books on the tickets of other libraries. These borrowers will have their "hometown" tickets. At one library these non-Westminster borrowers represent 10 per cent of the day's issue. For these the "Card" system will be adopted - and this demands description because it is our "line of retreat." For each day duplicate sets of dated numbered cards will be used. On one card (e. g. No. 52) will be written the book number; this card is kept and filed with the borrower's ticket. If the Card system were adopted instead of the Token system it would also be given the Reader's number. The counterpart card (also No. 52) is put in the book - where the book card was formerly kept. In case this card is lost, a different date stamp is used to show that this is not a Token issue. When the book is returned, it is "discharged", the borrower is given his ticket and the numbered card abstracted and cancelled. In the case of loans on non-Westminster tickets, overdue books will thus be automatically disclosed. Were the card system to be used instead of the Token system, the numbered cards abstracted from returned books would be filed and in due course checked with the set that had been originally retained, when any non-returns would be disclosed and the necessary "overdue" could be sent.

Dent, using the selective token system, also suggests an alternate procedure (574).

Normally-charged books are dealt with by the "delayed-discharging" method, the reader being given what appears to be an ordinary token but which is, in fact, numbered to correspond with the dummy book-card placed in the book. After delayed-discharging, the normal book-card is inserted in the book, and the dummy book card and reader's ticket are filed in a special slotted and numbered vertical filing tray on the exit counter. If the reader has already gone out, the book-card for his new book will already have been filed, in its numbered token, in the appropriate slot in the tray, awaiting the substitution of the reader's ticket for the token. If he is still in the library, the substitution takes place as he goes out.

McColvin stated in 1956, "we stand to lose perhaps a considerable number of books if many readers cease to borrow and if we cannot pursue them when their tickets expire;

and we shall certainly try to pursue them just as we often
have to pursue, unsuccessfully, some long overdue books under the Brown system (575)." Two years later, he was able
to give statistics on the problem (577).

> We all lose books, because people steal them. Obviously
> the extent of theft is not affected by the system in use.
> Losses of books attributable directly to the system would
> thus be of two kinds; (a) books borrowed and retained per-
> manently by readers who do not renew their tickets when
> they expire at the end of the year; and (b) books illegally
> retained by dishonest people who pretend they have lost a
> token when instead they have kept (i.e., stolen) a book....
> So, what have we lost?
> This year we have taken every reasonable step to "pur-
> sue" the borrower who has not renewed his membership,
> or returned his token, or cancelled his membership. As
> a result of these efforts, the "untraceable" and "untouch-
> able" borrowers have been reduced to a very small num-
> ber - and by the way, I doubt whether the effort is worth
> continuing - and the net result is that we may have lost,
> through this type of default, a total of some 230 books
> estimated to be worth about £80 (a figure based upon past
> charges for lost books, allowing for wear and tear, etc.).
> Secondly, how many books have we lost as a result of
> the deliberate dishonesty of those claiming to have lost to-
> kens when they have instead kept books? Obviously we do
> not know, as we do not know how many of our borrowers
> are dishonest. So let us take the blackest possible view
> of life.
> Between the inception of the scheme and last September,
> 1,035 tokens were lost. Of these 780 were paid for (us-
> ually at a reduced fine of 2_s instead of 10_s permitted by
> the Rules, because we were satisfied that the loss was due
> solely to carelessness). Another 200 were replaced free
> of charge as we were satisfied that they were lost through
> no fault of the borrower, (e.g., fire, theft, etc., even in
> two cases, through the capsizing of a boat), and for 55
> the borrowers refused to pay. But, against these losses,
> 327 tokens and 519 books were found, but could not be
> credited to specific readers - leaving a deficit of 189.
> Now, if all these 189 represented illicitly retained books
> - and the very thought is ridiculous - the maximum loss
> would be in the order of £100. In brief, the most we
> could have lost altogether would be some £200 and against
> this we must credit payments amounting to over £80, for
> lost tokens.

McColvin was able to see several advantages to this system. "...three or four assistants can handle any counter rushes that are ever likely to occur in the busiest library - and all the rest who were formerly needed are free for "proper" library work (575). Perhaps a 60-70 per cent saving in routine operations - a saving that, did we make it, would represent several thousands of pounds of manpower a year. I say 'did we make it'. We hope we shall make some saving in staff but we are much more interested in two longed-for results: one is that we shall be equipped to cope with any foreseeable increase in issues without any increase in staff; the other, that we shall at last be better able to give a real helpful service to our readers (575)."

Another advantage was mentioned in somewhat more delicate terms (576).

Let me first make it absolutely clear that we never intended the system to be an excuse for reducing staff....
Nevertheless, as there are observers who have expressed interest in our experiment in the belief that it can lead to staff reduction, I must emphasize this point .... Some small reduction might be possible in a large library which was already so well staffed that every operation was adequately performed, that there were no arrears of work, that every needed help was available for readers.

McColvin summed up the advances with this system in the following paragraph (578):

Therefore, whatever the other effects of the system may be - and we are sufficiently openminded to realize that every system has its intangible influence upon borrowing habits - we have lost nothing at all compared with what we have gained, both financially and in terms of a speedier, more efficient service and a staff better able to do their real work.

Dent reported these advantages with the selective token system (579).

Staff are handling the new processes with increasing facility, and the public, whose interest was aroused by the issue of a printed leaflet, have co-operated well. About 65 per cent of each day's issue is unrecorded. Two-thirds of the entrance counter surface is clear of issue trays, and the space is used for normally-charged books awaiting delay-discharging. Some of the time saved at the entrance counter on token-charged books is being dissipated on delayed-discharging the remainder. But for the desire to avoid confusing the public during the experimental period, delayed-discharging would be abandoned, for although it saves time at the point of contact with the reader and makes for greater accuracy, the whole process takes appreciably longer than normal discharging. However, this will have been a small price to pay if, after taking stock at the end of the year, we are able to demonstrate that the principle of selective token charging is sound, safe within reasonable limits of calculated risk, and worth adopting in a simpler and more permanent form.

L. M. Bickerton reported working out a system a year earlier, which was basically similar - "though with little practical resemblance" to McColvin's (580).

... The methods and results are based upon the issue of adult fiction only by this means....

Issue method. The tokens used... are retained by the reader only whilst he is in the library. Therefore at any one time a reader must have either a book or a ticket (at home) or a token (in the library).

On commencing to issue by the Worthing Token Scheme, the following routine is used:

(1) Change the color of the date stamp.
(2) Issue books by stamping the date of issue or return clearly [it will be the only evidence of date of issue] and file the reader's ticket in an alphabetical sequence.
(3) Discharge by exchanging one token for each book returned.
(4) Date stamp and issue further volumes in exchange for the tokens which are placed on a spike at the "out" counter. The spike is marked to indicate totals of, say, 50 tokens. As soon as this mark is reached, 50 issues are recorded on the daily issue sheet and the full spike transferred to the "in" counter.

Overdue checks. At Durrington [a branch library] checks for overdue books have been carried out at six-monthly intervals. At Westminster such checks are made annually, but I have preferred to have them more frequent to reduce the possibility of long-overdue books and heavy fines. In order to carry out the check, the following procedure is adopted:

(1) Change the colour of the date stamp. All books subsequently returned with the new colour stamp are charged and discharged by the normal method as outlined above.

(2) Place the alphabetical file of readers' tickets on the "in" counter and commence a new file on the "out" counter. As books with the old colour are returned, recover the reader's ticket(s) from the "in" file and give them to him in exchange for his books.

(3) As he leaves the library, stamp his books, recover the required number of tickets and insert them in the new file.

(4) A month after commencing the check, all tickets remaining in the "in" file will be at least a fortnight overdue, and notices can be sent demanding the return of "an overdue book"....

Advantages

(1) Savings in stationery.
   (a) No book pockets or book cards are required.
   (b) The number of overdues posted is greatly reduced.
   (c) Wear and tear of fiction tickets is greatly reduced.

(2) Savings in staff time.
   (a) Reduction in counter staff, since 90-95 per cent of the fiction issue can be charged and discharged with extreme rapidity. The remaining 5-10 per cent consists of overdue books and finding and returning tickets when books are not required.
   (b) Reduced clerical work in book preparation and sending overdue notices.
   (c) Automatic issue counting.
   (d) Queries resulting from crossed book cards and tickets are completely eliminated.

(3) Ease and cheapness of operation.
   (a) Staff and public rapidly become accustomed to the method.
   (b) Any type of existing membership ticket can be used.
   (c) Initial cost is negligible, 100 metal tokens and two correspondence spikes being the total equipment at the Durrington Branch, issuing about 60,000 adult fiction per annum.
   (d) Income from fines has been unaffected.

Disadvantages. Abandoning issue records can have results which some would regard as disadvantages, but

which others would not worry about.... Once we have decided that issue records are not providing information
which is vital to the service and which cannot be obtained
in any other way, their disappearance can cause little
concern.   In addition, it will be found that some apparent
disadvantages are less important in practice than they appear to be in theory.

(1) Regular overdue notices cannot be sent to readers. In
    practice this seems to have much less effect on the
    return or retention of books than might be expected.

(2) It is impossible to tell readers the titles of overdue
    books on loan to them.   Readers certainly find it
    much easier to search for a mislaid book when its
    title is known.   Results at Durrington show that very
    few books have not been traced.   In all cases read-
    ers have paid for them.

(3) Books found and returned to the library cannot be dis-
    charged and therefore cannot be connected with the
    person who borrowed them.   Overdue checks usually
    result in queries of this nature being sorted out quite
    easily.

(4) Writing of overdues and renewing of tickets is con-
    centrated in a short period of a few weeks in each
    six months instead of being spread out evenly.   Since
    we know that this will be the case, however, it is
    possible to plan duties in advance and make provision
    for the extra pressure.

(5) Errors by the staff, though much less frequent than
    in the Brown system, tend to be perpetuated until the
    next overdue check takes place.

(6) Staff must be trained to stamp issue dates clearly and
    to give tokens only for fiction.

(7) Lost books cannot be identified and records can only
    be corrected by stocktaking.

(8) Stocktaking must be timed to coincide with an overdue
    check.   This makes heavy demands on staff time
    whatever issue method is used, and librarians must
    decide for themselves whether the results justify the
    labour involved.

(9) Strict accuracy in filing readers' tickets is essential.

(10) Large fines can accumulate.   If the librarian feels
     that this is any part of his responsibility, impose a
     maximum fine of, say 2_s.
       . . . .

Applications to non-fiction and junior books.   The
Worthing Token System can be easily applied to non-fiction, and by using a different shape, colour or metal for

non-fiction tokens it would be possible to give a split between non-fiction and total fiction issues....

So far I have felt reluctant to abandon records of non-fiction issues, even though they account for one-third of the total; nor have I felt that it would be wise to dispense with regular overdue reminders for children.
Operation notes
. . . .
(2) Renewals. Renewals made by post or telephone should be entered in a desk diary. At the end of the day, the day's renewals can be added to the day's issue.
. . . .
(4) Lost books. In some cases readers will know the title of a lost book and, from the catalogue and accession register, a replacement price can be assessed. Should the library possess more than one copy of the title, added at widely differing dates, or should the reader have forgotten all details, there will be no means of assessing its value. It is recommended that a standard charge of, say 7_s6_d be made for novels which cannot be identified.

The system which W. G. Stiles suggests employs the token, but the system itself was based on the exchange principle (581).

Recreational literature could be dealt with on a simple exchange basis. In this category a pattern is noticeable in the borrowing habits of the public; to tabulate by factors:
(1) the approach is non-specific (i. e., "something to read" is required);
(2) the number of books borrowed often remains constant;
(3) the readers are often consistent library users;
(4) the reader attending primarily to acquire authentic literature might also desire recreational books. The reverse is seldom encountered. Thus variation in the borrowing pattern is seen more in the recreational category than in the other.
A scientific system will make use of these factors, to the full. Factor (1) indicates that a tracing mechanism is here of lesser importance; a token charging system is therefore the most economic. Factors (2) and (3) together indicate that the simplest means of effecting such a system is to use, as far as possible, the books themselves as the units of exchange. Factor (4) indicates that the serious reader might require the means of borrowing

from both categories, without recourse to cumbrous methods, such as duplicate sets of tickets....

A full-scale scheme for a municipal library will, however, require:

(a) variation of the specified quantity of books borrowed (which will then remain consistent for each individual);

(b) occasional variation of that quantity itself;

(c) temporary relinquishment of borrowing powers of recreational literature;

(d) reader-identification for the more complex conditions obtaining.

With (d) in mind, a small pass could be issued, similar to the convenient style used at Wandsworth for photocharging. It would bear the usual details plus the quantity of books which may be borrowed per visit (a figure specified by the borrowers). If this item could be made in detachable fashion, then it would be removed if the reader decided to forego borrowing for a period. (A transparent window is suggested, under which the quantity-tag could be inserted.) Thus requirements (a), (c) and (d) have been met. Requirement (b) is more difficult to satisfy.

The introduction of tokens to meet variation of the specified quantity can be considered in two stages.

1. Internal - a borrower presenting for discharge a lesser number of books than his specified quantity could be accommodated by the issue of a token bearing the lesser number. This will be handed in at the charging counter after presentation of a corresponding number of books.

2. External - a borrower presenting for charging a lesser number of books than was discharged can be issued with external tokens to make up the balance, and maintain the exchange principle. These may be surrendered at the discharging counter on future occasions in lieu of books.

Discharging and charging. To gain admittance the borrower is required to show at the discharge counter

(a) Reader's pass, complete with quantity tag;

(b) for surrender, a corresponding number of books and/or tokens (external).

Should a lesser number be presented, an internal token bearing the value of the lesser quantity is issued in exchange for the pass, which is then filed temporarily at the counter.

At the charging counter the reader presents:

(a) Pass, complete with quantity-tag; or an internal token;

(b) a corresponding number of books.

If a lesser quantity is presented, then external tokens to make up the balance are issued in lieu. The internal token, if this has been presented, is then exchanged for the pass.

It is necessary here to stress factor (2). The majority of recreational readers will pass through on a simple book-for-book basis, simply showing their passes.

Provision can be made for a reader temporarily to relinquish recreational borrowing privileges by extracting the quantity-tag and filing this with the "main-entry" registration form in a "temporarily relinquished" sequence. The reader is then relieved of the necessity of storing tokens, and his pass will still enable him to borrow, as desired, from the other category of literature. Thus the requirements of factor (4) are met.

Overdues. A periodical check (say, every six months) could be made as follows: as readers pass through, their tags are changed (by colour) and the expired tags set by temporarily. At leisure, these are matched up with the "main entry" registration forms and placed in a separate sequence. There will thus be three sequences (in the "main entry" forms);

(a) readers still using library with no overdue books;
(b) readers who have temporarily relinquished recreational privileges;
(c) remainder - i.e., readers not seen in library since new period began and known to possess books or tokens.

After the normal loan period has terminated, overdue notices could be sent out in the orthodox manner.

It would be advantageous to change the character of the tokens with the period, also, to prevent their transference between borrowers. If plastic tokens of the Westminster type were used, edge punching could be employed to denote the change of period. Then, once punched, a token could not be presented by another borrower listed as possessing overdues (or tokens).

Reserves. These could be dealt with by the scanning method used at Wandsworth - i.e., before shelving, returned books are placed in author order and scanned against a checklist of reserves, also in author order.

Renewals. Obviously these require a check against reserves, a list of which may be kept at the counter under author order. But it is felt that in this connection, at least, accession numbers may still have their uses.

The advantages of this system may be summarized:
(1) No tickets need be issued, only a conveniently sized pass.
(2) There is no need for a borrower to store tokens if recreational borrowing privileges are relinquished.
(3) The use of tokens is cut to an absolute minimum, and the maximum use is made of the book as the unit of exchange.
(4) No loose cards need be issued with loaned material.
(5) Methods exist of ultimately tracing overdues in all categories.
(6) The speed of the token system is retained for the category requiring it.
(7) Qualified staff are released to exploit the authentic elements of the collection.
(8) Works of value are properly accounted for by a signature.
(9) Records are cut to a minimum and therefore all effort can be centered on the authentic elements.
(10) Items (1), (2), (3) and (4) indicate possible savings in stationery.

The article by Stiles prompted K. R. Cox to outline a charging system which he thought of some years before (582).

Briefly, the scheme is to use the book as a unit of exchange and merely to exercise some control over the number of books held by the reader.

To achieve this control, each reader is issued with a card bearing his name and address, and printed with two parallel columns - one marked OUT - the other marked IN. . . .

When books are taken out, the number taken is marked in the "out" column, and when they are returned, the number returned is marked in the "in" column. . . .

The reader's card is held by the reader and must, of course, be brought to the library at each visit, as must the reader's ticket in token charging or photo-charging systems.

Since the number of books borrowed and returned over a period is recorded, it is immediately apparent when a reader has books not yet returned, since if four are borrowed and three returned, one is still to come, and readers can be asked to return the book outstanding. . . .

In the instances where it is not constant [each transaction cancelling itself] the number of books outstanding

could be recorded on the reader's card if this were
thought necessary.   Alternately, a periodic balance could
be struck at say, every five or even ten transactions.
Certainly the question of any books recorded as outstanding would be taken up with the reader when the card is
full and needs renewing.

Readers' cards would not need to be so large as might
at first be thought, since the item to be recorded at each
transaction is very small; and at one busy central lending
library the average number of books borrowed per year
by each reader is about 35.

Reserves could be dealt with by the panel system as
in token charging and photocharging.

Renewals could again be checked against reserved book
panels.

Charging becomes a quick and easy matter of entering
a number on a reader's card and stamping a date label.

Discharging becomes a matter of checking for fines
and entering a number on a reader's card.

Charging and discharging.   In considering the time
factor, it must be remembered that only one item has to
be recorded for each reader, regardless of the number of
books taken or returned.

If necessary, rubber stamps could be used to record
the number of books on the reader's card - no doubt a
card could be devised, but it is questionable whether it
would save time or work, though it would eliminate the
possibility of forgery.

Snags: (a) Readers coming to the library without their
readers' cards.   Both token charging and photo-charging
have shown this to be no real snag, and the scheme is
sufficiently flexible to permit a temporary card to be issued on the odd occasions when it is necessary.

(b) Loss of reader's card.   This is somewhat more
serious since this card is the only record of loan, but
again token charging has shown that the number of tokens
lost is small, and the method of a fairly high replacement charge could be adopted.... However, since the
number of books held by a reader can be controlled, even
total loss in the few cases where it will occur would not
be unduly serious.

Abuse.   It would be advisable to use a distinctive colour - marking pen or pencil, such as that used by aud-
itors when checking accounts, to ensure that the possibility of readers filling out their own cards is reduced to a
minimum....

Any advantages the scheme may have lie in its speed

and simplicity.

Conclusion

A glance into the future was made by Margery Quigley in her 1957 article, "Reporter at large." She wrote (583):

As research continues other mechanical aids adaptable to library circulation processes may be expected. Machines now popular will be improved, even superceded. Coming models may easily be small, portable, relatively cheap, and thus useful in bookmobiles, rural stations, and other service points removed from the main charging desks. Many of the present files and other records on cards or in code will surely be by-passed. ...

The main trouble with the circulation process today even with charging machines, microfilms and electronics is that, from registration on through the treatment of hopeless overdues, the process itself is not contemporary.

A suggested idea for the inventors was mentioned in 1936 by E. M. Fair. "The Photo-electric cell (the "electric eye") might, without stretching the imagination, be used to record books as they are borrowed or returned, matching symbol with symbol, just as it now rejects improperly labelled cans as they pass into review (345)."

Geer wrote of a machine which was available for book charging but no report has been given of its use. She gave the following description (584).

The Telecomputing Corporation of Burbank, California, has made available equipment for a system which uses punched tape for recording book charges. The borrower's card and the book card are pre-punched with holes which identify the reader and the book by means of a machine called the tag reader. When a book is charged out, the book card and borrower's identification card are entered in the tag reader, which automatically produces a punched tape. With the use of a tape-to-card converter, the information on the punched tape is transferred to punched cards. This tabulating equipment can be purchased or the tapes can be mailed to service bureaus, which can report periodically by mail the names of missing books. When a book is returned to the library the book card is entered in the tag reader which automatically credits the borrower with its return.

In July, 1957, R. H. Parker wrote of a "new piece of equipment, known as the Transceiver, which may make possible recording of loans in a central office from any lending unit in a library on perforated or magnetic tape (363)."

Shaw gives a few "implications for library service" in his discussion of the area of technical routines. Not every library can take advantage of mechanization. He summarizes his thoughts in this manner (585):

> To the extent that standardization has been achieved, it has been achieved in this field. To the extent that there are repetitive operations, they exist in this area; and to the extent that repetitive operations occur in relatively high frequency, they occur in this area. But here, again, the size of library units limits the level of mechanization that is useful....
>
> As a rule of thumb, it might be estimated that a machine that costs much over a thousand dollars (i.e., an amortized cost of $100 a year) would at best, have a potential field of usefulness of a few hundred of the thousands of libraries.

No issue method was found by E. W. Padwick to contain the panacea to all our problems. He elaborates (586):

> Each method has its advantages and disadvantages, which must be considered in relation to the peculiar problems that face each library. If one is prepared to trust the honesty of the vast majority of our readers and to accept such losses that are incurred and balance them against undoubted savings in staff time, stationery, and improved services to readers, then the token system may offer a lead into the future. If on the other hand, one feels that a stricter control of issues is necessary, then photocharging may well be the source of future development. Neither of these two methods has been fully developed, for in this new age of automation, it should be possible to devise an automatic self-charging system. The token system would seem particularly adaptable to this, as one can visualize the reader inserting his token into a ticket machine which would deliver him a pre-dated date card to slip in the pocket of his book. Whilst with self-charging it might not be possible to achieve the speed at which a trained assistant can charge books under present methods,

at least the reader would be issuing his own books and
staff time would be saved.

The new methods themselves will present their own
particular problems: for instance, to obtain the full benefit of photocharging it has been found necessary to redesign existing counters at Wandsworth.   Then again,
both with photocharging and the token system, because of
the speed of discharge, a problem arises over the quick
disposal of returned books.   They have, of course, to be
checked against the visible index of reservations before
they can be shelved, and thus need to be kept temporarily
out of range of the inquisitive public.   The solution might
be to install a simple conveyor belt to remove books from
the counter to an adjacent book reception room, where all
books are examined for wear and tear, and checked a-
gainst reservations before being passed to the lending library for further circulation.

The time is overdue for a more systematic approach
to issue methods in this country.   One has only to read
Geer to realize how much has been achieved in America,
and how little in comparison over here. What experiments
have taken place here, have been because of the personal
initiative of individual librarians working their own libraries.   But there is a limit to the value that can be achieved by personal enthusiasm, and the library service as a
whole will not benefit until research has been carried into
a wider field of investigation.   Experiments should be
made under working conditions in libraries of varying sizes and with differing issue problems, and it is difficult to
see how this could be achieved unless by a group of libraries willing to experiment and to cooperate for the
common good.

Charging methods are often expensive for scholarly libraries, according to Shaw, because of the intricacy of the
routines established.   A detailed study of present methods is
thought by Shaw to be desirable (587).

The cost of charging books in scholarly libraries is generally two to four times as much as that in popular libraries and may be as much as ten times as high.   Such re-
sonably adequate studies as are available indicate that the
cost of charging books in the college and university library,
when all of the related operations are included, is around
eleven or twelve cents in the average library which has
not done intensive   work on simplification of its charging routines.   This compares with two and a half to five

cents in the average popular library. In a number of
scholarly libraries the cost per book charged is twenty-
five or thirty cents or more, and in one case almost
seventy cents per charge....

Study of the cost of the charging process, no matter
how preliminary in nature, quickly reveals that the big
cost item in charging systems is labor. Supplies are almost negligible, whether they be punched cards, paper
coated with photographic emulsion, film, book cards or
other. There is a substantial labor cost in the preparation of multiple book cards and the replacement of book
cards, but the biggest labor cost comes in filing and re-
trieving the cards and reassembling them with the book.
The second biggest labor cost comes in searching the
files for location of copies on loan....

Regardless of whether research shows these to be justified or not, we must recognize the fact that we have established in most libraries of all types, a most intricate
pattern of routines and techniques for the process of charging books and the related operations. It is highly educational to put down, step by step, every one of the routines and variations on routines and sub-routines for special cases that we require our circulation people to do and
then to examine each of these in the light of the purposes
of the organization to determine which of them actually
contribute to the purposes for which the library exists,
and thus are essential. The first steps in a systems approach to the charging problem is the elimination of all
of the operations that do not contribute to the goal of the
library, and the provision for all of those operations
which are necessary to the goals.

Margaret Klausner believed that "in order to properly
evaluate any system it is necessary to know it in considerable detail. " She further stated (588):

Anyone studying circulation systems today finds it most
difficult to obtain valid information for comparative purposes. What we apparently need is a statement of policy
which defines the scope of the circulation department's
work and a compilation of statistics from which the work
loads in terms of man hours used can be determined.

A request was made by Ralph Blasingame for objectivity in analysis. In his thesis entitled The Application of
International Business Machines in Libraries, he noted this
lack of concrete evidence. He suggested the use of the

Breakeven Chart to aid in accomplishing this. [For more information on the Chart see Blasingame....pp. 32-39 and Rautenstauch and Villers: The economics of industrial management, pp. 104-34]. Blasingame felt that further study should be given to these problems of analysis (589).

> The general areas of the effect of mechanization upon the working force, the economic justifiability of machine methods, and the results which may be obtained through mechanical methods in the library are virtually unexplored at this time. Out of these three fields, any number of concrete hypotheses can be developed. Experimental work, collection of case studies, and further surveys of the existing methods of employing systems allied in some way to IBM or comparable machines are imperative if full advantage is to be taken of the experience gained by business, industry, and the academic fields. The unplanned and unco-ordinated use of machinery in libraries will continue to be less efficacious than it could be until more objective methods of reporting are applied to this wide field.
>
> It is believed that one of the most rewarding problems which this investigation has happened upon lies in the use of the Breakeven Chart: This method of prophesying the effect of new machinery upon profits has been extensively applied to business and industry, and holds considerable promise for the librarian. Internal standards, while admitedly not the best possible ones, are fairly easily determined with the use of techniques already described in library literature.
>
> Only one library which co-operated in this investigation has given concrete evidence of having made an objective study of the effect of IBM on its staff. That library has reported a considerable overall saving in money, and has also reported that its staff is now able to devote a larger percentage of its time to professional library tasks than it did before the installation of IBM. Here, again, techniques to be used in a personnel study are available in many sources. Yet even in this respect there is considerable room to prove the pudding.

Another word on analysis is given in this plea for a statement of standards, made by Blasingame (590).

> A possible means of developing standards by which an application of mechanical devices to the library may be judged as to economic performance lies in comparison

with other existing uses.   As has been demonstrated in
this study, the use of what may be termed "external
standards" is not feasible when considering IBM, since
those standards have not yet been developed.   Since libraries vary so widely in size, purpose, and general
make-up, it is doubtful whether external standards ever
will provide a good basis for comparison in this regard.
Another possibility lies in the use of "internal standards, "
or in using evidence which can be obtained through examination of the financial structure of the individual library
itself.

Chapter 6

Evaluation of Evidence for Statements
Made in the Literature

Systems of charging have been dealt with historically, described as to their minute workings, and explained as to their usefulness under certain standard conditions. Much of the material appearing in journals is merely descriptive. Often no attempt is made to record information concerning the circumstances under which the particular charging system was adopted. Costs and statistics are usually omitted. Advantages are normally given while disadvantages are many times explained away. Few writers include the facts as to what has been revealed by time tests or cost studies, although occasional mention is made that such surveys have been conducted.

The general subject of book charging has been summarized by many authorities in the field. However, we must look to the evidence given by only two studies for the critical picture of what systems were most often used and with what results.

In 1941, E. V. Baldwin and W. E. Marcus (587, 588) conducted a study of library costs and budgets. This is the evidence which they revealed as to library practice:

Twenty-seven (73 per cent) of the thirty-seven cost study participants reported that from a fourth to a little over a third (25 per cent to 35 per cent) of the total working time of the entire staff is now given to the routines connected with the distribution of books for use outside the building. Considering the apportionment from another angle, eight of the thirty-seven libraries spent in circulation routines 75 per cent or more of the total time they give to various types of direct service to the public.
This seems a disproportionately large amount of time for a function which, in most libraries, is more or less routine. As a possible defense of this record, it can be shown that in public libraries of the type studied, the

number of books distributed for home use represents by
far the heaviest demand made by the community upon the
library resources.

Baldwin and Marcus believed the process of actual
charging was simple, almost mechanical.   The time needed
for this operation when it included registration, filing of
cards, overdue work, renewal, reserves and compiling of
statistics was computed.

The average time required for the making and clearing of
an individual charge of a book (including all the incidental
work mentioned) is 2. 1 minutes and the average cost is
1. 8 cents.
A review of the individual records of the thirty-seven
libraries indicates, however, that there is still room for
improvement.   The shortest unit of time for the group
was 1. 2 minutes; the longest, 3 minutes, with fifteen of
the thirty-seven libraries reporting an average record below 2 minutes.

Baldwin and Marcus' findings were important in giving
basic percentages which could be compared with the results
of time and cost studies conducted by librarians of their own
practices.   This study became a rule of thumb by which the
various systems could be judged.

The report on work measurement in public libraries,
submitted by W. O'D. Pierce (589) in 1949, compared the
time spent on charging by seven groupings of libraries using
the systems then in vogue.   The evidence given by libraries,
grouped as to the amount of people served, was recorded by
Pierce in the following manner:

Library (Group)	Population Served	Questionnaire Sent	Replies
Group A	Over 500, 000	9	7
B	250, 000 to 500, 000	6	6
C	100, 000 to 250, 000	7	6
D	50, 000 to 100, 000	5	5
E	25, 000 to 50, 000	4	4
F	10, 000 to 25, 000	10	7
G	5, 000 to 10, 000	5	4
H	2, 500 to 5, 000	4	4
I	County libraries	10	10
		60	53

Charging Systems Used

Group N	Newark	Detroit	Gaylord	Manual	Other
A 7	2	4			1 Recordac
B 6	2	2	2		
C 6	3	1		1	
D 5	1		2	2	
E 4			1	2	1 IBM
F 7	1	1	3	2	
G 4	1			3	
H 4				4	
I 10	2			8	
Total	12	7	8	22	

The Gaylord systems reported an average of 8 seconds per book; the Detroit systems, 12 seconds; and the Newark systems 18 seconds. These figures are for charging at the desk and must be regarded as very tentative because of lack of definition.

The evidence revealed by this study by Pierce shows that the Newark and Detroit systems were more popular with the busiest libraries, Gaylord and Manual charging were often chosen by those serving ten thousand to one hundred thousand people and manual charging was most often used in the smallest libraries where speed of operation was not important. The conclusion as to the timing involved in actual charging is not as useful as is that given by the former study unless a librarian is faced with the problem of detaining the public during the charging operation. If the staff is sufficient to care for the behind-the-scenes mechanics then perhaps the great concern is to secure the speediest method at charging desk. Since 1949 other systems have been developed which could be subjected to scrutincy similar to that given by these two studies. These should be considered the forerunners of other objective attempts at detailed analysis.

Early Systems of Charging

During this so called "early period" librarians filled their journals with descriptions of new methods and worded defenses of the old. This time has been referred to as an age of invention in the library field and the great variety of charging procedures which were recommended witness to this theory. It would have been helpful if more of these innovators had studied their methods objectively and surrendered to the library world the results of their analysis.

A general report came from Carr (1) in 1889 which made known what charging methods were most in use. He gave the following facts:

Of the 203 libraries replying, 81 keep simple accounts (either by ledger or slips), in which the leading factor is the book number; ... one hundred and one libraries take a reverse method, and keep simple accounts (either by ledger or slips) in which the name or number of the taker is the chief basis for arranging the entry and subsequent reference to same. A more complete system is in vogue with 21 libraries, in which either a double or triple entry is made and both the number of the book and the taker alike made a leading factor in the accounts.

The facts revealed by Carr were useful in showing what methods were used most but gave no insight as to why they were popular or if they proved to be efficient or not. This study is important because it doubtless made librarians aware that this was a field for more study.

Evidently Estabrook (39) analyzed his permanent Card System in an objective fashion, because he gave the following facts concerning it.

We have about 12,000 v. Our force consists of a librarian and two assistants. We have delivered and charged 200 books in an hour. The cards do not cost half as much as the ledger and index formerly in use here.

Estabrook's study was a simple one, yet it yielded facts as to speed and cost which were indicative of the savings involved. A more detailed discussion would perhaps have been useful. Other librarians did not even supply this much information.

Two writers in the early 1900's gave some facts concerning indicators which were not easily accepted by most users of these devices.

Harris (93) in 1905 came up with some evidence. He found that to install an indicator for 20,000 volumes, allowing two 5 foot service spaces for the exchange of books, it would cost approximately as follows:

	L	s.	d.
Cost of indicators for 20,000 numbers at L6 per 1,000 numbers	120	0	0
Cost of counter, 35 foot long (minimum length) at L2 per foot	70	0	0
Cost of fitting indicator in frame (plain finish) at L1 per foot	25	0	0
	215	0	0

He further revealed that the

> cost of a Card Charging System, similar to those used in Safeguarded Open-Access Libraries would be a maximum of 30s. per 1,000 numbers. This includes all accessories as trays, guides, etc.

Cost of Card Charging System for 20,000 at 30s. per 1,000 numbers	30	0	0
Cost of counter (no fitting of system required) 24 feet at L2 per foot	48	0	0
	78	0	0

Of course his findings are not conclusive because he does not deal with the time involved in operating each type of system, but his evidence is useful when merely installational costs are considered.

Another writer considered the comparison of equipment needed with each of three types of charging procedures. Gill (91) gave the following statistics to back up his claims.

> A more detailed summary of the cost of the three systems for a library of 10,000 may be of use, and serves to bring out more emphatically the enormous difference involved in initial expenditure alone.

(a) Indicator

Indicator for 10,000 volumes	60	0	0
4,000 borrower's tickets	2	0	0
One reader's ticket-rack in oak		18	0
	62	18	0

(b) Card-charging

10,000 book pockets	2	0	0
4,000 do., for conjoining readers cards and book cards in issue tray		16	0

10,000 book-cards	2	5	0
10 issue trays	2	15	0
	7	16	0

This again is merely a cost study dealing with equipment and supplies. However, it as well as Harris' evidence possibly had much influence on librarians working in that time of transition to open-access methods of book circulation.

Two Trends in Card Charging

No evidence has been given by the users of the Browne Charging System for the claims of simplicity and speed of operation. However one of the possible forerunners of this system was commented on in 1893. Quinn wrote (118):

> With respect to the all-important question of staff, let me say that our issues in the lending library average some 450 daily, and at no time do we require more than one assistant for duty in the department, though in the evening we employ three school boys who, besides attending the borrowers, serve the boys' room - in itself a by no means light task - and obtain such books from the lending department as may be required by reference room readers. It speaks well for the system when these young inexperienced lads can work it in its entirety quite as expeditiously and as neatly as a trained assistant and without a single mistake worthy of the name, and which could not be readily rectified.

These comments can hardly be termed evidence of any tests or study conducted, but they do yield enough proof to make his claims convincing.

For the Newark System we again must note that no evidence was given although many claims were made that the discharging procedures were faster than with Browne. Evidence was lacking in all discussions of the Visible Record System in spite of the claims of speed.

Detroit System

Ulveling (186) was the first to make known the "time-saving" quality of the Detroit Charging System. He supplied the following proof:

Actual tests made show the Detroit Charging System requires only from one-quarter to one-half the time required by any of the other generally used systems for charging books. Because of the time thus saved long lines of patrons waiting to have books charged on busy nights have been practically eliminated. At busy branches, though we have only one person doing the verifying, rarely are there more than three or four people in line at one time, whereas formerly on busy days there would be from four to five times that many waiting while perhaps two or sometimes three assistants were charging.

In 1929, a Library Journal article (187) contained a note as to a time test conducted in Detroit.

Comparison of new and charging machine systems.
8 books charged by new system - 48 seconds
8 books charged by charging machine - 95 seconds

The writer further noted that because the "Dater is picked up only once for the entire day's stamping, whereas under the old arrangement it would be picked up from 500 to 1,000 times a day," stamping time is reduced. "A time check shows a page can stamp 1,000 date slips in seven minutes."

In recommending the Detroit Charging System, Field wrote (188):

A week after we had inaugurated the new way we had a 3,004 day, most of which was done in the hours between four and nine, but the lines were kept down. In fact we all felt that under the circumstances the new method had been worth installing just for what it did that day....
We have had an increase in circulation over last year of sixty thousand so far this year which puts us well over six hundred thousand for the year, and this circulation with the heavy increase, and its attendant extras in notices, registrations, repairs, etc., we have taken care of with five less members on the staff.

Ulveling's remarks as to the speed of the system were substantiated by time tests according to his note. Details as to these tests would have been of value. Ulveling did supply a picture of what the savings amounted to in the Detroit libraries. His remark as to the percentage of time saved was a bit vague.

The earlier article which appeared in 1929, gave the findings of the Detroit time study in a more exact manner, but again there were few facts given as to the conditions under which the study was conducted.

The evidence offered by Field gives an indication that saving in staff time was possible, although his facts are not concrete enough to be of definite value to other librarians seeking to make a comparison.

Dickman System

Soon after the Dickman charging machine was introduced a time test was recorded by Finney (201). She wrote:

> ....a recent test was made between machines and stamps of the two operators, - one uses the machines, the other is in a branch where stamps are used. The test were held at different times to avoid nervousness.
> Ten readers' cards and fifty books were used.
> A card was handed the assistant with the number of books to be issued, on each one varying in number and kind from five to ten. They included four weeks, two weeks, and seven-day books.
> The result of the test was:
>   Machine - 50 books in 9 minutes
>   Stamps - 50 books in 11 minutes

In an ALA Bulletin of 1930, Riggs gave the following report on some tests which had been made for a record of speed (221, 222).

> Twenty-five books were used, charged in various groups on six cards. Two books were rentals, four books were 7 day books, one was charged for 4 weeks. Time counted from the moment the first borrower put his book on the desk to the moment the last borrower took his away.
> Two assistants, working independently, made this test with the same books and cards, one in 3 minutes 20 seconds and the other in 3 minutes 30 seconds, or an average of 8 seconds per book for the fastest worker......5 or 6 minutes per hundred books.

McDougall, who claimed that they had issued over 1,200 books in three hours, gave this further bit of proof (216):

We staged a rehearsal of our Browne system and the Dickman system with the members of the Committee acting as
readers, and, on timing, it was established that the charging and discharging of thirty books was effected with the
Dickman by assistants who were unused to it, but were
used to the Browne, in less than half the time it took
with Browne.

Several isolated comments were made on the Toledo
method which could be regarded as evidence. The pamphlet
published by Library Efficiency Corp. in 1930 included the
following (221):

> One machine, operated by a page or a clerk, will charge
> a minimum of 2,000 books per day, with the Toledo
> Method. . . .
>   Improvement of service at charging desk will be appre-
> ciated. This will result in a reduction of at least 10 per
> cent in overdues. . . .
>   Uses every available space on all record cards, with
> a saving of from 25 to 50 per cent of the supplies, and
> the equivalent saving in the time required for re-writing
> said cards. . . .
>   Cost of installation. Maximum cost of one cent per
> year per borrower.

Both the test by Finney and the one by Riggs appear
to be objective in their methods of analysis. Of course it is
simply the act of charging which is timed. These two studies give evidence of the charging speed of the two methods
of Dickman charging. The earlier study is of value because
of its comparison with the stamping method. The study by
Riggs, of the Toledo Method, yielded information concerning
that method only.

McDougall's comparison of the Dickman System with
the formerly used Browne System gave convincing proof to
the Library Committee that Dickman charging was faster.
His statement of findings was vague and not exact enough to
be termed conclusive proof of great time savings.

The remarks on the Toledo Method are of varying
usefulness. The first statement is possibly evidence supplied
by a test, but this can only be assumed. The saving in overdues, until proven, can exist merely as theory. The
claims of supply and labor savings are open to question.
This saving would apply only to books which circulate a great

deal.   The low cost of installation would be based on the
fact that a library has more than a few borrowers.   The information could be more definite.

Gaylord System

Those using this charging system declined to show
any proof of its speed or efficiency.

Double Record Versus Single Record
Charging Systems

Only a few isolated studies have been done in this
field.   Problems such as time involved in filing cards, overdue routines, and reserve procedures have been dealt with in
the various discussions, but rarely has a librarian attempted
to substantiate claims by evidence.   This may be because
many of these systems are being used mainly by college and
university libraries and the expense of conducting such objective studies as are necessary would mean the allocation of
special funds.   It is fortunate that occasionally a master's
thesis will yield evidence of value to the study of charging
systems in college and university libraries.

Double Record Systems

Of those who found satisfaction in using the Double
Record Systems, most recommended the method because of
the controls possible and not because of speed and economy.
None of these writers recorded critical studies which may
have been given to this charging method.

Tab Systems

Many of the librarians using a tabbing system - employing signals, scotch tape, ink, or date tabs - claimed it
to be economical, simple or efficient.   Only Cooper recorded
that her Tab System (using the scotch tape method) had been
subjected to time studies (283).

Recent time trials show that an experienced operator can
tab accurately 16 cards a minute, or about 400 to 450
cards in 30 minutes.   A circulation of 200 or 300 cards
can be counted, arranged, tabbed, and ready to file in
little more than half the time it took when we used the

double entry system of indicator file and date due file.

Cooper gave enough evidence to substantiate her claims of speed of operations. We could only wish for more details of the study which was conducted and similar evidence from other users of Tab Systems with which to compare. Sister Helen (278) and M. Daniels (227) reported savings in using Signal Tabs, but gave no evidence of studies conducted. Daniels wrote:

> The reduction of files during the last five months has allowed for the transfer of one full time circulation assistant to work with public documents in the reference department. That signifies for the professional staff a 25 per cent increase in efficiency. In addition the student help assistance at the circulation desk has been reduced by one third.

Tab Pocket System

Rogers achieved a saving of over ten hours per month with the new overdue procedure of his Tab Pocket System (290). He gave the following analysis of the time which had been added in the circulation process.

Extra time needed for putting 2, 000
   charges in pockets and removing
   them at the time of discharge
   (per month) . . . . 2 hours
Time now needed to check overdues,
   (per month). . . . . 1 hour, 5 minutes
Time needed to sort 2, 000 pockets
   for reuse. . . . . 1 hour, 40 minutes

Total   4 hours, 45 minutes

This proof of actual savings is convincing. However, it would be useful to know the various procedures of the system which was formerly in use.

Notched Card System

When Stokes and Chapin (316, 328) contemplated using Keysort cards for circulation records in a university library they prepared the following table of statistics on which to base the possible expense of the system:

Labor that would be saved:
    The time necessary for writing duplicates of
    charges at present is 1 1/2 hours daily or 9
    hours a week. With Keysort cards the need-
    ling of overdues would probably take 1/2 hour
    on 3 days, or 1 1/2 hours a week. Therefore,
    with Keysort the difference, or 7 1/2 hours
    weekly, would be saved.

    A year of 52 weeks X 7 1/2 hours. . . . . 390 hours
    The time necessary for pulling duplicates
    of charges at present averages 15 hours
    a week. 52 weeks X 15 hours. . . . . . 780 hours
    A clerk's salary averages $1,380 for
    2,000 work hours or $.69 an hour.
    At that rate 1170 hours saved would be. . $807.30

Supplies that would be replaced by
    Keysort cards: 300,000 call slips at
    $63.32 per 100,000. . . . .$189.96
Supplies needed for Keysort annually:
    1. Cards for the location file; one
        year's average circulation. 150,000.00
    2. Cards to be used as call slips which
        will never become charges because
        the books they request are in other
        locations than the stacks. 150,000.00
Total card supply   300,000.00

    300,000 cards at $269.00 per
    100,000 $807.00
    The first year only 2 needles, 2
    punches   5.00
    An unpredictable charge for converting
    location file boxes to hold 3 1/4" cards   ---

Boardman (332) in writing to McGaw, noted that there
was a great saving in filing time. He gave the following information:

Our file of approximately 50,000 cards is contained in 29
19-inch trays. On an average the regular Wednesday
morning sorting takes one assistant one hour and a half.
Arranging the cards by first, second, and third notice requires about 15 minutes; rearranging and refiling, from
half an hour to an hour depending on the number of cards.

The estimates given by Stokes result from careful analysis of the situation at her library. The assumed savings of staff time were yet to be proved. The low cost of supplies had not yet been tested by a year's experience. After the system was in use, Stokes recorded that there were expenses she had not expected but also saving in labor which would "cancel the cost of the Keysort cards." We could wish for a similar tabling of expenses and savings which was composed after the system was in use for a considerable time.

The facts given by Boardman were sufficient to substantiate his claims.

Kilgour (327) noted possible saving in staff time by comparing the volume of circulation handled by the present staff, with the work accomplished under the old system in 1937 by the same number of employees. He assumed that four people would have had to be added to cope with the increased load. He also noted that annual expenses had been reduced about $3,500. Kilgour's remarks are convincing, but his evidence could be more concrete.

Punched Card System

Neither time tests nor cost studies were recorded for the punched call card systems used at University of Texas and University of Florida libraries. Callander (356), who wrote of the Powers-Samas equipment which had been installed at his library, gave some evidence of its accuracy and speed.

A sorter can, for instance, be put to arranging a pack of cards in a prescribed order, and will handle the cards at the rate of 24,000 per hour, while a tabulator will extract and print information from sorted cards at the rate of 80 cards per minute.

This information is useful to the prospective user of IBM as well as the user of Powers equipment. Perhaps it would have been of more value if there had been some mention made as to the source of the statistics. Did it result from studies that librarians had made or was it released from the company?

Leyland (362) had recommended to the larger libraries a charging method which would cut counter staff by 60 per cent. He gave the following facts, which he said he had proved:

The average time taken to sort and count the day's issue (the branch issues approximately 220,000 books a year), to deal with withdrawal cards and clear the overdue issues, was one and a half hours per day. This time has tended to decrease, and it is likely that after, say another three months' practice, it would drop to one hour....

The time taken to deal with borrowers, including time taken to reproduce two new cards per book, is approximately 60 per cent less than under the ticket and pocket method.

This evidence, offered by Leyland, resulted from his seemingly objective analysis. His experience with punched cards is unique - the only system of this type mentioned in the literature. Therefore any evidence which he could supply would be of interest. Facts as to the expense would also have been welcomed.

The various changes which were adopted at the Detroit Edison Company Library brought about time savings recorded by Bumgardner (408). He wrote that magazine circulation now takes thirty man-hours per week instead of the one hundred hours which were formerly involved in this job. He stated the fact, but did not give evidence of any time studies which were conducted.

Mullendore (340) mentioned time savings: less time "needed to answer questions and to discharge the books" and to sort cards for the overdue notices. No definite figures were given and no studies were mentioned. Hocker (331) also mentioned savings but his reference to taking "less than half the staff time used with our old system, " is indefinite in its implications.

The last bit of evidence for the effectiveness of punched cards was given in an analysis of the Montclair IBM system. W. O'D. Pierce gave the following information in his Work Measurement in Public Libraries, published by the Social Science Research Council in 1949, pp. 113-120. He mentioned that the "use of IBM machines for handling all circulation give a very high concentrated schedule of time distribution" when considering the non-professional staff. Pierce showed that the distribution of time for tabulation at Montclair was divided between a non-professional senior library tabulator with 52.8 and a non-professional library tabulator with 44.8 per cent. Under the heading of "circulation" he included the following percentages of time distribution:

	Junior Library Clerk	Junior Library Circulation Clerk	Junior Circulation Assistant	Junior Library Circulation Clerk
Registration	30. 5	7. 2	37. 6	5. 2
Circulation	58. 6	83. 6	46. 5	79. 6
Information	1. 5	2. 1	2. 0	
Publicity			5. 0	
Maintenance				3. 3
Miscellaneous	9. 4	6. 0	8. 9	10. 2

This study by Pierce reveals that much of the routine work of circulation was carried out by non-professionals which could indicate the possibility of either freeing the professional librarians for advisory work or reducing expenses by hiring less professional librarians than are normally needed to operate a circulation department. At Montclair the desire seemed to be one of giving superior service rather than reducing the expense involved in circulation. Pierce's study proves that routine can be handled by clerical employees.

Double Call Slip System (Columbia Method)

During the year of experimentation with this system at Columbia, before it was finally adopted, Forrest noted the results of various tests which were made. The evidence was yielded by time studies of routines under both the system in use and the experimental one. He gave the following facts as evidence:

Under both systems, for example, transaction cards are pre-dated, but under the trial system this card functions as a date due slip. Should it then be considered as part of the charging routine? At the same time it is part of the discharging operation both for books taken for home use and for books used in the building. Under the present system its function was a check to see that all books were either returned to the desk on the day taken or charged out for home use. The transaction card under this system is stamped with only one date, the date taken. Usually 300 transaction cards were taken each day; the time of this operation, including time used to replace missing numbers, was 14 minutes. Two types of cards were to be used in the experimental system, one set with date charged, and another with date due. By studying the requests at the Delivery Desk for several days it was de-

termined that the number of cards of the latter type would
be about twice the number needed of the former, that is,
approximately 200 with the two dates, 100 with the one.
The process involved stamping 500 dates; this process
averaged about 28 minutes including the time taken to
count them.   With a double stamp this could be reduced
to almost the same time as the old method, as only 300
separate dating operations would be involved.   Assuming
that the proposed system would be put into effect, it is
estimated that approximately 600 transaction cards would
be needed for the Stack Exit Desk.   The stamping operation would then consume about 45 minutes.   This could be
easily absorbed by the person at the special Stack Entrance
Desk.   [at present book cards were signed, no call slips
or t cds used]

Time records were made to determine how long it
takes under the present system to deliver a book to the
reader; that is, stamp transaction number on call slip,
place transaction card in book, and hand to reader and
how long it takes to charge a book at the charge desk, a
process that includes stamping book and card, checking
identification, and waiting for book card to be signed.
The Delivery Desk operation averaged 13 1/2 seconds and
the Charge Desk operation 27 1/2 seconds, making a total of 41 seconds.   The Delivery Desk operation of giving
a book to a reader under the trial system combined these
two operations; it included stamping transaction numbers
on card and call slip, placing transaction card in book
pocket, and dropping two parts of call slip into appropriate trays.   This operation averaged 22 seconds or 19 seconds less than the two operations under the present system.   It must be remembered, however, that about a
third of these books would not have been charged at the
Charge Desk under the present system.   Assuming an average day of 300 books given out at the Delivery Desk,
consuming 67 minutes, 30 seconds, approximately 200 of
these would have been charged for home use consuming
81 minutes, 40 seconds, making a total of 149 minutes,
10 seconds.   The Delivery Desk routine under the trial
system would consume 110 minutes; to this can be added
five more minutes which is consumed in dating the upper
portions of the call slip the following morning.   These
statistics do not, of course, account for the largest a-
mount of the desk assistants' time: receiving slips, sending for books, checking information, giving reports on
books.   These functions remain fairly constant under the
two systems, and no comparison was deemed necessary.

The transaction card routine under the present system involves arranging of the returned transaction cards, counting to detect missing numbers, searching of the shelves for books represented by these numbers and the sending of notices. The time consumed by these operations on an average day when 300 transaction cards are used is:

Counting and arranging	81 minutes
Searching	17 minutes
Notices	14 minutes
Total	112 minutes

Corresponding to this under the trial system would be the cancellation of lower and upper portions of call slips of books returned the same day as charged, searching of shelves for books represented by uncancelled slips and the sending of notices. The uncancelled slips marked by maltese crosses [those for reference use only] are pulled when the lower portions are dated. The time taken by dating is included although it might justifiably be included in the overdue routine. The arranging of the upper portions would correspond to the arranging of book cards under the present system; however, cards of books taken the same day must be arranged also before they are cancelled so that the difference in time taken in arranging under the two systems may be added to the cancellation procedure for books taken the same day. The time studies show the following results:

Cancellation of two portions of call slips including time to arrange cards (i. e. transaction)	23 1/2 minutes
Extra time taken in arranging upper portion	16 1/2 minutes
Searching (including dating)	25 minutes
Notices	3 minutes
Total	68 minutes

This time would not be greatly changed if the system were in use at the Stack Exit Desk for most of the books taken from the stacks are taken for home use and would not be returned the same day as taken. To these statistics of the daily transaction card routine could be added the time taken in the predating operation (discussed above):

Present system   126 minutes
Trial System   113 minutes

The person at the Return Desk also cancelled from the
date due file transaction numbers from previous dates.
There is some problem as to which routine to charge the
time taken in this operation: Should it be considered part
of the discharging or part of the overdue routine? As this
file is maintained in order to detect overdues the latter
routine might seem the logical place to put it. However,
by a similar logic, one could even consider the slipping
of books part of the overdue routine as it eliminates all
charges except the overdue ones. It has been decided to
compare the time taken in cancelling cards from date due
file plus the time taken cancelling cards from the charge
file with the time consumed in slipping books under the
present system. The latter operation averages about 50
seconds per book including the time taken in handling the
book. The two cancellation procedures under the trial
system consume only 35 1/2 seconds per book. In a day
on which 800 books were returned more than two hours
could be saved. During the fiscal year 1950-51, 185,775
books were slipped. Using the trial system during such
a year 348 hours could be saved, or slightly more than
a third of the working time of one person.

At the present time adequate statistics on overdues are
not available. Overdues have been sent only once on
books taken during the trial period. On April 25 notices
were sent on books taken on March 17, 18, and 19, which
were due on April 17, 18, and 19. It was decided to wait
one week as it is believed that a large proportion of overdues are returned within a few days after the due date.
This proved to be true. Of the overdues for April 17, 25
out of 67 were returned the first week; seven out of 34
and 13 out of 40 of the April 18 and 19 overdues came
back by April 25. The 96 remaining cards were pulled
from the charge file, and the remaining 86, after faculty
charges were marked, were checked on the shelves. Fourteen were found, eight with the transaction cards still in
the pockets. The number of books returned to the shelves
with the transaction cards not removed would undoubtedly
lessen were there only one kind of returns. The entire
process consumed about four and one half hours. It is
very difficult to say what amount would be spent were all
the charges made under the trial system. A large amount
of the charges at the Stack Exit Desk are to faculty members. Searching time per title decreases with the larger

amount to be searched.   Considering these factors an estimate of 28 hours per week for overdues is hazarded.
(Prompt action on overdues is expected to reduce second
and third notices to a small proportion.)   At present 19
hours a week is the average amount of time spent on overdues with the work months in arrears.   The extra eight
hours under the trial system which would be necessary to
keep the work up to date (if the estimate is correct) would
be more than balanced by the time saved in discharging
alone.

As to costs of the proposed system there are no prices
available at present; however, one can get some idea from
a comparison of the supplies used in the two systems. The
greatest cost increase would be in the call slip; it is estimated that the new one would be twice the price of the
present one.   (Mimeographed call slips were used in the
experiment so that no idea could be gained at that time.)
At the same time it must be remembered that the book
card will no longer be used which will constitute a saving
in time and money for the Cataloging Department.   The
Circulation Department itself now makes book cards to replace old ones that have been filled up.   The transaction
card will be smaller in size than the old one, perhaps
constituting a saving, but it can not be used as many
times.   More will be needed as it will be used at the
Stack Exit Desk as well as at the Delivery Desk and the
majority will not be returned the same day as used.   On
the other hand the need of date due slips will be eliminated.   A corner book pocket could be used instead of the
present one which is no doubt more expensive.

Stubblefield (388), the librarian at Columbia University
Library circulation department, gave this additional information:

In the time studies it was found that the operation of giving a book to a reader under the old system averaged 13
seconds and the Charge Desk operation averaged 27 seconds, making a total of 40 seconds.   Now that both operations are combined the time averages 22 seconds.   A
difference of 18 seconds may sound negligible but a reader
may take several books at once, and these figures do not
show the time wasted in waiting at another desk.   From
reader reaction we know that they appreciate this time
saving.

The material supplied by the study conducted by

Stubblefield and Forrest would easily satisfy the circulation expert. An attempt was made to correlate past activities with present ones, thus recording the comparison of time involved. Cost studies would have been of equal value.

Wayne County System

At the Wayne County Library where registration files were eliminated, the claim was made that less books were lost than under the former system. W. H. Kaiser gave this as evidence (519, 520):

> At one library after seventeen months and 80,000 circulations, only one book has been lost which can be attributed to the new procedures. In analyzing reports from branch librarians, fourteen cases were reported involving illegible handwriting, "no such address," and ficticious names, for a period averaging six months at all branches. For a comparable period under the old system, seventy-three cases were noted involving card numbers copied incorrectly, "no such address," illegibly written book cards, and incorrect address due to failure to notify of change of address.

Five years later results were recorded of studies which were made at Wayne County concerning registration and borrowers' cards. Kaiser found this evidence supported two conclusions:

1. Losses of books, issued under the circulation procedures employed in the Wayne County Library Charging System, neither increased nor decreased as a result of eliminating both registration and library cards....
2. When excessive losses occurred they were probably due more to such identifiable socio-economic factors as low educational level and low income than to circulation procedures.

He gave a table which helped to explain the percentage of books not returned during the years in which both systems were in use.

Number and Per Cent of Unreturned Books

Period	Total Circulation	Number of Unreturned books	Books to circulation o/o of unreturned
1944-1949	3, 229, 745	2, 321	. 07186 of 1 per cent
1951-1954	3, 506, 631	2, 517	. 07177 of 1 per cent

Kaiser received answers to a questionnaire which he sent out to librarians who had eliminated registration. One of the questions was, "Have you made any estimates of savings or drawn any conclusions as to improvements of library services as a result of the elimination of registration?" Kaiser gave the following listing of the answers which he received.

Berkley: estimates an annual savings of $1500 annually in clerical help, plus small material savings.

Cuyahoga County: able to handle increased circulation with present personnel; reduced book mobile staff by four clerical assistants. (Comments relate primarily to adoption of Wayne County Charging System, but partly to elimination of registration!)

Hamtramck: $1200 annually. Patrons have expressed appreciation for registration elimination.

Kern County: elimination of registration has eliminated one and one-half clerical positions at Headquarters.

Long Beach: reports a tentative saving of $9, 480 annually.

Pomora: one clerical position was eliminated.

Queens Borough: reduced from a total of five and one-half to three at central registration and "I cannot begin to estimate the amount of clerical time saved in the branches. "

St. Louis County: convinced that savings run at least $15, 000 per year in labor, equipment and materials. We're sold on it completely.

Kaiser supplied the proof needed to show that registration would be an unnecessary expense for his library and went further revealing that other librarians agreed with him. Other mechanics of the charging system were not supported by proof. He and other librarians using the Wayne County method neglected to give evidence for the remarks which they made as to the speed and simplicity of charging. Kaiser did make a study of the time taken in sorting of cards. This is covered under the material on Notched Transaction Card

Systems.

Notched Transaction Card System

Newton did not record having made a study of the relative cost of Keysort cards used with his charging procedure or of the time taken for charging books. However, W. H. Kaiser (535) reported having used notched cards with his Wayne County System. He described the study which he had made of their use.

For full comprehension of the data below it is necessary to note conditions which may be at variance with those in other libraries using marginal punched cards as a transaction card. Seven separate, serially numbered decks of cards are used, a different deck, with distinguishing colors, being used each week. All books issued fall due on the same day of the week regardless of the day on which the books may have been drawn. The transaction cards are punched or coded for transaction number color and agency or branch number. Color is also indicated by a small color band on the two side edges of each card to facilitate identifying overdue books.

The study involved five libraries and was carried on over a period of four weeks. Reports by each library were made weekly. The sorting was usually done by one person in each library but occasionally by two. Instructions to those participating in the study cautioned against speed-up or anything else which would affect the objectivity of the study. As an additional control, a training supervisor of the McBee Company was requested to make an independent time study involving the same process at one of the libraries.

The following four tables of statistics were offered by Kaiser as evidence for the speed of sorting.

Table I

Number of Cards, Sorted, Checked and Recorded for Missing Numbers per Hour

Library	Number of Cards per Hour
Fastest speed	1,300
Slowest speed	780
Average speed	1,100

Training supervisor of	
McBee Company	1, 176
1952 test	1, 200

Table II

Average Weekly Time Required to Perform
Processes (Each participating library timed
weekly operations for four weeks. The
data for each library represented the
average of four separate timings for the
various processes.)

Time in Minutes and Seconds

	Library A	Library B	Library C	Library D	Library E
Color Sort	7:07	(10:26)*	11:19	10:48	1:44
Breakdown Sort (100's-1, 000's)	13:10	10:05	14:34	10:44	3:42

*This library did not color sort; time derived from average of other four libraries.

	Library A	Library B	Library C	Library D	Library E
Numerical Sequence Sort	26:14	34:35	18:40	19:30	8:35
Total Time for all sorts	46:31	55:01	44:33	41:02	14:01
Checking and Recording Missing Numbers	38:30	42:28	27:50	39:07-	22:27
Total time for sorting, checking and recording missing numbers	85:01 (1:25:01)	97:29 (1:37:29)	72:23 (1:12:23)	80:09 (1:20:09)	36:28
Number of Cards Sorted	1, 857	1, 702	1, 500	1, 086	608

Table III

Sorting Time: average of all libraries (more accurately, averages of averages.)

Process	Time in Minutes and Seconds
Color Sort	8:17
Breakdown Sort (100's and 1,000's)	10:19
Numerical Sequence Sort	21:31
Total for All Sorts	40:07
Checking and Recording Missing Numbers	34:04
Total time for sorting, checking and recording missing numbers	74:11 (1:14:11)
Number of Cards Sorted	1,351

Table IV

Performance Record of McBee Company Training Supervisor

Process	Time in Minutes and Seconds	Number of Cards	Number of Holes	Total Number of Holes
Color Sort	8:15	3,000	5	16,500
Breakdown Sort	19:08	1,616	13	21,008
Numerical Sequence Sort	24:58	1,616	13	21,008
Total time for all Sorts	52:21			58,516
Checking and Recording Missing Numbers	30:08			
Total time for sorting, checking and recording missing numbers	82:29 (1:22:29)			
Number of Cards Sorted	1,616			

He explained these statistics in an adequate manner, well substantiating his claims. His findings are of value to those choosing transaction or data cards and to others selecting the fastest sorting method.

Table IV indicates that 58, 516 holes were involved in the sorting process with an elapsed time of 52 minutes and 21 seconds or at the rate of 67, 000 holes per hour. A McBee Company representative informed the writer that an acceptable standard for the type of sorting required in this use of a marginal punched card is 60, 000 holes per hour, not including, of course, the checking and recording missing numbers.

Table IV indicates that the Color Sort, a Direct Sort, is three times faster than Sequence Sorting, the slowest of all sorts, and twice as fast as Breakdown Sorting.

Important: in comparing the time necessary to check and record missing numbers, it must be realized that the amount of elapsed time is affected by the number of overdues to be recorded. Thus, a library having fewer overdues - hence fewer numbers to record in preparation for sending overdue notices - will find the elapsed time less for this process, other things being equal....

Since the above data have been carefully compiled and checked, and since the findings of the current study are similar to those of an independent experimenter and of a test conducted five years ago, considerable confidence in the findings of this study seems justified.

IBM Transaction Card System

The IBM Circulation Control System installed at Stockton, California was recommended as being flexible and a saving, reducing operational costs. Klausner (547) gave much information to support her claims. The initial costs were given in the article appearing in California Library Bulletin, September, 1948, p. 13.

An initial cost of 2, 500 purchased card stock for eight operating agencies, two stamping machines (the other two were bought by local communities), book slips, posters, and mimeographed announcement forms. This transaction card stock, which is used over and over, has an estimated life of ten years and provides for a maximum circulation of over 700, 000 volumes, allowing for future growth.

Cost of Old System

Personnel	11, 103. 84
Supplies, equipment, etc.	410. 00
	11, 513. 84

Cost with IBM

Personnel	8, 873. 44
Supplies, equipment	950. 00
	9, 823. 44

The initial cost can be amortized over a ten year period at $250 a year. Operating expense includes rental on the sorting machine and the price of book slips. These costs appear to total about $700 a year. Thus the yearly cost is $950.

In explanation of these cost figures, this librarian gave the following information in a chapter which was included in R. S. Casey's book, Punched Cards, Their Application to Science and Industry, 1951, pp. 227, 228.

Before operating with punched cards, the main circulation department was using 151. 5 man-hours weekly for circulation, registration, overdues, and reserves, and was unable to fill one vacancy which allowed an additional 37. 5 hours a week. During December, 1948 a work week of 146 man-hours handled a circulation increase of 5. 2 per cent and a registration increase of 8 per cent over 1947.

.... Stockton was able to allocate a circulation clerk, allowed in its 1948 budget to another hard pressed department, and at the same time was able to do more work with less staff in a reorganized circulation department using "IBM" methods.

In 1950, the Library Journal article, entitled "Stockton Public Library Appraises IBM Operation, " p. 512, contained this table of statistics:

.... these latest statistics on our operation with the IBM system. During the calendar year 1949 these are the results:

Man hours used with the IBM Circulating System
    (including charging and discharging books,
    operating IBM machine, handling overdues,
    complete registration process, reserve
    book routines at Main Desk)   141 hours per week
Total books handled and circulat-
    ed (main desk)   164, 400
Volumes per worker (3. 76 persons)   43, 723
Overdues handled   12, 977
Reserves   3, 089
Registrations taken and renewed   5, 741
Total book cards sorted (includes
    runs for 8 outlets)   336, 879
        Main Desk   164, 400
        Branches   172, 479
Machine time used (hours and
               minutes)   203' 25"

    The December, 1952 report "IBM circulation control, "
submitted to the Library Journal contained this evidence on
page 2166-2168.

    The Circulation Department personnel answer the telephone
calls; they check books in and out; register borrowers;
maintain the borrowers' file (alphabetic only); operate the
IBM equipment and prepare overdue lists for the main library and seven agencies; maintain files, handle the overdue routine for the main library; and maintain the reserve
book file.
    The staff is composed of one department head, one
senior clerk, and three junior clerks, totaling 187. 5 man-
hours a week. Following is a comparison of the work
loads handled by this system:

	1948-9	1951-52
Books issued with IBM	320, 384	441, 874
Main Desk	158, 943	190, 641
Children's Room	39, 060	50, 734
ElDorado Branch	21, 302	45, 590
Fair Oaks Branch	26, 408	38, 188
Escalon Branch	12, 545	22, 822
Manteca Branch	19, 065	24, 823
Ripon Branch	18, 455	35, 136
Tracy Branch	24, 606	33, 940
New cards issued (registration)	5, 059	6, 223
Reserves handled	2, 971	4, 156
Overdues sent	177, 900	170, 186

We use 187.5 man-hours a week to service this load.
Until early 1952 the man-hours used were 150. Then an
additional person was added to the staff.... At this time
the work load at the main desk is 38,000 issues per worker per year, plus the other work outlined. When additional help was added in early 1952 the work load was 44,210
per worker. The maximum load in this situation appears
to be 40,000-42,000....
In our system the following percentages of books overdue have been established, according to records which
have been in use since 1948-49. Slightly more than 6 per
cent of the total books issued become overdue. (The loan
period is two weeks and first notices are sent at the end
of the third week.) Of the 6 per cent overdue only 28 per
cent to 30 per cent need a second notice; 42 per cent of
the second overdue must be followed up, and 22 per cent
of these become delinquent. Our total loss of books for
a circulation of 190,641 during 1951,52 was 208 volumes.

A similar tabling of statistics was given for the years
October, 1947 to May 1, 1955 in the July, 1955 issue of
News Notes of California Libraries, pp. 468-9.

In 1953 eighteen additional hours were added to the staff..
.. At this time the personnel in the Circulation Department appear to be carrying a peak load. The work load
at the main desk is 39,000 issues per worker per year
plus the other work outlined.
The total cost of the operation, including all machinery,
cards, service and replacements from 1947 to 1955 has
been $12,018.86.

IBM Costs - October 1947 to May 1, 1955

Capital Costs:
   Original punched card stock for
      total system (754,814 cards)   2,170.86
   9 time machines and one re-
      placement   2,877.92

                              5,048.78

Operation and Maintenance Costs:
   Sorter and Punch rental   4,304.83
   Replacement cards   94.15
   Book slips   1,805.00
   Time clock ribbons   87.90

Service on equipment   678. 20
                                       ‾‾‾‾‾‾‾‾
                                        6, 970. 08

Costs

Average cost per year   929. 34
Average cost per unit of
  circulation (the circulation   . 002
  handled to date totals 3, 174, 956)

Circulation Department Work Loads
1947-1954

	1946-47	1949-50	1952-53	1953-54
Books issued - Main Desk	123, 941	166, 075	189, 935	207, 830
IBM cards monitored for system	not in use	365, 403	510, 255	636, 391
Telephone calls monitored	no record	no record	25, 336*	32, 285
Overdue notices sent	no record	14, 584	14, 918	14, 783
Reserves taken	2, 523	2, 347	3, 882	4, 748
Reserves filled	2, 301	2, 220	3, 934	4, 507
People using adult areas	no record	no record	267, 025	274, 621
Man-hours used per week	187. 5	150	187. 5	205. 5

*Partial tally only.

A wealth of material has been given by Klausner. According to her record of the initial expenses involved the IBM system was less expensive than the former system used. However she assumed that the IBM equipment and supplies would be used for ten years, applying only $250 of the total cost to this first year. She has presented convincing proof of the great savings in staff time and has revealed that over an eight year period the operational and maintenance costs can be amazingly low, amounting to $929. 34 per year or . 002 per unit circulated. The fact remains that the high initial expense will deter many librarians from installing IBM.

The Los Angeles Public Library (548) gave evidence

of the costs and savings effected when IBM was coupled with Recordak in a Photo-lending System.

Monthly costs of L. A. P. L. Photo-Lending

International Business Machine equipment used in Tab Room	Monthly Rental	Total
2 Sorters (No. 080) at $50.00 per month	$100	
2 Collators (No. 077) at $100.00 per month	200	
1 Reproducer (No. 513)	80	
1 Interpreter (No. 551)	65	
1 Duplicating punch (No. D16)	18	
		$463.00

Recordak equipment used at charging desks and in workrooms		
37 Recordaks JA or JC Models at $17.50 per month	$547.50	
6 Recordaks JC-1 Model at $20.00 per month	120.00	
4 Recordak Readers Model. P-10 and PD at $5.00 per month	20.00	
2 Recordak Readers Model P-40 at $8.50 per month	17.00	
		$704.50

Supplies		
60 rolls of film at $7.00 per roll (including cost of developing)	420.00	
44,000 (approx.) IBM cards	45.00	

Salaries		
3 Tab Room operators (cost based on middle salary step)	895.00	
Total monthly expense	$2,547.50	

Because of the cost of an IBM installation, it is obvious its use in relation to mechanical charging is economical only when a large circulation is involved.

The monthly expense involved seems great but savings were recorded in staff time, amounting to eight hundred dollars per month. The cost of equipment is much higher when that equipment is rented than when it is bought and "amor' tized over a ten year period" but the initial investment when on a rental basis is perhaps more reasonable.

Other Systems

Concrete evidence is lacking for the claims made for Accession Number Charging and the Indefinite Loan System. Merely descriptive information was given for the circulation of non-book materials.

Audio-Charging System

Detailed cost studies were not reported for audio-charging by any of the librarians using this system.

Smith (497) gave evidence for the fact that he judged the recording equipment relatively low in cost. This adequately supported his statement.

In the case of a tape recorder the same tape may be erased and used over and over again without apparent wear. Discs and cylinder may be reprocessed and re-used. While it is too early for us to compute costs exactly, we anticipate our expense for discs at about .09¢ per book charged, or $9.00 for every 100,000 of circulation.

Bailey (504, 507) believed the audio-charging system slower than photocharging particularly when author and title of book were read into the machine.

The average time spent with this audio method was 22 seconds for one book to one person and 42 seconds for three books to one person.

After a few changes were made he released the following facts as to the expense of the system and time involved in charging. Some comparison is made with photocharging and the modified Newark.

A book can be charged to a borrower in 11 1/3 seconds.

At this rate, 350 charges can be made on an hour record which costs 13 cents. These records can be reprocessed at 5 cents a record and used over again up to forty times. This means the cost of materials for charging with the Audograph has been cut to a fraction of the microfilm cost. Using new discs exclusively the cost is .0015 per book charged. If the discs are reproduced up to twenty times, the cost goes down to .00015 per book charged.

Using a quadruplicate type of overdue notice has cut the time of sending overdue notices to 3.4 minutes for combination of first and second notices. "This cuts the time from approximately 7 minutes for first and second notice to 3.4 minutes for the two notices." It was further stated that the circulation desk could be operated for 72 hours a week with two and one fifth persons instead of the three persons which it took at one time. The following tables were given as more evidence of the comparisons which were made:

Table of Statistics

Time Spent in Charging Books

Microfilm	Audio	Modified Newark
7 1/3 seconds per book	11 1/3 seconds per book	11 1/4 seconds per book

Time Spent in Discharging Books

Microfilm	Audio	Newark and Gaylord
.5 seconds per book	.5 seconds per book	30 seconds per book

Time Spent in Sorting & Filing Cards

Plain Numerical Transaction Card	Keysort Transaction	Book Card with Dewey Decimal No.
4 cards per minute	25 cards per minute	9 cards per minute

Time Spent in Sending Overdues

Newark System	Quadruple Notice Cards Keysort Transaction Card Audio-Charge	Quadruple Notice Cards Keysort Transaction Cards Microfilm Charge
4 minutes 1st notice 3 minutes 2nd notice	3-4 minutes both notices	3-4 minutes both notices

Costs of Machines and Materials

Recordak Junior	Audograph
$15.00 monthly rental	$338.60 Recorder
6.00 200 ft. roll film	280.28 Transcriber
(microfilm readers	.13 Initial cost disc
vary in cost)	

The information is useful and is sufficient to back up his claims. However a description of the actual tests is not given, nor is an attempt made to present a detailed picture of the expense involved.

Other writers failed to mention similar studies, if these studies were made.

Selective Charging Token Systems

Studies were made by two librarians who had worked with the Token System of book circulation. These studies dealt with the matter of lost books and overdues, which could be problems with a selective charging system. McColvin (577) gave his findings on "lost books."

Another librarian, L. M. Bickerton (580) gave the results of the overdue checks at Durrington where another system was in effect. He submitted the following as proof of the security of the system.

Period overdue at least	August 1955 check No. of overdues	Notices sent	February 1956 check No. of overdues	Notices sent
2 weeks	191		202	
3 weeks	133		115	
4 weeks	101		94	
5 weeks	82	64 1st applications	67	56 1st applications
6 weeks	42	28 2nd applications	44	29 2nd applications
7 weeks	31	14 final notices	30	11 final notices
8 weeks	16		22	
6 months	2		--	

Eventual reduction of the August 1955 overdues to two
must be regarded as highly satisfactory under any system and
the February check seems to be following the same course.
Having regard to the high number of overdues at the beginning of the check I am satisfied that such checks are necessary in order to prevent the accumulation of too many serious overdues and queries.

The amount of books lost under McColvin's system
were considerably higher than under Bickerton's but much
less time had been spent in recovering them.   The evidence
given by both of these writers seems sufficient to prove their
claims.   A librarian must determine whether the expense
caused by the loss of books would be balanced by a sufficient
saving in staff time and supplies.

Bickerton claimed savings of time spent on book charging as well as on overdue procedures although he does not
supply evidence to substantiate this.   McColvin's evidence on
this point reflected a different conclusion (576).   He wrote:

> Before introducing the system, we made, with expert O.
> and M. assistance, various studies.   For example, we
> analyzed in detail a typical rush hour - how many brought
> one book, how many two, how many had fines to pay and
> of how much and which coins were proffered in payment,
> etc., and we made a "mock up" of this and tested it with
> the token system; we tried out our present method of
> handling reserves... with the conventional methods as re-
> gards both timing and efficiency.   And one of the things
> we discovered was that only 32 per cent of the total time
> of the lending library staff was spent on counter duties.
> In other words, even if the token system reduced counter
> duties by half, at least 84 per cent of the existing man
> hours would still be necessary.

McColvin seemed to feel that reduction of staff time
would only be possible in a large library where all activities
were accomplished up-to-date.   The fact that normal charging procedures must be carried out for part of the books
while others are merely exchanged for tokens makes added
care necessary.   This selective charging was proven to be
a saving in two library situations.   To accept it, other librarians must recognize that lack of book control is a risk.

References

1. Carr, H. J. Report on charging systems. Library journal, 14:212, May-June 1889.
2. Brown, J. D. History and description of charging systems. Library world, 2:2, 1899.
3. Geer, H. T. Charging systems. Chicago, ALA, 1955. p. 1.
4. Flexner, J. M. Circulation work in public libraries. Chicago, ALA, 1927. pp. 75, 76.
5. Schwartz, J. Charging systems. Library journal, 5:73, March 1880.
6. Dewey, M. More about charging systems. Library journal, 5:75, 1880.
7. Bolton, C. K. Charging systems and statistics. Library journal, 19:225, 226, 1904.
8. Brown, J. D. History and description of charging systems. Library world, 1:19, 1898.
9. Ibid., 33, 35.
10. Dewey, M. Charging systems: accounts with books. Library journal, 3:288, 1878.
11. Bostwick, A. E. An old New England method of book distribution. A. L. I. papers and proceedings, 10-13, 1921.
12. Stetson, W. K. Practical notes: charging. Library journal, 11:121, April 1886.
13. Arnold, G. U. Charging by day-books. Library journal 11:167, 1886.
14. Easy charging system. Vermont library bulletin, 10:6, 1914.
15. Ref. 1, p. 204.
16. Dewey, M. Charging systems based on an account with borrowers. Library journal, 3:252, 1878.
17. Ibid., 254.
18. Ref. 10, p. 285.
19. Ref. 8, p. 75.
20. Ref. 1, pp. 206, 207.
21. Wheatley, B. R. Hints on library management. Library journal, 2:214, 1878.
22. Newburgh, N. Y. library. Charging system of a novel sort. Library journal, 3:119, 1878.
23. The Sunday-school library. Library journal, 6:288, 289,

1881.
24. Ref. 1, p. 205.
25. Hulls, C. H.   Issue methods.   New Zealand libraries,
    4:9, Aug. 1940.
26. Ref. 8, p. 19.
27. Peck, A. L.   Charging by means of baggage checks.
    Library journal, 13:315, 316, 1888.
28. Fletcher, W. I.   Public libraries in America.   Boston,
    Roberts, 1894.   p. 66.
29. Ref. 1, p. 205, 206.
30. Schwartz, J.   A 'combined' charging system.   Library
    journal, 4:276, 1879.
31. Ibid., 277.
32. Cadwallader, B.   Record blanks of books loaned.   Library
    journal, 1:254, 255, 1876.
33. Cutter, M. S.   Charging systems in foreign libraries.
    Library journal, 16:52, 1891.
34. Brown, J. D.   Charging systems.   Library, 3:391, 392,
    1891.
35. Parr, G.   Card-ledger, a charging system without writ-
    ing.   Library association transactions, 2:73-75, 1879.
36. Davis, O. S.   Y. M. C. A. library, Albany, charging sys-
    tem.   Library journal, 16:232, 1891.
37. Ref. 10, p. 288.
38. Plummer, M. W.   Hints to small libraries.   Brooklyn,
    Pratt Institute free library, 1894.   pp. 40-43.
39. Estabrook, C.   More about charging systems.   Library
    journal, 5:72, 73, 1880.
40. Ref. 34, p. 292.
41. Cutter, C. A.   Mr. Cutter's charging system.   Library
    journal, 4:445, 1879.
42. Foster, W. E.   New charging system.   Library journal,
    5:320, 1880.
43. Massey, A. P.   Coloured cards for recording loans.
    Library journal, 6:34, 1881.
44. Linderfelt, K. A.   Charging systems.   Library without
    the walls.   Ed. Laura M. Janzow.   N. Y., Wilson,
    1927.
45. Hasse, A. R.   New charging system of Los Angeles li-
    brary.   Library journal, 19:195, 196, 1894.
46. Bolton, H. C.   Dated book marks.   Library notes, U. S.
    2:218, 1887.
47. Bolton, C. K.   Bettering circulation in small libraries -
    the 'two-book' system.   Library journal, 19(5):161,
    May 1894.
48. Jones, G. M.   Cards for the 'two-book' system.   Library
    journal, 20(5):168, May 1895.

49. Ref. 10, p. 286.
50. Vinton, **F.** Hints for improving library economy. Library journal, 2:56, 1877.
51. Ref. 1, p. 206.
52. Cutter, C. A. Another charging plan. Library journal, 4:17-18, 1879.
53. Winsor, **J.** Charging loans at Harvard. Library journal, 3:338, 1878.
54. Ref. 16, pp. 254, 255.
55. Plummer, M. W. Loan systems. Library journal, 18: 244, 1893.
56. Ref. 52, p. 18.
57. Circular of the board of library commissioners, State of New Hampshire. Library journal, 18:42, 1893.
58. Woodham, W. H. Peplow system of recording issues. Librarian and book world, 29:9-11, Sept. 1939.
59. Buhre, M. E. Charging systems. Public library, 1: 132, 133, 1896.
60. Meisoner, **J.** A charging system for a university library Pacific northwest library association: proceedings. 63, 1910.
61. Poole, W. **F.** Organization and management of public libraries. Public libraries in the United States: special report. Washington, Government printing office, 1876. pp. 501, 502.
62. Ref. 16, p. 255.
63. Rae, W. S. C. Public library administration. London, Routledge, 1913. pp. 73-75.
64. Dewey, **M.** Charging loans combined plan. Library journal, 3:359, 360, 1878.
65. Chamberlain, L. **T.** Charging methods for Sunday-school libraries. Library journal, 6:159, 160, 1881.
66. Little, G. **T.** A charging system for small libraries. Library journal, 11:212, 213, 1886.
67. Vitz, C. Circulation work. Manual of library economy :21. Rev. ed. Chicago, ALA, 1927. p. 4.
68. Ref. 2, pp. 1, 2.
69. Ref. 2, pp. 2, 3.
70. Pollitt, W. Principles of book charging. Library world 15:340-343, 1913.
71. Ref. 2, p. 3.
72. Ref. 2, pp. 30, 31.
73. Ref. 2, p. 59.
74. Yates, **J.** The Leed's indicator. Library journal 1:443, 1876.
75. Ref. 2, p. 116.
76. Ref. 2, p. 114.

77. Ref. 63, p. 65.
78. A new indicator, a description of the Chiver's indicator. Library, 7:318, 319, 1895.
79. Brown, J. D. Library appliances. Library, 3:386, 387, 1891.
80. Robertson, A. W. On library indicators, with special reference to the 'Duplex' indicator. Library 2:23-26, 1890.
81. The Robertson or the Aberdeen indicators. Librarian and book world, 30:64, 1940.
82. Robertson, A. W. The duplex indicator. Library journal, 14:42, 1889.
83. Devices for recording book loans. Ontario library review, 19:153, 154, 1935.
84. Plummer, M. W. Western libraries visited by the ALA party. Library journal, 16:335, 1891.
85. Meesham, E. W. Cotgreave indicator; an adaptation. Library world, 11:79, 115, 116, 1908.
86. Librarians' workshop - indicators: method of dealing with duplicate books. Library world, 1:43, 1899.
87. Brown, J. D. Suggestions for a new form of library indicator. Library, 8:98-100, 1896.
88. Davis, C. T. Indicators versus card charging. Library 5:291, 292, 1893.
89. Ibid., 292, 293.
90. Ref. 87, p. 101.
91. Gill, A. K. Indicator considered as a modern library appliance. Library world, 9:314-316, March 1907.
92. Cotgreave, A. Comments on an article concerning library indicators, by A. Kirby Gill. Library world, 9:404, May 1907.
93. Harris, W. J. Indicators vs. card charging. Library world, 7:211, Feb. 1905.
94. Oswald, W. K. Indicator: a patience exerciser, or obstructor. Library world, 9:289, 291, Feb. 1908.
95. Ref. 63, p. 73.
96. Cole, F. C. Card charging and appliances. Library world, 10:118, 1907.
97. Ref. 34, p. 390.
98. Ref. 34, p. 391.
99. Quinn, J. H. A card-charging system for lending libraries. Library, 5:35, 1893.
100. Browne, N. E. Another charging system. Library journal, 20:168, 1895.
101. Ref. 4, p. 78.
102. Harrod, L. M. Lending library methods. London, Grafton, 1933. p. 117.

103. Hill, F. P.   Preparing a book for issue; and charging systems.   Library journal, 21:52, 53, Dec. 1896.
104. Schwartz, J.   Combined charging system.   Library journal, 22:428, 1897.
105. Dana, J. C.   ALA primer.   Public libraries, 1:79-81, 1896.
106. Crunden, F. M.   How things are done in one American library.   Library, n. s. 1:393, 1900.
107. A new method of charging books.   Wisconsin library bulletin, 13:163, June 1917.
108. Identification vs. borrower's card.   Wisconsin library bulletin, 18:89, 1922.
109. Ulveling, R. A.   Detroit charging system.   Libraries, 35:393, 1930.
110. Bostwick, A. E.   The library and the public.   American public library.   New York, Appleton, 1929. p. 57.
111. Lehman, G. I.   The Dickman bookcharging system.   Library journal, 56:302, 1931.
112. Finney, G.   Dickman charging system.   ALA bulletin, 22:428, 1928.
113. Patterson, S.   The Gaylord electric automatic charging machine.   Library journal, 56:304-305, 1931.
114. Book charging in England.   Library journal, 56:612, 1931.
115. Ref. 102, p. 115.
116. Brown, C. H. and Bousfield, H. G.   Circulation work in college and university libraries.   Chicago, ALA, 1933. p. 142.
117. Ref. 34, pp. 390, 391.
118. Ref. 99, pp. 35-39.
119. Tapley-Soper, H.   Charging system in use at Exeter public library, England.   Public library, 16:328, Oct. 1911.
120. Ibid., 329.
121. McDonald, B.   Browne charging system.   Ontario library association, proceedings. p. 69, 1909.
122. Cutter, C. A.   Charging simplified.   Library journal, 28:664, 1903.
123. Browne, N. E.   Comparison of Newark and Browne charging systems: a correction.   Public library, 13:403, Dec. 1908.
124. Book issue methods.   Librarian and book world, 24:219, Apr. 1935.
125. Six-day wickets.   Librarian and book world, 22:119, Jan. 1933.
126. Doubleday, W. E.   Manual of library routine.   London, Allen, 1933. pp. 154, 155.

127. Ref. 123, O. 402.
128. Clarke, E. P.   Browne charging system, a further
     word.   Library journal, 24:478, 1899.
129. Pennock, B. W.   Browne charging system.   Library
     journal, 22:296, 1897.
130. Ibid., 295.
131. Ibid., 295, 296.
132. Smith, C. W.   Seattle charging case.   Library journal,
     30:350, June 1905.
133. Hyde, M. E.   Comparison of charging systems.   Public
     library, 13:344, Nov. 1908.
134. Maidment, W. R.   Book issue methods: a systematic
     approach.   Library association record, 57:54, 55,
     Feb. 1955.
135. Johnston, C. D.   Modifications of the Browne system.
     Library journal, 26:873, 1901.
136. Ref. 105, pp. 79, 80.
137. ALA committee on library administration.   Report,
     1912.   ALA bulletin, 6:108, 109, 1912.
138. Van de Carr, S. C.   The lending department.   In
     Dana, J. C., Modern American library economy,
     rev. ed., Chicago, ALA, 1927.   p. 38.
139. Ibid., 58, 59.
140. Ref. 105, p. 80.
141. Ref. 137, p. 110.
142. Ref. 4, p. 89.
143. Ref. 3, p. 7.
144. Ref. 138, pp. 55, 56.
145. Ref. 103, p. 55.
146. Ref. 4, pp. 80, 82, 85.
147. Corwin, E. F.   Charging system in use at Elkhart.
     Library occurrent, 5:112, 113, 1919.
148. Severance, H. O.   Charging system of the University
     of Missouri library.   Public library, 17:117, 118,
     1912.
149. Ref. 147, p. 113.
150. Ref. 4, pp. 79, 80.
151. Lansden, E. A.   Cairo's charging system.   Illinois
     libraries, 1:50, 1919.
152. New borrower's voucher.   Librarian and book world.
     27:107, Dec. 1937.
153. Clement, C. B.   New charging system at Manchester.
     New Hampshire bulletin, 27:152, 1931.
154. Woodruff, J. L.   Labor saving method.   Public library
     15:58, Feb. 1910.
155. Ref. 138, p. 39.
156. Wood, H. M.   Charging system.   Public libraries, 4:

376, 1899.
157. Ref. 106, pp. 399, 401.
158. Ref. 3, p. 8.
159. Ref. 147, p. 113.
160. Gaillard, E. W.   Charging system wanted.   Public libraries, 3:262, 1898.
161. Browne charging system: possible improvements suggested.   Library journal, 24:202-204, 1899.
162. Drake, J. M.   Elimination of the use of readers' cards in a public library.   ALA bulletin, 12:220, 1918.
163. Roth, R. S.   Visible borrower's record.   South Dakota library bulletin, 25:19, 20, Sept. 1939.
164. Something new.   Kansas library bulletin, 2:7, June 1933.
165. The Newark system simplified.   Wisconsin library bulletin, 16:51, Apr. 1920.
166. Roth, R. S.   Self charging system.   South Dakota library bulletin, 24:3, March 1938.
167. Ref. 107, p. 164.
168. Ref. 166, p. 4.
169. Ref. 166, p. 2.
170. Murdock, M. H.   Signatures instead of library cards. California library association bulletin, 7:119, March, 1946.
171. Ulveling, R. A.   The Detroit charging system.   Demco library supplies, 1930.   p. 1.
172. Detroit charging system.   Illinois libraries, 12:38, 39, 1930.
173. Comstock, R.   Self charging system.   Vermont bulletin, 31:2, June 1935.
174. Ref. 109, pp. 393, 394.
175. Ann Arbor, Michigan public library.   Self charging system satisfactory.   Library journal, 56:308, 1931.
176. Baker, E. G. H.   Self charging. Wilson library bulletin, 15:508, Feb. 1941.
177. Strieby, Irene M.   Books...borrowed, lost or stolen. Special libraries, 43:86, March 1952.
178. Wright, I. F.   The Detroit charging system.   Illinois libraries, 12:117, 1930.
179. Field, P. I.   Detroit charging system as used at Legler branch.   Illinois libraries, 12:175, 1930.
180. Ref. 109, pp. 395, 396.
181. Ref. 175, p. 307.
182. Charge your own.   Library journal, 54:944, 1929.
183. Ref. 172, p. 39.
184. Ref. 109,. pp. 394, 395.
185. Ref. 171, p. 10.
186. Ref. 171, p. 2, 5

187. Ref. 182, pp. 943, 944.
188. Ref. 179, pp. 175, 176.
189. Ref. 175, p. 307.
190. Ref. 175, p. 308.
191. Ref. 176, p. 508.
192. Houghton, Amy. The Detroit charging system. Illinois libraries, 12:178, 1930.
193. Ref. 109, p. 395.
194. Brewitt, T. R. Detroit system not a barrier. Library journal, 56:615, 1931.
195. Ref. 178, p. 176.
196. Shaw, R. R. Gary charging system. Library journal, 64:198-199, March 1939.
197. Ref. 171, p. 11
198. ALA committee on library administration. Charging methods. ALA bulletin, 13:67, 1919.
199. Gaillard, E. W. Charging desk problems. Library journal, 43:462, 463, 1918.
200. Ref. 4, p. 7.
201. Ref. 112, pp. 428, 429.
202. The Toledo method of the Dickman book charging system. Library efficiency corp., 1930. pp. 2, 4, 8.
203. Harrod, L. M. Dickman charging system in England. Library world, 38:107, Nov. 1935.
204. Riggs, W. Dickman book charging system as used in the Toledo public library. ALA bulletin, 24:492, 1930.
205. Christopher, H. G. T. Dickman book charging system. Library world, 41:231-233, May 1937.
206. Ibid., 232.
207. Trudeau, E. C. The Dickman bookcharging system in use. Massachusetts library club bulletin, 20:87, 1930.
208. Ref. 202, p. 19.
209. Ref. 204, pp. 492, 493.
210. Smith, K. Dickman system and interavailability. Librarian and book world, 37:326, Dec. 1948.
211. Ibid., 329, 330.
212. McDougall, D. Lending library technique with special reference to the Dickman system. Library association record, 41:169, 1937.
213. Ref. 205, p. 234.
214. Ref. 207, p. 86.
215. Principles and practice of lending. Library world, 38: 135, Dec. 1935.
216. Ref. 212, pp. 166, 168.
217. Ref. 210, pp. 325, 326.
218. Ref. 203, p. 109.

219. Ref. 212, pp. 166, 167.
220. Ref. 205, pp. 232-235.
221. Ref. 202, pp. 20, 31, 32.
222. Ref. 204, p. 493.
223. Ref. 212, p. 168.
224. Ref. 113, p. 305.
225. Daniels, M. How it is done at Washington University. Library journal, 64:397-399, 1939.
226. Mrs. Brewster's inspiration. Syracuse, N. Y., Gaylord Bros., 1938. p. 9.
227. Ref. 225, p. 398.
228. A new tempo in book charging. The Gaylord electric-automatic book charging machine. Syracuse, N. Y., Gaylord Bros., n.d., p. 5.
229. The Gaylord electric-automatic book charging machine. Syracuse, N.Y., Gaylord Bros., 1946. p. 3.
230. Ref. 228, title page.
231. The mechanical charger on the bookmobile. ALA bulletin, 51:521-522, Aug. 1957.
232. Kilgour, F. A new punched card for circulation records. Library journal, 64:131, Feb. 15, 1939.
233. Ambrose, L. A study of college libraries. Library journal, 18:116, 1893.
234. Koch, T. W. Student circulation in a university library. Library journal, 31:758-761, Nov. 1906.
235. Wright, J. E. Manual of special library techniques. London, Aslib, 1946. p. 55.
236. Hood, M. Circulation work. In Lyle, Guy. The administration of the college library. N.Y., Wilson, 1944. p. 141.
237. Bousfield, H. G. Circulation systems. Library trends, 3:165, Oct. 1954.
238. Ref. 3, p. 153.
239. Parker, R. H. Library applications of punched cards: a description of mechanical systems. Chicago, ALA, 1952. pp. 25-26.
240. Adaptation of machines to book charging. Library trends, 6:39, July 1957.
241. Trotier, A. H. Introduction to mechanization in libraries. Library trends, 5:192, Oct. 1956.
242. Jesse, W. H. and Goehring, E. E. University library charging systems. College and research libraries, 6:53, 57, Dec. 1944.
243. Dove, J. The common round. Librarian and book world, 42:7-10, Jan. 1953.
244. Cook, O. V. Some unsolved problems in circulation service; abridged. ALA bulletin, 32:846-847, Oct. 15,

1938.
245. Randall, W. M.   Principles of college library adminis-
     tration.   Chicago, ALA, 1941.   p. 129.
246. Ref. 137, p. 107.
247. Schwartz, T. G.   Books, clientele, and the charging
     system.   Wilson bulletin, 12:601, May 1938.
248. Smith, A. L.   Circulation records department of the
     Illinois state library.   Illinois libraries, 20(9):n. p.
     Sept. 1938.
249. Ref. 3, p. 87.
250. McHale, C. J.   An experiment in university library
     circulation files.   Library journal, 56:427-428, 1931.
251. McGaw, H. F.   Self-charging system.   Wilson library
     bulletin, 16:658-660, Apr. 1942.
252. Cooper, D. M.   College library revises its circulation
     routines.   Library journal, 73:381, March 1948.
253. Thomas, J.   Circulation activities and methods in the
     research center library.   Louisiana library associa-
     tion bulletin, 20:24, Winter 1957.
254. Duck, L. W.   The multiple issue system in the Henry
     Watson music library.   Library association record,
     52:118, 119, 1950.
255. Voos, H. and Costello, M. A.   Role of a technical
     information section in a government research and de-
     velopment organization.   Special libraries, 48:327,
     Sept. 1957.
256. Gosset, M.   The library of the atomic energy research
     establishment.   Aslib proceedings, 1:222, 223, Nov.
     1949.
257. Browning, E. W.   A time saving filing system.   Library
     journal, 54:39, 1929.
258. Marvin, P. A.   Circulation in the divisional library:
     the new plan of service.   College and research librar-
     ies, 12:241-244, July 1951.
259. Woledge, G. and Page, B. S.   A manual of university
     and college library practice.   London, Library assoc-
     iation, 1940.   pp. 72, 73, 129.
260. Sandall, F. A.   Simple triple-entry charging scheme.
     New Zealand libraries, 2:47, 48, Jan. 1939.
261. Gauntlett, M. D.   The use of continuous-form station-
     ery for library loan records.   Aslib proceedings, 5:
     129-130, May 1953.
262. Ref. 67, p. 3.
263. Ref. 65, p. 5.
264. Dewey, M.   Delinquent notices and check boxes.   Li-
     brary journal, 3:370, 371, 1878.
265. Hood, M. and Lyle, G. R.   A new system of book

charging for college libraries. Library journal, 65:
18, Jan. 1940.

266. Peebles, M. Charge it, please. Southeastern librarian, 3:65, Summer 1953.

267. Ref. 265, p. 19.

268. Ref. 266, p. 66.

269. Ref. 265, p. 18.

270. Ref. 3, p. 91.

271. Ref. 265, p. 20.

272. Ref. 3, p. 92.

273. Shumar, N. Cards and tabs provide records. Library
journal, 74:525, Apr. 1949.

274. Sister Helen. Simplified circulation records for a college library. Library journal, 66:201, 202, March
1941.

275. Ref. 273, p. 526.

276. Ref. 274, p. 202.

277. Ref. 274, pp. 202, 203.

278. Ref. 274, p. 203.

279. Belton, E. J. A charging system for a university library. South African libraries, 19:13-16, July 1951.

280. Tollefson, H. A. Reid Scotch tape tabs serve any size
of circulation. Library journal, 73:181, 182, Feb.
1948.

281. Cooper, D. M. University of Washington adopts
Michigan tabbing system. Library journal, 75:1424,
Sept. 1950.

282. Ref. 280, p. 182.

283. Ref. 281, p. 1425.

284. Ref. 281, p. 1426.

285. Hamlin, A. T. and Wright, W. W. Goodbye to the
book card. Library journal, 73:1717, 1718, Dec. 1948.

286. Ibid., 1717-1719.

287. Ibid., 1718-1820.

288. Ref. 3, p. 109.

289. Ref. 3, p. 132.

290. Rogers, R. D. Charging pocket solution for overdues.
Library journal, 66:1072-1074, Dec. 1941.

291. McGaw, H. F. Marginal punch cards in college and
university libraries. N. Y., Scarecrow press, 1952.
p. 101.

292. Ibid., p. 121, 122, 139.

293. Voight, M. J. Trend toward mechanization in libraries. Library trends, 5:195, Oct. 1956.

294. Perry, J. M. Punched-card systems and their application to library and technical work: 1. The use of
punched cards in American libraries. Aslib, twenty-

second annual conference, p. 41, 1947.
295. Ref. 239, p. 78.
296. Ref. 239, p. v.
297. Ref. 3, p. 110.
298. Ramsey, E. W.   Use of the marginal punched card in
     tabulating vital statistics data.   American journal of
     public health, 29:907, Aug. 1939.
299. Ref. 291, pp. 16-18.
300. Ref. 232, pp. 131, 132.
301. Stream-lined charging.   Headlight on books at Pennsyl-
     vania State, 9:12, May 1940.
302. Stokes, K. M.   Librarian looks at Keysort.   Library
     journal, 72:899, June 1947.
303. Ibid., 900.
304. Ref. 291, p. 91.
305. Ref. 302, pp. 899, 900.
306. Ref. 302, pp. 900, 911.
307. Stokes, K. and Chapin, R. E.   On using Keysort.
     Library journal, 72:170, 171, Feb. 1952.
308. Hocker, M. L.   Punched-card charging system for a
     small college library.   College and research libraries
     18:120-122, Mar. 1957.
309. Ref. 302, p. 954.
310. Upchurch, G.   Punched cards for circulation records.
     Arkansas libraries, 5:8, Oct. 1948.
311. Ref. 291, p. 86.
312. Ref. 291, p. 94.
313. Ref. 232, p. 132.
314. Ref. 308, p. 121.
315. Ref. 302, p. 953.
316. Ref. 307, pp. 169-172.
317. Ref. 307, pp. 171-172.
318. Ref. 308, p. 122.
319. Ref. 232, p. 133.
320. Ref. 232, pp. 132, 133.
321. Ref. 291, pp. 86, 87.
322. Ref. 291, p. 89.
323. Ref. 291, p. 92.
324. Ref. 291, pp. 125, 126.
325. Ref. 291, pp. 100, 101.
326. Ref. 291, p. 101.
327. Ref. 232, p. 133.
328. Ref. 307, p 173.
329. Ref. 307, p. 170.
330. California state library, Sacramento.   Budget stretch-
     ing through more efficient technical processes; a
     workshop for practical libraries.   News notes Calif-

ornia libraries, 50:442, July 1955.
331. Ref. 308, p. 131.
332. Ref. 291, pp. 87, 88.
333. Ref. 308, pp. 122, 131.
334. Ref. 302, p. 955.
335. Stokes, K. M.   Library applications of punched card systems.   Special libraries, 38:207, Sept. 1947.
336. Mullendore, J. M.   Punched cards for circulation records.   Medical library association bulletin, 38:261, 262, July 1950.
337. Ref. 291, p. 117.
338. Ref. 336, pp. 262-264.
339. Ref. 291, p. 119.
340. Ref. 336, p. 265.
341. Ström, I.   Registrering av utlan (Translation: Registration of loans).   Tidskrift för dokumentation, 13(2):13-16, 1957.
342. Orton, F. E.   Let's look at paper work.   Library journal, 75:368, 384, March 1950.
343. Ref. 291, pp. 114-116.
344. Kilgour, F. G.   A circulation records system using marginal-punched cards.   Yale medical library annual report 1954-55.   New Haven, Conn., Yale University school of medicine, 1955.
345. Fair, E. M.   Inventions and books - what of the future.   Library journal, 61:48, Jan. 1939.
346. Modern business methods as applied to library administration.   Library association record, 13:223, 1946.
347. Morey, L.   A president's suggestion.   Problems and prospects of the research library, ed. E. Williams.   N. Y., Scarecrow, 1955.   p. 21.
348. Geer, H. T.   Charging machines.   Library trends, 5:250, Oct. 1956.
349. Ref. 239, pp. 27, 28.
350. Duer, M. D.   How we use IBM.   Library journal, 78:1289, Aug. 1953.
351. Ref. 239, p. 28.
352. Callander, T. E.   Punched card systems: their application to library technique.   Library association record, 13:171, 172, July 1946.
353. Pratt, E. C.   International business machines used in circulation department, University of Florida library.   Library journal, 67:302, Apr. 1942.
354. Ibid., 303.
355. Parker, R. R.   Mechanical aids in college and university libraries.   ALA bulletin, 32:819, Oct. 1938.
356. Ref. 352, p. 172.

357. Ref. 239, p. 29.
358. Sharp, J. R.   Punched card charging - a suggested system.   Library association record, 59:151-155, May 1957.
359. Obear, L.   Punch card charge records.   Library of Congress bulletin, 10:11-12, Nov. 1951.
360. Leyland, E.   Mechanized book issue.   Library association record, 52:112, 113, Apr. 1950.
361. Ibid., 113, 114.
362. Ibid., 114.
363. Parker, R. H.   Adaptation of machines to book charging.   Library trends, 6:40, July 1957.
364. Quigley, M.   Library facts from International Business Machine cards.   Library journal, 66:1066, Dec. 1941.
365. Quigley, M.   Business machines in a public library save space and time of public and staff and in effect make the library larger.   American city, 60:101, May 1945.
366. Automatic book charging.   Library journal, 66:803, Sept. 1941.
367. Quigley, M.   Ten years of IBM.   Library journal, 77:1152, 1153, July 1952.
368. Hirsch, F. E.   Business machine - tool of library progress.   ALA bulletin, 38:291, Sept. 1944.
369. Ref. 365, p. 102.
370. Ref. 367, p. 1155.
371. Parker, R. H.   Punched card method in circulation work.   Library journal, 61:905, Dec. 1936.
372. Beeler, E. L.   Mechanical device versus the personal touch.   Wilson library bulletin, 25:382, Jan. 1951.
373. Hand, W. J.   Special library of the future.   Special libraries, 42:13, 16, Jan. 1951.
374. Ref. 3, p. 136.
375. McNiff, P. J.   The charging system of the Lamont library.   Harvard library bulletin, 3:438-440, Autumn 1949.
376. Ibid., 440.
377. Adams, T. R.   Machines Library journal, 75:1023, June 1950.
378. Ibid., 1024.
379. Ref. 3, p. 140.
380. Ref. 3, pp. 140-143.
381. Stubblefield, L. M. and Forrest, F. H.   Columbia's new charging system.   College and research libraries, 14:381, 382, Oct. 1953.
382. Forrest, F. H.   An experiment in charging in the circulation department, Columbia University library, un-

published Master's essay. N. Y., Columbia University, school of library service, 1952. p. 14.

383. Ref. 381, p. 383.
384. Ref. 381, pp. 383, 384.
385. Ref. 381, p. 384.
386. Ref. 382, pp. 20-21.
387. Ref. 382, pp. 20, 32.
388. Ref. 381, p. 385.
389. Ref. 382, pp. 32-37.
390. Ref. 382, p. 38.
391. Ref. 382, pp. 38-39.
392. Ref. 381, pp. 384, 385.
393. Ref. 382, pp. 39, 40.
394. Ref. 381, p. 386.
395. Ref. 381, pp. 385, 386.
396. Ref. 3, p. 151.
397. Komidar, J. S. Indefinite time system of book loans in a college library. College and research libraries, 4:250, June 1943.
398. McGaw, H. F. Circulation system based on an indefinite loan period. Wilson library bulletin, 17:452, Feb. 1943.
399. Ref. 397, p. 251.
400. Ref. 398, pp. 452, 453.
401. Restricted reference books. Library notes, 2:216-218, Dec. 1887.
402. Rideout, J. D. University of New Hampshire library has worked out a reserve plan. Library journal, 73: 643, Apr. 1948.
403. Tanner, E. F. Rental service. Library journal, 60: 674-675, Sept. 1935.
404. Wofford, A. Circulating non-book materials. Wilson library bulletin, 15:652-653, 655, Apr. 1941.
405. Fargo, L. F. The library in the school, 4th ed. rev. and enl. Chicago, ALA, 1947. p. 323.
406. Jackson, L. Technical libraries. N. Y., SLA, 1951. pp. 68, 70.
407. Campbell, D. J. The control and utilization of periodicals. Library association record, 54:9, Feb. 1952.
408. Bumgardner, H. E. Labor-saving methods applied to magazine circulation. Special libraries, 43:92, 93, 102, March 1952.
409. Clapp, V. W. Scientific libraries. Antiquarian bookman, 15: 1 , Jan. 29, 1955.
410. Tauber, M. F. Technical services in libraries. N. Y., Columbia University press, 1954. p. 354.
411. Shaw, R. R. Reducing the cost of the lending process.

ALA bulletin, 35:507, Oct. 1, 1941.
412. Bailey, T. A. Charlotte experiments with audio charging. Library journal, 75:1065, June 15, 1950.
413. Ref. 330, p. 445.
414. Goldhor, H. Criteria for an ideal circulation system. Wilson library bulletin, 29:637, 649, 650, Apr. 1955.
415. Dinnan, L. T. Voice for the small library. Wilson library bulletin, 30:323, 324, Dec. 1955.
416. Bauer, H. C. Circulation service and public relations. Library trends, 6:62, July 1957.
417. Van Horne, B. Portland drops transaction cards. ALA bulletin, 52:635, Sept. 1958.
418. Charging systems instituto. Odds and book ends, 28:40, Fall 1957.
419. Corbett, E. V. Wandsworth's experiment with photocharging. Library association record, 57:1345, Sept. 1955.
420. Bloss, M. Transaction charging. Library journal, 78:1286, Aug. 14, 1953.
421. Diebold, Inc. The Philadelphia story, a new book-lending technique at the free public library of Philadelphia. N. Y., Diebold, n.d. p. 2
422. Diebold, Inc. Portable microfilm camera revolutionizing office procedure. N. Y., Diebold, n.d. pp. pp. 2, 3
423. Bowen, E. M. E. An experiment in photocharging in Toronto. Library association record, 60:147, May 1958.
424. Shaw photocharger announced. Library journal, 72:1513, Nov. 1, 1947.
425. The Remington Rand photocharger. N. Y., Remington Rand, n.d. pp. 9, 14.
426. Ibid., 4.
427. Ref. 421, p. 1288.
428. Matson, C. Six months of the Recordak. Minnesota libraries, 16:74, 76, Sept. 1949.
429. Andres, M. Practical aspects of photographic charging. University of Illinois library school occasional papers, 39:3, June 1954.
430. Ref. 420, pp. 1285, 1286.
431. Corbett, E. V. Photocharging: its operation and installation in a British public library. London, James Clarke, 1957. pp. 85, 86.
432. Ref. 424, p. 1515.
433. Ref. 411, p. 508.
434. Photographic charging machine. Gary, Ind., Gary public library, n.d. pp. 1, 2, 8, 9.

435. Ref. 419, p. 346.
436. Martell, H. D. Speeding photographic book charging. Library journal, 83:53, Jan. 1, 1958.
437. Corbett, E. V. Wandsworth's experiment with photo-charging; a second report. Library association record, 58:136, April 1956.
438. Hepworth, P. Provincial photocharging installation. Library association record, 59:163, May 1957.
439. Ref. 431, p. 31.
440. Martin, A. B. Tulsa finds new aid in photographic charging. Library journal, 74:1474, 1475, Oct. 1, 1949.
441. Ref. 437, p. 346.
442. Ref. 431, p. 49.
443. Ref. 429, pp. 6, 7.
444. Robinson, E. S. The technique of photocharging. Canadian library association bulletin, 10:116, Feb. 1954.
445. Hacker, H. S. Erie county bookmobile carries first photocharger. Library journal, 74:871, June 1949.
446. Ref. 424, p. 1514.
447. Ref. 434, p. 3.
448. Circulation by camera clicks. Pioneer, 21 (1):3, 4, Jan. - Feb. 1958.
449. Ref. 421, p. 5.
450. Ref. 428, p. 76.
451. Ref. 411, pp. 508, 509.
452. Ref. 440, p. 1475.
453. Ref. 440, p. 1476.
454. Murray, C. E. Installation of Recordak photocharging, Queensborough public library. N. Y., Recordak, n.d. . p. 1.
455. Ref. 411, p. 509.
456. Blasingame, R. W. Gadgets: Miscellanea, but not all trivia. Library trends, 5:239-243, Oct. 1956.
457. Ref. 420, p. 1288.
458. Tucker, H. W. Circulation breakdown with electric counter. Library journal, 82:1731-1732, July 1957.
459. Mamalakis, M. J. More gadgets, please! Wilson library bulletin, 16:350, Jan. 1942.
460. Pragan, O. Photographic charging of books. Library journal, 68:1059, 1060, Dec. 15, 1943.
461. Ref. 424, pp. 1515, 1521.
462. Miller, B. A. Photographic charging versus manual charging. Library journal, 76:977, 978, June 1, 1951.
463. Henselman, F. Which charging machine for you. California librarian, 19:105, 131, Apr. 1958.

464. Ref. 423, p. 149.
465. Ref. 412, p. 1066.
466. Tucker, H. W.   Photographic charging machine.   Library journal, 71:1782, Dec. 15, 1946.
467. Robertson, E. L.   Photocharging at Glendale.   California library bulletin, 10:104, March 1949.
468. Library automation: cheaper and quicker.   Times education supplement, 2235:460, March 21, 1958.
469. Photocharging comes to Britain.   Publishers' circular, 169:1340, Oct. 22, 1955.
470. Ref. 437, pp. 345-347.
471. Ref. 431, p. 89.
472. Ref. 438, p. 164.
473. Ref. 429, pp. 4, 5.
474. Ref. 428, pp. 76, 77.
475. Foutts, J. C.   Recordak, in the mechanical charger on the bookmobile.   ALA bulletin, 51:520, July-Aug. 1957.
476. Ref. 454, pp. 1, 2.
477. Donaldson, M. C.   Progress at Pasadena.   Pioneer, 12:7, July-Aug. 1949.
478. Ref. 445, p. 870.
479. Ref. 444, p. 168.
480. Microphotography and book charging.   Journal of documentary reproduction, 3:119, June 1940.
481. Ref. 448, p. 4.
482. Ref. 454, p. 2.
483. Ref. 412, pp. 1065, 1066.
484. Ref. 437, pp. 346, 347.
485. Ref. 428, p. 77.
486. Shawkey, D. R.   Remington Rand photocharger in the mechanical charger on the bookmobile.   ALA bulletin, 51:521, July-Aug. 1957.
487. Ref. 429, pp. 7-11.
488. Ref. 411, pp. 509, 510.
489. Ref. 462, p. 977.
490. Ref. 445, p. 870.
491. Ref. 437, p. 347.
492. Ref. 423, p. 148.
493. Ref. 437, p. 137.
494. Ref. 431, pp. 9, 10, 56-60.
495. Shaw, R. R.   Photographic charging in scholarly libraries.   Catholic library world, 24:46-47, Nov. 1952.
496. Burke, A.   Evaluation by photocharger.   Catholic library world, 24:47-50, Nov. 1952.
497. Smith, S. W.   ---and a few machines.   Library journal, 74:1046, July 1949.
498. Ibid., 1046, 1047.

499. Ref. 348, p. 248.
500. Speer, L. M. Charging books the audio way. Wilson
     library bulletin, 25:58, Sept. 1950.
501. Eggen, J. A. Audio charging works here. Library
     journal, 77:1292-1294, Aug. 1952.
502. Ref. 412, p. 1068.
503. Ref. 501, p. 1292.
504. Ref. 412, p. 1067.
505. Ref. 500, p. 59.
506. Ref. 501, p. 1294.
507. Ref. 412, pp. 1067, 1068.
508. Ref. 501, pp. 1293, 1294.
509. Parks, A. Mechanical chargers. Library journal, 79:
     1577-1578, Sept. 1954.
510. Ref. 497, p. 1047.
511. Ref. 501, p. 1294.
512, Audio-charging in the library. Minnesota libraries, 16:
     293, June 1951.
513. Kaiser, W. H. Wayne County library charging system:
     a manual of installation, operation and evaluation.
     Detroit? , Wayne County library, 1950. planographed
     p. 1.
514. Witmer, E. M. New book-charging scheme. Library
     journal, 74:1173, Sept. 1, 1949.
515. Kaiser, W. H. No machines used in this charging sys-
     tem. Library journal, 74:513, March 15, 1950.
516. Kaiser, W. H. No cards; no registration. Library
     journal, 77:1042, June 15, 1952.
517. Kaiser, W. H. Are registration and library cards
     musts? Library journal, 82:1394, June 1, 1957.
518. New charging system saves time. Michigan library
     news, 9:8, Jan. 1950.
519. Ref. 516, p. 1043.
520. Ref. 517, pp. 1393, 1394, 1398.
521. Ref. 513, p. 8.
522. Ref. 513, p. 7.
523. Ref. 515, pp. 513, 514.
524. Ref. 515, p. 514.
525. Bacon, W. This charging system not held a panacea.
     Library journal, 75:1219, 1220, July 1950.
526. Benton, W. Dunedin's new issue system, photographic
     without photography. New Zealand libraries, 11:257-
     261, Nov. 1948.
527. Pike, J. A new lease of life. Library world, 56:86-
     87, Dec. 1954.
528. Rift, L. R. Inexpensive transaction number charging
     system with book record. College and research li-

braries, 18:112-118, March 1957.

529. Newton, M. L. and Blackburn, R. H.   Punched card
     charging system.   Canadian library association, 6:40,
     Sept. 1949.
530. Ibid., 40, 41.
531. Ref. 291, p. 129.
532. Ref. 529, p. 42.
533. Ref. 291, pp. 132, 133.
534. Ref. 291, p. 133.
535. Kaiser, W. H.   Time study..... Wayne County library
     charging system; a manual of installation, operation,
     and evaluation.   Detroit? , Wayne County library,
     1950.   pp. 2758, 2759.
536. Ref. 529, p. 42.
537. Ref. 291, p. 134.
538. Ref. 239, p. 26.
539. International business machines corporation.   Circula-
     tion control for libraries.   N. Y., IBM, 1953.   pp.
     3-6.
540. Los Angeles public library.   Photo-lending.   Los
     Angeles, that library, 1951 .   p. 1.
541. Ref. 539, pp. 7, 9.
542. Ref. 540, p. 2.
543. Klausner, M.   Routine library operations - application
     of machine-sorted cards, in Punched cards; their ap-
     plications to science and industry.   Ed. R. S. Casey.
     N. Y., Reinhold, 1951.   p. 226.
544. Ibid., 226, 227.
545. Klausner, M.   IBM circulation control at Stockton.
     California library bulletin, 10:12, Sept. 1948.
546. Ref. 543, p. 227.
547. Ref. 543, pp. 222-226.
548. Ref. 540, pp. 3, 4.
549. Young, G. G.   Borrower merely signs his name.   Li-
     brary journal, 74:12, 13, Jan. 1, 1949.
550. Ibid., 13-16.
551. Young, G. G.   Embossed plate book charging.   Library
     journal, 71:1773, 1774, Dec. 15, 1946.
552. Ibid., 1774, 1775.
553. Ibid., 1777.
554. Ibid., 1775.
555. Ibid., 1775, 1776.
556. Ibid., 1778.
557. Ref. 3, p. 153.
558. Addressograph-Multigraph takes pride in presenting
     today's most modern book charging system - Booka-
     matic.   Cleveland, O. , Addressograph-Multigraph,

n. d. .   p. 5.

559. Ibid., 6-8.
560. Ibid., 9.
561. Ibid., 9, 10.
562. Ibid., 10.
563. Ibid., 3.
564. Ref. 3, p. 158.
565. Ref. 558, p. 2.
566. Harlan, H. O.   Charge plate charging at Midland.
     Michigan library news, 17:11, Fall 1957.
567. Brodac, Bro-Dart's automatic charging system.   Newark,
     N. J., Bro-Dart industries, n. d. .   p. 2 .
568. Ibid., 3 .
569. Ibid., 4 .
570. McColvin, L. R.   Westminster token charging scheme.
     Library association record, 56:259, July 1954.
571. Ref. 134, p. 55.
572. Ref. 134, p. 56.
573. Mason, D. L.   Token charging at Westminster.   Mari-
     time library assocation bulletin, 21:5, Fall 1956.
574. Dent, J.   Selective token charging.   Library associa-
     tion record, 58:139, Apr. 1956.
575. Ref. 570, p. 260.
576. McColvin, L. R.   Progress report on the Westminster
     token system.   Library association record, 58:15,
     Jan. 1956.
577. Ibid., 15, 16.
578. Ibid., 16.
579. Ref. 574, p. 140.
580. Bickerton, L. M.   Worthing token system.   Library
     association record, 58:265-268, July 1956.
581. Stiles, W. G.   Charging by a simple exchange principle.
     Library association record, 59:397-399, Dec. 1957.
582. Cox, K. R.   Controlled issue - charging system for
     lending libraries.   Library association record, 60:
     225-226, July 1958.
583. Ref. 55, p. 242.
584. Wilson, L. R. and Tauber, M. F.   The university li-
     brary.   N. Y., Columbia University press, 1956.
     p. 222.
585. Ref. 237, p. 164.
586. Ref. 237, p. 173.
587. Baldwin, E. V. and Marcus, W. E.   Library costs and
     budgets.   N. Y., Bowker, 1941.   pp. 85-86.
588. Ibid., 123-126.
589. Pierce, W. O'D.   Work measurement in public librar-
     ies.   N. Y., Social science research council, 1949.

pp. 24, 36.
590. Shepherd, G. F. Methods and procedures. Library
   trends, 6:22, 23, July 1957.
591. Ref. 411, p. 505.
592. Yenawine, W. S. Current trends in circulation service;
   introduction. Library trends, 6:3, July 1957.
593. Ibid., 4.
594. Gwynn, S. E. Departmentalization and circulation
   works; problems and relationships. Library trends,
   6:91, 92, July 1957.
595. Dudley, Edward. Go forth, my little book. Assistant
   librarian, 49:28, 29, Feb. 1956.

Supplementary Bibliography

596. ALA Committee on library administration. Report 1913, ALA proceedings. ALA bulletin, 7:128-131.

597. The Audograph story. Gray audograph electronic soundwriter, n. d.

598. Austen, W. Banking method of charging books. Library journal, 30:144-146, March 1905.

599. Balcke, C. The German library world and its system. Library association record, n. s. 5:101-121, 1927.

600. Barlow, S. H. Method for simplifying reserved book chasing. Library world, 52:77-78, Nov. 1949.

601. Barnes, A. M. Manual for the circulation division of the general library of the University of Georgia. A. M. L. S. thesis typewritten. Ann Arbor, University of Michigan, 1944.

602. Barrett, F. T. Book notation and an indicator. Library world, 4:281-286, 1902.

603. Bond, H. Some features of recent library practice in Great Britain. Library association record, 17:227-243, 1915.

604. Borrower's cards: charging a book. Library news bulletin, 10:7-9, Dec. 1942.

605. Brown, W. Chiver's indicator adapted as an author indicator for fiction. Library world, 11:243-244, Dec. 1908.

606. Brown, Zaidee. Reading list on loan work. Wilson library bulletin, 2:102-104, 1923.

607. Callander, T. E. The application of the punched card system to library technique. The Powers magazine, 12:2-5, 1946.

608. Carson, W. O. Newark (modified) charging system. Ontario library association proceedings of annual meeting, 68-69, 1909.

609. Charging and circulation: The standard Dickman machines. Newark, N. J., Library efficiency corp., n. d. . p. 39.

610. Charging system for a college library. Library journal, 44:616, Sept. 1919.

611. Clark, John W. The care of books. London, Cambridge University press, 1909. 352 p.

612. Cochran, M. A. University of Texas package loan li-

brary. M. L. S. thesis. Austin, University of Texas, 1914-1954. 206 p.

613. Cotgreave, Alfred. Indicators versus bookkeeping and notes on Cotgreave's library indicators. London, John Bale, 1885. 23 p.

614. Cotgreave, Alfred. Library economics - a modified Kennedy indicator. Library world, 11:363, March 1909.

615. Cotgreave, Alfred. Library indicator: pro and con. Library association record, 4:333-339, 360-361, 1902.

616. Cotgreave, Alfred. Open access versus indicators. Library world, 11:196-200, Nov. 1908.

617. Cutter, C. A. Inconveniences of library cards. Library journal, 10:48, 1885.

618. Dana, J. C. A library primer. Boston, N. Y., etc. Library bureau, 1920. pp. 149-159.

619. Dana, J. C. Public library handbook. Denver, Colo., Carson-Hurst, 1895. pp. 46-57, 62-64, 75-80, 86-90.

620. Davis, Winifred L. School library routines visualized. New Haven, Conn., Demco library supplies, 1948. pp. 30-34.

621. The Demco self-charging system. Library journal, 56:305-306.

622. Demco visible charging and Demco visible registration. New Haven, Conn., Demco library supplies, 1951.

623. Demco visible charging and Demco visible registration. Library supplies, catalog no. 53. New Haven, Conn. Demco library supplies, 1953. pp. 28-29.

624. The Detroit system. Library mercury, 3:57, 1931.

625. Dewey, M. Books and readers' accounts. Library journal, 4:131, 1879.

626. Dickman system. Librarian and book world, 25:95, Dec., 1935.

627. Diehl, Katharine Smith. One librarian. N. Y., Scarecrow press, 1956.

628. Discussion on charging systems by Massachusetts library club. Library journal, 19:173-174, 1894.

629. Douglas, Mary Peacock. The teacher-librarian's handbook. 2nd ed. Chicago, ALA, 1949. pp. 43-46.

630. Dow, A. Photocharging; recording issues on microfilm. Scottish library association news, 25:12-15, Sept.-Oct. 1957.

631. Faculty book loan policies. Bookmark (Idaho), 9:14-15, Sept. 1956.

632. Farrow, T. E. Graham indicator. Library world, 11:29-31, July 1908.

633. Ferris, L. A.   Bibliography on the uses of punched
     cards.   Journal of documentation, 3:258-262, March
     1948.

634. Foltz, Laura.   Mechanical charging systems.   Library
     news bulletin, 18:240-243, Oct. -Dec. 1951.

635. Calvin, Hoyt R.   Charging system for public libraries.
     Charlotte, N. C., the author c/o Public library, 1949.
     5 p.

636. Gardner, John L.   Some impressions of working in an
     American public library.   Open access, 3:8, Jan.
     1955.

637. Gates, M. L.   Installing a new book charging system
     in the Newark library system.   Newark public library:
     The library, 4:6-7, 1931.

638. Gates, M. L.   Punched cards for library records.   Li-
     brary journal, 71:1783-1784, Dec. 15, 1946.

639. Gaylord electric automatic: Book charging machine in-
     struction book.   Syracuse, N. Y., Gaylord Brothers,
     1949.   8 p.

640. Green, S. S.   Administration.   Library journal, 6:108-
     109, 1881.

641. Greenwood, T.   Public libraries.   4th ed.   London,
     Cassell, 1891.   pp. 413-417.

642. Gull, C. D.   Summary of applications of punched cards
     as they affect special libraries.   Special libraries 38:
     208-212, Sept. 1947.

643. Hatcher, A. F.   New method of indicator charging.
     Library association record, 10:419-420, 1908.

644. Hobson, M. B.   Introducing punched cards.   Cape li-
     brarian, 1:5-11, Jan. 1958.

645. Instruction for student assistants.   5th ed.   New Bruns-
     wick, Maine, Bowdoin college library, 1945.   p. 7.

646. International business machines corporation.   IBM ac-
     counting; circulation control for public libraries.
     N. Y., IBM, 1947.   11 p.

647. Jackson, F.   Systems of charging loans and an improved
     slip-case.   Library journal, 3:230-231, 1878.

648. Jast, L. S.   Charging checks.   Library world, 2:16-17,
     1899.

649. Kite, W.   Book registry for small libraries.   Library
     journal, 8:40-41, 1883.

650. Koch, T. W.   Some phases of the administrative history
     of college and university libraries.   ALA bulletin, 6:
     274, 1912.

651. Lehman, Barbara M.   A comparison of non-manual
     charging systems in libraries.   M. L. S. thesis.
     N. Y., Pratt Institute library school, 1952, 111 p.

652. Library association. Small municipal libraries. A manual of modern methods. Edinburgh, T. and A. Constable, 1931. pp. 92-100.
653. Library book-charging transformed to fast routine with aid of needle bearings. Bearings engineer, 15:6, July-Aug. 1955.
654. Livingston, Jane. A manual for the installation and operation of the Kaiser charging system for the Door-Kewaunee Regional library. Madison, Wisconsin free library commission, 1950. 15 p.
655. Loan system for rural, village and school libraries. Ontario library review, 4:60-63, 1920.
656. Lynn, C. Lawrence. We do it this way. Catholic library world, 12:190-191, March 1941.
657. Machine aids to librarianship. Special libraries association, Alabama chapter bulletin, 4:39, Sept. 1957.
658. Mash, M. H. B. Recording of issues. Croydon crank, 2:42-44, July 1909.
659. Maxfield, D. K. Library punched card procedures past experience and future possibilities. Library journal, 71:902-905, June 15, 1946.
660. Mr. Smith goes to the library. The pioneer, 5:2-3, Feb. 1942.
661. Municipal library circulation; mechanical charging and signature systems. News notes of California libraries, 45:298, Apr. 1950.
662. New charging system at the California State library. News notes of California libraries, 50:313-314, Apr. 1955.
663. New method of charging books. Library mercury, 2(6): 3-4, 1930.
664. Open access versus indicators. Library world, 11:101-103, Sept. 1908.
665. Parker, J. Brown charging system. Vermont free public library commission bulletin, 2:1-2, June 1906.
666. Pencil entries now recorded automatically on punched cards. Journal of accountancy, 81:332, 1946.
667. Perkins, F. B. Registration and delivery service. How to make town libraries successful. Special libraries report, U. S. Office of education. Public libraries of the United States, 1878. pp. 426-427.
668. Perry, F. C. Charging systems. School librarian, 2:33-39, March 1939.
669. Plastic cards for charging books. Library journal, 83: 3062-3063, Nov. 1, 1958.
670. Property accounting: Charlotte library uses audio-charging system. Audograph news, 3-4, Oct. 1950.

671. Punch card system tested. Library journal, 66:625, July 1941.

672. Quigley, M. C. Trees and the woods. Louisiana library association bulletin, 11:43-44, Jan. 1948.

673. Randall, W. M. and Goodrich, Francis L. D. Principles of college library administration. 2nd ed. Chicago, ALA and University of Chicago press, 1941. pp. 229, 232.

674. Rees, Stephen A. A survey of the literature relating to the use of punched cards in the public and special libraries of the U. S. A. London, Library association, 1948. pp. 1-4.

675. Reid, Jennie. Charging system. Ontario library association, proceedings of annual meeting. 71. 1909.

676. Roebuck, C. E. and Thorne, W. B. Primer of library practice. London, G. P. Putman, 1904. pp. 38-46.

677. Schwartz, J. Apprentice's library charging system. Library journal, 14:468-469, 1889.

678. Self-charging system. Michigan library bulletin, 23:91-92, 1932.

679. Sharp, H. A. Lending library routine work. Primer of librarianship by W. E. Doubleday. London, Allen & Unwin, 1931. pp. 78-94.

680. Shaw, Ralph R. Photocharging in public library. N. Y., Library bureau, 1947.

681. Sheldon, H. G. An elementary talk on charging systems. Library journal, supplement, 22:63-64, 1897.

682. Shepley, Gladys. Work simplification in public libraries: photographic charging. Ontario library review, 38:206-208, Aug. 1954.

683. A simple card charging system. The red book. 4th ed. Syracuse, N. Y., Gaylord, 1923.

684. Simple forms for the loan system. Library occurrent, 2:5-8, Oct. 1908.

685. Some methods of recording issues. School library review, 1(4):105-108, Easter term 1937.

686. Spaulding, F. B. The old charging method defended. Library journal, 56:434, 1931.

687. Staley, G. F. Ledger charging. Library world, 10: 35-37, July 1907.

688. Steenberg, A. S. A Danish charging system. Library, 6:78-79, 1894.

689. Stokkeland, M. C. Use of punched cards for recording information. M. L. S. thesis. Pittsburgh, Carnegie Institute of Technology, 1950. 63 p.

690. Stott, C. A. On reorganizing a school library. School libraries, 3:68-76, July 1943.

691. Token charging: methods and results in the Midlands; the Westminster method at Shrewsbury, John L. Hobbs; the Worthing method at Dudley, A. Wilson. Open access, 5:6-8, Jan. 1957.

692. Tollefson, Horace A. A charging system for college and university libraries. n.d., 17 leaves. (Not located.)

693. Waugh, D. Business machines in the public library. Wilson library bulletin, 16:366-377, Jan. 1942.

694. Webb, A. Modified Kennedy indicator. Library world, 11:281-284, Jan. 1909.

695. Welles, Jessie. Some twentieth century lending methods. Wisconsin library bulletin, 16:45-51, Apr. 1920. Also in Wilson bulletin, 2:323-328, Dec. 1924.

696. Wick, D. E. Durrington. Branch library system. Wessex bookman, 4:13, Summer-Winter 1955.

697. Wright, Edward. Methods and techniques of library surveys. Library trends, Louis Wilson, ed. Chicago, University of Chicago press, 1937. pp. 353-360.

698. Williamson, W. L. New circulation system at Baylor University. News notes, 24:28, Apr. 1948.

Index

A

Accession number, 28, 72, 73, 114, 118, 188-190.
Act of Parliament (England), 48.
Adams, T. R., 189-190.
Adressograph, 291.
----Model 60, 288, 292.
----Tag, 289.
Adressograph Bookamatic charge imprinter, 293.
Adressograph-Multigraph corporation (Cleveland, O.) Pamphlet, 292-296.
Albany Y. M. C. A. library, 32, 83.
Ambrose, Lodilla, 113.
American library association, 97.
----Bulletin (1930), 329.
----Committee on library administration, 74, 96.
----Convention, 62.
----Primer, 72.
American library institute, 21.
Amherst College, 23.
Andres, Marianna, 221, 228, 242, 247.
Ann Arbor, 89, 90, 92, 93, 137, 138.
Application of international business machines in libraries, 319.
Arkansas, University of, 163.
Arnold, G. W., 21.
Athenaeum library, 34.
Atomic energy research library, 124.

Audio-charge method, 213, 258-266, 352-354.
Audograph, 262, 354.
Automatic key punch, 180.

B

Bacon memorial library (Wyandotte, Mich.), 225.
Bacon, W., 271.
Bailey, T. A.
----Borrower's card, 260.
----Overdues, 261.
----Transaction cards, 212, 213, 245.
Baker, E. G., 92.
Baldwin, E. V. (and Marcus, W. E.), 12, 322.
Baldwin-Marcus study, 236, 322.
Ballou, Hubbard, vii.
Barlow, Mr., 118.
Bassett, N. D., 96.
Bauer, H. C., 216.
Beeler, E. L., 187.
Belton, E. J., 135-137.
Bentley, George F., 163.
Benton, W., 273.
Berkeley, 342.
Berthel, John H., 146.
Bethany (library), 135.
Bethesda, (Md.), 211.
Bickerton, L. M., 308, 354, 355.
Bigelow, Dr. Julian H., v.
Blackburn, R. H., 276-279.
Blasingame, Ralph, 167, 233, 319-321.
Bloss, M., 221, 230, 234,

385